KEY TO THE B[...] W9-DHS-190

LIST OF BOXES

 Key Points Boxes

For **LANGUAGE AND CULTURE** and **TECH NOTE** listings, see page 592. For **ESL NOTE** and Source Shot listings, see page 593.

5TH EDITION

Keys for Writers

Ann Raimes

Hunter College, City University of New York

Houghton Mifflin Company
Boston   New York

Publisher: Patricia Coryell
Editor-in-Chief: Carrie Brandon
Marketing Manager: Tom Ziolkowski
Marketing Assistant: Bettina Chiu
Senior Development Editor: Meg Botteon
Senior Development Editor: Martha Bustin
Associate Editor: Jane Acheson
Editorial Assistant: Sarah Truax
Senior Project Editor: Rosemary Winfield
Editorial Assistants: Katherine Leahey, Andrew Laskey
Art and Design Coordinator: Jill Haber
Cover Design Director: Tony Saizon
Photo Editor: Jennifer Meyer Dare
Composition Buyer: Chuck Dutton

Cover photograph: © 2006 Ralph Mercer, ralphmercer.com

Credits continue on page 590, which constitutes an extension of the
copyright page.

Copyright © 2008 by Houghton Mifflin Company. All rights reserved.
No part of this work may be reproduced or transmitted in any form or by any means, electronic
or mechanical, including photocopying and recording, or by any information storage or retrieval
system without the prior written permission of Houghton Mifflin Company, unless such copying
is expressly permitted by federal copyright law. Address inquiries to College Permissions,
Houghton Mifflin Company, 222 Berkeley Street, Boston, MA 02116-3764.

Printed in China   Library of Congress Catalog Card Number 2006922366
5 6 7 8 9 -SDP-10 09 08

Instructor's exam copy ISBN 0-618-75659-0 or 978-0-618-75386-4
For orders, use student text ISBN 0-618-75386-9 or 978-0-618-75386-4

Preface

I began the first edition of *Keys for Writers* in 1993, and it was published in 1996. Some may think that sounds like the Dark Ages. At that time, students used mostly books and print articles for research, they did not have the vast resources and distractions of the Internet so widely available, they were more familiar with words on a page than images on a screen—and they certainly did not carry around cell phones, flash drives, and iPods. In fact, at the time of the first edition, the dominant medium was print, and the Web was not a significant research tool. The word *Web* wasn't even indexed in the book.

Every new edition has a story to tell, and for the fifth edition it is now the story of globalization, diversity, mind-boggling technological innovations, and a proliferation of the *multi* prefix. Students, communities, colleges, and courses are multicultural and multilingual. The concept of literacy has expanded as our world embraces multimedia, integrating print with visuals, audio, and video. Perspectives on English are changing, too, as the language becomes more global, more fluid, reinventing itself as local Englishes and providing the opportunity for even more multiliteracies. And the understanding of writing as a way of learning and not just of communicating ideas has expanded its scope from one required college course into multiple courses across the curriculum.

These ongoing global and technological developments redirect our attention to written communication—via Web sites, e-mail, instant messaging, texting, online discussion lists, online courses, blogs, wikis, and so on. The multitasking we all do necessarily means that we use writing more in our daily lives.

This new fifth edition, then, is specifically written for today's students, citizens of a changing world, and so includes broad rhetorical contexts for writing while still guiding students to produce essays that meet the goals and requirements of college courses.

But although the story of this fifth edition involves such dramatic global and technological shifts, I continue to believe that the best handbook is one that students will use. It is one that not only keeps pace with their changing needs but also invites use and is easy to use. The success of the previous editions of *Keys for Writers* tells me to keep this handbook's distinctive navigation and its two (yes, only two) color-coded and descriptively labeled rows of tabs entailing no mastery of codes, the coaching tone that students see as lively but respectful, and the concise explanations and examples of grammar and style that have delighted many users. Yet *Keys for Writers* has also changed because both teachers and students have conveyed in person, sent, and e-mailed invaluable suggestions to help the book keep pace with current trends in writing and be as accurate and timely as a handbook should be. I am grateful for those shared ideas and delighted to incorporate them.

So you have in your hand a handbook that provides solid instruction and lively examples in a brand-new design, keeps up with change, insists on authentic examples of student writing, and conveys the challenges of writing for multiple audiences in multiple settings. I'd like to hear your reactions. You can write to me at <college_English@hmco.com >.

New to the Fifth Edition

As well as thoroughly updating examples of Internet citations, research methods, and linguistic developments necessary today, this edition of *Keys* offers the following new materials:

Expanded and updated MLA, APA, CSE, and *Chicago* guidelines Parts 3 and 4 now include an At a Glance Index for all four documentation styles. They also include side-by-side examples of in-text citations with their corresponding entries in a list of works cited and updated and expanded examples of how to cite Web sources. Guidelines for CSE style are those of the seventh edition (2006) of *Scientific Style and Format.*

Source Shots The seven Source Shots in Parts 3 and 4 provide examples from different media that show what to cite and where to find the necessary information on a page or screen. Special emphasis has been given to how to cite from online databases, with several examples.

New student papers New papers illustrate APA style (on addiction to virtual worlds) and *Chicago Manual* style (on slang dictionaries). The sample papers for MLA, APA, and *Chicago* are annotated in different colors to show both content/argument issues and formatting. In addition, you'll find an example of a student's blog, along with examples of students' online discussions on the *Keys* Web site, a new literature paper (on identity in stories by Sherman Alexie and Edwidge Danticat), and a new argument paper (on the benefits of a vegan diet).

Enhanced discussion of argument   In addition to the new student argument paper and the argument-specific annotations on the sample research papers, the argument chapter includes more examples of appeals to an audience and more on using visuals to enhance or present an argument.

Expanded chapter on plagiarism   The chapter now includes a focus on the ethical use of sources along with a new memorable feature, "The Seven Sins of Plagiarism." By popular request, the section on quoting has been moved to the plagiarism chapter.

More on writing across the curriculum   Expanded coverage of writing and researching in the humanities, sciences, and social sciences occurs throughout the book, with links to sample student essays at the Online Study Center at the *Keys* Web site.

Expanded coverage of visuals and media   This edition contains information on how to read visuals critically, how to locate them, and how to use them ethically in research papers ("Honesty in Visuals" in 21d). It also includes a student's Web site prepared for a community service project (23e) and an example of a student's e-portfolio (24c). A valuable addition to Part 2 (Research) is a flow chart and illustrative screenshot on "How to Read a Web Site" (8e).

Other new features   Among the many other new features in the fifth edition the following are especially notable:

- an editing guide to vernacular Englishes (59e), which recognizes the increasing number of students who come from a variety of language backgrounds
- a section on how punctuation shows meaning (beginning of Part 8)
- more coverage of critical reading of text and images, integrated throughout (such as in 1b, 4a, 4l, 10f, 21c, and 21d)
- screenshots to help with recording research sources (7a, 7c, 7d, and 8e)
- a chart that takes the guesswork out of recording source information: "Source Essentials: What to Record" (9d)
- a section on "Not Rigging the Evidence" when quoting (9g)

Helpful Contents Designed for Easy Access

A vibrant new design for the fifth edition of *Keys for Writers* enhances those user-friendly visual features that have been a hallmark of the book's accessibility and ease of use.

Two rows of color-coded divider tabs   The simplicity and clarity of two rows of tabs make it easy to find information quickly. The first row is red, for writing and research issues; the second row is gold, for sentence-level issues.

Unique KeyTabs®   Found in the back of the handbook, the five moveable, custom-fit KeyTabs® serve as bookmarks, extended margins, and note cards. Students and instructors simply insert these locator cards into the binding, with the top of the KeyTab® extending from the top of book, to mark easy access to information that is often consulted. The URL for the *Keys* Web site is helpfully printed at the bottom of each KeyTab®.

Bracketed labels on selected sample citations in all styles   These show at a glance what types of information to include and how to format, arrange, and punctuate that information.

182   **12e**   Sample MLA Entries: Works in Online Library Subscription Databases

30. Magazine article in a library database
See Source Shot 3 for an example.

31. Scholarly article in library database
Lowe, Michelle S. "Britain's Regional Shopping Centres: New Urban Forms?"
volume number for print version of scholarly article
Urban Studies 37.2 (2000): 261–. MasterFile Premier. EBSCO. Brooklyn
persistent URL
Public Lib., Brooklyn, NY. 20 Feb. 2005 ‹http://search.epnet.com/login
.aspx?direct=true&db=f5h&an=2832704›.

Whole part on style, including the Five C's of Style   *Keys for Writers* continues to devote a full part (Part 6) to the important area of style, covering sentence- and word-related style issues in a unified presentation. The popular Five C's of Style advises students in straightforward, memorable fashion to Cut, Check for Action, Connect, Commit, and Choose the Best Words.

Thorough and clear coverage of grammar, in one convenient part   Part 7, Common Sentence Problems, gives students one central place to turn to when they have grammar questions. Grammar coverage is not divided confusingly over several parts, as in other handbooks. Handy sections on students' frequently asked grammar questions and top ten sentence problems begin Part 7.

Distinctive approach to ESL, Englishes, and vernaculars   *Keys for Writers* features clear coverage of language issues for multilingual and multicultural writers, along with a unique opening segment that places this instruction within a supportive framework. It includes a useful editing guide to multilingual transfer errors as well as an editing guide for speakers of vernacular Englishes. ESL Notes throughout the book provide additional and immediate coverage to help with editing (they are listed on page 593).

Helpful tips for using technology   For a list of Tech Notes, useful ideas and resources for writing, using the Web, and researching with technology, see page 592.

Coverage of writing and communicating across and beyond college   *Keys for Writers* prepares students for a range of writing and communicating tasks they may meet in college as well as in the community and the workplace. With many model documents, Web pages, PowerPoints, tips for oral presentations, and other resources, Part 5 covers writing, communicating, and document design in a range of media for diverse audiences.

A Complete Support Package

Free Resources for Student Writers

Online Study Center *Online Study Center*   Access the Online Study Center for this text by visiting <http://college.hmco.com/keys.html>. Resources at this site include the following:

- Samples of student essays, journals, PowerPoint slides, and online conversations
- Tutorials on coherence, narrowing a topic, identifying logical fallacies, using PowerPoint, and more
- A sentence-problem log sheet
- Interactive editing and grammar exercises
- Research templates for keeping track of different types of sources
- A research paper schedule
- Sources in twenty-seven subject areas, with fully updated lists and links to frequently used reference works in print, print and electronic indexes, and Web sites. This extensive time-saving research source list, updated for this edition of *Keys* by research librarian Trudi Jacobson at the University at Albany, SUNY, remains a tool that students can use throughout their college career as they work on papers across the curriculum.

Internet Research Guide   Online at <http://college.hmco.com/ English/students/composition.html>, the second edition of this online guide by Jason Snart of College of DuPage presents extended learning modules with practice exercises (tutorials) for using the Internet as a research tool. Topics include evaluating Web site information, building an argument with Web research, and plagiarism and documentation.

e-Exercises   This rich e-library of enjoyable self-quizzes at <http:// college.hmco.com/english/students/composition.html> lets students hone their grammar skills, go at their own pace, and work wherever is convenient for them—home, computer lab, or classroom. Exercises cover thirty areas within the broad categories of punctuation, mechanics, parts of speech, spelling, and sentence problems.

Plagiarism Prevention Zone   Online at <http://college.hmco.com/ english/students/composition.html>, this "crash course" of compelling tutorials teaches students how to recognize and avoid plagiarism.

Premium Technology Tools for Student Writers

The multimedia edition of *Keys for Writers*—the print textbook packaged with the new Technology Guide ensemble of technology products—provides convenient and powerful aids for self-paced and personalized writing instruction on the computer.

Digital Keys 5.0   This newly revised resource has a host of interactive tools and tips to help students work on all aspects of their writing, including documentation, style, using visuals, revising, and editing (with animation and audio explanations). Students use an online passkey for a twelve-month subscription to the Digital Keys site. The core of this writing aid is an easily navigated handbook of writing instruction, practice exercises, examples, diagnostic tests, KeyTabs® for bookmarking, and hotlinks. When students look up a topic, they have two choices: they can read a brief explanation, or they can click a button for more detailed explanation and annotated examples. From either the brief screen or the detailed explanation screens, students can instantly access exercises and model documents with pop-up annotations.

WriteSpace   WriteSpace is an online course management system with teaching and learning materials designed to enhance and extend your course. It is accessed through a registration code. It offers the following:

- **Re:Mark,** an innovative online grading tool
- **Peer Re:Mark,** a new-generation peer review environment that offers instructors and students easy-to-use, flexible, and effective tools for collaborative writing
- **My DropBox Safe Assignment** plagiarism prevention that checks papers against four databases
- **Digital Keys 5.0,** a concise, complete handbook full of examples and exercises, four diagnostic tests, and model student papers
- **HM Assess,** an assessment program that provides diagnostic tests that, when graded, automatically offer each student in the course a personalized study plan
- **twenty-four multimedia interactive news reports** from the Associated Press, presented with context-building introductions and follow-up questions designed to develop visual literacy and critical thinking
- **writing modules, or tutorials,** covering the writing process, rhetorical modes, argument and persuasion, and research
- a wide array of **suggested writing assignments** as well as **exercises**

Technology Tools for Writing Instructors

Access the Online Teaching Center *Online Study Center* at <http://college .hmco.com/keys.html>. Resources at this site include the following:

Instructor's Resource Manual Housed in the Online Teaching Center in five parts, the Instructor's Resource Manual provides an overview of the handbook and ideas on how to use it, a section on teaching composition to ESL and multilingual students, advice on using the Internet both within the composition classroom and throughout the course, diagnostic test handouts on five main areas of grammar, and answers to numbered items in the *Exercise Booklet.*

PowerPoint slides Based on selected content of the Instructor's Resource Manual, the PowerPoint slides allow instructors to adapt presentations for individual classroom needs.

Print Supplements for Students

Raimes and Flanagan, *Exercise Booklet,* Fifth Edition This well-regarded print booklet contains eighty-two well-crafted editing exercises. It has been carefully revised to match *Keys for Writers,* Fifth Edition, and make a good companion to it.

THEA and CLAST Preparation Manuals   These manuals include practice tests to help students pass the Texas Higher Education Assessment Test and Florida's College Level Academic Skills Test.

The American Heritage College Dictionary, Fourth Edition   This best-selling reference is an indispensable tool and desk reference.

The American Heritage English as a Second Language Dictionary This reference is specially designed with additional sample sentences to suit the needs of intermediate to advanced ESL students.

Print Supplements for Instructors

Teaching Writing with Computers: An Introduction   Edited with an introduction by Pamela Takayoshi and Brian Huot, this is an up-to-date resource on integrating technology into writing instruction.

Finding Our Way: A Writing Teacher's Sourcebook   Edited by Deborah Coxwell Teague and the late Wendy Bishop, this is a unique and powerful collection of essays for new or relatively new composition instructors.

The Essentials of Tutoring: Helping College Students Develop Their Writing Skills   A supportive and comprehensive guide for writing tutors by Paul Gary Philips and Joyce B. Philips.

Exercises to Accompany *Keys for Writers*

Exercises to accompany *Keys for Writers*, Fifth Edition, may be found on Digital Keys 5.0; in WriteSpace, an easy-to-use Web-based writing program with hundreds of interactive exercises on grammar, writing, punctuation, and usage topics; and in the print *Exercise Booklet*, Fifth Edition, which contains eighty-two editing exercises.

Acknowledgments

For all their help with this book, I am grateful to teachers and students across the country. When I travel to do workshops and attend conferences, faculty members have been unfailingly generous with their feedback. Suggestions from Glen McClish, Jackie Giordano, Gordon Bastian, Alice Horning, Michael Underwood, and others have led me to rethink some material in the book. For his expert advice on technological matters and prompt replies to my many e-mails, I am again grateful to Manfred Kuechler, a colleague in the sociology department at Hunter College, whose knowledge of the workings of the Internet

Thanks go, too, to Hunter College librarians Tony Doyle and Jean Jacques Strayer for keeping me up to date on databases and search engines and to Trudi Jacobson at the University at Albany, SUNY, for so ably updating the listing of resources in twenty-seven subject areas. Scot Ober, Ball State University, generously contributed the documents in the section on writing for work. For help in locating good online materials by students, I am grateful to James T. Spencer at Syracuse University, Aaron Delwiche at Trinity University, San Antonio, Texas, and Hector Graciano at LaGuardia Community College, City University of New York. I make a point of insisting that the student writing included in my handbooks is authentic. For giving me permission to use their work in this new edition or on the Web site, I offer many thanks to the following students, all of whom were responsive, helpful, and a pleasure to work with: Katelyn Davies, Daniel Sauve, Charles Mak, Mara Lee Korngold, Brian Cortijo, Lindsay Camp, Catherine Turnbull, Tiffany Brattina, Emily Luo, Jennifer Martinez, Eva Hardcastle, Patricia Lee, Angela Tolano, Tatyana Shchensek, Juana Mere, Mariana Gonzalez, Zhe Chen, and Christel Hyden.

The writing process was much in evidence, as both the fourth edition and the drafts of the new edition were reviewed by composition instructors. They gave the manuscript the benefit of their experience, wisdom, and critical eyes. I am grateful to all of the following:

B. Cole Bennett, Abilene Christian University
Candace Boeck, San Diego State University
Cheryl Bohde, McLennan Community College
Laura B. Carroll, Abilene Christian University
David D. Dzaka, Messiah College
Murray A. Fortner, Tarrant County College
Charles Eric Hoffman, Northern Illinois University
John Hyman, American University
Lindsay Lewan, Arapahoe Community College
Nancy McTaggart, Northern Virginia Community College
Sarah O'Connor, James Madison University
Greg Rubinson, UCLA
Julia Ruengert, Pensacola Junior College
John Silva, LaGuardia Community College of CUNY
Wayne Stein, University of Central Oklahoma
John Stovall, National-Louis University
Eleanor Swanson, Regis University
Brian Walker, Pulaski Technical College
Fredel Wiant, University of San Francisco
Pavel Zemliansky, James Madison University

In addition I extend my grateful thanks to the following, who helped at earlier stages of composition:

Joseph A. Alvarez, Central Piedmont Community College
Akua Duku Anokye, University of Toledo
Jennie Ariail, University of South Carolina
Janet Badia, Marshall University
Pamela J. Balluck, University of Utah
Lona Bassett, Jones County Junior College
Jennifer Beech, Pacific Lutheran University
Robin A. Benny, Chicago State University
Linda Bergman, Illinois Institute of Technology
Clair Berry, State Technical Institute at Memphis
Curtis W. Bobbit, College of Great Falls
Candace A. Boeck, San Diego State University
Darsie Bowden, Western Washington University
Laurie Bower, University of Nevada, Reno
Terry Brown, University of Wisconsin, River Falls
Stephen M. Byars, University of Southern California
Jeffrey P. Cain, Sacred Heart University
Bettina Caluori, DeVry Institute, New Brunswick
Karen A. Carlton, Humboldt State University
Gina Claywell, Murray State University
Linda Clegg, Cerritos College
Robert Cousins, Utah Valley State College
Ned Cummings, Bryant and Stratton College
Lisa Davidson, Passaic County Community College
Ben Davis, Cuyahoga Community College
Judith Davis, Old Dominion University
Virginia B. DeMers, Ringling School of Art and Design
Rob Dornsife, Creighton University
Darlynn R. Fink, Clarion University of Pennsylvania
Katherine Frank, University of Southern Colorado
Muriel Fuqua, Daytona Beach Community College
David W. Furniss, University of Wisconsin, River Falls
Lynée Lewis Gaillet, Georgia State University
Philip Gaines, Montana State University
Dennis Gartner, Frostburg State University
Dorothy Gilbert, California State University, Haywood
Thomas Goodman, University of Miami
Katherine Green, Albuquerque Technical-Vocational Institute
John Gregorian, Contra Costa Community College

Claudia Gresham-Shelton, Stanly Community College
Elizabeth Grubgeld, Oklahoma State University
Keith Gumery, Temple University
Jane E. Hardy, Cornell University
D. Alexis Hart, University of Georgia
Beth L. Hewett, Community College of Baltimore
    County, Essex
Christopher Z. Hobson, State University of New York,
    College at Old Westbury
Franklin E. Horowitz, Columbia University
Michael Hricik, Westmoreland City Community College
Margaret Hughes, Butte College
Mary L. Hurst, Cuyahoga Community College
John Hyman, American University
Ernest H. Johansson, Ohio University
Ted E. Johnston, El Paso Community College
Karen Jones, St. Charles Community College
Mary Kaye Jordan, Ohio University
Ann Judd, Seward County Community College
Susan Kincaid, Lakeland Community College
Martha Kruse, University of Nebraska, Kearney
Sally Kurtzman, Arapahoe Community College
Joseph LaBriola, Sinclair Community College
Lindsay Lewan, Arapahoe Community College
Daniel Lowe, Community College of Allegheny County
Kelly Lowe, Mount Union College
Dianne Luce, Midlands Technical Community College
Mike MacKey, Community College of Denver
Mary Sue MacNealy, The University of Memphis
Gina Maranto, University of Miami
Louis Martin, Elizabethtown College
JoAnne Liebman Matson, University of Arkansas, Little Rock
Ann Maxham-Kastrinos, Washington State University
Michael G. Moran, University of Georgia
Marie Nigro, Lincoln University, Pennsylvania
Carolyn O'Hearn, Pittsburgh State University
Liz Parker, Nashville State Technical Institute
Sally Parr, Ithaca College
Kathy Parrish, Southwestern College
Jane Peterson, Richland College
Lillian Polak, Nassau Community College
Nelljean M. Rice, Coastal Carolina University

Kenneth Risdon, University of Minnesota at Duluth
Mark Rollins, Ohio University
Cheryl W. Ruggiero, Virginia Polytechnic Institute
Kristin L. Snoddy, Indiana University at Kokomo
James R. Sodon, St. Louis Community College at Florissant Valley
Ellen Sostarich, Hocking College
Jami M. Taylor, ECPI College of Technology
Michael R. Underwood, San Diego State University
Amy Ulmer, Pasadena City College
Jane Mueller Ungari, Robert Morris College
Margaret Urie, University of Nevada
Thomas Villano, Boston University
Brian K. Walker, Pulaski Technical College
Colleen Weldele, Palomar College
Barbara Whitehead, Hampton University
Stephen Wilhoit, University of Dayton
Debbie J. Williams, Abilene Christian University
James D. Williams, University of North Carolina, Chapel Hill
James Wilson, LaGuardia Community College,
   City University of New York
Sallie Wolf, Arapahoe Community College
Randell Wolff, Murray State
Martin Wood, University of Wisconsin, Eau Claire
Randal Woodland, University of Michigan, Dearborn
Pamela S. Wright, University of California, San Diego
Laura W. Zlogar, University of Wisconsin, River Falls

My colleagues at Houghton Mifflin have once again been a pleasure to work with. Unfailingly, they are warm, supportive, responsive, knowledgeable about textbook publishing, and unflappable when I get in a flap. Special thanks go to Pat Coryell, Vice President and Publisher, and Suzanne Phelps Weir, for their leadership and enthusiasm for the project; to Carrie Brandon, Editor in Chief, for her energetic support; to Meg Botteon, Senior Development Editor, for her tactful and thoughtful guidance through the new edition; to Martha Bustin, Senior Development Editor, for her timely advice and warm encouragement; to Rosemary Winfield, Senior Project Editor, for coping so calmly with challenging deadlines during the production process; and to Cindy Graff Cohen, Tom Ziolkowski, and Annamarie Rice, for keeping me attuned to market needs. I also gratefully acknowledge the help and professionalism of others on the large *Keys* team: Jane Acheson, Janet Edmonds, John McHugh, Sarah Truax, Katherine Leahey, Andrew

Laskey, Jill Haber, Jerilyn Bockorick, Maria Sas, Bruce Carson, Jennifer Meyer Dare, Lisa Jelly Smith, Mary Dalton Hoffman, Marianne L'Abbate, Susan Zorn, Mary Kanable, Vici Casana, Sherri Dietrich, Priscilla Manchester, and Stephanie Gintowt's miracle workers at New England Typographic Service.

Warmest thanks go once more to my friends in Brooklyn and Chatham, New York, for the good meals, distractions, and fun that writers need in order to survive. For all her good cheer and innovative ideas, I am grateful to Maria Jerskey, colleague, friend and now my new partner in this esoteric enterprise of textbook writing. Our conversations make talking about writing seem like pleasure, not work. Close family members—Emily, Dave, Lucy, and Matt—have been unfailingly supportive and ingenious in finding things to say and do to alleviate the stress of deadlines. And as always, thanks to my husband of forty-two years, James Raimes, now also a Houghton author. A colleague once noted how my acknowledgments to him have escalated in intensity with each book. Quite right. He not only comments on what I write but also cooks great meals, makes sure work is balanced by play ("Enough of this! Let's go to the movies!"), and is always there to make me laugh and laugh with me. His contributions to this fifth edition are enormous.

Ann Raimes

Through writing, you do not just *display* what you know; you can also *discover* what you know and think. The process of writing helps you have ideas, make connections, and raise questions, whether you are producing an e-mail message, a research report, or a Web document. Use the time and solitude that the writing process affords to discover as well as to present, to learn as well as to fulfill an assignment. Expect writing to be not a linear or step-by-step procedure, but a messy adventure, one that you control but that often surprises you with your own insights.

Though virtually no one marches neatly through the process in a set sequence, writing does involve several overlapping and recurring activities:

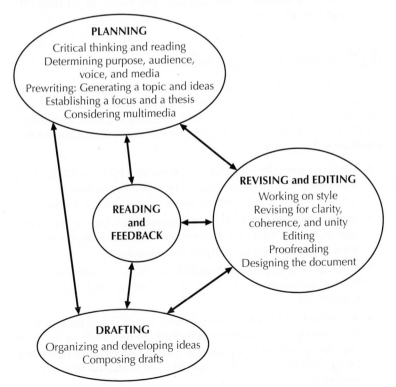

PLANNING
Critical thinking and reading
Determining purpose, audience,
voice, and media
Prewriting: Generating a topic and ideas
Establishing a focus and a thesis
Considering multimedia

READING and FEEDBACK

REVISING and EDITING
Working on style
Revising for clarity,
coherence, and unity
Editing
Proofreading
Designing the document

DRAFTING
Organizing and developing ideas
Composing drafts

In the multitasking common in today's wired or wireless world, the need to keep all those tasks in mind all at once will probably not seem too taxing.

 Chapter **1**

Ways into Writing

Getting started can be hard if you think of a piece of writing as a permanent document. A blank page or an empty screen with its blinking cursor can be daunting, but the act of writing offers an advantage over speaking: you can go back and make changes. You are not locked into what you have written—not until you decide to turn your finished work over to readers. You can also present whatever image of yourself you choose. You have the freedom to invent yourself anew. As journalist Adam Gopnik says fondly of writing, "It's you there, but not quite you."

1a   Writing in today's world

Just as writing allows you to present yourself in multiple ways, the act of writing (or composing) is not a single, easily definable act but one that thrives on the complexity of today's global and digital world. In fact, look at how the prefix *multi-* characterizes the writing situation today:

- Writing, especially online or supplemented by presentation software, uses *multi*media—images, color, audio, animation, video— not just print and is produced and read in a nonlinear way.

- Writers and readers today are therefore developing the necessary *multi*modal literacy to cope with the many modes that are used in preparing and interpreting today's texts.

- Patterns of migration and globalization have created *multi*cultural communities made up of *multi*ethnic and *multi*lingual individuals.

- As writers and readers move in and out of countries and local communities or experience them through the media or the Web, they necessarily develop the *multi*literacies that derive from language diversity (see 37c and 59a on Standard English and Englishes).

Add to these the fact that writers today engage in *multi*tasking—writing an essay while talking on the phone, sending an IM, checking e-mail, listening to music, and downloading MP3 files—and you get a picture of the complex world writers and readers inhabit. Grappling with these multiplicities is part of the challenge and excitement of writing today. You'll find them mentioned often in this book.

1b What it means to read critically

Just as we think critically about what we read, readers think critically when they read what we write, sometimes making comments like these: "I wonder where she gets that from?" "I don't understand that point." "She hasn't convinced me at all."

When we read and write, we engage in a process of locating and entering an ongoing conversation about an issue, examining critically the ideas expressed by others and asking questions about those ideas. For example, we may find ourselves nodding and agreeing with or even admiring a text. Or we may be triggered to use the word "*But . . .*" as we read—either saying it in our head or writing it in the text itself—a sign of our critical evaluation of a writer's ideas and a mark of our entry into the swirl of ideas around the topic. As we read, we learn what the threads are in the discussion around the issue, scrutinize the ideas we find, and adjust our own ideas accordingly. During the process of writing, we think critically about our own position and the position others take. That critical thinking helps shape our writing.

Thinking critically does not, however, mean thinking negatively in order to criticize—though if what you read is badly written, that could well be the result. Instead, it means questioning, discussing, and looking at words and images from a number of sides. It also means looking for points of connection and agreement with a writer's views.

For more on thinking critically about arguments, see 4a.

KEY POINTS
Critical Thinking and Reading of Text and Images

1. *Do close readings.* Read more than once; examine a text or an image slowly and carefully, immersing yourself in the work.

2. *Look for common ground.* Note places where you are impressed by the points made in the text or image—that is, places where you nod in approval. *(Continued)*

(Continued)

3. *Question and challenge.* Take on the role of a debater. Ask, for example, where an idea comes from, what biases the writer reveals, whether the writer provides you with enough information in an interesting way, what evidence a writer provides, whether the writer's logic is sound, and whether opposing views are taken into account.

4. *Write as you read.* Interact with a text or image by writing comments and questions in the margins of a page, between the lines in an online document saved to your word processor, or on self-stick notes. In this way, you start a conversation with anything you read. The text you are reading will look messy—but that is a good sign.

5. *Keep a reading journal and write summaries and reactions.* See 1d on using journals and blogs.

6. *Remember that readers will read critically what you write.* It is not enough to read critically. Be aware that your own writing has to stand up to readers' careful scrutiny and challenge, too.

While reading the following passage about the Ultimatum Game, a student annotated the passage as she read it with comments, questions, and challenges, increasing her interaction with the article.

I like the direct approach!

Imagine that somebody offers you $100. All you have to do is agree with some other anonymous person on how to share the sum. The rules are strict. The two of you are in separate rooms and cannot exchange information. A coin toss decides which of you will propose how to share the money. Suppose that you are the proposer. You can make a single offer of how to split the sum, and the other person—the responder—can say yes or no. The responder also knows the rules and the total amount of money at stake. If her answer is yes, the deal goes ahead. If her answer is no, neither of you gets anything. In both cases, the game is over and will not be repeated. What will you do?

Critical point Ha! Why anonymous

Authors use feminine pronoun here

Instinctively, many people feel they should offer 50 percent, because such a division is "fair" and therefore likely to be accepted. More daring people, however, think they might get away with offering somewhat less than half the sum.

Or more greedy?

Have the authors researched this assumption

Before making a decision, you should ask yourself what you would do if you were the responder. The only thing you can do as the responder is say yes or no to a given amount of

ut the
rganizers
iil know
shat I offer,
o it's not
intirely
etween two
anonymous people.

money. If the offer were 10 percent, would you take $10 and let someone walk away with $90, or would you rather have nothing at all? What if the offer were only 1 percent? Isn't $1 better than no dollars? And remember, haggling is strictly forbidden. Just one offer by the proposer; the responder can take it or leave it.

So what will you offer?

—Karl Sigmund, Ernst Fehr, and Martin A. Nowak,
"The Economics of Fair Play" (copyright © 2002 by
Scientific American, all rights reserved)

1c Considering purpose, audience, voice, and media

Your purpose   As you read, try to articulate what you see as the writer's purpose. Then, before you begin writing, consider your own main purpose. Use the questions in the Key Points box as a guide.

> **KEY POINTS**
> **Asking about Purpose in Your Writing**
>
> 1. Is your main purpose to explain an idea or provide information? Writing with this purpose is called *expository writing.*
>
> 2. Is your main purpose to persuade readers to see things your way or move readers to action? This aim leads to *persuasive writing* or *argumentation.*
>
> 3. Is your main purpose to describe an experiment or a detailed process or to report on laboratory results? Writing with this purpose is frequently referred to as *scientific* or *technical writing.*
>
> 4. Is your main purpose to record and express your own experience, observations, ideas, and feelings? In the humanities, such accounts are known as *expressive, autobiographical,* or *personal writing.*
>
> 5. Is your main purpose to create an original work of art, such as a poem, story, play, or novel? Writing with this purpose is called *creative writing.*

Among the categories the overlap can be considerable. Some assignments may require you to explore and test concepts and opinions against what you already know. Other assignments may ask you to blend explanation with persuasion. Creative nonfiction, which includes memoir, biography, and travel writing, crosses categories to present information in a literary and original way, adding the art of storytelling to the accurate reporting of information. Whatever you determine to be the main purpose or purposes of a given assignment should guide you as you begin writing.

Your audience and discourse community   A good writer connects with his or her audience and keeps readers in mind at all times, as if in a face-to-face communication. Achieving this connection, however, often proves challenging because not all readers have the same characteristics. Readers come from different discourse communities—that is, from different regions, communities, ethnic groups, organizations, and academic disciplines, all with their own linguistic and rhetorical conventions (see 4f). Ask yourself the following questions about your readers.

LANGUAGE AND CULTURE
Assessing Your Readers' Expectations

- Who will read your piece of writing? What will those readers expect in terms of length, format, date of delivery, technical terms, and formality of language?

- What kinds of texts do your readers usually read and write, and what are the conventions of those texts? For example, if you are writing a business letter to a company in another country, consult a business communications book to find out what readers there expect.

- What characteristics do you and your readers have in common: nationality, language, culture, race, class, ethnicity, gender? Consider what limitations writing for these readers places on your use of dialect, punctuation, vocabulary, and political and cultural comments. Cultivate common ground, and try not to alienate readers.

- Is your instructor your main reader? If so, find out about the expectations of a reader in his or her academic discipline. Be sure to ask what background information you should include and what you can safely omit, and ask to see a model paper. In most cases, regard your instructor as a stand-in for an audience of general readers, not as an individual expert.

TECH NOTE

Taking Accessibility Issues and Disabilities into Account

For documents you prepare for online viewers or for oral and multimedia presentations, issues of accessibility are important.

- Consider whether readers have a dialup or a broadband connection before you post large image files online.

- For any vision-impaired viewers, increase type size, provide a zoom function, and limit the number of visuals or describe them in words.

- Pay attention to color in visuals: contrasting shades work better for some viewers than different colors.

- Use online sites such as WebAim and Bobby to test your documents for accessibility.

Online Study Center   **Design** Accessibility

Your voice   Closely connected to your purpose and audience is the voice or persona you present to readers. How do you want to come across to them? What impression do you want them to form of you as a person, of your values and opinions? One of the first considerations is whether you want to draw attention to your opinions as the writer by using the first person pronoun "I," or whether you will try the more objective-seeming approach of keeping that "I" at a distance. Even if you do the latter, though, as is often recommended for academic and especially for scientific writing, you know that readers will still see what you write as ultimately presenting you and your work. Professor Glen McClish at San Diego State University has pointed out how the voice—and, consequently, the effect—of a text such as the one below changes significantly when the first fourteen words, including the first person pronouns, are omitted:

> In the first section of my paper, I want to make the point that the spread of technology is damaging personal relationships.

Your instructor or work supervisor may have strong ideas about the voice, the level of formality, and the amount of authorial intervention expected, so ask him or her what is preferred.

The media you'll use   A printed document? Print and images? An online document with hyperlinks, images, sound, or video? A presentation of your work using the bells and whistles available in presentation software, such as bulleted items appearing one by one or flying onto the screen? As you work through the process of choosing and developing a topic (1d) for a defined purpose and audience, you'll also need to consider simultaneously the communication means available to you, especially if you are presenting your work online or with the help of presentation software. Keep in mind throughout the process of writing where you can enhance your point with the design of your document and the use of images, graphs, or multimedia tools wherever appropriate (chapters 20, 21, 24, and 28).

1d Ways to generate a topic and ideas

Whether you have to generate your own idea for a topic or you already have a clear sense of purpose and topic, you need strategies other than staring at the ceiling or waiting for inspiration to fly in through the window. Professional writers use a variety of prewriting techniques to generate ideas at various stages of the process. In her article "Oh Muse! You Do Make Things Difficult!" Diane Ackerman reports that the poet Dame Edith Sitwell used to lie in an open coffin, French novelist Colette picked fleas from her cat, statesman Benjamin Franklin soaked in the bathtub, and German dramatist Friedrich Schiller sniffed rotten apples stored in his desk.

Perhaps you have developed your own original approach to generating the mess of ideas that will help you write a draft. Perhaps you were taught a more formal way to begin a writing project, such as by constructing an outline. If what you do now does not seem to produce good results, or if you are ready for a change, try some of the following methods and see how they work. Not every method works equally well for every project or for every writer. Experimenting with prewriting is a good idea.

The tools described in the rest of this section can be used for generating a topic or discovering ideas on a specific topic—or both.

Generating a topic   "What on earth am I going to write about?" is a question frequently voiced or at least thought in college classrooms, especially in those classrooms in which students are free to write about any topic that interests them.

Using the strategies in 1d will help you find topics. In addition, think about what matters to you. Reflect on issues raised in your college courses; read newspapers and magazines for current issues; consider campus, community, city, state, and nationwide issues; and look at the Library of Congress Subject Headings to get ideas (see also 7d). Sometimes, browsing an online library catalog, a Web directory, or the site of an institution devoted to research can produce good ideas for choosing a topic, but it is usually better to begin with something that has caught your interest elsewhere and has some connection to your life.

TECH NOTE

Using Web Directories to Find a Topic

Academic Web directories assembled by librarians and academic institutions provide reliable sources for finding good academic subjects. For links to the Librarians' Index to the Internet, Academic Info, and Voice of the Shuttle, a University of California at Santa Barbara directory for humanities research, go to the Online Study Center.

Online Study Center   **Writing Process** Finding a topic

General Internet search engines and directories such as Yahoo! at <http://www.yahoo.com> and Google at <http://www.google.com> offer subject categories that you can explore and successively narrow down to find a topic suitable for an essay. For example, one Yahoo! search beginning with "Education" produced forty different categories, with links to twenty-one site listings (such as *computers as tutors, National Clearinghouse for Comprehensive School Reform, EducationReform.net,* and *No Child Left Behind*), with further links to sites with bibliographies.

What if you are assigned a topic that you are not interested in? That can happen, but do not despair. Read as much as you can on the topic until something strikes you and captures your interest. You can try taking the opposite point of view from that of one of your sources, challenging the point of view. Or you can set yourself the task of showing readers exactly why the topic has not grabbed people's interest—maybe the literature and the research have been just too technical or inaccessible? If you can, find a human angle.

For more on topics, see 4c and 6d.

TECH NOTE

Web Sites for Generating Ideas and Planning

The *Purdue University Online Writing Lab* at <http://owl.english.purdue.edu> and other online resources include information on generating ideas and planning.

Journals, blogs, and online conversations   A *journal* can be far more than a personal diary. Many writers carry a notebook and write in it every day. Journal entries can be observations, references, quotations, questions for research, notes on events, and ideas about assigned texts or topics, as well as specific pieces of writing in progress. A journal can also serve as a review for final examinations or essay tests, reminding you of areas of special interest or subjects you did not understand.

The *double-entry* or *dialectical journal* provides a formalized way for you to think critically about readings and lectures. Two pages or two columns or open windows in your word processor provide the space for interaction. On the left-hand side, write summaries, quotations, and accounts of readings, lectures, and class discussions—that is, record as exactly and concisely as you can what you read or heard. The left-hand side, in short, is reserved for information about the material. On the right-hand side, record your own comments, reactions, and questions about the material.

Online Study Center   **Writing Process** Double-entry reading journal

A *blog* also gives you the opportunity to think aloud—in public. Not only can others read your posting; they can respond to it as well. (It is easy to set up a blog using an automated publishing system.) Blogs are posted in reverse chronological order but otherwise function similarly to a writer's journal, but with responses. The unedited blog entitled "The *Life* of a Salesman" (p. 13) was posted on a writing course blog site by Tiffany Brattina, a student at Seton Hall University. Here she works out a personal, original, and critical point of view as, after a missed class, she considers an interpretation of the character Willie Loman in Arthur Miller's play *Death of a Salesman*. Brattina largely avoids the colloquial nature of instant messaging and informal e-mail and begins to move to the conventions of public discourse suitable for her academic audience. Knowing that other students in her English course will be reading her blog, Brattina openly asks what others think.

Online Study Center   **Writing Process** Blogging/online conversations

A student's blog on a course site

March 16, 2004

The *Life* of a Salesman

Ok. So, I'm sure during class today everyone talked about how crazy Willie was, and I am the first to agree. Willie was insane, in the end. However, what about his life?

In *Death of a Salesman* we see the end of Willie's life as a salesman. He went through his entire life working on the road selling things to buyers, he didn't know how to do anything else. Don't you think that would make you go crazy? If a company you worked for your entire life took you off of salary and put you on commission like you were just starting out wouldn't you feel like you were unworthy? Then there is the fact that Willie and his family didn't really have any money to their names at all. Willie kept borrowing money from Charley so that Linda wouldn't know that he wasn't getting paid anymore. Then the company he worked for fired him! I feel bad for Willie, I really do. His kids thought that he was insane and wanted nothing to do with him. The people he worked for his entire life turned him away. Willie was old, tired, and worn out and people including his family turned their backs on him.

Let me make this personal for a minute. My dad recently went through something very similar at his place of work. The company he worked for came into new management and they tried to put my dad on commission. My dad has major tenure where he works considering he is now 56 and has been working there for 40 years making him the longest member still working at the company. He took the new management to court and won his case. I know that while my dad was going through that time he was a total mess, so seeing my dad I can understand what Willie was going through.

What do you guys think? Do you feel bad for Willie or do you think he was just a jerk? Why or why not?

Posted by Tiffany Brattina at March 16, 2004 06:49 PM

Comments

Do you remember Greek Tragedy? I do, and let me say that Willie is the tragic hero. I kept wanting him to succeed, and he didn't. I really felt that there was a chance for him to make something of himself, and couldn't. I had the feeling that Willie was going to kill himself, but something kept telling me that he was going to get out of the severe skid that he was in.

Posted by The Gentle Giant at March 16, 2004 08:58 PM

Never thought of that Jay ... you are right though. I did feel like he was going to succeed, especially there at the end ... Oh well.
Tiff

Posted by Tiffany at March 16, 2004 09:57 PM

Freewriting If you do not know what to write about or how to approach a broad subject, try doing five to ten minutes of *freewriting* either on paper or on the computer. When you freewrite, you let one idea lead to another in free association, without concern for correctness. The important thing is to keep writing. If you cannot think of a word or phrase while you are freewriting, simply write a note to yourself inside square brackets, or put in a symbol such as #, as Zhe Chen does when she questions her use of the word *puttering* and can't remember the word *windowpanes*. On a computer, use the Search command to find your symbol later, when you can spend more time thinking about the word.

Zhe Chen did some unedited freewriting in class on the topic "name and identity," which led her eventually to an essay topic examining the effects of the Cultural Revolution on family identity.

> I have a unusual name, Zhe. My friends in China say it's a boys name. My friends in America think it has only one letter. Most of my American friends have difficulty pronouncing my name.
>
> Some people ask me why don't I Americanize my name so it would be easier to pronounce. But I say if I change my name, it will not be me any more. What else can I write? When I was seven years old, I asked my mother what my name meant. "Ask your father," she said as she washed dishes. It was raining outside, and the room was so quiet that I could hear the rain puttering [? Look this up] on the #. My father's thoughts returned to another rainy day in 1967 when the Cultural Revolution just begun. Thousands of people had been banished to countryside and all the schools were closed. My grandparents fled to Hong Kong but my father and aunt stayed in China. Life was difficult. Gangs sent them to the countryside to work. It was here that my parents met.
>
> Back to name again. My father named me Zhe. In Chinese my name means remember and hope. He wanted me remember the Cultural Revolution and he wanted me to finish college. He didn't have that chance.

Brainstorming Another way to generate ideas is by *brainstorming*—making a freewheeling list of ideas as you think of them. Brainstorming is enhanced if you do it collaboratively in a group, discussing and then listing your ideas. (See also 1h, Writing collaboratively.) You can then, by yourself or with the group, scrutinize the ideas, arrange them, reorganize them, and add to or eliminate them.

One group of students working collaboratively made the following brainstorming list on the topic "changing a name":

voluntary changes—hate name
escape from family and parents
show business
George Eliot (Mary Ann Evans)
Woody Allen (Allen Stewart Konigsberg)
P. Diddy (Sean Combs aka Puff Daddy)
writers and their pseudonyms
married women
writers and their pseudonyms—who?
some keep own name, some change, some use both names and
   hyphenate
Hillary Clinton/Hillary Rodham Clinton
immigrants
Ellis Island
forced name changes
political name changes
name changes because of racism or oppression
criminals?

Once the students had made the list, they reviewed it, rejected some items, expanded on others, and grouped items. Thus, they developed a range of subcategories that led them to possibilities for further exploration and essay organization:

Voluntary Name Changes

authors: George Eliot, Mark Twain, Isak Dinesen
show business and stage names: Woody Allen, Bob Dylan, Ringo Starr,
   P. Diddy, Eminem, Pink
ethnic and religious identification: Malcolm X, Muhammad Ali

Name Changes upon Marriage

reasons for changing or not changing
Hillary Clinton
problem of children's names
alternative: hyphenated name

Forced Name Changes

immigrants on Ellis Island
wartime oppression
slavery

Mapping *Mapping,* also called *clustering,* is a visual way of generating and connecting ideas. It can be done individually or in a group. Write your topic in a circle at the center of a page, think of ideas related to the topic, and write those ideas on the page around the central topic. Draw lines from the topic to the related ideas. Then add details under each of the ideas you noted. For a writing assignment that asked students to respond to something they had read, a student created the following map. She saw that it indicated several possibilities for topics, such as the increasing casualness of American society and the power of uniforms to both camouflage and identify their wearers. (See her drafts in 3e.)

Using journalists' questions   Journalists check the coverage of their stories by making sure that they answer six questions—Who? What? When? Where? Why? How?—though not in any set order. A report on a public transit strike, for example, would include details about the union leaders (who they were), the issue of working conditions and benefits (what the situation was), the date and time of the confrontation (when the strike occurred), the place (where it occurred), what caused the confrontation (why it happened), and how the people involved behaved and resolved the strike (how it evolved and ended). If you are telling the story of an event, either as a complete essay or as an example in an essay, asking the journalists' six questions will help you think comprehensively about your topic. If you are writing creative nonfiction, you will move beyond the objective reporting of facts to the inclusion of dramatic and poetic details and language.

Using prompts   Sometimes you might find it helpful to use a formal set of directions (known as *prompts*) to suggest new avenues of inquiry. Write down responses to any of the prompts that apply to your topic, and note possibilities for further exploration. A topic assigned by your instructor may also include these terms. See 2c for examples of ideas developed in these and other ways.

DEFINE YOUR TERMS   Look up key words in your topic (like *success, identity, ambition,* and *ethnicity*) in the dictionary, and write down the definition you want to use. Consider synonyms, too.

GIVE EXAMPLES OR FACTS   Think of facts and stories from your reading or experience that relate to your topic.

INCLUDE DESCRIPTIONS   Whatever your topic, make your writing more vivid with details about color, light, location, movement, size, shape, sound, taste, and smell. Help your reader "see" your topic, such as a person, place, object, or scientific experiment, exactly as you see it.

MAKE COMPARISONS   Help your reader understand a topic by describing what it might be similar to and different from. For example, how is learning to write like learning to juggle?

ASSESS CAUSE AND EFFECT   Convey information on what causes or produces your topic and what effects or results emerge from it. For example, what are the causes and effects of dyslexia? inflation? acid rain? hurricanes? asthma?

CONSIDER WHAT OTHERS HAVE SAID   Give your reader information, facts, and statistics on what others say about your topic in interviews, surveys, reading, and research.

1e   Developing a focus and a thesis

You might be given any of the following types of assignments for an essay, arranged here from the broadest in scope to the narrowest:

- a free choice of subject
- a broad subject area, such as "genetic engineering" or "affirmative action"
- a focused and specific topic, such as "the city's plans to build apartments on landfill" or "the treatment of welfare recipients in California"
- an actual question to answer, such as "In what ways is age an issue in cases of driving accidents?"

If you are given a free choice of subject, you will need to narrow your focus to a specific subject area, to a topic, to a question. After that, still more narrowing is necessary to formulate a thesis.

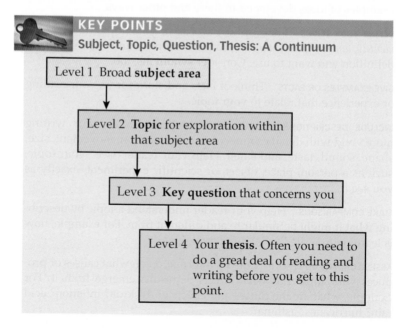

KEY POINTS

Subject, Topic, Question, Thesis: A Continuum

Level 1 Broad **subject area**

Level 2 **Topic** for exploration within that subject area

Level 3 **Key question** that concerns you

Level 4 Your **thesis**. Often you need to do a great deal of reading and writing before you get to this point.

Your thesis, or claim, is your statement of opinion, main idea, or message that unifies your piece of writing, makes a connection between you and the subject area, lets your reader know where you stand in relation to the topic, and responds to the question posed.

Here is one student's movement from subject to thesis over several days of reading, discussion, freewriting, and note-taking:

Subject: College admissions policies

Topic: Affirmative action in college admissions

Question: How do people react to students who are accepted by colleges under affirmative action policies?

Thesis: The public and the press often unjustly question the abilities of students accepted into colleges under affirmative action policies.

If you choose a topic and a question that are too broad, you will find it difficult to generate a thesis with focused ideas and examples. Whenever you find yourself thinking, for instance, "There's so much to say about affirmative action—its history, goals, practice, criticisms, successes—that I don't know where to start," narrow your topic. If you begin by choosing a topic and a question that are too narrow, you probably will not find enough material and will end up being repetitive. Whenever you feel you have enough material to fill only a page and can't imagine how you will find more ("What else can I say about how my cousin got into college?"), broaden your topic. Above all, stay flexible: you may want to change your topic or your question as you discover more information.

Formulating a working thesis—and why you need one
Suppose someone were to ask you, "What is the main idea that you want to communicate to your reader in your piece of writing?" The sentence you would give in reply is your *thesis statement,* also known as a *claim.* Your claim tells readers what stand you are going to take. It is not enough to say, "I am writing about bilingual education." Are you going to address bilingual education in elementary, secondary, or higher education? Which readers do you regard as your primary audience? Which geographical areas will you discuss? Will you be concerned with the past or with the present? What do you intend to propose about the area of bilingual education you have selected? In short, what point do you want to make about which aspect of bilingual education—for which readers? You don't have to know exactly where to put your thesis statement in your essay right now, but having a thesis will focus your thoughts

as you read and write. See 4d for more on the thesis in an argument paper.

A good thesis statement may be one or more of the following:

1. a generalization needing supporting evidence

    ▶ **Students benefit when they learn in two languages.**

2. a strong, thought-provoking, or controversial statement

    ▶ **Bilingual education has not fulfilled its early promise.**

3. a call to action

    ▶ **All inner-city schools should set up bilingual programs.**

4. an analytical statement that sets up the structure of the essay

    ▶ **Bilingual education suffers from two main problems: a shortage of trained teachers and a lack of parental involvement.**

After you have formulated your working thesis, write it on a self-stick note or an index card and keep it near you as you write. The note or card will remind you to stick to the point. If you still digress as you write, you may need to consider changing your thesis.

KEY POINTS
Thesis Checklist

You should be able to put a checkmark next to each quality as you examine your draft.

☐ Your thesis is worth presenting and is the answer to a question that could be debated (is not an obvious truism or vague generalization).

☐ Your thesis narrows your topic to the main idea that you want to communicate.

☐ Your thesis makes a claim or states your view about your topic.

☐ Your thesis can be supported by details, facts, and examples within the assigned limitations of time and space.

☐ Your thesis stimulates curiosity and interest in readers and prompts them to think, "Why do you say that?" and then to read on and be convinced by what you have written.

☐ Your thesis forecasts and unifies all that follows in your essay; it does not include ideas or points that you do not intend to discuss in your essay.

☐ Your thesis is expressed concisely in one or two complete sentences (though you will come across many variations as you read).

Stating your thesis in your paper   In most academic writing in the humanities and social sciences, a thesis is stated clearly in the essay, usually near the beginning. See your thesis statement as a signpost—both for you as you write your draft and, later, for readers as they read your essay. A clear thesis prepares readers well for the rest of the essay. If you use key words from your thesis as you write, you will keep readers focused on your main idea.

Sometimes, though, particularly in descriptive, narrative, and informative writing, you may choose to imply your thesis and not explicitly state it. In such a case, you make your thesis clear by the examples, details, and information you include. You may also choose to state your thesis at the end of your essay instead of the beginning, presenting all the evidence to build a case and then making the thesis act as a climax and logical statement about the outcome of the evidence.

On not falling in love with your thesis   A good thesis often takes so long to develop that you might be reluctant to change it. Be willing, however, to refine and change your thesis as you find more information and work with your material. Many writers begin with a tentative working thesis and then find that they come to a new conclusion at the end of the first draft. If that happens to you, start your second draft by focusing on the thesis that emerged during the writing of the first draft. Be flexible: it's easier to change a thesis statement to fit new ideas and newly discovered evidence than to find new evidence to fit a thesis. Note that your final thesis statement should take a firm stand on the issue. Flexibility during the writing process is not the same as indecision in the final product.

LANGUAGE AND CULTURE
Language, Identity, and the Thesis Statement

Often writers who have developed their writing skills in one language notice distinct differences in the conventions of writing in another, particularly with respect to the explicit statement of opinion in the thesis. A Chinese writer, Fan Shen, for example, sees the explicit thesis statement favored in Western writing as "symbolic of the values of a busy people in an industrialized society, rushing to get things done" (*College Composition and Communication* [Dec. 1989]: 462). It is difficult to determine how much of a role one's culture plays in the way one writes and to separate culture's role from the roles of gender, socioeconomic status, family background, and education. However, always consider what approaches your anticipated readers are likely to be familiar with and to value.

1f   Using outlines

A *scratch outline* is a rough list of numbered points that you intend to cover in your essay. A scratch outline lets you see what ideas you already have, how they connect, what you can do to support and develop them, and what further planning or research you still need to do. One student in the group that made the brainstorming list on pages 15–16 developed the following scratch outline and formulated a tentative thesis:

Topic: Changing a name

Question: Why do people change their names?

Tentative thesis: People change their names because they either have to or want to.

Points:

1. Some are forced to make name changes in a new country or a new school.
2. Some change a name to avoid discrimination or persecution.
3. Some (women only?) change a name upon marriage.
4. Show business personalities often change their names.
5. Some people change a name to avoid recognition.
   a. Criminals—witness protection program
   b. Writers

When this student began to write his draft, however, he changed direction and unified some of his points, developing a more focused thesis (see the formal outline below).

A *formal outline* spells out, in order, what points and supportive details you will use to develop your thesis and arranges them to show the overall form and structure of the essay. You may produce a formal outline before you begin to write, but you are likely to find that making an outline with a high level of detail is more feasible after you have written a draft. Done at this later point, the outline serves as a check on the logic and completeness of what you have written, revealing any gaps, repetition, or illogical steps in the development of your essay.

The student who did the brainstorming (1d) and made the scratch outline finally settled on a thesis and made this topic outline of an essay draft, using complete sentences for the first three levels of the outline.

Thesis: A voluntary name change is usually motivated by a desire to avoid or gain recognition.

I. The desire to avoid recognition by others is one motive for a name change.
   A. Criminals change their names.
   B. Writers use pseudonyms.
      1. Women writers adopt men's names.
         a. George Eliot (Mary Ann Evans)
         b. George Sand (Amandine Aurore Lucie Dupin)
         c. Isak Dinesen (Karen Blixen)
      2. Some writers adopt a pseudonym.
         a. Mark Twain (Samuel Clemens)
         b. Lewis Carroll (Charles Dodgson)
         c. Amanda Cross (Carolyn Heilbrun)
   C. Some change a name to avoid ethnic identification.
II. Married women and entertainers may change a name to join a group and gain recognition.
   A. Married women mark membership in a family.
      1. They want to indicate married status.
      2. They want the same name as their children.
   B. Entertainers choose eye-catching names.
      1. Marilyn Monroe (Norma Jean Baker)
      2. Woody Allen (Allen Stewart Konigsberg)
      3. Ringo Starr (Richard Starkey)
      4. P. Diddy (Sean Combs) and Eminem (Marshall Mathers)

Making an outline is a useful tool for revision. This student saw that his draft was basically well structured but that he needed to find out more about criminals and their aliases (I.A.) and about people who change a name to avoid ethnic identification (I.C.). You may find, however, that purpose statements and proposals are often more easily created in the early stages of planning than are outlines (6f).

1g　Overcoming writer's block

Most of us, even if we write a great deal or profess to like writing, have at some time or another felt blocked. We sit and stare at the blank page or screen or at our notes and keep going to the refrigerator or vending machine for solace. If you feel overwhelmed with the task of organizing your research findings, frustrated because your writing doesn't seem to "sound right," or blocked for any reason, take comfort from the fact that you are not alone. The following questions and strategies may help.

KEY POINTS
Overcoming Writer's Block

1. Do you have a set of rules that you try to follow in your writing process, such as "Always begin by writing a good introduction," "Check everything as soon as you write it," or "Always start with a complete outline"? If you do, consider whether your rules are too rigid or even unhelpful. As you gather ideas and do your preparatory drafting, try ignoring any self-imposed rules that hinder you.

2. Do you edit as soon as you write, and do you edit often? If you answer yes, your desire to write correctly might be preventing you from thinking about ideas and moving forward. Try journal writing, freewriting, brainstorming, or mapping (see 1d).

3. Do you feel anxious about writing, even though you have knowledge of and interest in your topic? If you do, try using some of the freewriting and brainstorming strategies in 1d, or begin writing as if you were talking about your topic with a friend.

4. Do you feel that you do not yet know enough about your topic to start writing, even though you may have done a great deal of research? If so, try freewriting or try drafting the sections

you know most about. Writing will help show you what you know and what you need to know.

5. Do you find you need more information, insight, or background knowledge than you have so far gathered? If so, set aside more time and devote yourself to reading, interpreting, taking notes, and critical thinking. What you think is writer's block may miraculously disappear once you feel in control of your topic.

1h Writing collaboratively

Writing is not necessarily a solitary process. In the academic or business world, you will often have to work collaboratively with one or more classmates or colleagues. You might be part of a group, team, or committee assigned to draft a proposal or a report. You might be expected to produce a document reflecting the consensus of your section or group. Or you might need to draft and circulate a document and then incorporate into it the comments of many people, as was the case with the student drafts in 3e and in chapter 35.

In group settings, make sure that every member of the group has the opportunity to contribute and does contribute. You can do this by assigning each person a set of specific tasks, such as making lists of ideas, drafting, analyzing the draft, revising, editing, assembling visuals, and preparing the final document. Schedule regular meetings, and expect everyone to come with a completed written assignment. Build on strengths within the group. For example, ask the member skilled in document design and computer graphics to prepare the visual features of the final document.

However, make sure that you work collaboratively only when doing so is expected. An instructor who assigns an essay will not always expect you to work on it with your sister, classmate, or tutor. If collaborative peer groups are encouraged, you may find the peer response form in 3b useful.

TECH NOTE

Writing Collaboratively on the Computer

Word processing programs provide useful tools for collaboration. You can work on a text, make and highlight changes, and attach the revised text to an e-mail message to a colleague, who can then accept or reject the changes. See 3b for more details.

1i Tips for writing a first draft

Writing provides what speech can never provide: the opportunity to revise your ideas and the way you present them. The drafting process lets you make substantive changes as you progress through drafts. You can add, delete, and reorganize sections of your paper. You can rethink your thesis and support. You can change your approach to parts or all of the paper. Writing drafts allows you to work on a piece of writing until it meets your goals.

KEY POINTS
Tips for a First Draft

1. Plan the steps and set a schedule (6b). Work backward from the deadline, and assign time in days or hours for each of the following: deciding on a topic, generating ideas, making a scratch outline, writing a draft, getting feedback, analyzing the draft, making large-scale revisions, finding additional material, editing, proofreading, formatting, and printing.

   Online Study Center   **Research** Sample research schedule

2. Don't automatically begin by writing the introduction. Begin by writing the essay parts for which you already have some specific material. Then you will know what you need to introduce.

3. Write in increments of twenty to thirty minutes to take advantage of momentum.

4. Write your first draft as quickly and fluently as you can and print it triple-spaced. Write notes to yourself in capitals or surrounded by asterisks to remind yourself to add or change something or to do further research.

   ### TECH NOTE
   #### Using Comment and AutoCorrect

   Some word processing programs have a Comment function that allows you to type notes that appear only on the screen, not in a printout. These notes are easily deleted from later drafts. In addition, if you use a term frequently (for example, the phrase "bilingual education"), abbreviate it (as "b.e.") and use a tool like AutoCorrect and Replace to substitute the whole phrase throughout your draft as you type.

5. Avoid obvious, vague, or empty generalizations (such as "All people have feelings"). Be specific, and include interesting supporting details.

6. Resist the lure of Copy and Paste. Copying a passage from an online site and pasting it into your own document may seem like a good solution when you are facing a looming deadline and surfing for good Web sources. However, the penalties for plagiarism are far worse than those for lateness (see 9a). So the bottom line here is ***DON'T DO IT.***

 Chapter **2**

Developing Paragraphs and Essays

Sentences make up paragraphs, and paragraphs are the building blocks of essays. See chapters 4, 5, 13, 16, and 19 for more on organizing essays across the curriculum and for sample essays.

2a Writing a paragraph: The basics

The first line of a paragraph is indented five spaces from the left margin or, in business and online documents, begins after a blank line. A good paragraph makes a clear point, supports your main idea, and keeps to one topic.

Some paragraphs have more to do with function than with content. They serve to take readers from one point to another, making a connection and offering a smooth transition from one idea to the next. These transitional paragraphs are often short.

For introductory and concluding paragraphs, see 2e.

KEY POINTS
When to Begin a New Paragraph

1. To introduce a new point (one that supports the claim or main idea of your essay)

2. To expand on a point already made by offering new examples or evidence *(Continued)*

(Continued)

3. To break up a long discussion or description into manageable chunks that readers can assimilate

Both logic and aesthetics dictate when it is time to begin a new paragraph. Think of a paragraph as something that gathers together in one place ideas that connect to each other and to the main purpose of the piece of writing.

2b Composing a unified paragraph

A *unified paragraph,* in academic writing, includes one main idea that the rest of the piece of writing (paragraph or essay) explains, supports, and develops. Just as a thesis statement helps readers of an essay keep your main idea in mind, a *topic sentence* in a body paragraph lets readers know what the main idea of the paragraph is. Readers should notice a logical flow of ideas as they read through a paragraph and as they move from one paragraph to another through an essay.

When you write a paragraph, imagine a reader saying, "Look, I don't have time to read all this. Just tell me in one sentence (or two) what point you are making here." Your reply would express your main point. Each paragraph in an academic essay generally contains a controlling idea expressed in a sentence (a topic sentence) and does not digress or switch topics in midstream. Its content is unified.

The following paragraph is devoted to one broad topic—tennis—but does not follow through on the promise of the topic sentence to discuss the *trouble* that the *backhand* causes *average* players (the key words are italicized).

> The backhand in tennis causes average weekend players more trouble than other strokes. Even though the swing is natural and free-flowing, many players feel intimidated and try to avoid it. Serena Williams, however, has a great backhand, and she often wins difficult points with it. Her serve is a powerful weapon, too. When faced by a backhand coming at them across the net, mid-level players can't seem to get their feet and body in the best position. They tend to run around the ball or forget the swing and give the ball a little poke, praying that it will not only reach but also go over the net.

What is Grand Slam winner Serena Williams doing in a paragraph about average players? What relevance does her powerful serve have to the average player's problems with a backhand? The student revised by cutting out the two sentences about Serena Williams.

Serena Williams

When placed first, as it is in the paragraph on the troublesome backhand, a topic sentence makes a generalization and serves as a reference point for the rest of the information in the paragraph. When placed after one or two other sentences, the topic sentence focuses the details and directs readers' attention to the main idea. When placed at the end of the paragraph, the topic sentence serves to summarize or draw conclusions from the details that precede it.

Some paragraphs, such as the short ones typical of newspaper writing or the one-sentence paragraphs that make a quick transition, do not always contain a topic sentence. Sometimes, too, a paragraph contains such clear details that the point is obvious and does not need to be explicitly stated. However, in academic essays, a paragraph in support of your essay's claim or thesis (main point) will usually be unified and focused on one clear topic, whether or not you state it in a topic sentence.

2c   Strategies for developing ideas

Whether you are writing a paragraph or an essay, you will do well to keep in mind the image of a skeptical reader always inclined to say something challenging, such as "Why on earth do you think that?" or "What could possibly lead you to that conclusion?" Show your reader that your opinion is well founded and supported by experience, knowledge, logical arguments, the work of experts, or reasoned examples, and provide vivid, unique details. Here are illustrations of some rhetorical strategies you can use to develop ideas in paragraphs and essays. They may serve as prompts (1d) to help you generate ideas.

Give examples. Examples make writing more interesting and informative. The paragraph that follows begins with a topic sentence that announces the controlling idea: "Ant queens . . . enjoy exceptionally long lives." The authors could have stopped there, expecting us to assume that they were right. We might wonder, however, what "exceptionally long" means about the life of an ant (a month? a year? seven years?). Instead of letting us wonder, the authors develop and support the controlling idea with five examples, organized to build to a convincing climax. Beginning with a generalization and supporting it with specific illustrative details is a common method of organizing a paragraph, known as *deductive organization.*

> Ant queens, hidden in the fastness of well-built nests and protected by zealous daughters, enjoy exceptionally long lives. Barring accidents, those of most species last 5 years or longer. A few exceed in natural longevity anything known in the millions of species of other insects, including even the legendary 17-year-old cicadas. One mother queen of an Australian carpenter ant kept in a laboratory nest flourished for 23 years, producing thousands of offspring before she faltered in her reproduction and died, apparently of old age. Several queens of *Lasius flavus,* the little yellow mound-building ant of European meadows, have lived 18 to 22 years in captivity. The world record for ants, and hence for insects generally, is held by a queen of *Lasius niger,* the European black sidewalk ant, which also lives in forests. Lovingly attended in a laboratory nest by a Swiss entomologist, she lasted 29 years.
>
> —Bert Hölldobler and Edward O. Wilson, *Journey to the Ants*

In addition, you may decide to provide an apt example or illustration of an idea in a visual image inserted into your text.

Tell a story.   Choose a pattern of organization that readers will easily grasp. Organize the events in a story chronologically so that readers can follow the sequence. In the following paragraph, the writer tells a story that leads to the point that people with disabilities often face ignorance and insensitivity. Note that she uses *inductive organization,* beginning with background information and the specific details of the story in chronological order and ending with a generalization.

> Jonathan is an articulate, intelligent, thirty-five-year-old man who has used a wheelchair since he became a paraplegic when he was twenty years old. He recalls taking an ablebodied woman out to dinner at a nice restaurant. When the waitress came to take their order, she patronizingly asked his date, "And what would he like to eat for dinner?" At the end of the meal, the waitress presented Jonathan's date with the check and thanked her for her patronage. Although it may be hard to believe the insensitivity of the waitress,

this incident is not an isolated one. Rather, such an experience is a common one for persons with disabilities.

—Dawn O. Braithwaite, "Viewing Persons with Disabilities as a Culture"

Describe with details appealing to the senses. To help readers see and experience what you feel and experience, describe people, places, scenes, and objects by using sensory details that recreate those people, places, scenes, or objects for your readers. In the following paragraph from a memoir about growing up to love food, Ruth Reichl tells how she spent days working at a summer camp in France and thinking about eating. However, she does much more than say, "The food was always delicious" and much more than "I looked forward to the delicious bread, coffee, and morning snacks." Reichl appeals to our senses of sight, smell, touch, and taste. We get a picture of the campers, we smell the baking bread, we see and almost taste the jam, we smell and taste the coffee, and we feel the crustiness of the rolls. We feel that we are there—and we wish we were.

When we woke up in the morning the smell of baking bread was wafting through the trees. By the time we had gotten our campers out of bed, their faces washed and their shirts tucked in, the aroma had become maddeningly seductive. We walked into the dining room to devour hot bread slathered with country butter and topped with homemade plum jam so filled with fruit it made each slice look like a tart. We stuck our faces into the bowls of café au lait, inhaling the sweet, bitter, peculiarly French fragrance, and Georges or Jean or one of the other male counselors would say, for the hundredth time, *"On mange pas comme ça à Paris."* Two hours later we had a *"gouter,"* a snack of chocolate bars stuffed into fresh, crusty rolls. And two hours later there was lunch. The eating went on all day.

—Ruth Reichl, *Tender at the Bone: Growing Up at the Table*

Develop a point by providing facts and statistics. The following paragraph supports with facts and statistics the assertion made in its first sentence (the topic sentence) that the North grew more than the South in the years before the Civil War.

While southerners tended their fields, the North grew. In 1800, half the nation's five million people lived in the South. By 1850, only a third lived there. Of the nine largest cities, only New Orleans was located in the lower South. Meanwhile, a tenth of the goods manufactured in America came from southern mills and factories. There were one hundred piano makers in New York alone in 1852.

In 1846, there was not a single book publisher in New Orleans; even the city guidebook was printed in Manhattan.

—Geoffrey C. Ward, *The Civil War: An Illustrated History*

Here, too, visual representations in the form of tables, charts, and graphs would help present data succinctly and dramatically.

Define key terms.   Sometimes writers clarify and develop a topic by defining a key term, even if it is not an unusual term. Often they will explain what class something fits into and how it differs from others in its class: for example, "A duckbilled platypus is a mammal that has webbed feet and lays eggs." In his book on diaries, Thomas Mallon begins by providing an extended definition of his basic terms. He does not want readers to misunderstand him because they wonder what the differences between a diary and a journal might be.

> The first thing we should try to get straight is what to call them. "What's the difference between a diary and a journal?" is one of the questions people interested in these books ask. The two terms are in fact hopelessly muddled. They're both rooted in the idea of dailiness, but perhaps because of *journal*'s links to the newspaper trade and *diary*'s to *dear,* the latter seems more intimate than the former. (The French blur even this discrepancy by using no word recognizable like *diary*; they just say *journal intime,* which is sexy, but a bit of a mouthful.) One can go back as far as Dr. Johnson's *Dictionary* and find him making the two more or less equal. To him a diary was "an account of the transactions, accidents, and observations of every day; a journal." Well, if synonymity was good enough for Johnson, we'll let it be good enough for us.
>
> —Thomas Mallon, *A Book of One's Own: People and Their Diaries*

Analyze component parts.   Large, complex topics sometimes become more manageable to writers (and readers) when they are broken down for analysis. The *Columbia Encyclopedia* online helps readers understand the vast concept of life itself by breaking it down into six component parts:

> Although there is no universal agreement as to a definition of life, its biological manifestations are generally considered to be organization, metabolism, growth, irritability, adaptation, and reproduction. . . . Organization is found in the basic living unit, the cell, and in the organized groupings of cells into organs and organisms. Metabolism includes the conversion of nonliving material into cellular components (synthesis) and the decomposition of organic matter (catalysis), producing energy. Growth in living matter is an

increase in size of all parts, as distinguished from simple addition of material; it results from a higher rate of synthesis than catalysis. Irritability, or response to stimuli, takes many forms, from the contraction of a unicellular organism when touched to complex reactions involving all the senses of higher animals; in plants response is usually much different than in animals but is nonetheless present. Adaptation, the accommodation of a living organism to its present or to a new environment, is fundamental to the process of evolution and is determined by the individual's heredity. The division of one cell to form two new cells is reproduction; usually the term is applied to the production of a new individual (either asexually, from a single parent organism, or sexually, from two differing parent organisms), although strictly speaking it also describes the production of new cells in the process of growth.

Classify into groups.   Dividing people or objects into the classes or groups that make up the whole gives readers a new way to look at the topic. In the following paragraphs, the writer develops his essay on cell phones by classifying users into three types and devoting one paragraph to each.

> Cell phone use has far exceeded practicality. For many, it's even a bit of an addiction, a prop—like a cigarette or a beer bottle—that you can hold up to your mouth. And each person is meeting a different psychological need by clinging to it.
>
> As I see it, the pack breaks down something like this: Some users can't tolerate being alone and have to register on someone, somewhere, all of the time. That walk down [the street] can be pretty lonely without a loved one shouting sweet nothings in your ear.
>
> Others are efficiency freaks and can't bear to lose 10 minutes standing in line at Starbucks. They have to conduct business while their milk is being steamed, or they will implode. The dividing line between work and home has already become permeable with the growth of telecommuting; cell phones contribute significantly to that boundary breakdown.
>
> Then there are those who like to believe they are so very important to the people in their personal and professional lives that they must be in constant touch. "Puffed up" is one way to describe them; "insecure" is another.
>
> —Matthew Gilbert, "All Talk, All the Time"

Compare and contrast.   When you examine similarities and differences among people, objects, or concepts, different types of development achieve different purposes.

1. You can deal with each subject one at a time in a block style of organization, perhaps summarizing the similarities and differences at the end. This organization works well when each section is short and readers can easily remember the points made about each subject.

2. You can select and organize the important points of similarity or difference in a point-by-point style of organization, referring within each point to both subjects.

The following example uses the second approach in comparing John Stuart Mill, a British philosopher and economist, and Harriet Taylor, a woman with whom Mill had a close intellectual relationship. The author, Phyllis Rose, organizes the contrast by points of difference, referring to her subjects' facial features, physical behavior, ways of thinking and speaking, and intellectual style. (A block organization would deal first with the characteristics of Taylor, followed by the characteristics of Mill.)

John Stuart Mill

You could see how they complemented each other by the way they looked. What people noticed first about Harriet were her eyes—flashing—and a suggestion in her body of mobility, whereas his features, variously described as chiselled and classical, expressed an inner rigidity. He shook hands from the shoulder. He spoke carefully. Give him facts, and he would sift them, weigh them, articulate possible interpretations, reach a conclusion. Where he was careful, she was daring. Where he was disinterested and balanced, she was intuitive, partial, and sure of herself. She concerned herself with goals and assumptions; he concerned himself with arguments. She was quick to judge and to generalize, and because he was not, he valued her intellectual style as bold and vigorous where another person, more like her, might have found her hasty and simplistic.

—Phyllis Rose, *Parallel Lives: Five Victorian Marriages*

Harriet Taylor

2d Using transitions and links for coherence

However you develop your individual paragraphs, readers expect to move with ease from one sentence to the next and from one paragraph to the next, following a clear flow of argument and logic. When you construct an essay or paragraph, do not force readers to grapple with "grasshopper prose," which jumps suddenly from one idea to another without obvious connections. Instead, make your writing *coherent*, with all the parts connecting clearly to one another with transitional expressions, context links, and word links. (See also 40j for examples of the contribution of parallel structures to coherence.)

Transitional words and expressions Make clear connections between sentences and between paragraphs either by using explicit connecting words like *this, that, these,* and *those* to refer to something mentioned at the end of the previous sentence or paragraph or by using transitional expressions.

KEY POINTS
Transitional Expressions

Adding an idea also, in addition, further, furthermore, moreover

Contrasting however, nevertheless, nonetheless, on the other hand, in contrast, still, on the contrary, rather, conversely

Providing an alternative instead, alternatively, otherwise

Showing similarity similarly, likewise

Showing order of time or order of ideas first, second, third (and so on), then, next, later, subsequently, meanwhile, previously, finally

Showing result as a result, consequently, therefore, thus, hence, accordingly, for this reason

Affirming of course, in fact, certainly, obviously, to be sure, undoubtedly, indeed

Giving examples for example, for instance

Explaining in other words, that is

Adding an aside incidentally, by the way, besides

Summarizing in short, generally, overall, all in all, in conclusion

For punctuation with transitional expressions, see 47e.

Though transitional expressions are useful to connect one sentence to another or one paragraph to another, do not overuse these expressions. Too many of them, used too often, make writing seem heavy and mechanical.

Context links   A new paragraph introduces a new topic, but that topic should not be entirely separate from what has gone before. Let readers know the context of the big picture. If you are writing about the expense of exploring Mars and then switch abruptly to the hazards of climbing Everest, readers will be puzzled. You need to state clearly the connection with the thesis: "Exploration on our own planet can be as hazardous and as financially risky as space exploration."

Word links   You can also provide coherence by using repeated words or connected words, such as pronouns linked to nouns; words with the same, similar, or opposite meaning; or words linked by context. Note how Deborah Tannen maintains coherence: not only by using transitional expressions (*for example, furthermore*) but also by repeating words and phrases (blue) and by using certain pronouns (red)—*she* and *her* to refer to *wife*, and *they* to refer to *Greeks*.

> Entire cultures operate on elaborate systems of indirectness. For example, I discovered in a small research project that most Greeks assumed that a wife who asked, "Would you like to go to the party?" was hinting that she wanted to go. They felt that she wouldn't bring it up if she didn't want to go. Furthermore, they felt, she would not state her preference outright because that would sound like a demand. Indirectness was the appropriate means for communicating her preference.
>
> —Deborah Tannen, *You Just Don't Understand*

2e   Writing introductions and conclusions

Introduction   Imagine talking to others at a party. Someone you have never met before comes up to you and says, "Capital punishment should be abolished immediately." You're surprised. You wonder where this position came from and why you are being challenged with it. You probably think this person rather strange and pushy. Now imagine readers picking up a piece of your writing. Just like people at a party, readers like to know why a topic is worthy of discussion before you pronounce on it. Think of your introduction as providing a social function between writer and reader. If you find it difficult to write an introduction because you are not yet clear about your thesis or how you will support it, wait until you have written the body of your essay. You may find something concrete easier to introduce than something you have not yet written.

When you write an essay in the humanities, keep the following points in mind. (For other disciplines, see 4i, 5d, and 5e.)

KEY POINTS
How to Write a Good Introduction

Options

- Make sure your first sentence stands alone and does not depend on readers' being aware of the essay title or an assigned question. For instance, avoid beginning with "This story has a complex plot."
- Provide context and background information to set up the thesis.
- Indicate what claim you will make in your essay, or at least indicate the issue on which you will state a claim.
- Define any key terms that are pertinent to the discussion.
- Establish the tone of the paper: informative, persuasive, serious, humorous, personal, impersonal, formal, informal.
- Engage the interest of your readers to make them want to explore your topic with you.

What to Avoid

- Avoid being overly general and telling readers the obvious, such as "Crime is a big problem" or "In this fast-paced world, TV is a popular form of entertainment" or "Since the beginning of time, the sexes have been in conflict."
- Do not refer to your writing intentions, such as "In this essay, I will . . ." Do not make extravagant claims, such as "This essay will prove that bilingual education works for every student."
- Do not restate the assigned essay question.

To engage readers' interest, try the following:

surprising statistics	a challenging question
a pithy quotation	interesting background details
an unusual fact	an intriguing opinion statement
a relevant anecdote	

In the following example, the author introduces the theme of multinationalism in the United States with a hook, an anecdote that leads readers to expect the city he describes to be in an unfamiliar part of the world. Then he surprises them in the last sentence—the city is Detroit— and prepares them for his discussion of a multinational continent.

> On the day before Memorial Day, 1983, a poet called me to describe a city he had just visited. He said that one section included mosques, built by the Islamic people who dwelled there. Attending his reading, he said, were large numbers of Hispanic people, forty thousand of whom lived in the same city. He was not talking about a fabled city located in some mysterious region of the world. The city he'd visited was Detroit.
>
> —Ishmael Reed, "America: The Multinational Society"

Conclusion   Think of your conclusion as completing a circle. You have taken readers on a journey from presentation of the topic in your introduction, to your thesis, to supporting evidence and discussion, with specific examples and illustrations. Remind readers of the purpose of the journey. Recall the main idea of the paper, and make a strong statement about it that will stay in their minds. Readers should leave your document feeling satisfied, not turning the page and looking for more.

KEY POINTS
How to Write a Good Conclusion

Options

- Frame your essay by reminding readers of something you referred to in your introduction and by reminding readers of your thesis.

- End on a strong note: a quotation, a question, a suggestion, a reference to an anecdote in the introduction, a humorous insightful comment, a call to action, or a look to the future.

- Leave readers with a sense of completion of the point you are making.

What to Avoid

- Do not use the obvious "In conclusion."

- Do not apologize for the inadequacy of your argument ("I do not know much about this problem") or for holding your opinions ("I am sorry if you do not agree with me, but . . .").

- Do not use the identical wording you used in your introduction.

- Do not introduce a totally new direction. If you raise a new point at the end, readers might expect more details.
- Do not contradict what you said previously.
- Do not be too sweeping in your conclusions. Do not condemn the whole medical profession, for example, because one person you know had a bad time in one hospital.

A long article on the health care system and insurance (or lack of it) in the United States concludes with a paragraph that summarizes the complex issues discussed in the article. The author condenses the issues to several rhetorical questions, ending by reiterating strongly his thesis concerning the assumptions made about health care in the United States and in the rest of the world.

> The issue about what to do with the health-care system is sometimes presented as a technical argument about the merits of one kind of coverage over another or as an ideological argument about socialized versus private medicine. It is, instead, about a few very simple questions. Do you think that this kind of redistribution of risk is a good idea? Do you think that people whose genes predispose them to depression or cancer, or whose poverty complicates asthma or diabetes, or who get hit by a drunk driver, or who have to keep their mouths closed because their teeth are rotting ought to bear a greater share of the costs of their health care than those of us who are lucky enough to escape such misfortunes? In the rest of the industrialized world, it is assumed that the more equally and widely the burdens of illness are shared, the better off the population as a whole is likely to be. The reason the United States has forty-five million people without coverage is that its health-care policy is in the hands of people who disagree, and who regard health insurance not as the solution but as the problem.
>
> —Malcolm Gladwell, "The Moral-Hazard Myth"

Chapter **3**

Revising, Editing, and Formatting

Always allow time in your writing schedule for putting a draft away for a while before you look at it with a critical eye.

Revising—making changes to improve a piece of writing—is an essential part of the writing process. It is not a punishment inflicted on inexperienced writers. Good finished products are the result of careful revision. Even Leo Tolstoy, author of the monumental Russian novel *War and Peace,* commented: "I cannot understand how anyone can write without rewriting everything over and over again."

As you revise and edit, address both "big-picture" and "little-picture" concerns. Big-picture revising involves making changes in content and organization. When you revise, you may add or delete details, sections, or paragraphs; alter your thesis statement; vary or strengthen your use of transitions; move material from one position to another; and improve clarity, logic, flow, and style. Little-picture editing involves making adjustments to improve sentence variety; vary sentence length; and correct errors in grammar, spelling, word choice, mechanics, and punctuation. Both are necessary, but most people like to focus first on the big picture and then on the details.

3a Developing strategies for revising

For college essays and important business documents, always allow time in your schedule for a second draft, and more drafts if possible. Develop systematic strategies for examining the drafts and revising.

- Print out a draft triple-spaced so that you can easily write in changes and comments. Revise for ideas, interest, and logic; do not merely fix errors. It is often tempting just to correct errors in spelling and grammar and see the result as a new draft, but revising entails more than that. You need to look at what you have written, imagine a reader's reaction to your thesis and title, and rethink your approach to the topic.

- Create distance and space. Put a draft away for at least a few hours or days, and then read it again with fresher, more critical eyes.

- Highlight key words in the assignment. Mark passages in your draft that address the words. If you fail to find any, that could signal where you need to revise.

- Read your draft aloud. Mark any places where you hesitate and have to struggle to understand the point. Go back to them later. Alternatively, ask somebody else to read a copy of the draft and to note where he or she hesitates or feels unsure about the meaning.

- Make an outline of what you have written to discover gaps or repetitions (see 1f).

- Use the "Triggers for Revision" Key Points box to alert yourself to things to look for as you read your draft.

TECH NOTE

Computer Tools for Writing and Revising

- Copy and paste first sentences. Select the first sentence of each paragraph, and use the Copy and Paste features to move the sequence of sentences into a new file. Then examine these first sentences to check for logical progression of ideas, repetition, or omission.

- Write multiple drafts and save every draft under a separate file name, one that clearly labels the topic and the draft. Some people prefer to save deleted sections in a separate "dump" file so that they can retrieve deleted parts.

- The Find feature helps you find words and phrases that you tend to overuse. Use it to look for instances of "there is" or "there are," for example, and you will see if you are using either phrase too often.

- The Insert Comment feature allows you to write a note in the middle of a draft. The place where a comment is inserted will be highlighted on your screen, and you can see the comment appear at the end of your document. You can then choose to print your document with or without the comments showing.

KEY POINTS

Triggers for Revision

Any of the following should alert you to a need for revision:

1. A weak or boring introductory paragraph

2. A worried frown, a pause, or a thought of "Huh? Something is wrong here" in any spot as you read your draft

3. A paragraph that never makes a point

4. A paragraph that seems unrelated to the thesis of the essay

5. A phrase, sentence, or passage that you cannot immediately understand (if you have trouble grasping your own ideas, readers surely will have trouble, too)

6. Excessive use of generalizations—*everyone, most people, all human beings, all students/lawyers/politicians,* and so on (use specific examples: *the students in my political science course this semester*)

7. A feeling that you would have difficulty summarizing your draft (maybe it is too vague?) *(Continued)*

(Continued)

8. An awareness that you have just read the same point earlier in the draft

9. Failure to find a definite conclusion

3b Giving and getting feedback

Ask a friend, colleague, or tutor to read your draft with a pencil in hand, placing a checkmark next to the passages that work well and a question mark next to those that do not. Ask your reader to tell you what main point you made and how you supported and developed it. This process might reveal any lack of clarity or indicate gaps in the logic of your draft. Your reader does not have to be an expert English teacher to give you good feedback. If you notice worried frowns (or worse, yawns) as the person reads, you will know that something in your text is puzzling, disconcerting, or boring. Even that simple level of feedback can be valuable. See 3e and chapter 35 for examples of student writing revised after feedback.

If you are asked to give feedback to a classmate or colleague, use the following guidelines.

KEY POINTS
Giving Feedback to Others

1. When you are asked to give feedback to a classmate, don't think of yourself as an English teacher armed with a red pen.

2. Read for positive reactions to ideas and clarity. Look for parts that make you think, "I agree," " I like this," or "This is well done."

3. As you read, put a light pencil mark next to one or two passages that make you pause and send you back to reread.

4. Try to avoid comments that sound like accusations ("You were too vague in paragraph 3"). Instead, use *I* to emphasize your reaction as a reader ("I had a hard time visualizing the scene in paragraph 3").

Here is a sample peer response form that can be used to provide feedback.

Online Study Center   **Writing Process** Peer response form

Draft by _____   Date _____

Response by _____   Date _____

1. What do you see as the writer's main point in this draft?

2. What part of the draft interests you the most? Why?

3. Where do you feel you would like more detail or explanation? Where do you need less?

4. Do you find any parts unclear, confusing, or undeveloped? Mark each such spot with a pencil question mark in the margin. Then write a note to the writer with questions and comments about the parts you have marked.

5. Give the writer one suggestion about one change that you think would improve the draft.

TECH NOTE

Using Track Changes

The Tools/Track Changes feature allows you to mark and highlight additions and changes to your own document or one received via e-mail that you want to work on collaboratively and have copied into your word processing program. This feature lets you see clearly on the screen and on the printed page the changes you have made. Going to Tools/Options allows you to set the color of the inserts and to label each insert with your user name, which will appear as a pop-up with the added text. The Accept or Reject Changes option allows you to accept or reject all the changes or each change separately, and it will make the changes to your document automatically.

3c Writing and revising a title

A good title captures the reader's attention, makes the reader want to read on, and lets the reader know what to expect in a piece of writing. You might have a useful working title as you write, but after you finish writing, brainstorm several titles and pick the one you like best.

WORKING TITLE **The Benefits of Travel**

REVISED TITLE **From Katmandu to Kuala Lumpur: A Real Education**

3d Editing and proofreading

Examine your draft for grammar, punctuation, and spelling errors. Often, reading your essay aloud will help you find sentences that are tangled, poorly constructed, or not connected. Looking carefully at every word and its function in a sentence will alert you to grammatical problem areas. Turn to 37a–37c for help with Standard English and methods for correcting common errors.

TECH NOTE
Computer Tools for Editing

- A *spelling checker* will flag any word it does not recognize, and it is very good at catching typographical errors such as *teh* for *the* or *responsability* for *responsibility*. However, it will not identify grammatical errors that affect only spelling, such as missing plural or *-ed* endings. Nor will it flag an omitted word or find a misspelled word that forms another word, such as *then* for *than*, *their* for *there*, or *affect* for *effect*.

- An online *thesaurus* will prompt you with synonyms and words close in meaning to a highlighted word; check suggested words in a dictionary for their connotations.

- The *Tools/Word Count* feature is handy when you are given a word limit; it provides an immediate, accurate count.

- *Grammar-check programs* will analyze your sentences and make suggestions about what might need to be fixed, tightened, or polished. However, these programs cannot take context or meaning into account, so their capabilities are limited. For example, if you wrote "The actors were boring" but meant to write "The actors were bored," the grammar-check programs would not reveal your mistake.

ESL NOTE
The Dangers of Grammar-Check Programs

Never make a change in your draft at the suggestion of a grammar-check program before verifying that the change is really necessary. A student from Ukraine wrote the grammatically acceptable sentence "What he has is pride." Then, at the suggestion of a grammar-check program, he changed the sentence to "What he has been pride." The program had not recognized the sequence "has is."

Proofreading Even after editing carefully and getting as much help from computer tools as you can, you still need to proofread your final draft to make sure no errors remain.

KEY POINTS
Proofreading Tips

1. Do not try to proofread on the computer screen. Print out hard copy.
2. Make another copy of your manuscript, and read it aloud while a friend examines the original as you read.
3. Use proofreading symbols to mark typographical and other errors (see last page of book).
4. Put a piece of paper under the first line of your text. Move it down line by line as you read, focusing your attention on one line at a time.
5. Read the last sentence first, and work backward through your text. This strategy will not help you check for meaning, logic, pronoun reference, fragments, or consistency of verb tenses; but it will focus your attention on the spelling, punctuation, and grammatical correctness of one sentence at a time.
6. Put your manuscript away for at least a few hours after you have finished it. Proofread it when the content is not so familiar.

3e Revising an essay: A student's drafts

With her class, student Catherine Turnbull was assigned to read a chapter of Paul Fussell's book *Uniforms: Why We Are What We Wear* and respond to it. After she wrote a first draft, she read it aloud to a group of classmates and took note of their comments. She also received feedback from her instructor in a conference. Turnbull's first rough draft of her first two paragraphs and her conclusion shows her notes and annotations for revision. Following that is her second draft, in which she moved material from the end to the beginning for a clearer thesis statement; fine-tuned her style, sentence structure, word choice, and accuracy; and cited her source. Her major changes are noted. She did not include MLA identification format (3f) or works-cited information until she wrote her final edited draft.

FIRST DRAFT

Shift from self to topic — Reader Response Essay: Nonmilitary Uniforms *Think up better title*

get readers interested! I read the wedding gown chapter from Paul Fussell's assigned book. This chapter covered the history of the white tradition, cost, fanciness, and saving the dress afterwards, etc. This chapter and the idea of the book made me look at the uniforms of people around me. While wedding dresses are intended to be incredibly special and are basically heavy, tight, and uncomfortable, *— say how?* many "real" uniforms are intended to be comfortable, casual, and *Move to end?* are team- or job-related. *Expand this point.*

Change this   My first example is my aunt, a nurse at a hospital. She wears colorful, baggy, easy-wash scrubs most days, like pajamas with pockets, badge, and a stethoscope. Her name and credentials (RN) are on her badge. She wears super-comfortable shoes because she has to walk miles in the course of making *add More details* her rounds, day or night. Her uniform says, I am part of the hospital team and am (hear) to help you. *sp*

[Two more paragraphs were included: on her brother's basketball uniform and a train conductor's uniform.]

Move to beginning. Make Stronger   In sum, Paul Fussell writes on wedding dresses in his uniform book, but they are not really uniforms in the sense most working people mean the term. More commonly, uniforms are functional and comfortable garments, symbolizing an active day-to-day role played *thesis* for the larger good. They make you one with your team and also stand out from the rest of the general populace. Unlike a wedding dress, an average uniform is not so special that it needs special storage. It is what people do and their role in society that are special. *choppy*

SECOND DRAFT

Title revised to include word *everyday*

Comfortable Shoes: Everyday Uniforms and the People Who Fill Them

New intro: third person voice (1b)

How many people would call a bridal gown a uniform?

Paul Fussell makes this somewhat startling claim in a chapter in a recent book in which he examines the so-called uniform of the formal wedding gown, its history, cost, and traditions, particularly the way it is often stored carefully away for future generations (167–69). He may justify his classification of the wedding dress as a uniform, but that is not the way most people mean the term. Surely it is more common to see uniforms as functional and comfortable garments, symbolizing an active day-to-day role played for a larger good.

Cites author and page

Thesis moved here from last ¶ of first draft (1e)

Deletes reference to "my first example" (29c)

My aunt, for instance, a nurse at Boston City Hospital, wears colorful, baggy, cotton medical scrubs to work, like pajamas with pockets, a badge, and a stethoscope. She says this outfit is easy to wash, which is important in the hygienic hospital setting. She wears the most comfortable rubber-soled shoes she can find since her job involves a lot of walking in the course of a day, making her rounds. Her name and credentials (RN) are on her badge, letting people know her official status and role as well-trained caregiver. In the past, nurses might have had to dress in white or wear more formal outfits and hats, but today the code is relaxed, with an emphasis on comfort and ease of laundering. Still, no matter how casual, her uniform definitely communicates the message, "I am an

Has added descriptive details of uniforms

experienced member of the hospital team. I am here to help you."

[Turnbull included two more paragraphs.]

Paul Fussell stretches the definition of uniform when he includes wedding gowns. He correctly points out that wedding dresses conform to many set features, but even so they are meant to be as out of the ordinary and beautiful as possible. They are usually expensive, heavy, and snugly fitting, made with impractical fabrics and beads. In contrast, however, most everyday uniforms are loose, comfortable, and inexpensive; they identify wearers as part of a particular team with a particular mission, thus making them stand out from the crowd. Unlike a wedding dress, an average uniform is not so valuable that it needs to be preserved in a special garment bag. It is what people *do* in their uniforms and the role they have taken on within their larger community that has special value.

Makes a strong point about Fussell

Synthesis of role of uniforms in 3 examples

Ends with a strong claim.

3f Formatting a college essay (print)

Once you have written, revised, and edited your document, you need to prepare it for presentation to readers. Guides are available for presenting essays in specific disciplines and media. Frequently used style guides are those published by the MLA (Modern Language Association), APA (American Psychological Association), CSE (Council of Science Editors), and *The Chicago Manual of Style*. The features of these guides are covered in this handbook. However, commonalities exist among the differences. Basic guidelines follow for preparing your essay on paper, whichever style guide you follow. See 20a for how Word functions can help with formatting. For online presentations, see chapter 24.

KEY POINTS

Guidelines for College Essay Format

Paper   White bond, unlined, $8^1/_2'' \times 11''$; not erasable or onion-skin paper. Clip or staple the pages.

Print   Dark black printing ink—an inkjet or laser printer if possible.

Margins   One inch all around. In some styles, one and one-half inches may be acceptable. Lines should not be justified (aligned on the right). (In Microsoft Word, go to Format/Paragraph or to the formatting toolbar to adjust alignment.)

Space between lines   Uniformly double-spaced for the whole paper, including any list of works cited. Footnotes (in Chicago style) may be single-spaced.

Spaces after a period, question mark, or exclamation point   One space, as suggested by most style manuals. Your instructor may prefer two in the text of your essay.

Type font and size   Standard type font (such as Times New Roman or Arial), not a fancy font that looks like handwriting. Select a regular size of 10 to 12 points.

Page numbers   In the top right margin. (In MLA style, put your last name before the page number. In APA style, put a short version of the running head before the page number.) Use Arabic numerals with no period (see p. 50; 20a shows the header formatting tools available in Word).   *(Continued)*

(Continued)

Paragraphing Indent one-half inch (5 spaces) from the left.

Title and identification On the first page or on a separate title page. See the examples that follow.

Parentheses around a source citation MLA and APA style, for any written source you refer to or quote, including the textbook for your course (for an electronic source, give author only); then add at the end an alphabetical list of works cited.

Your instructor may prefer a separate title page or ask you to include the identification material on the first page of the essay.

Title and identification on the first page The following sample of part of a first page shows one format for identifying a paper and giving it a title. The MLA recommends this format for papers in the humanities.

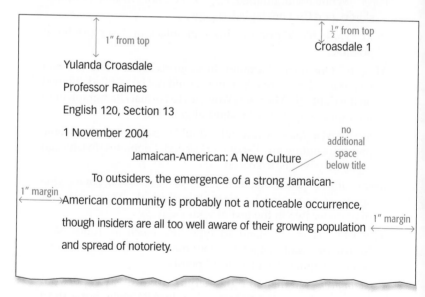

At the top of subsequent pages, write the page number in the upper right corner, preceded by your last name (20a shows you how to make this header). No period or parentheses accompany the page number.

Title and identification on a separate title page In the humanities, include a title page only if your instructor requires one or if you include an outline. On the title page include the following, all double-spaced:

Title: Centered, about one-third of the way down the page. Do not enclose the title in quotation marks, do not underline it, and do not put a period at the end.

Name: Centered, after the word *by,* on a separate line.

Course information: Course and section, instructor, and date, each centered on a new line, either directly below your name or at the bottom of the title page.

With a title page, you do not need the title and identification on your first page. Chapter 16 shows a sample title page in APA style.

Chapter **4**

Constructing an Argument

When you argue a point, you present your opinions on an issue as clearly and convincingly as you can. This type of writing is frequently assigned in courses in the humanities and social sciences. Choose an issue that is interesting and debatable. You will probably want to persuade readers to adopt your point of view; but even if they don't, you will want them to acknowledge that your claim rests on solid evidence and that you have good reasons for your position. A written argument is frequently called for outside college, too—in letters to the press or to government agencies or business organizations, in business reports, and in community service.

4a Thinking critically about arguments

Whatever your topic, approach it by thinking critically both as you read and do research and as you write (see 1b). Thinking critically means keeping an open mind and asking probing questions. It is a good habit to step back and read an argument critically, whether it is your own or somebody else's, in order to identify its merits and faults.

In your reading, develop a system of inquiry. Do not assume that because something is in print, it is accurate. Be aware that readers will use the same care when they read an argument that *you* write. So put yourself in a critical reader's shoes when you evaluate your own arguments. Here are questions to ask while analyzing an argument:

1. What am I reading? A statement of fact, an opinion, an exaggeration, an attack, an emotional belief?

2. Where does the information come from? Do I trust the sources?

3. How reliable are the writer's statements? Are they measured, accurate, fair, and to the point? Do I feel the need to interject a challenge, using "But . . ."?

4. Can I ascertain the writer's background, audience, and purpose? What biases does the writer reveal?

5. What assumptions does the writer make? If a writer argues for a college education for everyone, would I accept the underlying assumption that a college education automatically leads to happiness and success? (For more on assumptions, see 4h.)

6. Does the writer present ideas in a convincing way, relying on rational presentation of evidence rather than on extreme language or name-calling?

For more on critical thinking, go to 5b (literary texts), 8e and 9e (research sources), and 4l (visuals).

4b Formulating a good argument

When you are writing an argument, the goal is to persuade readers to adopt your point of view on your chosen or assigned topic. At the very least, you will want readers to acknowledge that the claim you make about your topic rests on solid, reliable evidence and that you provide a fair, unbiased approach to this evidence. Let readers discover that you have good reasons for your position.

KEY POINTS
The Features of a Good Argument

A good argument

- deals with an arguable issue (4c)

- is not based on strong gut reactions or beliefs but on careful analysis of reliable information (4c)

- stands up to a critical reading (4a)
- takes a position on and makes a clear claim about the topic (4d)
- supports that position with detailed and specific evidence (such as reasons, facts, examples, descriptions, and stories) (4e)
- establishes common ground with listeners or readers and avoids confrontation (4f)
- takes opposing views into account and either refutes them or shows why they may be unimportant or irrelevant (4g)
- presents reasons logically (4h, 4i, 4j)
- is engaged and vital, a reflection of your thinking rather than just a marshalling of others' opinions

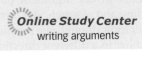
Online Study Center **Writing Process** Online resources for writing arguments

4c Selecting a topic

Choose an issue that is fresh. Avoid topics such as the death penalty, drug laws, and abortion that have been written about so often that original or interesting arguments are hard to find. Beware of saying that you intend to write about "the importance of family," "the church and morality," or "racial prejudice." Such issues might mean a great deal to you personally, but you will have difficulty structuring a logical argument around them.

Brainstorming; reading books, magazines, and newspapers; and browsing on the Internet in search directories, informational sites, or online discussion groups can help you discover novel and timely issues. When you find an interesting issue and your instructor has approved it (if necessary), begin by writing the issue as a question and then considering the arguments on both or all sides.

Student Mara Lee Kornberg decided to tackle the issue of the health effects of a vegan diet. As a vegan, she was interested in examining the facts of a case in which a child who had been fed a vegan diet had to be hospitalized. Envisioning her classmates, instructor, and a wider general audience as her readers, she began with a topic and a focused research question:

Topic: A vegan diet for children

Research question: Does a vegan diet supply adequate nutrition for children?

As she read and researched, took notes, and discussed her topic, she eventually developed her working thesis (4d), which guided her further research and the content and organization of her argument. (Her paper is in 4m.)

4d Formulating an arguable claim (thesis)

The position you take on a topic constitutes your thesis or claim. Mara Lee Kornberg knew that the claim in her argument paper should be debatable, so after some reading and research, she formulated a preliminary working thesis on her topic, though she remained prepared to change it if her research led her in a different direction.

Working thesis: A vegan diet is a healthy diet for children.

Avoid using any of the following as claims, as they are not debatable:

- a neutral statement, which gives no hint of the writer's position
- an announcement of the paper's broad subject
- a fact, which is not arguable
- a truism (statement that is obviously true)
- a personal or religious conviction that cannot be logically debated
- an opinion based only on your own feelings
- a sweeping generalization

Here are some examples of nondebatable claims, each with a revision.

NEUTRAL STATEMENT	**There are unstated standards of beauty in the workplace.**
REVISED	**The way we look affects the way we are treated at work and the size of our paychecks.**

TOO BROAD	**This paper is about violence on TV.**
REVISED	**TV violence has to take its share of blame for the violence in our society.**

FACT	*Plessy v. Ferguson,* **a Supreme Court case that supported racial segregation, was overturned in 1954** by *Brown v. Board of Education.*
REVISED	**The overturning of** *Plessy v. Ferguson* **by** *Brown v. Board of Education* **has not led to significant advances in integrated education.**

TRUISM	**Bilingual education has advantages and disadvantages.**
REVISED	**A bilingual program is more effective than an immersion program at helping students grasp the basics of science and mathematics.**

PERSONAL CONVICTION	**Racism is the worst kind of prejudice.**
REVISED	**The best weapon against racism is primary and secondary education.**

OPINION BASED ONLY ON FEELING	**I think water-skiing is a dumb sport.**
REVISED	**Water-skiing should be banned from public beaches.**

SWEEPING GENERALIZATION	**Women understand housework.**
REVISED	**The publication of a lengthy guide to housekeeping and its success among both men and women suggest a renewed interest in the domestic arts.**

Avoiding loaded terms In your claim, avoid sweeping and judgmental words—for instance, *bad, good, right, wrong, stupid, ridiculous, moral, immoral, dumb,* and *smart.*

Modifying or changing your claim Sometimes you will have an instant reaction to an issue and immediately decide which position you want to take. At other times, you will need to reflect and do research before you take a stand. Whenever you decide what your position is, formulate a position statement that will serve as your working thesis—for example, "Undocumented aliens should (or should not) have to pay higher college tuition fees than citizens or other immigrants." However, keep an open mind. Be prepared to find out more about an issue so that you can make an educated claim with concrete support, and be prepared to modify, qualify, or even change your original claim as you do your research.

Mara Lee Kornberg began with a working thesis that guided her research. However, as she did more reading and research and as she examined her assumptions (see 4h) and got feedback on her ideas, she began to refine her thesis to take counterarguments into account. The following shows how she progressed in her planning:

Topic: A vegan diet for children

Research question: Does a vegan diet supply adequate nutrition for children?

Working thesis: A vegan diet is a healthy diet for children.

Revised thesis: A vegan diet can be healthy for children provided that it is supplemented with vitamins and minerals.

You can read a draft of her essay in 4m to see how she supports her claim with evidence, appeals to her readers, establishes common ground, and discusses opposing views.

LANGUAGE AND CULTURE

Arguments across Cultures: Making a Claim and Staking a Position

The types of arguments described in this section are those common in academic and business settings in North America and the Western world. Writers state their views directly, arguing for their viewpoints. The success of their arguments lies in the credibility and strength of the evidence they produce in support. But such an approach is not universal. Other cultures may prefer a less direct approach, one that begins by exploring and evaluating all options rather than by issuing a direct claim. One of the basic principles of writing well—know your audience's expectations—is especially relevant to writing arguments in cultures different from your own.

4e Supporting the claim with reasons and concrete evidence

Supporting your claim means telling your readers what reasons, statistics, facts, examples, and expert testimony bolster and explain your point of view. If a reader asks, "Why do you think that?" about your claim, then the support you offer answers that question in detail.

Reasons Imagine someone saying to you, "OK. I know your position on this issue, but I disagree with you. What led you to your position?" This is asking you to provide the reasons for your conviction. To begin to answer the question, add at least one "because clause" to your claim.

> **Claim:** Colleges should stop using SAT scores to determine admissions.
>
> **Reason:** (because) High school grades predict college success with more accuracy.
>
> **Claim:** Organized hunting of deer is necessary in suburban areas.
>
> **Reason:** (because) With a diminishing natural habitat, deer are becoming an otherwise uncontrollable hazard to people and property.
>
> **Claim:** A large coal-fired cement factory in a rural scenic region could be an ecological disaster.
>
> **Reason:** (because) Its operation would threaten water, wildlife, and the residents' health.

Once you have formulated a tentative claim, make a scratch outline listing the claim and developing and expanding your reasons for supporting it. As you work more on your argument, you will then need to find specific and concrete evidence to explain and support each reason. Here is an example of a scratch outline (see 1f) developed to argue against building a cement factory in a rural scenic region. Note the revised, more detailed claim, the expanded list of reasons, and the inclusion of visual arguments to make a strong point.

> **Claim:** Although a large, coal-fired cement factory on the Hudson River would satisfy the increased demand for building materials and might help boost the local economy, the danger is that it could not only

pollute air and water but also threaten the wildlife and the natural beauty of the area.

Reasons:

1. Drilling, blasting, and mining pose dangers to the local aquifer and to the nearby city's water supply.

2. Every year, a 1,800-acre coal-burning plant with a 406-foot stack would emit just under 20 million pounds of pollution, including arsenic, lead, and mercury.

3. Smokestack emissions could affect birds; barge traffic and discharge into the river could affect fish.

4. Views portrayed by the Hudson River school of painters would be spoiled.

Billboards sponsored by Scenic Hudson, Inc., and Columbia Action Now to oppose the plans for a cement plant.

Concrete evidence   You need reasons, but reasons are not enough. You also need to include specific evidence that supports, illustrates, and explains your reasons. Imagine a reader saying, after you give one of your reasons, "Tell me even more about why you say that." The details you provide are what will make your essay vivid and persuasive.

Add to the outline any items of concrete evidence you will include to illustrate and explain your reasoning. What counts as evidence? Facts, statistics, stories, examples, and testimony from experts can all be used as evidence in support of your reasons.

ESL NOTE

Evidence Used to Support an Argument

The way arguments are structured, the concept of *expertise,* and the nature of evidence regarded as convincing may vary from one culture to another. In some cultures, for example, the opinions of religious or political leaders may carry more weight than the opinions of a scholar in the field. Be sure to consider the readers you will be writing for and the type of evidence they will expect.

4f   Appealing to the audience and establishing common ground

Ask who your readers are.   Consider the readers you are writing for. Assess what they might know, what assumptions they hold, what they need to know, how they can best be convinced to accept your position, and what strategies will persuade them to respect or accept your views.

If you are writing for readers with no specific prior knowledge, biases, or expertise—a *general audience*—remember to include background information: the place, the time, the context, the issues. Do not assume that a general reader knows a great deal more than you do. For more on audience, see 1c.

Appeal to readers.   Aristotle classified the ways that writers appeal to readers in arguments. Your profile of readers will help you decide what types of appeal to use. Within one extended argument, you may find it necessary to use more than one type of appeal to reach all readers' needs. The examples of the appeals below, for example, were used by Nicholas Kristof in a *New York Times* op-ed argument for hunting to control the deer population ("For Environmental Balance, Pick Up a Rifle," 4 December 2005: 4:12).

RATIONAL APPEAL (LOGOS)   A rational appeal bases an argument's conclusion on facts, examples, and authoritative evidence. Such an appeal is appropriate for educated readers and useful when readers are uninformed or hostile.

Examples: Kristof presents as evidence for his argument the fact that in the United States, deer kill 150 people a year in car crashes and cause damage amounting to $1 billion (presumably to property and crops, though this is not specified). In addition, a square mile of New Jersey alone could be inhabited by up to 200 deer. To show the decline in hunting, he cites a report that gives figures for the decreasing numbers of hunters.

ETHICAL APPEAL (ETHOS)   You make an ethical appeal to readers when you represent yourself or any sources you refer to as reliable, experienced, thoughtful, objective, and evenhanded, even when considering opposing views. Such an appeal is appropriate for formal situations in business and academic worlds. In advertising, too, ethical appeals often include testimony from famous people, whether they are experts or not—for example, American Express uses Robert De Niro to promote its credit card.

Examples: Kristof presents himself as knowledgeable about country issues: he was raised on a farm and was even, as he says, "raised on Bambi," as well as on eating meat such as venison. He cites as a reliable source the New Jersey Audubon Society, which emphasizes the ecological need for deer hunting. He pays attention to counterarguments by granting that in the suburbs it is not feasible to hunt in backyards or to bring in wolves as natural predators, but he does advocate an increase in wilderness preservation and in hunting elsewhere to restore an ecological balance.

EMOTIONAL APPEAL (PATHOS)   You make an emotional appeal when you try to gain the empathy and sympathy of your readers by assessing their values and to persuade them by using descriptions, anecdotes, case studies, and visuals in order to appeal to those values. Such an appeal is less common in academic writing than in journalism and the other media. It is appropriate when readers are regarded as either already favorable to particular ideas or apathetic toward them.

Examples: Kristof assesses his readers' values. He sees *New York Times* readers as being opposed to hunting, so when he proposes encouraging hunting, he speaks to readers head-on: "Now, you've probably just spilled your coffee." He ends his article with an anecdote aimed to gain his readers' empathy: a 200-pound man in Arkansas whose home was broken into by a buck fought with it for 40 minutes until he eventually had to kill it with his bare hands.

Within one extended argument, you will probably find it necessary to use all types of argument to reach the maximum number of readers, each with individual expectations, preferences, and quirks. See 4m for examples of these appeals in a student's argument essay.

Establish common ground.   Remember that readers turned off by exaggerations or extreme language have the ultimate power to stop reading and ignore what you have to say.

KEY POINTS
Ways to Establish Common Ground with Readers

1. Avoid extreme views or language. Do not label someone's views as *ridiculous, ignorant, immoral, fascist,* or *crooked,* for example.

2. Write to convince, not to confront. Recognize shared concerns, and consider the inclusive use of *we.*

3. Steer clear of sarcastic remarks, such as "The company has come up with the amazingly splendid idea of building a gigantic cement factory right in the middle of a natural beauty spot."

4. Use clear, everyday words that sound as if you are speaking directly to your readers.

5. Acknowledge when your opponents' arguments are valid, and work to show why the arguments on your side carry more weight.

6. If possible, propose a solution with long-term benefits for everyone.

4g Refuting opposing views

It is not enough to present your own reasons and evidence for your claim. When you take into account any opposing arguments and the reasons and evidence that support those arguments, you present yourself as objective and evenhanded, furthering your ethical argument. Examine opposing arguments; describe the most common or convincing ones; evaluate their validity, applicability, and limitations; and explain what motivates people to take those positions. Then discuss the ways in which you see your reasons and evidence as more pertinent and convincing than those in opposing arguments.

Be careful to argue logically and rationally without insulting your opponents. Take pains to explain rationally why your views differ from theirs. You may choose to do this by following each one of your own points with a discussion of an opposing view. Or you may prefer to devote a whole section of your essay to dealing with opposing views.

4h Asking Toulmin's four questions

The four questions in the Key Points box, derived from Stephen Toulmin's *The Uses of Argument,* will provide you with a systematic way to construct a logical argument.

KEY POINTS
Four Questions to Ask about Your Argument

1. What is your point? (What are you claiming?)
2. What do you have to go on? (What support do you have for your claim, in the form of reasons, data, and evidence?)
3. How do you get there? (What assumptions—Toulmin calls them *warrants*—do you take for granted and expect readers to take for granted, too?)
4. What could prevent you from getting there? (What qualifications do you need to include, using *but, unless,* or *if* or adding words such as *usually, often, several, mostly,* or *sometimes* to provide exceptions to your assumptions?)

Here is an example showing how the Toulmin questions can be used to develop the claim and supporting reason introduced in 4e:

CLAIM **Colleges should stop using SAT scores in their admissions process.**

SUPPORT **(because) High school grades and recommendations predict college success with more accuracy.**

ASSUMPTION/ WARRANT **Colleges use SAT scores to predict success in college.**

QUALIFIER **. . . unless the colleges use the scores only to indicate the level of knowledge acquired in high school.**

REVISED CLAIM **Colleges that use SAT scores to predict college success should use high school grades and recommendations instead.**

Examine your assumptions. Pay special attention to examining assumptions that link a claim to the reasons and evidence you provide. Consider whether readers will share those assumptions or whether you need to explain, discuss, and defend them. For example, the claim "Telemarketing should be monitored because it preys on the elderly and the gullible" operates on the assumption that monitoring will catch and reduce abuses. The claim "Telemarketing should be encouraged because it benefits the economy" operates on the assumption that benefiting the economy is an important goal. These different assumptions will appeal to different readers, and some may need to be persuaded of the assumptions before they attempt to accept your claim or the reasons you give for it.

Note that if your claim is "Telemarketing should be encouraged because it is useful," you are saying little more than "Telemarketing is good because it is good." Your reader is certain to object to and reject such circular reasoning. That is why it is important to ask question 3 from the Key Points box. That question leads you to examine how you get from your evidence to your claim and what assumptions your claim is based on.

4i Reasoning logically

Another way to check the logic of your arguments is to assess that they are valid examples of deductive or inductive reasoning.

Deductive reasoning The classical Aristotelian method of constructing an argument is based on a reasoning process (a syllogism) that moves from true premises to a certain and valid conclusion.

MAJOR PREMISE	**Coal-fired factories can cause significant damage to the environment.**
MINOR PREMISE	**The proposed cement plant will use coal for fuel.**
CONCLUSION	**The proposed cement plant could cause significant damage to the environment.**

Even if the major premise is not stated, readers must nevertheless accept it as the truth:

MAJOR PREMISE NOT STATED	**Since the new proposed cement plant will be coal-fired, it could cause significant damage to the environment.**

The premises must be true for a conclusion to be valid.

Inductive reasoning   An inductive argument begins with details that lead to a *probable* conclusion. Inductive arguments are used often in the sciences and social sciences. Researchers begin with a tentative hypothesis. They conduct studies and perform experiments; they collect and tabulate data; they examine the evidence of other studies. Then they draw a conclusion to support, reject, or modify the hypothesis. The conclusion, however, is only probable and not necessarily certain. It is based on the circumstances of the evidence. Different evidence at a different time could lead to a different conclusion. Conclusions drawn in the medical field change with the experiments and the sophistication of the techniques—eggs are called good for you one year, bad the next. That is because the nature of the evidence changes.

4j   Recognizing logical fallacies

Faulty logic can make readers mistrust you as a writer. Watch out for some common flaws in logic (called *logical fallacies*) as you write and check your drafts.

Sweeping generalization   Generalizations can sometimes be so broad that they fall into stereotyping. Avoid them.

▶ All British people are stiff and formal.

▶ The only thing that concerns students is grades.

The reader will be right to wonder what evidence has led to these conclusions. Without any explanation or evidence, they will simply be dismissed. Beware, then, of the trap of words like *all, every, only, never,* and *always.*

Hasty conclusion with inadequate support   To convince readers of the validity of a generalization, you need to offer enough evidence—usually more than just one personal observation. Thoughtful readers can easily spot a conclusion that is too hastily drawn from flimsy support.

▶ My friend Arecelis had a terrible time in a bilingual school. It is clear that bilingual education has failed.

▶ Bilingual education is a success story, as the school in Chinatown has clearly shown.

Non sequitur *Non sequitur* is Latin for "It does not follow." Supporting a claim with evidence that is illogical or irrelevant causes a non sequitur fallacy.

▶ **Maureen Dowd writes so well that she would make a good teacher.** [The writer does not establish a connection between good writing and good teaching.]

▶ **Studying economics is a waste of time. Money does not make people happy.** [Here the writer does not help us see any relationship between happiness and the study of a subject.]

Causal fallacy You are guilty of a causal fallacy if you assume that one event causes another merely because the second event happens after the first. (The Latin name for this logical flaw is *post hoc, ergo propter hoc:* "after this, therefore because of this.")

▶ **The economy collapsed because a new president was elected.** [Was the election the reason? Or did it simply occur before the economy collapsed?]

▶ **The number of A's given in college courses has increased. This clearly shows that faculty members are inflating grades.** [But does the number of A's clearly show any such thing? Or could the cause be that students are better prepared in high school?]

Examine carefully any statements you make about cause and effect.

Ad hominem attack *Ad hominem* (Latin for "to the person") refers to unfair ethical appeals to personal considerations rather than to logic or reason. Avoid using arguments that seek to discredit an opinion through criticizing a person's character or lifestyle.

▶ **The new curriculum should not be adopted because the administrators who favor it have never even taught a college course.**

▶ **The student who is urging the increase in student fees for social events is a partygoer and a big drinker.**

Argue a point by showing either the logic of the argument or the lack of it, not by pointing to flaws in character. However, personal considerations may be valid if they pertain directly to the issue, as in "The two women who favor the abolition of the bar own property on the same block."

Circular reasoning   In an argument based on circular reasoning, the evidence and the conclusion restate each other, thus proving nothing.

> ► **Credit card companies should be banned on campus because companies should not be allowed to solicit business from students.**

> ► **That rich man is smart because wealthy people are intelligent.**

Neither of these statements moves the argument forward. They both beg the question—that is, they argue in a circular way.

False dichotomy or false dilemma   Either/or arguments reduce complex problems to two simplistic alternatives without exploring them in depth or considering other alternatives.

> ► **After September 11, New York could do one of two things: increase airport security or screen immigrants.**

This proposal presents a false dichotomy. These are not the only two options for dealing with potential terrorism. Posing a false dilemma like this will annoy readers.

TECH NOTE

Logical Fallacies on the Web

Go to *Stephen's Guide to the Logical Fallacies* for lists of many more types of logical fallacies, all with explanations and examples. A link to this site and additional practices for identifying logical fallacies are at the Online Study Center.

Online Study Center   **Writing Process** More on logical fallacies

4k Structuring an argument essay

General to specific   The general-to-specific structure is used frequently in the humanities and arts. It moves from the thesis to support and evidence. Obviously, writers find many variations on this structure, but it is one you can turn to for help.

KEY POINTS
Basic Structure for a General-to-Specific Argument

- *Introduction:* Provide background information on the issue, why it is an issue, and what the controversies are. After you have introduced your readers to the nature and importance of the issue, announce your position in a general statement of your claim or thesis statement, perhaps at the end of the first paragraph or in a prominent position within the second paragraph, depending on the length and complexity of your essay.

- *Body:* Provide evidence in the form of supporting points for your thesis, with concrete and specific details. For each new point, start a new paragraph.

- *Acknowledgment of opposing views:* Use evidence and specific details to describe and logically refute any opposing views.

- *Conclusion:* Return to the topic as a whole and your specific claim. Without repeating whole phrases and sentences, remind readers of the point you want to make. End on a strong note.

Specific to general Alternatively, you might choose to begin with data and points of evidence first and then draw a conclusion from that evidence, providing that the evidence is relevant and convincing. A basic specific-to-general argument on the topic of driving with a cell phone looks like this:

Introduction: background, statement of problem and controversy

Data:

1. Cell phone users admit to being distracted while driving (cite statistics).
2. Many accidents are attributable to cell phone use (cite statistics).
3. Several states have passed a law against using a handheld cell phone while driving.
4. NPR talk show hosts Click and Clack (Tom and Ray Magliozzi) criticize the small sample size used by the AAA (only forty-two cases) to claim that only very few (8.3 percent) car crashes are caused by driver distraction, with even fewer of those distractions (1.5 percent of 8.3 percent) attributable to cell phone use (<http://www.newsfactor.com/perl/story/12502.html>).

Conclusion: Discussion of data and presentation of thesis (generalization formed from analysis of the data): All states should pass laws prohibiting use of handheld cell phones while driving.

In an argument in the sciences or social sciences (as in the APA paper in chapter 16), writers often begin with a hypothesis that they can test: they list their findings from experimentation, surveys, facts, and statistics. Then, from the data they have collected, they draw conclusions to support, modify, or reject the hypothesis.

Problem and solution If your topic offers solutions to a problem, you probably will find it useful to present the details of the problem first and then offer solutions. Consider where the strongest position for the solution you consider most desirable would be: at the beginning of your solutions section or at the end? Do you want to make your strong point early, or would you rather lead up to it gradually?

Cause and effect Writers of arguments in history, art history, and social movements often examine the causes and effects of events and trends to enhance their point of view. The reasoning behind an analysis of causes and effects is far from simple, involving many variables and interpretations. Take care not to reduce your analysis to one simple cause, and avoid the logical fallacy of assuming that one event causes another simply because it precedes it (see 4j).

4l Using visual arguments

We commonly think of arguments as being spoken or written, and 4a–4k deal largely with the features of written arguments. However, another type of argument is widespread—an argument that is presented visually. Think, for example, of arguments made in cartoons, advertisements, and works of art. Think of photographs of hurricane devastation or of starving children in Africa in appeals for donations. And the two visuals shown in 4e offer a strong visual argument to support a writer's thesis and make an emotional impact.

Pictures that tell a story You can supplement your written arguments with visual arguments: maps, superimposed images, photographs, charts and graphs, political cartoons—vivid images that will say more than many words can to your readers.

An argument essay on the media, for example, would make a strong visual impact if its argument included this image from Adbusters.com.

It says that children see what their parents watch and challenges us to consider how much the media dictate what we see.

Visual arguments make their appeals in ways similar to written arguments, appealing to logic, showcasing the character and credentials of the author, or appealing to viewers' emotions. When you write an argument, consider adding to the impact of your thesis by including a visual argument.

SHE'S GOT YOUR EYES

TECH NOTE

Finding Images on the World Wide Web

A comprehensive Web site, constructed by librarian Heidi Abbey of the University of Connecticut Libraries, provides demystifying information on digital image formats; a primer on basic copyright issues; links to search engines; and best of all, links to several annotated image Web sites, including image resources for specific subjects.

Interactive multimedia: The language of words, sound, and images Present-day technology allows for a new way to express ideas. No longer limited to using type on a page, writers now can use screens to present an interaction of words, color, music, sound, images, and movies to tell a story and make a point.

In preparing a multimedia presentation, consider, then, the effectiveness of juxtaposing images and conveying emotion and meaning through colors and pictures, as well as using words. If you use media imaginatively, you can do what writing teachers have long advised: Show, don't just tell.

An outstanding example of a multimedia visual argument was created by undergraduates at the University of Southern California for a course in Near Eastern and Mediterranean archeology. The students chose the ancient city of Troy as the subject of their presentation. Using excavation records, archaeological findings, and Homer's texts (as well as architectural modeling software, audio, and virtual reality techniques), the students reconstructed "the citadel as it may have appeared at the time of the Trojan War in the 13th century B.C."

 **Online Study Center**   **Design Media** Student multimedia project

4m A student's argument essay

Here is a draft of Mara Lee Kornberg's argument paper on a vegan diet, annotated to point out the strategies in her argument. Note how she presents her thesis, supports it, considers and refutes opposing views, and varies appeals to readers. For final draft format, see 3f.

Dispelling the Media Myth: Vegan Diet Is Safe for Children

In April 2003, a Queens couple was convicted of assault and related charges for nearly starving their young daughter to death by feeding her only vegan foods. Silva and Joseph Swinton placed their daughter on a strict, meat- and dairy-free diet shortly after her birth. By the time Ilce Swinton was fifteen months old, she weighed only ten pounds, had no teeth, had suffered broken bones and internal injuries, and was diagnosed as being severely malnourished. She was taken into foster care in 2001, and almost immediately the media swarmed, focusing not on the fact that this child had obviously been abused and neglected and never once given medical care, but on the fact that she had been fed—when she was fed at all—a vegan diet. Before long, the case was being referred to in newspapers as "the Vegan Baby Diet" (Retsinas).

Emotional appeal: story of a sick child

Definition of term

A vegan is, according to <u>Merriam-Webster Medical Dictionary</u>, a "strict vegetarian who consumes no animal food or dairy products." While it is not uncommon to be a vegetarian nowadays, "knowledge on adequacy and nutritional effects of vegan diets is still limited," according to the German Vegan Study

(GVS) of 154 vegans, a scholarly study conducted in 2003, which has greatly helped in shedding light on this still widely unknown way of eating (Waldmann et al. 947). Because it is uncommon, the practice of veganism was not received well by the general public when the Swinton case became headline news. As is often the case, a way of life was perceived as problematic simply because it was not well understood, and this vegan diet was very quickly assumed to be the cause of the baby's medical problems. However, veganism can be a very healthful dietary choice for parents to make for their children, provided they see to it that the diet is properly employed and therefore sufficient in vitamins and minerals.

Claim—with qualifier (4h)

While the mainstream media, in the wake of the Swinton case, has painted a portrait of veganism as a risky alternative lifestyle, it is for the most part simply a dietary decision a person makes, similar to the decision one may make to eat kosher. While the choice to observe a kosher diet is almost certainly a religious one, those who observe a vegan diet tend to fall into two schools of reasoning. Of the 154 vegans participating in the GVS, more than 90 percent of them admitted to becoming vegan for one of the following two reasons: ethics or health (Waldmann et al. 951). Those who subscribe to the first set of reasons choose to eliminate animal by-products because of moral concerns. They feel that animals should not be used to feed human beings. Often, people who subscribe to this belief also choose to eliminate leather, wool, and other animal-based materials from their wardrobes. According to People for the Ethical Treatment of Animals (PETA), adhering to a vegan diet is one way of living a "cruelty-free" lifestyle ("Cruelty").

Scholarly research cited

The second group of vegans excludes animal products for health reasons. Many people are lactose intolerant and therefore choose not to consume animal milk or similar products that may act as allergens upon their systems. Others eliminate foods such as red meat and cheese from their diets because of their high fat content. These vegans tend to regard veganism as a dietary option only and do not usually eliminate animal products from their wardrobes. Vegans who employ such a diet for their children tend to see the diet as a moral choice. Similar to those who encourage a kosher diet in their offspring because of their religious beliefs, these vegans attempt to pass down their set of beliefs and moral concerns to their children.

Veganism has gained exposure in recent years, especially after the details of the Swinton case brought it to the forefront of debates among nutritionists. This extends outside the medical field as well and has brought to society's attention both an opposition to and advocacy of veganism. Many celebrities, including singer Moby and Olympic gold-medal runner Carl Lewis, have claimed to be vegans. During the filming of the movie <u>Gladiator</u>, actor Joaquin Phoenix insisted that his costumes be made entirely of synthetic materials, as he not only excludes animals from his diet but from his wardrobe as well ("Joaquin Phoenix"). A crop of new vegan-friendly restaurants has popped up, offering both healthful vegetable dishes and more traditionally meaty fare in soy and grain-based forms. Moby's restaurant, Teany, specializes in sandwiches and desserts such as a soy "turkey" club and vanilla bean strawberry shortcake, among others, all of which once called for animal ingredients like eggs and milk (Pepe).

Ethical appeal: testimony from well-known people

For children, the diet rightly comes under more scrutiny. For a child's diet to be a healthy one in the eyes of pediatric medicine, it should adhere to the recommendations made in the long-established food guide pyramid (U.S. Dept of Agriculture). According to medical journalist Karen Sullivan, the diet should be balanced and include at the very least "the required number of fruits and vegetables" as well as "good sources of protein and carbohydrates" (76). Sullivan lists some of what she calls "good-quality protein" as including "fish, lean meat, chicken, turkey, cheese, milk, yogurt, tofu, nuts, nut butters, seeds, and legumes" (77). Perhaps most important in a child's diet is variety, which is precisely the problem that many nutritional experts express with the practice of veganism. "The keyword is balance," writes Sullivan (76). As long as a child eats a fair amount of foods from each group in the food guide pyramid and consumes a balanced group of nutrients and minerals, there should be no harm done to his or her general health. Almost half of the twelve items on Sullivan's

Expert testimony to support thesis

list of proteins are appropriate for the very strictest vegan diet. Were a parent to eliminate meat, dairy, and fish from the sum of protein-rich foods he or she serves a child, there would still be a number of healthy proteins to choose from, as is shown in the legumes and nuts section of the vegan pyramid in Figure 1.

Use of image to make a visual argument

Fig. 1   The vegan food pyramid (Source: Vegsource.com at <http://vegan.uchicago.edu/nutrition/01.html>)

While veganism is gaining some acceptance in today's society in spite of opposition, a stigma still attaches to those who choose to raise their children this way. This is evident in the way the media has focused on young Ilce Swinton's vegan diet, despite the fact that she was obviously otherwise neglected and abused. Such a restrictive diet appears on the surface to be dangerous for young, developing bodies; however, if the diet is applied properly, a baby or toddler can live a perfectly healthy young life eating only vegan foods. Dr. Spock's Baby and Child Care, a text long regarded as the foremost authority on parenting and pediatric health, plainly states that "children can thrive on

1st opposing argument about diet

vegetarian and vegan diets" (Spock and Needleman 338), with the cautionary note that children should also receive vitamin and mineral supplements.

Authority refute opposing view—wit qualifier

2nd opposing argument about vitamin deficiency

In fact, adequate amounts of vitamins and minerals are a concern often associated with veganism. A mother's breast milk is allowed on even the strictest of vegan diets, but there have been cases in which babies fed breast milk of mothers on vegan diets suffered from malnutrition and/or vitamin B12 deficiency. Vitamin B12 "occurs naturally only in animal products" (Lawson). However, according to Maria Elena Jefferds, an epidemiologist who worked with the Centers for Disease Control in monitoring the babies involved in the aforementioned cases, vitamin B12 deficiency is a problem "that doesn't just affect vegetarians" (Lawson). Amy Joy Lanou, the nutrition director of Physicians for Responsible Medicine, who in fact testified during the 2003 Swinton case, warns that a vitamin B12 deficiency "is becoming more common among infants of vegan and vegetarian as well as meat-eating parents." She notes, however, that families who are vegetarians or vegans "generally take in much higher levels of important vitamins and minerals." And the GVS researchers found that only a few vitamins and minerals (calcium, iodine, and cobalamin) needed to be supplemented in the diets of the vegans they studied (Waldmann et al. 954).

Refutation of 2nd opposing argument

Logical appeal of facts from research

3rd opposing argument about additives

Those who oppose implementing vegan diets in children worry not only about what is lacking in the diet but also about the unnecessary additives that may interrupt a child's system. Soy milk, a staple of a vegan diet, may contain added sugar or artificial sweeteners, which can be disruptive to a child's body chemistry. Soy milk also contains phytoestrogens, hormonal compounds that, though helpful in preventing some cancers in adults, are unnecessary for children and may adversely affect their hormones (Sullivan 350). In addition, just as a child can develop an allergy to cow's milk, too much soy milk can lead to similarly unfavorable reactions.

However, these problems that could potentially arise from a vegan diet are easily remedied. Sugar-free soy milks are available, and as long as they are not used as a child's sole source of protein and calcium, there is no problem with their inclusion in a pediatric

Solutions to counter 3rd opposing argument

diet plan. As to the lack of vitamin B12 and other important vitamins and minerals in a vegan diet, "parents need to take special care that their children are getting enough," advises Dr. Spock, which he thinks is easily achieved: "A multivitamin and mineral supplement can offer the needed insurance" (Spock and Needleman 338). Lucy Moll, author of The Vegetarian Child, agrees: "Including B12 in your diet is easy . . . the solution is as simple as a bowlful of fortified breakfast cereal" (18).

support for esis: egan diet healthy

Not only does a vegan diet satisfy a child's health needs; it also "offers significant protection from many health complications" (Lanou). Many sources of traditional proteins, the food group most often lacking in a vegetarian or vegan diet, are very high in saturated and trans fats, which can lead to obesity in children, which in turn can lead to a variety of other medical ailments. Soy proteins are generally lower in fat and cholesterol than their animal-based counterparts, and there is some evidence that soy proteins actually help lower levels of bad cholesterol, a substance in the blood that, in abundance, can lead to such medical conditions as heart disease (Sullivan 350).

Dr. Spock has alerted parents to the dangers of animal milks: "Milk may actually pose health risks" (Spock and Needleman 340). Traditional animal milk is high in saturated fat and low in iron and essential fats. These healthy fats are more often found in vegetable sources, such as avocados, vegetable oils, and nut butters. Furthermore, cow milk is a common allergen in children, and just as many adults avoid animal milks because of lactose intolerance, it may be safest for children to avoid cow milk as well. Milk-based products can contribute to headaches and stomach ailments like diarrhea and constipation and can increase the risk of developing genetic diseases such as asthma, eczema, and juvenile onset diabetes (Spock and Needleman 341). Sullivan also addresses issues surrounding pediatric milk consumption. The recent use of genetically engineered bovine somatotrophin, a hormone naturally present in cow milk, to increase milk production in dairy cows has led to concern about human consumption of such chemically enhanced milk (29). While the use of this hormone was banned in Canada and the United Kingdom ten years ago, it is still in use in the

Support: dangers of dairy products

United States. Because children generally take in a much greater amount of milk than their parents, the youngest Americans make up the group most at risk.

Although most of the blame for Ilce Swinton's poor health was laid on the vegan diet her mother and father fed her, it should be noted that although Silva Swinton admitted in court to feeding her daughter according to a vegan diet plan, she was not applying the diet properly. Because breast milk is not derived from animals, and none are harmed in its production, it is perfectly acceptable for a vegan baby to consume. Mrs. Swinton, however, chose not to feed Ilce with breast milk and chose instead to mix homemade soy formulas, which were obviously inadequately prepared. If a vegan diet is sensibly employed, it can be perfectly healthy, both for adults and children. In fact, vegans generally lead much healthier lifestyles than meat-eaters. The GVS reports that only three percent of the vegans studied were smokers (Waldmann et al. 949), and just one-quarter of participants regularly drank alcohol. The implication here is that vegans possess a greater awareness than the general population as to what are the building blocks of a healthy lifestyle. The GVS study concludes reassuringly with this: "Our data show that the participants of the GVS had an above average healthy lifestyle" (Waldmann et al. 955). Moreover, according to Dr. Spock, a meat-free diet, when set up with care, may be able to "offer even more long-term health benefits to you and your children" (Spock and Needleman 338). It is important that parents instill in their young children a sense of what is and what is not healthful so that they will make educated diet and lifestyle choices throughout their lives.

In light of the issues surrounding animal foods and the proven benefits of a meat-free diet, a viable dietary choice is to eliminate animal sources of nutrition from one's diet. This is especially true in the case of children, who are considerably more susceptible to the ills of poor nutrition and obesity. While there is still a great deal of opposition to veganism for children, much of it derived from society's general ignorance of the diet, raising a child as a vegan, with careful supplements of necessary vitamins and minerals, can be a safe and healthy choice.

Margin notes:

Lead-in to conclusion: return to the introductory story

Strong logical appeal of data from research study

Conclusion

Reiteration of thesis

Works Cited

"Cruelty-Free Living." People for the Ethical Treatment of Animals.
22 Nov. 2004 <http://peta.org/living/>.

"Joaquin Phoenix." Internet Movie Database. 20 Nov. 2004
<http://imdb.com/name/nm0001618/bio>.

Lanou, Amy Joy. "Vegan's Bad Wrap." Psychology Today Sept./Oct.
2003: 6. Academic Search Premier. EBSCO. Hunter College
Lib. 8 Nov. 2004 <http://search.epnet.com/login.aspx?
direct=true&db=aph&an=10602091>.

Lawson, Willow. "Brain Food." Psychology Today May/Jun. 2003:
22– . Academic Search Premier. EBSCO. Hunter College
Lib. 8 Nov. 2004 <http://search.epnet.com/login.aspx?
direct=true&db=aph&an=9625534>.

Moll, Lucy. The Vegetarian Child. New York: Perigee, 1997.

Pepe, Michelle. "Teany: Moby's Tiny Tearoom." AOL City Guide.
2004. 30 Nov. 2004 <http://www.digitalcity.com/
newyork/dining/venue.adp?sbid=116500935>.

Retsinas, Greg. "Couple Guilty of Assault in Vegan Case." New York
Times.5 Apr. 2003, late ed.: 1. Academic Universe: News.
LexisNexis. Hunter College Lib. 13 Nov. 2004
<http://web.lexis-nexis.com>.

Spock, Benjamin, and Robert Needleman. Dr. Spock's Baby and
Child Care. 8th ed. New York: Pocket, 2004.

Sullivan, Karen. The Parent's Guide to Natural Health Care in
Children. Boston: Shambala, 2004.

United States Dept. of Agriculture. Food Guide Pyramid. 5 Nov.
2004 <http://usda.gov/cnpp/images/pyramid.gif>.

"Vegan." Merriam-Webster Medical Dictionary. Medline Plus. 12
Nov. 2004 <http://www.nlm.nih.gov/medlineplus/
mplusdictionary.html>.

Waldmann, A., J. W. Koschizke, C. Leitzmann, and A Hahn. "Dietary
Intakes and Lifestyle Factors of a Vegan Population in
Germany: Results from the German Vegan Study." European
Journal of Clinical Nutrition 2003: 947–955. Academic Search
Premier. EBSCO. Hunter College Lib. 8 Nov. 2004
<http://search.epnet.com/login.aspx?direct=true&db=
aph&an=10344856>.

st includes
ly works
tually
ed in the
per

New page
for list of
works cited

Documented
in MLA style:
Chapters 11
and 12

Chapter **5**

Writing in All Your Courses

5a Writing under pressure: Essay exams and short-answer tests

In an examination setting, you have to write quickly and on an assigned topic. Learn how to cope with these tests so that you can choose the facts and ideas you need and present them clearly.

KEY POINTS

Guidelines for Essay Exams

1. For a content-based essay test, review assigned materials and notes; assemble facts; underline, annotate, and summarize significant information in your textbooks and other assigned materials; predict questions on the basis of the material your instructor has covered in detail in class; and draft some answers.

2. Highlight or underline key terms in the assigned questions (see the list on p. 79).

3. Think positively about what you know. Work out a way to emphasize the details you know most about. Stretch and relax.

4. Make a scratch outline (see 1f) to organize your thoughts. Jot down specific details as evidence for your thesis.

5. Focus on providing detailed support for your thesis. In an exam, this is more important than an elaborate introduction or conclusion.

6. Check your essay for content, logic, and clarity. Make sure you answered the question.

In short-answer tests, use your time wisely. So that you know how long you should spend on each question, count the number of questions and divide the number of minutes you have for taking the test by the number of questions (add 1 or 2 to the number you divide by, to give yourself time for editing and proofreading). Then for each answer, decide which points are the most important ones to cover in the time you have available. You cannot afford to ramble or waffle in short-answer tests. Get to the point fast, and show what you know. To increase your confidence, answer the easiest question first.

For essay exams and short-answer tests, always read the questions carefully, and make sure you understand what each question asks you to do. Test writers often use the following verbs:

analyze: divide into parts and discuss each part

argue: make a claim and point out your reasons

classify: organize people, objects, or concepts into groups

compare: point out similarities

contrast: point out differences

define: give the meaning of

discuss: state important characteristics and main points

evaluate: define criteria for judgment and examine good and bad points, strengths and weaknesses

explain: give reasons or make clear by analyzing, defining, contrasting, illustrating, and so on

illustrate: give examples from experience and reading

relate: point out and discuss connections

 **Online Study Center**   **Across/Beyond College** Student essay exam

5b Writing about literature

Before you begin writing, pay careful attention to the content and form of the work of literature by reading the work more than once and highlighting significant passages. Then use the Key Points box on page 80 to analyze the work systematically.

Here are some guidelines for writing about literature, followed by more specific guidelines for analyzing fiction, nonfiction, poetry, and drama.

- Assume a larger audience than your instructor. Think of your readers as people who have read the work but not thought of the issues you did.

- Make sure that you formulate a thesis. Do not devote a large part of your essay to summary; assume that readers have read the work. Occasionally, though, you may need to include a brief summary of the whole or of parts to orient readers. Make sure you tell them not just what is in the work but also how you perceive and interpret important aspects of the work.

■ Turn to the text for evidence, and do so often. Text references, in the form of paraphrase or quotation, provide convincing evidence to support your thesis. But do not let your essay turn into a string of quotations.

KEY POINTS
Ten Ways to Analyze a Work of Literature

1. *Plot or sequence of events*   What happens, and in what order? What stands out as important?

2. *Theme*   What is the message of the work, the generalization that readers can draw from it? A work may, for example, focus on making a statement about romantic love, jealousy, sexual repression, courage, ambition, revenge, dedication, treachery, honor, lust, greed, envy, social inequality, or generosity.

3. *Characters*   Who are the people portrayed? What do you learn about them? Do one or more of them change, and what effect does that have on the plot or theme?

4. *Genre*   What type of writing does the work fit into—parody, tragedy, love story, epic, sonnet, haiku, melodrama, comedy of manners, or mystery novel, for example? What do you know about the features of the genre, and what do you need to know? How does this work compare with other works in the same genre? What conventions does the author observe, violate, or creatively vary?

5. *Structure*   How is the work organized? What are its major parts? How do the parts relate to each other?

6. *Point of view*   Whose voice speaks to the reader and tells the story? Is the speaker or narrator involved in the action or an observer of it? How objective, truthful, and reliable is the speaker/narrator? What would be gained or lost if the point of view were changed?

7. *Setting*   Where does the action take place? How are the details of the setting portrayed? What role, if any, does the setting play? What would happen if the setting were changed?

8. *Tone* From the way the work is written, what can you learn about the way the author feels about the subject matter and the theme? Can you, for example, detect a serious, informative tone, or is there evidence of humor, sarcasm, or irony?

9. *Language* What effects do the following have on the way you read and interpret the work: word choice, style, imagery, symbols, and figurative language?

10. *Author* What do you know, or what can you discover through research, about the author and his or her time and that author's other works—and does what you discover illuminate this work?

Writing about prose As you read novels, short stories, memoirs, and biographies or autobiographies, consider these basic questions for thinking about what you read: What happened? When and where did it happen? Who did what? How were things done? Why? Then extend your inquiry by considering the ten points in the preceding Key Points box, in addition to the following:

narrator: author's attitude to and depiction of the narrator: omniscient, deceived, observant, truthful, biased, crazy?

style: word choice, sentence length and structure, significant features

imagery: effect of figures of speech, such as similes and metaphors (see pp. 82–83 and section 33e)

symbols: objects or events with special significance or with hidden meanings

narrative devices: foreshadowing, flashback, leitmotif (a recurring theme), alternating points of view, turning point, and dénouement (outcome of plot)

Writing about poetry In addition to using some of the suggestions relating to prose, you can consider the following factors when you analyze a poem.

stanza: lines set off as a unit of a poem

rhyme scheme: system of end-of-line rhymes that you can identify by assigning letters to similar final sounds—for example, a rhyme scheme for couplets (two-line stanzas), *aa bb cc;* and a rhyme scheme for a sestet (a six-line stanza), *ababcc*

meter: number and pattern of stressed and unstressed syllables (or *metric feet*) in a line. Common meters are trimeter, tetrameter, and pentameter (three, four, and five metric feet). The following line is written in iambic tetrameter (four metric feet, each with one unstressed and one stressed syllable):

Whŏse woŏds / thĕse aŕe / Ĭ thínk / Ĭ knów.   —Robert Frost

foot: unit (of meter) made up of a specific number of stressed and unstressed syllables

Writing about drama   As you prepare to write about a play, use any of the relevant points listed for prose and poetry, and in addition, focus on the following dramatic conventions:

structure of the play: acts and scenes

plot: episodes, simultaneous events, chronological sequence, causality, climax, turning point

characters: analysis of psychology, social status, relationships

setting: time, place, and description

time: real time depicted (all action takes place in two hours or so of the play) or passage of time

stage directions: details about clothing, sets, actors' movements, expressions, and voices; information given to actors

scenery, costumes, music, lighting, props, and special effects: purpose and effectiveness

presentation of information: recognition of whether the characters in the play know things that the audience does not or whether the audience is informed of plot developments that are kept from the characters

Online Study Center   **Across/Beyond College**   Student essays on literature

Figurative language   The writers of literary works often use figures of speech to create images and intensify effects.

simile: a comparison, with two sides stated

Like as the waves make towards the pebbled shore,
So do our minutes hasten to their end.

—William Shakespeare

The weather is like the government, always in the wrong.

—Jerome K. Jerome

Playing for teams other than the Yankees is "like having a crush on Cinderella but dating her ugly stepsisters."
—David Wells (when Yankees pitcher)

A woman without a man is like a fish without a bicycle.
—Attributed to Gloria Steinem

metaphor: an implied comparison, with no *like* or *as*

The still, sad music of humanity   —William Wordsworth

The quicksand of racial injustice   —Martin Luther King, Jr.

alliteration: repetition of consonant sounds

He bravely breach'd his boiling bloody breast.
—William Shakespeare

assonance: repetition of vowel sounds

And feed deep, deep upon her peerless eyes   —John Keats

onomatopoeia: sound of word associated with meaning

murmuring of innumerable bees   —Alfred, Lord Tennyson

personification: description of a thing as a person

rosy-fingered dawn   —Homer

zeugma: use of a word with two or more other words, forming different and often humorous logical connections

The art dealer departed in anger and a Mercedes.

For more on using figurative language, see 33e.

KEY POINTS
Common Conventions in Writing about Literature

Tense   Use the present tense to discuss works of literature even when the author is no longer alive (41e).

Authors' Names   Use an author's full name the first time you mention it: "Stephen King." Thereafter, and always in parenthetical citations, use only the last name: "King," not "Stephen," and certainly not "Steve."

Author/Narrator Distinction   Make a clear distinction between author and narrator. The narrator is the person telling a story or serving as the voice of a poem and does not necessarily express the author's views. Often the author has invented the persona of the narrator. Keep the terms distinct.   *(Continued)*

(Continued)

Titles of Works Underline or italicize the titles of books, journals, and other works published as an entity and not as part of a larger work. Use quotation marks to enclose the title of a work forming part of a larger published work: short stories, essays, articles, songs, and short poems.

Quotations Integrate quotations into your text, and use them for help in making your point (10e). Avoid a mere listing and stringing together: "Walker goes on to say. . . . Then Walker states. . . ." When quoting two or three lines of poetry, separate lines by using a slash (/). When using long quotations (more than three lines of poetry or four typed lines of prose), indent one inch, but do not add quotation marks; the indentation signals a quotation (10f).

5c A student's literature paper

The following essay draft was written by sophomore Brian Cortijo for a course on multicultural American literature. The assignment was to compare and contrast two collections of stories according to the way they present a concept of identity and to focus on the texts themselves without turning to secondary sources. Cortijo was writing for his instructor and classmates, all of whom were familiar with the stories, so summary was unnecessary. He decided to focus on three of the ten areas in the Key Points box on pages 80–81: theme, setting, and language, specifically symbols. The draft is documented according to MLA style. For more on this and MLA format for a final draft, see 3f and chapters 11–13.

Identity and the Individual Self

While distinct in their subject matter, the collections of stories presented in Sherman Alexie's The Lone Ranger and Tonto Fistfight in Heaven and Edwidge Danticat's Krick? Krack! are strikingly similar in the responses they evoke and in their ability, through detached or seemingly detached narratives, to create a sense of collective selfhood for the peoples represented in those narratives. Through connected stories, repetition of themes and events, shifting of narrative voice and honest, unapologetic discussion of the problems and the beauty of their personal experiences, Danticat and Alexie provide frank, cohesive portrayals of a Haitian and Native American peoplehood, respectively.

Introduces the works with complete names of authors

States thesis, emphasizing similarity

Refers to setting and theme

Now uses last names only

While it may not be the intention of these authors to address such a collective identity, it is clear that each is working from some conception of what that identity is, if not what it should be. Each author has symbols and characters that are used to display the identity in all its glory and shame, all its beauty and horror. For Alexie, both characters and objects are used, each for its own purpose. Most notable among these are Thomas Builds-the-Fire, a symbol of spirituality; Norma, who remains uncorrupted by the life imposed on the Indian peoples; and the seemingly ubiquitous drum, a symbol of religion that, if played, "might fill up the whole world" (23). Danticat, by contrast, concentrates more on objects than on characters to embody the ideals and the fears of the identity she is constructing through her narrative. The most prominent among these symbols are the bone soup, braids, and, more generally, hair.

Danticat's use of the bone soup in her last story, "Caroline's Wedding," and of the braids in her "Epilogue: Women Like Us" is of paramount importance to any claim of Haitian peoplehood, or Haitian womanhood, that she might try to make. The use of these elements is indicative of the loving imposition and inclusion of past generations into one's own, as well as the attempt to pass down all that has gone before to those who will one day bear the burden of what that past means. Thus, Hermine's soup is her daughter Gracina's soup as well, not because she eats of it but because those bones—that ancestry—are a part of her and she will one day be responsible for passing them (and it) on. Likewise, Danticat's reader in the epilogue must know her history and her lineage, not only to know how to braid her daughter's hair but for whom those braids are tied.

Not surprisingly, as both books deal greatly with ancestry, they also deal with the transition and maintenance of an identity over time. Both authors assert that the collective self represented by the past is part and parcel of that embodied by the future—bound to it and inseparable. The one serves to define the other. Likewise, there is a call to make the efforts and struggles of the past worthwhile—to do better, if simply for the sake of one's ancestors.

In Tonto, Alexie goes as far as to suggest that time is unimportant, if even existent, with respect to reality. Watches and keeping track of time are of no consequence. One's past will

Points out how theme is addressed

Integrates quotation

Points to differences

Uses present tense

Analyzes symbols

Provides specific references to the text and to characters

Returns to similarities in theme

Gives specific references

always be present, and the future always ahead, so there is no need to dwell on either, but that does not mean that they do not matter. A person lives in the now, but every "now" was once the future and will become the past (22). Alexie makes extensive use of the period of five hundred years, as though that is a length of time perceptible to the human consciousness, if appreciated more by the Indian.

Danticat's twisting of time is less blatant than Alexie's, but that may be because it is not necessary to speak of things in terms of hundreds of years. A few generations suffice, and the connections between her characters rely so heavily on the similarities between their stories that their relations are obvious. The suicide of the new mother in the first story is mirrored perfectly in the last, though they might take place fifty years apart. The question and answer game played by the sisters forces one to wonder whether Caroline and Grace's mother went through an experience similar to Josephine's mother's. Then there is Marie, who finds and claims the dead baby Rose, who very well may be the daughter of Josephine, who is connected to at least two of the other tales. Beyond the characters themselves, the re-use of the symbols of hair and the bloody water is striking. The Massacre River, which took the lives of many who attempted to cross it, is named (44), but it is also implied in the bloody stream of Grace's dream with her father, even though the character may know nothing of it. After years, generations, and physical separation, the events at that river seem to pervade the collective consciousness of the Haitian people.

Clearly, these authors make no attempt to glorify the identity that they are helping to define. What is vital to the presentation of these collective identities is that they are transcendent of both time and location and that they are honest, if not visceral, in their telling. As beautifully told as these pieces of fiction are, they aim for truth and are unapologetic in presenting the faults and difficulties inherent in that truth. By telling these tales honestly and without pretense, Alexie and Danticat help to reveal what many may not be willing to admit or acknowledge about others or about themselves—the importance, beauty, and complexity of a collective selfhood.

Focuses on structure of work

Provides specific details about characters

Points out relevance of symbols

Draws threads together with term "collective identities"

Ends on a strong note affirming thesis of "peoplehoo

Works Cited

Alexie, Sherman. <u>The Lone Ranger and Tonto Fistfight in Heaven</u>.
New York: HarperCollins, 1994.

Danticat, Edwidge. <u>Krick? Krack!</u> New York: Vintage-Random, 1996.

New page in
final MLA draft

Follows MLA
for citing
books (12a,
12c)

5d Writing about community service

Service learning projects link a college to the community. For such projects, students volunteer for community service, often related to the content of a discipline or a particular course. They then must demonstrate
to the college instructor what they learned from the service experience.
There are three main types of writing for community service projects:

1. writing done initially with the site supervisor to outline the goals,
   activities, and desired outcomes of the service project

2. writing done during the service work, such as reports to a supervisor, daily records, summaries of work completed, and documents such as flyers and brochures (25b).

3. writing done for the college course—usually reflective reports
   describing the service objectives and the writer's experiences and
   assessing the success of the project

To reflect fully on the work you do, keep an ongoing journal of your
activities so that you can provide background about the setting and
the work and give specific details about the problems you encounter
and their solutions. Link your comments to the goals of the project.

The following paragraph is from Joanne L. Soriano's reflective
journal. While enrolled in a microbiology course at Kapi'olani
Community College in Hawaii, Soriano worked at an arboretum (a
place to study trees) propagating endangered plant species.

Through Service Learning, I am able to contribute to the Lyon
Arboretum's efforts. I made my first visit on February 5th, and was
taken to their micropropagation lab. In it, my supervisor, Greg Koob,
showed me racks and racks of test tubes filled with plantlets. They
were either endangered or native Hawaiian, or both. The endangered
ones were clones; in some cases they were derived from only a few
remaining individuals. A major function of the lab is to perpetuate
these species by growing them in the test tubes and then splitting
each individual into more test tubes as they grow. Thus one specimen
can become hundreds, under the right conditions. They can be planted

on the Arboretum's grounds or sent to various labs to be studied. I am thrilled to be given the opportunity to participate in the process.

Section 23e shows an example of a Web site designed by a student in a course devoted to community service.

TECH NOTE

Students' Writing in Service Learning Courses

For samples of student community service writing, go to *The Writing Center: Michigan State University* site.

5e Preparing a portfolio

Portfolios are used by artists, writers, and job hunters. In a college writing course, selecting work to include in a portfolio gives you and your instructor an opportunity to review your progress over time and to assess which pieces of writing best reflect your abilities and interests. Choose pieces that indicate both the range of topics covered in the course (or in your course of study) and the types of writing you have done. To show readers that you are able to produce more than one type of writing, include pieces on different topics, written for different purposes. If your instructor does not issue specific guidelines for presenting your portfolio, use those in the following Key Points box.

KEY POINTS

Presenting a Writing Portfolio

1. Number and date drafts; clip or staple all drafts and final copy together.

2. To each separate package in your portfolio add a cover sheet describing the contents of the package (for example, "In-class essay" or "Documented paper with three prior drafts").

3. Include a brief cover letter to introduce the material and yourself.

4. Pay special attention to accuracy and mechanics. Your semester grade may depend on the few pieces of writing that you select to be evaluated, so make sure that the ones you include are carefully edited and well presented.

E-portfolios are discussed and illustrated in 24b and 24c.

5f Writing and researching across the curriculum

One semester you may be writing about *Hamlet,* and the next semester you may move to exploring the census, writing about Chopin's music, discussing geological formations, researching the history of the civil rights movement, or preparing a paper on Sigmund Freud and dreams. You may be expected to write scientific laboratory reports or to manipulate complex statistical data and to use a style of documentation different from one you learned in an English course.

Find out what way of writing and documenting is expected in each of your courses. Although each one may call for some adaptation of the writing process and for awareness of specific conventions, in general, you will engage in familiar activities—planning, researching, drafting, revising, and editing.

LANGUAGE AND CULTURE
The Cultures of the Academic Disciplines

When you take a course in a new discipline, you are joining a new "discourse community" with established conventions and ways of thinking and writing. Use the following strategies to get acquainted with the discipline's conventions.

1. Listen carefully to lectures and discussion; note the specialized vocabulary used in the discipline. Make lists of new terms and definitions.

2. Read the assigned textbook, and note the conventions that apply in writing about the field.

3. Use subject-specific dictionaries and encyclopedias to learn about the field. Examples include *Encyclopedia of Religion* and *Encyclopedia of Sociology.*

4. Subscribe to e-mail discussion lists (22a) in the field to discover what issues people are concerned about.

5. When given a writing assignment, make sure you read samples of similar types of writing in that discipline.

6. Talk with your instructor about the field, its literature, and readers' expectations.

┌───┐
TECH NOTE
Useful Sites for Writing across the Curriculum
Try these Web sites for useful advice on writing in all your courses and for
more links to other sites:

- The Dartmouth College site with advice to nonmajors on writing in the
  humanities, sciences, and social sciences

- The George Mason University Writing Center site on writing in public
  affairs, management, psychology, biology, and history
└───┘

Online Study Center   **Research** Sources in 27 subject areas

Writing and researching in the humanities and arts

Guidelines for writing research papers in the humanities and arts

- Consult primary sources, such as original works of literature, or
  attend original performances, such as plays, films, poetry readings, and concerts.

- Form your own interpretations of works. The first person *I* is used
  in personal and expository writing more than in other disciplines.

- Use secondary sources (works of criticism) only after you have
  formed your own interpretations and established a basis for
  evaluating the opinions expressed by others.

- Look for patterns and interpretations supported by evidence, not
  for one right answer to a problem.

- Use the present tense to refer to what writers have said (*Emerson
  points out that . . .*).

- Use MLA guidelines (chapters 11–13) or *The Chicago Manual of
  Style* (chapter 18) for documentation style.

You will find examples of students' humanities and arts research
papers in 4m, 5c, and chapters 13 and 19. Additional papers in the
humanities and arts are available at our Online Study Center.

Online Study Center   **Across/Beyond College** Student papers in the
humanities and arts

Writing and researching in the sciences   Most writing in the natural sciences (such as astronomy, biology, chemistry, and physics)

and applied sciences (agriculture, engineering, environmental studies, computer science, and nursing, for example) concerns itself with empirical data—that is, with the explanation and analysis of data gathered from a controlled laboratory experiment or from detailed observation of natural phenomena. Frequently, the study will be a replication of a previous experiment, with the new procedure expected to uphold or refute the hypothesis of that previous experiment.

Guidelines for writing research papers in the natural sciences and mathematics

- Focus on empirical data.

- Avoid personal anecdotes.

- Report firsthand original experiments and calculations.

- Present a hypothesis.

- Give background information in the introductory section of your paper, a section sometimes called "Review of the Literature."

- Use the present perfect tense to introduce a survey of the literature (*Several studies have shown that . . .*).

- Use the past tense for details of specific studies (*Cocchi et al. isolated the protein fraction . . .*).

- Use the passive voice more frequently than in other types of writing (*The muscle was stimulated . . .*) (42a).

- Be prepared to write according to a set format, using sections with headings: Abstract, Method, Results, Discussion, Conclusion (see chapter 16).

- Use APA (chapters 14–16) or CSE (chapter 17) documentation style, or follow specific style manuals in scientific areas.

KEY POINTS

A Model for the Organization of an Experimental Paper in the Sciences

1. Title page: running head, title, author's name, institution

2. Table of contents: necessary for a long paper or for a paper posted online

3. Abstract: a summary of your research and your conclusions (about 100–175 words) *(Continued)*

(Continued)

4. Title, followed by background information: why the study is necessary, your hypothesis, review of other studies

5. Method: with headed subsections on participants, apparatus, procedures

6. Results: backed up by statistics or survey data, with tables, charts, and graphs where appropriate

7. Discussion: evaluation of the results from the perspective of your hypothesis

8. Conclusion and recommendations: implications of the results of the study and suggestions for further research

9. References: a list of the works cited in the paper

10. Tables and figures: check with your instructor about placing these at the end or within your text.

The following annotated excerpt is from Natasha Williams's lab report on microbial genetics conjugation, written for a cell biology course.

Discussion

Conjugation involves transfer by appropriate mating types. F+ and Hfr are donor cells with respectively low and high rates of genetic transfer. F- cells are recipients. Contact between the cell types is made by a conjugation bridge called an F pilus extending from the Hfr cell. The donor chromosome appears to be linearly passed through the connecting bridge. Sometimes this transfer is interrupted. The higher the frequency of recombination, the closer the gene is to the beginning of the circular DNA. In this way one can determine the sequence of genes on the chromosome.

Table 1 shows consistently that histidine is the last amino acid coded with the smallest number of recombinants,

Major section heading centered

Passive voice common in lab reports

Use of one for general reference

and arginine is the second to last coded with the next smallest number of recombinants. However, the results obtained for proline and leucine/threonine vary.

Discussion
of table
included in
paper

Online Study Center   **Across/Beyond College** Excerpts from student papers in the sciences.

Writing and researching in the social sciences

The social sciences (anthropology, business, economics, geography, political science, psychology, and sociology) examine how society and social institutions are constructed, how they work (or don't work), and what the ramifications of structures, organizations, and human behavior are.

Two types of writing prevail in the social sciences. Some writers, for instance, use empirical scientific methods similar to those used in the natural sciences to gather, analyze, and report their data, with a focus on people, groups, and their behavior. Then there are writers in the social sciences who are more social philosophers than scientists. In fields such as public policy and international relations, researchers examine trends and events to draw their conclusions. Ethnographic studies are common, too, with researchers taking detailed notes from observing a situation they want to analyze—the behavior of fans at a baseball game, for example, or the verbal reactions of constituents to a politician's tax-cut proposals.

When you are given a writing assignment in the social sciences, it will be helpful if you can ascertain (from the approach taken in class—or just ask) whether your instructor leans toward the humanities or the sciences and whether an empirical study or a philosophical, interpretive essay is more appropriate.

Guidelines for writing research papers in the social sciences

- Understand that the research method you choose will determine what kind of writing is necessary and how you should organize the writing.
- Decide whether your purpose is to describe accurately, measure, inform, analyze, or synthesize information.

- Decide on what kind of data you will use: figures and statistics from experimental research, surveys, the census, or questionnaires; observational data from case studies, interviews, and on-site observations; or your reading.

- For an observational study, take careful field notes that describe accurately everything you see. Concentrate on the facts rather than interpretations. Save the interpretive possibilities for the sections of your paper devoted to discussion and recommendations.

- Examine research studies in the field, evaluate their methodology, compare and contrast results with those of other studies, and draw conclusions based on the empirical evidence uncovered. Devote a section of the paper to a review of the literature. (If your field is public policy, international relations, or ethnography, however, your writing will examine trends and draw conclusions, an approach closer to the humanities than to the natural sciences.)

- Look for accurate, up-to-date information, and evaluate it systematically against stated criteria.

- Use sections and headings in your paper. See the APA paper in chapter 16 written for an undergraduate course in Interactive Media (in the communication department).

- Report facts and data. Add comments and expressions such as "I think" only when this is a specific requirement of the task.

- Use the past tense to refer to another researcher's work (*Smith's study (2004) showed that . . .*).

- Use the passive voice when it is not important for readers to know the identity of the person performing the action: "The participants were timed. . . ."

- Present statistical data in the form of tables, charts, and graphs whenever possible (chapter 21).

- Follow the APA *Publication Manual* or whichever style manual is recommended.

 **Online Study Center** social sciences **Across/Beyond College** Student paper in the

Chapter 6

Beginning a Research Project

What is research and why do it? You think you might have chronic fatigue syndrome, and you try to find out what the symptoms are and the best way to treat them. That's research. You want to buy an XM satellite radio player, but you don't know anything about the features, brands, and prices. You order catalogs, talk to salespeople, go to stores, ask friends what they recommend, read consumer magazines, and roam the Web. That's research, too. And when your English professor asks you to write a paper on, say, the role of government in protecting the environment, research helps you do that. Doing research is finding out as much as possible about an issue, finding good questions to ask, formulating a research question, and then attempting to find answers to that question. Entering into the ongoing debates around an issue is a vital part of daily life; contributing to the discussion is an essential part of academic and scholarly work.

6a What's involved in a research paper

1. Know the requirements, and set a realistic schedule. Find out what the demands of the assignment are, such as length, due date, information you should include, number and types of sources, documentation style, and manuscript format. Set a week-by-week or day-by-day schedule for the steps in the process (see 6b).

2. Assemble the tools you will need. Have on hand a research notebook, a flash drive or disks, printer cartridges, index cards, highlighting pens, folders, paper clips, a stapler, self-stick notes, and a card for the library copier. Set up computer folders for all your research files, such as "Drafts," "Notes from Sources," and "Works Cited."

3. Do preliminary research to establish your topic. Make sure you understand and answer the assigned question or address the assigned topic. If you select your own topic, check with your instructor to make sure it is appropriate. Narrow the topic so that it is manageable for the number of pages you intend to write (see 1e). Make sure, too, to choose a topic that will engage and sustain not only readers' interests but also your own. Connect your topic to your own experience whenever possible. If your topic is assigned, make sure you understand the terms used in the assignment (5a).

4. Develop your research question. For a full-scale research paper, design a research question that gets at the heart of what you want to discover. The answer you find as you do research is likely to become your thesis. See 6d.

5. Write a statement of purpose or a proposal. See 6e for how to do this.

6. Determine types of sources and how to find them. Decide which types of primary and secondary sources will give you the best results (6c, chapter 7); then draw up a plan of action. Allow large blocks of time for research. This work cannot be done in just an hour or two.

7. Evaluate sources, make copies, and keep full and accurate records. Select only reliable sources (chapter 8). Record full bibliographical information for every source you consult (see 9d). Download, print, or make photocopies of your source material whenever possible so that you can annotate and make notes later.

8. Make precise notes. Paraphrase and summarize as often as possible while taking notes (9f). Be sure to use your own words and write down why the information is useful or how you might integrate it into your paper (10e). Make sure you copy quotations exactly as they are written (9g), using quotation marks or a colored font. In your notes, record all page numbers of print sources. Copy and save Web addresses.

9. Establish your thesis or hypothesis. Digest your material, and determine your focus. Your paper should not string together what others have said, with no commentary from you. Especially in the humanities, use your research to help yourself form opinions and arrive at conclusions about your topic. Readers want to find *you* and your ideas in your paper (10c). Develop a working thesis as soon as you can, and make lists of supporting evidence and specific details from what you know and what you read. In the sciences and social sciences, it is more usual to form a hypothesis, present the evidence, and draw conclusions (10g).

10. Write drafts. Write more than one draft. As with almost all writing for college and beyond, revision is an essential step in the writing process. You should not expect to produce a perfect first draft. Make an outline of each draft to check on the logic of your argument (3a, 10a).

11. Acknowledge all your sources. Avoid plagiarism by providing information in your text every time you not only quote but also refer to the ideas you find in a source (9f, 9g).

12. Prepare a list of works cited. Follow a clear and consistent set of conventions (spacing, indentation, names, order, and punctuation of entries) when you prepare a list of works cited (see chapters 12–13 and 15–19). Then compare your citations with your list. Make sure that every item on your list appears in your paper and that every work referred to in your paper appears in your list. Use a system of checkmarks in both places as you read a draft.

6b Setting a schedule

Get started as early as you can. As soon as a project is assigned, set a tentative schedule, working backward from the date the paper is due and splitting your time so that you know when you absolutely must move on to the next step. On the next page is a sample time block schedule that you can download, print, or adapt. You will find that in reality, several tasks overlap and the divisions are not neat. If you finish a block before the deadline, move on and give yourself more time for the later blocks.

Online Study Center   **Research** Sample research schedule

RESEARCH SCHEDULE

Starting date:

Date final draft is due:

Block 1: Getting started

Understand the requirements.

Select a topic or narrow a given topic.

Determine the preliminary types of sources to use.

Do preliminary research to discover the important issues.

Organize research findings in computer files.

Write a research question.

Complete by _____

Block 2: Reading, researching, and evaluating sources

Find and copy print and online sources.

Annotate and evaluate the sources.

Write summaries and paraphrases and make notes.

Set up a working bibliography.

Complete by _____

Block 3: Planning and drafting

Formulate a working thesis.

Write a purpose statement, proposal, and/or an outline.

Write a first draft.

Complete by _____

Block 4: Evaluating the draft and getting feedback

Put the draft away for a day or two—but continue collecting useful sources.

Outline the draft and evaluate its logic and completeness.

Plan more research as necessary to fill any gaps.

Get feedback from instructor and classmates.

Complete by _____

Block 5: Revising, preparing list of works cited, editing, presenting

Revise the draft.

Prepare a list of works cited.

Design the format of the paper.

Edit.

Proofread the final draft.

Complete by _____

(final deadline for handing in)

6c Considering types of sources: Primary and secondary

First-year college writing assignments often ask student writers to engage with and respond to *primary sources*—a poem, scientific data, or a photograph. First-year research assignments typically require students to consider and include *secondary sources*—a literary analysis of the poem, an interpretation of the data, an art critic's commentary on the photograph—in order to expand, enrich, and challenge the writer's topic.

Primary sources Primary sources are the firsthand, raw, or original materials that researchers study and analyze. You can consult historical documents, visuals, journals and letters, autobiographies, memoirs, government statistics and studies, and speeches. You can examine works of art, literature, and architecture or watch or listen to performances and programs. You can study or initiate case studies or scientific experiments and take extensive field notes. You can also conduct interviews and use data collected from questionnaires. The use of such primary sources can bring an original note to your research and new information to your readers.

INTERVIEWS Interview people who have expert knowledge of your topic. Plan a set of interview questions, but do not stick so closely to your script that you fail to follow up on good leads in your respondent's replies. Ask permission to tape-record the interview; otherwise, you will have to take quick and accurate notes, particularly if you want to quote. Check the functioning of your tape recorder beforehand. Make note of the date, time, and place of the interview. See chapter 16 for a student's research paper using interviews.

QUESTIONNAIRES Designing useful questionnaires is tricky since much depends on the number and sample of respondents you use, the types of questions you ask, and the methods you employ to analyze the data. Embark on questionnaire research only if you have been introduced to the necessary techniques in a college course or have consulted experts in this area. You may also need permission to conduct research on human subjects.

Secondary sources Secondary sources are analytical works that comment on and interpret other works, such as primary sources. Examples include reviews, discussions, biographies, critical studies, analyses of literary or artistic works or events, commentaries on current and historical events, class lectures, and electronic discussions.

6d From research question to working thesis

At the planning stage, you need to move from establishing a topic to narrowing it into a workable research question, as shown in 1e.

Designing a research question For a research paper, design a research question that gets at the heart of what you want to discover. Your question should contain concrete keywords that you can search (see 7a) rather than general terms or abstractions. The answer you find as you do research is likely to become your thesis. If you find huge amounts of material on your question and realize that you would have to write a book (or two) to cover all the issues, narrow your question.

Questions Needing Narrowing	Revised Questions
How important are families? *Too broad: important to whom and for what? No useful keywords to search.*	In what ways does a stable family environment contribute to an individual's future success?
What problems does the Internet cause? *Too broad: what types of problems? What aspects of the Internet?*	What types of Internet controls would protect individual privacy?
What are the treatments for cancer? *Too wide-ranging: volumes could be and have been written on this.*	For which types of cancer are the success rates of radiation therapy the most promising?

Formulating a working thesis As you do your preliminary work of examining the task, planning which types of sources to use, and moving toward a topic, you will probably have in mind the point you want to make in your paper. If your research question is "Should Internet controls be established to protect individual privacy?", you probably favor either a "yes" or "no" answer to your question. At this point, you will formulate a working thesis in the form of a statement of opinion, which will help drive the organization of your paper. See also 1e.

KEY POINTS
Writing a Working Thesis

1. Make sure the thesis is a statement. A phrase or a question is not a thesis: "Internet controls" is a topic, not a thesis statement. "Are Internet controls needed?" is a question, not a thesis statement.

2. Make sure the thesis statement is not merely a statement of fact: "About 50% of U.S. residents are active users of the Internet" is a statement that cannot be developed and argued. A statement of fact does not let readers feel the need to read on to see what you have to say.

3. Make sure the thesis statement does more than announce the topic: "This paper will discuss Internet controls." Instead, your thesis statement should give information about or express an opinion on the topic: "Service providers, online retailers, and parents share the responsibility of establishing Internet controls to protect an individual's privacy."

4. Above all, be prepared to change and refine your thesis as you do your research and discover what your topic entails.

6e Writing a purpose statement or a proposal

A purpose statement is useful to focus your ideas and give yourself something to work with. Write a simple statement of purpose after you have done some preliminary research. This statement may become more developed or later even change completely, but it will serve to guide your first steps in the process. Here is an example:

> The purpose of this documented paper is to persuade general adult readers that historical films—such as Gladiator —should give precedence to a good story over historical accuracy because readers expect entertainment rather than education when they go to the movies.

Your instructor may also ask for an outline (1f) or for a fuller proposal with a working bibliography attached (9d). Once you have your brief purpose statement, you can use it as a basis for a proposal in narrative or list form, covering background information, establishing your connection to the topic, addressing what you regard as your purpose and audience, and including your research question.

Chapter **7**

Searching for Sources

The Internet has opened access to knowledge. From a computer you can do so much more than search Google or AOL. A click of the mouse on a computer linked to a library can take you to academic sources such as reference works, the full text of articles, online books, historic government documents, and vast databases of scholarly research.

Get to know your college or community library, its layout, and what its holdings include. What online databases and indexes does it subscribe to? Can you access the online holdings from your home? Should you print, save, or e-mail sources you find online? Your best resources are the reference librarians at your library's reference desk. Get to know them, too, and don't be afraid to ask for their help.

7a Online searching

Keyword searches   Use keywords to search for any material stored electronically. Keyword searching is especially effective for finding material in journal and newspaper articles in databases such as *EBSCO, InfoTrac, LexisNexis,* and specialized subject-area databases because a computer can search not only titles but also abstracts (when available) or full articles. See 7c for more on searching databases.

Keywords are vital for your Web searches, too. Spend time thinking of the keywords that best describe what you are looking for. If a search yields thousands of hits, try requiring or prohibiting terms and making terms into phrases (see the Key Points box on pages 106–109). If a search yields few hits, try different keywords or combinations, or try another search engine or database. In addition, try out variant spellings for names of people and places: *Chaikovsky, Tchaikovsky, Tschaikovsky.* Some search engines, such as Google, automatically suggest alternate spellings.

Use the results to help refine your search. If your search produces only one useful source, look at the terms used in that one source and its subject headings and search again, perhaps using those terms with a different search engine or on a different database. Above all, be flexible. Each database or search engine indexes only a portion of what is available in the published literature or on the Web. Once you find a promising reference to a source that is not available online in full text, check whether your library owns the book or journal.

If your search yields a source available only on microfilm or microfiche, you might need a librarian's help to learn how to use the reading machines and how to make copies.

URLs If you already know the Web address (the uniform resource locator or URL) of a useful site, type it exactly, paying attention to spaces (or, more often, lack of spaces), dots, symbols, and capital or lowercase letters. Just one small slip can prevent access. Whenever you can, copy and paste a URL from a Web source so that you do not make mistakes in typing. If you ever get a message saying "site not found," check your use of capitals and lowercase letters (and avoid inserting spaces as you type an address), and try again. Or try adding "l" to an .htm suffix—or deleting "l" from .html. You may find, however, that the site is no longer available.

Search engines and directories If you do not know the exact Web site you want, you need to use search tools. Some search the whole Web for you; some search selected sites; some search only the first few pages of a document; still others search only a specific site, such as a university library system or a noncommercial organization; or they search other search engines (these are called *metasearch engines*). Some (Google, Yahoo!, and academic sponsors) offer subject directories to help you search by topic (see also 1d). Make sure you try all types to find information on your topic. You will miss many useful sources if you do only a Google search.

TECH NOTE
Advice on Search Engines and Directories
For useful information and search tips, go to <http://www.searchenginewatch.com>.

SOME USEFUL SEARCH ENGINES

- Google (the favorite of many academics) searches more than eight billion Web pages and other search engines. It organizes and ranks results by the number of links to a site. Google also offers a directory of sites grouped by topic and an image search. Google Book Search, a new feature, helps you find books addressing your search terms.

- Google Scholar offers searching limited to scholarly content on the Web, though the site's interpretations of what is scholarly may not always agree with your instructor's interpretation.

- INFOMINE provides scholarly resources (for example, in medical sciences, business, and visual arts) and general references, selected and annotated.

- Internet Public Library is run by librarians. It includes a guide to subject collections and an "Ask a question" feature, which allows you to e-mail a question about a research project to librarians for evaluation and possible response within three days.

- A useful free resource for general questions is Answers.com at <http://www.answers.com>.

- Metasearch engines extend your search by searching the results of other search engines. Recommended are Dogpile, which searches Google, Yahoo!, and others, and jux2, which searches two chosen search engines at one time and presents "best results."

SOME USEFUL DIRECTORIES

- WWW Virtual Library is a directory of sources in a large number of academic disciplines.

- Yahoo! is a subject index and directory of the Web. You can keep narrowing down your subjects, or you can use specific keywords. Such a tool is particularly useful when you are trying to find a topic. Yahoo! Picture Gallery finds images.

- University of Michigan's Documents Center Directory supplies statistical, legal, and government documents.

- Librarians' Internet Index is a directory of academic sources.

In addition, consider using subject-specific start pages for more efficient searches than those using general search engines. For links to search engines and directories and to further examples, go to the Online Study Center.

KEY POINTS

Doing a Keyword Search

1. *Know the system used by the database or search engine.* Use the Search Tips or Help link to find out how to conduct a search. Systems vary. Some search for any or all of the words you type in, some need you to indicate whether the words make up a phrase (item 4), and some allow you to exclude words or search for alternatives (items 3, 6, and 8).

2. *Use Advanced Search features in a search engine or database.*
Google (<http://www.google.com/help/refinesearch.html>)
provides a simple grid to indicate whether you want to find
results with all the words, with the exact phrase, with at least
one of the words, or without the words, as shown in the screenshot below. In addition, databases often provide ways to limit
results, such as a box you can check to retrieve only full-text or
"peer-reviewed" articles (scholarly articles, approved for publication by peer reviewers). See the EBSCO screenshot in 7c.

Google Advanced Search

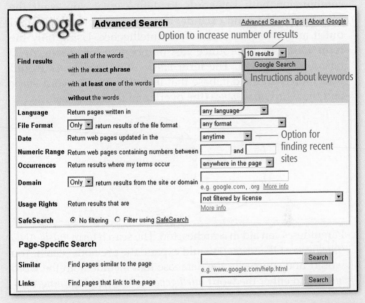

3. *Use a wildcard character to truncate a term and expand the
search.* A wildcard allows you to use at the end of a phrase a
character that indicates that more letters can be attached.
Common wildcard characters are * for several characters and ?
for one character. The truncated search term *addict** will produce references to *addict, addicts, addiction, addictive,* and so on.

4. *Narrow a search by grouping words into phrases.* You can
use quotation marks (or in some cases parentheses) to surround
search terms to group the words into a phrase, a useful technique

(Continued)

(Continued)

for finding titles, names, and quotations. A half-remembered line from a poem by Wordsworth ("the difference to me") entered as a Google search without quotation marks does not produce a Wordsworth poem on the first page of hits. However, putting quotation marks around this phrase produces a hit to the full text of Wordsworth's Lucy poem right on the first page of results.

5. *Use Boolean terms to narrow or expand a search.* Some advanced searches operate on the Boolean principle, which means that you use the "operators" *AND, OR,* and *NOT* in combination with keywords to define what you want the search to include and exclude. Imagine that you want to find out if and how music can affect intelligence. Using only the term *music* would produce vast numbers of hits. Using *AND* narrows the search. The term *music AND intelligence* would find sources in the database that include both the word *music* and the word *intelligence* (the overlap in the circles below).

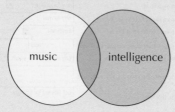

Parentheses can aid in searches, too. The search term *music AND (intelligence OR learning)* would expand the previous search. You would find sources in the database that include both the word *music* and either the word *intelligence* or the word *learning.*

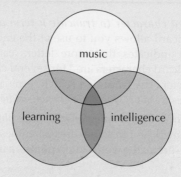

In Boolean searches, *AND* and *NOT* narrow the search: *chicken AND salmonella; tigers NOT Detroit.* The operator *OR* expands the search: *angiogram OR angioplasty.* Not all databases and search engines use this system. Google, for instance, deliberately ignores the words *and* and *not* in a search, so there the search string *tigers NOT Detroit* actually produces sites dealing with the baseball team the Detroit Tigers. Google recommends using the minus sign (always after a space) to exclude a term, as in *tigers −Detroit.* Always check the instructions with each search engine or database.

6. *Require or prohibit a term to narrow a search.* Many search engines allow you to use a symbol such as + (plus) before a term that must be included in the document indexed; a − (minus) symbol prohibits a term: + "Civil War" − Gettysburg.

7. *Take advantage of the "proximity" search feature if available.* Some search engines and many databases let you indicate when you want your search terms to occur close to each other in the text, a useful feature when you can remember only part of a quotation. Check in the Help or Tips file to determine whether the engine you are using has this feature. Proximity is indicated in various ways in various search engines. *NEAR* or *ADJ* (adjacent) are common: "Virginia Woolf" *NEAR* "Bloomsbury group" would search for the two phrases near each other in the text.

8. *Be flexible.* If you don't get good results, try using synonyms—in Google, type a tilde (~) immediately before the search term, as in *~intelligence.* Or try a different search engine or database.

7b Basic reference works

The reference section of your college or local library is a good place to gather basic information. Reference books cannot be checked out, so they are in the library at all times. Also, more and more reference works are being made generally available online, so the accessibility of material from a library or home computer increases. Check Google or your school's online resource page to find out which sources are available online, or ask a librarian.

Reference works provide basic factual information and lead to other sources. However, use reference works only to get started with basic information; then quickly move beyond them. See 7d–7e for details on finding sources other than basic reference works. Check to see if your library subscribes to the huge online database for reference works *xreferplus*.

Encyclopedias   Encyclopedias can help you choose or focus a topic. They provide an overview of the issues involved in a complex topic. Some may also provide extensive bibliographies of other useful sources, so they can also help you develop your research and formulate a research proposal if you are asked to provide one.

General print and online encyclopedias such as *Columbia Encyclopedia, Encyclopaedia Britannica,* and subject-specific encyclopedias such as the *Internet Encyclopedia of Philosophy* or *Berkshire Encyclopedia of World History* can help you get started. The online *Wikipedia* is also useful, but be aware that it is a work in progress and constantly subject to error and revision.

In any case, use encyclopedias only as a way to start your investigations; do not rely on them for most of your project. Instead, move on to more substantial sources.

Bibliographies (also known as *guides to the literature*)   You can find lists of books and articles on a subject in online bibliographic databases such as the following: *Books in Print, International Medieval Bibliography, MLA International Bibliography of Books and Articles on the Modern Languages and Literature, New Books on Women and Feminism,* and *Political Science Bibliographies.*

Biographies   Read accounts of people's lives in biographical works such as *Who's Who, Dictionary of American Biography, Biography Index: A Cumulative Index to Biographic Material in Books and Magazines, Contemporary Authors, Dictionary of Literary Biography, African American Biographies, Chicano Scholars and Writers, Lives of the Painters,* and *American Men and Women of Science.*

Directories   Directories provide lists of names and addresses of people, companies, and institutions. These are useful for setting up interviews and contacting people when you need information. Examples are *Jane's Space Directory* and *Communication Media in Higher Education: A Directory of Academic Programs and Faculty in Radio-Television-Film and Related Media.*

Dictionaries For etymologies, definitions, synonyms, and spelling, consult *The American Heritage Dictionary of the English Language,* 4th edition; *Oxford English Dictionary* (multiple volumes—useful for detailed etymologies and usage discussions); *Facts on File* specialized dictionaries; and other specialized dictionaries such as *Dictionary of Literary Terms* and *Dictionary of the Social Sciences.*

Dictionaries of quotations For a rich source of traditional quotations, go to *Bartlett's Familiar Quotations;* for more contemporary quotations, searchable by topic, go to *The Columbia World of Quotations* (both are available online at <http://www.bartleby.com>). Also, consult specialized dictionaries of quotations, such as volumes devoted to chess, law, religion, fishing, women, and Wall Street.

Collections of articles of topical interest and news summaries *CQ (Congressional Quarterly)* weekly reports, *Facts on File* publications, and *CQ Almanac* are available in print and online by subscription. *Newsbank* provides periodical articles on microfiche, classified under topics such as "law" and "education," and *SIRS (Social Issues Resources Series)* appears in print and online.

Statistics and government documents Among many useful online sources are *Statistical Abstract of the United States, Current Index to Statistics, Handbook of Labor Statistics, Occupational Outlook Handbook,* U.S. Census publications, *GPO Access, UN Demographic Yearbook, Population Index,* and *Digest of Education Statistics.*

Almanacs, atlases, and gazetteers For population statistics and boundary changes, see *The World Almanac, Countries of the World,* or *Information Please.* For locations, descriptions, pronunciation of place names, climate, demography, languages, natural resources, and industry, consult a gazetteer such as *Columbia-Lippincott Gazetteer of the World* and the *CIA World Factbook* series.

General critical works Read what scholars have to say about works of art and literature in *Contemporary Literary Criticism* and in *Oxford Companion* volumes (such as *Oxford Companion to Art* and *Oxford Companion to African American Literature*).

Indexes Indexes of articles appearing in periodicals will start you off in your search for an article on a specific topic. Print indexes, such as *Readers' Guide to Periodical Literature,* will list works published before 1980. More recent publications are listed in online indexes, such as *Applied Science and Technology Index, Engineering Index,* and *Art Index.* An index will provide a complete citation: author, title, periodical, volume, date, and page numbers, often with an abstract. That information will narrow your search. Then you have to locate the periodical in a library or a database and find the actual article.

Online Study Center   **Research** Reference works online

7c Databases

Online databases of journal articles provide sources that have been previously published and referred to by experts.

Online databases and citation indexes owned or leased by libraries can be accessed in the library itself. Many libraries also make the databases they subscribe to available on the Internet through their home pages. For example, many libraries provide online access to the following:

- databases of abstracts in specific subject areas, such as *ERIC* (for education), *PAIS* (for public affairs), *PsycINFO* (for psychology), and *SocIndex* (for sociology)

- general databases of full texts of articles published in the last twenty or thirty years, such as *InfoTrac Expanded Academic ASAP, LexisNexis Academic Universe,* and *EBSCO Academic Search Premier*

- databases of abstracts (with some full texts) of general, nonspecialized magazine articles, such as the Wilson *Readers' Guide to Periodical Literature*

- databases devoted to quantitative statistics, such as the Millennium Development Goal Indicators Database, or to images such as works of art at the J. Paul Getty Trust Web site.

- the *JSTOR* database, providing access to less-recent sources

Access to databases in university library Web sites, from both library and home computers, is often limited to enrolled students, who need to verify their status when they log on. Check with your college library to learn which databases it subscribes to. Articles that you find in a database have for the most part been previously published in print, so evaluate them as print sources for currency, objectivity, and reputation (see 8c).

Before you begin a search, read the instructions on the database to learn how to perform a simple search and an advanced search. Knowing what you are doing can save you a great deal of frustration! Generally, begin a search by using keywords or subject terms, if you know them. Use what the database provides to limit a search as to type of source, date, full-text articles or not, and scholarly, peer-reviewed articles, as shown in the accompanying screenshot.

**Advanced Search Screen: EBSCO Academic
Search Premier Database**

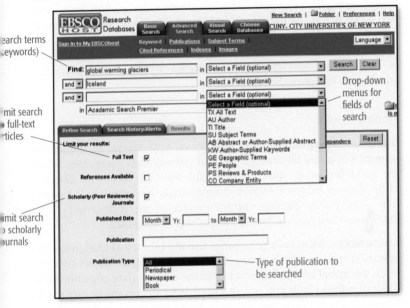

7d Searching for print sources: Books and articles

For library catalogs and periodical databases, decide whether to search by title, author, subject, or keyword (7a). Exact wording and exact spelling are essential for all these searches.

Subject searches To find sources focused on one topic, try subject searching. For that, you need to know the specific subject headings the catalogers used to identify and classify material. Consult a reference source such as *Library of Congress Subject Headings*, or ask a librarian for help. For example, you won't find *cultural* *identity* or *social identity* in *Library of Congress Subject Headings,* but you can look up *culture* and find a list of thirty-two associated headings, such as "language and culture" and "personality and culture."

In addition, these subject headings show related terms, which can suggest ways to narrow or broaden a topic and can help you in other searches, particularly in electronic keyword searches. *Bilingualism,* for example, takes you to topics such as "air traffic control," "code-switching," and "language attrition." An entry in a library catalog will appear with the subject descriptors, so if you find one good source, use its subject classifications to search further. A search in a library online catalog using the keywords *bilingual, education,* and *politics* finds forty-two records. One of these (on p. 115) provides some subject terms to help with further searching: *education and state, educational change,* and *educational evaluation.* Similarly, a keyword search of an online database of full-text articles will produce articles with subject descriptors attached, as in Source Shot 3 in 12e.

Finding books

ONLINE LIBRARY CATALOGS The Web gives you access to the online resources of many libraries (actual and virtual) and universities, which are good browsing sites. Some useful sites are *Library of Congress* <http://lcweb.loc.gov>, *LibWeb* <http://sunsite.berkeley.edu/Libweb>, *New York Public Library* <http://www.nypl.org/index.html>, and *Smithsonian Institution Libraries* <http://www.sil.si.edu>.

CALL NUMBER Most college libraries use the Library of Congress classification system, which arranges books according to subject area and often the initial of the author's last name and the date of publication. The call number tells you where a book is located in the library stacks (the area where books are shelved). Write this number down immediately if a book looks promising, along with the book's title and author(s) and publication information (9d). If a library has open stacks, you will be able to browse through books on a similar topic on the same shelf or on one nearby.
Note: If your college library does not own a book you want, ask a librarian about an interlibrary loan. This option is helpful, of course, only if you begin your search early.

INFORMATION IN THE CATALOG The screens of electronic catalogs vary from one system to another, but most screens contain the name of the system you are using; the details of your search request and of the search, such as the number of records found; and detailed bibliographical information.

Library Catalog Screen: City University of New York

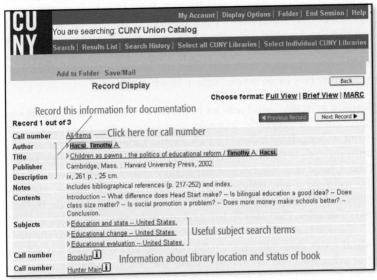

Courtesy of the City University of New York.

The screen shown here, which extends to links to the call number (LC89.H215202) and the locations of the holdings (places where the book is housed), provides all the essential information you will need to document the source at the end of your paper: author, title, place of publication, publisher, and date of publication. In addition, it lets you know the number of pages in the book and shows that the book contains a bibliography and an index—useful research tools. The subject search terms shown can help structure further searches.

Once you find a book that seems to be related to your topic, you do not have to read the whole book to use it for your paper. Learn what you can from the catalog entry; then skim the table of contents, chapter headings, and bibliography. Your best time-saver here is the index. Turn to it immediately, and look up some key words for your topic. Read the section of the book in which references to your topic appear; take notes; annotate a photocopy of the relevant pages (9e). A book's bibliography and references are useful, too. The research the author has done can help you in your search. It is a good idea to make a copy of the title page and the page on which the copyright notice appears. If you find nothing remotely connected to your research question, do not cite the book as a resource, even though you looked at it.

BOOKS IN PRINT AND ALTERNATIVES If you want to find a book or check on bibliographical details, use *Books in Print* (available in print and online). If your library does not subscribe to the online version, you can use the Amazon.com site at <http://www.amazon.com> or any other large commercial online bookseller to look up the details of a book—free. Amazon does not, however, list the place of publication, but it may be visible if you "search inside the book."

Finding articles Find articles in periodicals (works issued periodically, such as scholarly journals, magazines, and newspapers) by using a periodical index. Use electronic indexes for recent works, print indexes for earlier works—especially for works written before 1980. Check which services your library subscribes to and the dates the indexes cover. Indexes may provide abstracts; some, such as *EBSCO, LexisNexis Academic Universe,* and *InfoTrac,* provide the full text of articles. (See also 7b for more on indexes.)

Search methods are similar to those in book searches. If the periodical index does not provide the full text, you will need to find out first whether your library owns the periodical and then in which form it is available: in files, in bound volumes, or in film form with pages shown in a strip (microfilm) or on a sheet (microfiche), which you will need to read with a special machine. The catalog for your library will tell you on the screen which issues are available in the library and in which format and location. For articles in journals not available in your library, ask about interlibrary loan.

7e Finding Web sources

The democratic nature of the Internet means that many Web pages have no editorial control, so although you will probably find a great deal of material, much of it could be mindless and inaccurate (8d). On the plus side, you will find vast resources, current material, and frequent updates—all without leaving your computer. As you plan your research, consider which of the following Internet resources might be the most appropriate for your topic. A reference librarian can help you decide.

Online magazines and online scholarly journals Online magazines and journals are proliferating. You'll find a useful directory at <http://www.lii.org/pub/topic/magazines>. Some scholarly journals have no print versions. For examples of such journals, see links in the Online Study Center. Some online journals and magazines are available free; some allow you to view only the current issue at no cost.

Many, however, require a subscription through your library computer network or a personal subscription. Several university libraries, such as Albany and Houston, include a directory of journals in their sites.

Online literary texts   Literary texts that are out of copyright and in the public domain are increasingly available online for downloading. The following are useful sites to consult, although the versions of texts you see may not always be authoritative: *Project Bartleby* <http://www.bartleby.com>, *Project Gutenberg* <http://www.promo.net/pg/index.html>, *University of Virginia's Electronic Text Center* <http://etext.lib.virginia.edu>.

E-books   Many books are becoming available as e-books, either to be read online at a computer or to be downloaded and read in an e-book reader. If your library subscribes to e-book databases, check their offerings when you are looking for a book.

Online news sites   The Web sites of major newspapers, magazines, and television networks provide up-to-date news information; some offer archived information but often only to subscribers. See, for example, *New York Times on the Web* and *CNN Interactive*. *LexisNexis* also provides access to articles from many newspapers.

Online Study Center   **Research** Online texts and news

Nonprofit research sites   Many nonprofit sites offer valuable and objective information. For example, see *Public Agenda Online*, *American Film Institute*, and *San Francisco Bay Bird Observatory*.

Web pages and hypertext links   Universities and research institutes provide information through their own Web home pages, with hypertext links that take you with one click to many other sources. Individual Web pages can provide useful information, too, but need careful evaluation since anyone can publish anything on the Web (8d).

E-mail discussions   With e-mail, you have access to many discussion groups. Messages go out to a list of people interested in specific topics. Without charge, you can join a list devoted to a topic of interest (22b). However, most of the lists are not refereed or monitored, so you have to evaluate carefully any information you find.

For academic research, personal blogs, Usenet newsgroups, and chat rooms provide little that is substantive. Evaluating the reliability of a contributor's comments can be difficult.

7f Research sources in twenty-seven subject areas

Twenty-one college librarians from eighteen colleges in thirteen states helped with compiling a list of useful print and online starting points for research across the curriculum in twenty-seven subject areas—from "Art and Architecture" to "Women's Studies." That list, with links available online, has recently been updated and revised by Professor Trudi Jacobson, Coordinator of User Education Programs at the University Libraries of the University at Albany, State University of New York.

 Online Study Center   **Research** Sources in 27 subject areas

Chapter 8

Evaluating Sources

How can you identify good, relevant sources? Use the following guidelines.

8a Reading sources critically

Reading what others write always provides ideas, but not just the ideas you absorb from the page or screen. If you read critically, you will generate ideas of your own as you read and make your own contributions to the issues under discussion. The principles of critical analysis discussed in 1a and 4c can be extended to critical reading of sources.

KEY POINTS
Reading Sources Critically

▪ Ask questions about the credentials and reputation of the author and the place of publication. What do you learn about the writer's purpose and the audience whom the author is addressing? Make sure you subject any material you find on Web pages to especially careful scrutiny (8d).

- Ask questions about the ideas you read. An easy way to do this is to write your annotations in the margin. If you find yourself thinking "But . . ." as you read, go with that sense of doubt, and make a note of what troubles you. Examples of annotated readings are in 1b and 9e.

- Be on the lookout for assumptions that may be faulty. If you are reading an article on home-schooling and the writer favors home-schooling because it avoids subjecting students to violence in schools, the unstated assumption is that all schools are violent places. For more on the logic of argument, see 4h and 4i.

- Make sure the writer's evidence is adequate and accurate. For example, if the writer is making a generalization about all Chinese students based on a study of only three, you have cause to challenge the generalization as resting on inadequate evidence.

- Note how the writer uses language. Which terms does the writer use with positive—or negative—connotations, signaling the values the writer holds? Does the writer flamboyantly denigrate the views of others with such phrases as "a ridiculous notion" or "laughably inept policies"?

- Be alert for sweeping generalizations, bias, and prejudice: "Women want to stay home and have children." "Men love to spend Sundays watching sports."

Do your reading when you can write—not on the treadmill or while watching TV. Note any questions, objections, or challenges on the page, as in the annotated text shown in 9e; on self-stick notes; on index cards; in a response file on your computer; or in a journal. Your critical responses to your reading will provide you with your own ideas for writing.

8b Recognizing a scholarly article

Learn to distinguish scholarly from nonscholarly articles. A scholarly article is not something you are likely to find in a magazine in a dentist's office. A scholarly journal is peer reviewed—that is, other scholars read all the articles and approve them for publication.

KEY POINTS
What a Scholarly Article Does

A scholarly article

- refers to the work of other scholars (look for in-text citations and a bibliographical list of works cited, footnotes, or endnotes)
- names the author and usually describes the author's credentials
- includes notes, references, or a bibliography and may include an abstract
- deals with a serious issue in depth
- uses academic or technical language for informed readers
- appears in journals that do not include colorful advertisements or eye-catching pictures (a picture of two stunning models is an indication that you are not looking at a scholarly article)

When you read scholarly articles, look for any section headings, read the abstract and any section headed "Summary" or "Conclusions," and determine the author's main idea to find out whether the article addresses your topic. If you are working on a topic related to current events, you probably will need to consult newspapers, magazines, and online sources as well as or in place of scholarly journals. See 12d, item 20, for the cover of a scholarly journal.

Recognizing scholarly articles in general databases Some databases are specialized and will yield only research articles (or only abstracts) published in scholarly journals. Other databases, such as those hosted by *EBSCO* and *InfoTrac,* are more general, including popular magazines as well as serious and scholarly peri-

TECH NOTE
Databases of Journal Information

- Genamics JournalSeek provides links to the Web sites of journals to help you identify journals as scholarly or not.
- The Cornell University Web site *Distinguishing Scholarly Journals from Other Periodicals* provides definitions and examples of four categories of periodical literature: scholarly, substantive news and general interest, popular, and sensational.

odicals. In several databases, you can search for scholarly articles by opting to find "peer-reviewed" articles; these are articles that have been approved by an editorial board. *EBSCO* databases provide this feature.

Online Study Center   **Research** Journal information

8c Evaluating works originating in print

Before you make detailed notes on a book or an article that began its life in print, be sure it will provide suitable information to help answer your research question.

Print books Check the date of publication, notes about the author, table of contents, and index. Skim the preface, introduction, chapter headings, and summaries to give yourself an idea of the information in the book and the book's theoretical basis and perspective. Do not waste time making detailed notes on a book that deals only tangentially with your topic or on an out-of-date book (unless your purpose is to discuss and critique its perspective or examine a topic historically). Ask a librarian or your instructor for help in evaluating the appropriateness of sources you discover. If your topic concerns a serious academic issue, readers will expect you to consult books and not limit your references to popular magazines, newspapers, and Internet sources.

Periodical articles in print Take into account the type of periodical, any organization with which it is affiliated, and the intended audience. Differentiate among the following types of articles (listed in descending order of reliability, with the most reliable first):

- scholarly articles (see 8b)
- articles, often long, in periodicals for nonspecialist but serious, well-educated readers, such as *New York Review of Books, Atlantic Monthly, Economist, Scientific American,* and *Nation*
- shorter articles, with sources not identified, in popular magazines for a general audience, such as *Ebony, Time, Newsweek, Parents, Psychology Today,* and *Vogue,* or in newspapers
- articles with dubious sources, written for sensational tabloid magazines, such as *National Enquirer, Globe,* and *Star*

KEY POINTS

Questions to Evaluate a Print Source

1. *What does the work cover?* It should be long enough and detailed enough to provide adequate information.

2. *How objective is the information?* The author, publisher, or periodical should not be affiliated with an organization that has an ax to grind—unless, of course, your topic entails reading critically and making comparisons with other points of view.

3. *How current are the views?* Check the date of publication. The work should be up-to-date if you need a current perspective.

4. *How reputable are the publisher and author?* The work should be published by a reputable publisher in a source that is academically reliable, not one devoted to gossip, advertising, propaganda, or sensationalism. Check *Books in Print, Literary Market Place,* or ACQWEB's *Directory of Publishers and Vendors* for details on publishers. The author should be an authority on the subject. Find out what else the author has written (in Google, in *Books in Print,* or at Amazon.com) and what his or her qualifications are as an authority.

Newspaper articles   The *New York Times, Washington Post,* and *Los Angeles Times,* for example, provide mostly reliable accounts of current events; daily editorial comments; and reviews of books, film, and art. Be aware that most newspapers have political leanings, so reports of and comments on the same event may differ.

8d Evaluating Web sources: Developing junk antennae

What makes the Internet so fascinating is that it is wide open, free, and democratic. Anyone can "publish" anything, and anyone can read it. For anyone looking for information and well-presented, informed opinion, however, the Internet can pose a challenge.

If you find an article in a subscription database (*InfoTrac* or *LexisNexis,* for example), you will know that the article has been published in print, so you can use the criteria for print works (8c) to evaluate it. If the article has been published in a reputable periodical or in an online journal sponsored by a professional organization or a university, you can assume that it is a valid source for a research paper.

For works devised specifically for the Web, use the strategies in the following Key Points box to separate the information from the junk.

KEY POINTS
Developing Your Junk Antennae

1. *Scrutinize the domain name of the URL.* Reliable information can be found on .gov and .edu addresses that are institutionally sponsored (but see item 2). With .com ("dot com") or .org sources, always assess whether the source provides factual information or advocates a specific point of view on an issue.

2. *Assess the originator of an .edu source.* Check that the institution or a branch of it is sponsoring the site. A tilde (~) followed by a name in the URL indicates an individual posting from an academic source. Try to ascertain whether the individual is a faculty member or a student. Increasingly, though, individuals are setting up Web sites under their own domain name.

3. *Check the About page or the home page.* Always take the link from a Web site to its "About" page or its home page, if you are not already there. These pages often provide more information about the author, the sponsor, the purpose, and the date of posting.

4. *Determine the author, and discover what you can about him or her.* Look for a list of credentials, a home page, a résumé, or Web publications. In Google or Google Scholar, use the author's name as a search term to see what the author has published on the Internet or who has cited the author. If no individual author or institutional author is to be found anywhere, check the purpose and sponsor of the site.

5. *Investigate the purposes of a Web page author or sponsor.* Objectivity and rationality are not necessarily features of all Web pages. The sponsor of a site may want to persuade, convert, or sell. Even if the message is not obviously biased and extreme, be aware that most authors write from some sense of conviction or purpose. (Note, though, that a Web site can be oriented toward a specific view without necessarily being irresponsible.)

6. *Evaluate the quality of the writing.* A Web page filled with spelling and grammatical errors should not inspire confidence. If the language has not been checked, the ideas probably haven't been given much time and thought, either. Don't use such a site as a source. Exceptions are discussion lists and Usenet postings. They are written and posted quickly, so even if they contain errors, they can also contain useful ideas to stimulate thinking on your topic.

(Continued)

(Continued)

7. *Follow the links.* See whether the links in a site take you to authoritative sources. If the links no longer work (you'll get a 404 message: "Site Not Found"), the home page with the links has not been updated in a while—not a good sign.

8. *Check for dates, updates, ways to respond, and ease of navigation.* A recent date of posting or recent updating; information about the author; ways to reach the author by e-mail, regular mail, or phone; a clearly organized site; easy navigation; and up-to-date links to responsible sites are all indications that the site is well managed and current.

9. *Corroborate information.* Try to find the same information on another reliable site. Also look for contradictory information elsewhere.

TECH NOTE

Web Sites on Evaluating Sources

Useful information on evaluating sources is available at a Widener University (Chester, PA) site. In addition, an interactive tutorial on evaluating Internet sources can be found at the Online Study Center.

Online Study Center   **Research** Evaluating sources

8e Anatomy of a Web site

Using the flowchart   Use the following flowchart to find on a Web site the information that will help you evaluate its reliability. In addition, if you record the information for every accessed site that you might refer to or quote from in your paper, you will then be able to construct your citation without retracing your steps (see 9d). Although different styles of documentation, such as MLA and APA, ask for different chunks of information in different configurations, the five items listed in the chart are common to most of them. As you read the chart, refer to the accompanying annotated screenshot of a site with an explicitly stated agenda, "dedicated to restoring democratic authority over corporations, reviving grassroots democracy, and revoking the power of money and corporations to control government and civic society."

How to Read a Web Site

What to Look For and Record; Where and How to Find It	Additional Things You May Need to Do

1. Name of author

Look at the top or bottom of the page. For Web documents with no author named, look for an organization, government agency, or business that serves as the author.

- Follow any links on the document page to a résumé, publications, purpose statement, or home page. Try to establish the purpose of the site.
- Do a Google search for details about the author, whether an individual, institution, organization, business, or government agency.
- Do not confuse the Web site manager or the person maintaining the site with the author of the information.
- If you cannot find an author, look on the "Home" or "About" page, or go to #2, "Title."

2. Title of document

Find it at the top of the page. Note, though, that some sites will contain documents with titles, and some will not.

- For online sources previously in print form, record any print publication details provided.
- Record page numbers only for PDF documents, in which page numbers appear on the screen.
- Record the name of the document section in which relevant information appears (e.g., Introduction).
- Record paragraph numbers *only* when they are part of the document and appear on the screen.

3. Name of site

If it is not visible at the top or bottom of the page, go to "Home" or "About." Or delete the URL progressively back to each single slash, and click to see which part of the site you access.

Also record what you can of the following, if available:

- name of the organization in charge of the content of the site (owner or sponsor)—usually indicated in the root domain of the URL (before the first single slash)
- for an online journal, the volume and issue numbers
- the date when material was posted online or updated (often not available)

4. Your date of access

Because Web sites come and go and change, always record the exact date on which you access the site.

Save any page that provides you with crucial information or is likely to update or change its content, such as blogs or files ending with *.php, .asp,* or *.shtml.*

5. URL

Copy and paste this from your browser into your working bibliography. Copying by hand may introduce errors.

If a page is divided into sections ("frames"), and you want to refer to one frame only, right-click in the frame, and select "Save (or Add) as Favorite"; then retrieve the material in the frame with its own URL.

Web Page

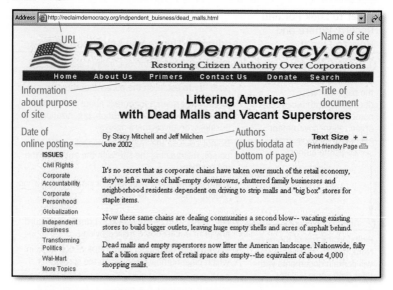

Recognizing the difficulties   Note that on many sites, you may have difficulty finding a date of posting, a document title as well as a Web site name, or an exact identification of the author of the material, whether an individual or an organization. Just record whatever you can find on a thorough search of the site, always scrolling down to the bottom of a page. Try using the root domain of the URL—the material just before the dot preceding the first single slash (as in <http://www.library .ucla.edu/>)—to identify the owner, also referred to as the *publisher* or *sponsor,* of the site, who is responsible for its content. If the "Home" and "About" links provide no useful information, consider whether you should use a source if you are unsure about the identity of the author, the author's credentials, or the owner and purpose of the site.

Chapter **9**

Avoiding Plagiarism

The convenience and comfort of researching online are not without a downside. The ease of finding, copying, and downloading information from the screen has its attendant dangers: that researchers lose sight of what is theirs and what isn't, that they forget where they read something, that information seems so prolific that surely it must be there for the taking. Unfortunately, though, that is not the case, especially in the academic world, where presenting somebody else's words or ideas without acknowledging where those words and ideas come from is a punishable offense.

The word for the offense, *plagiarism*, is derived from a Latin verb meaning "to kidnap," and if you use someone else's words and ideas without acknowledging them, you are in effect kidnapping or stealing those words and ideas.

9a The seven sins of plagiarism— and the consequences

KEY POINTS
The Seven Sins of Plagiarism

1. *Intentional grand larceny* Presenting as your own work a whole essay bought from paper mills, "borrowed" from a friend, or intentionally copied and pasted from an online source (where such a practice may be compared to ordering "a takeout essay"—see 9e)

2. *Premeditated shoplifting* Using passages from a book, article, or Web site that you intentionally insert in your paper without any attribution (a type of plagiarism differing from point 1 only in that passages, not the whole paper, are copied)

3. *Tinkering with the evidence* Using unattributed source material, making only a few word changes, and trusting that those changes are enough to avoid charges of plagiarism

4. *Idea kidnapping* Using ideas written by others (even if you do use your own words) and neglecting to cite the source of the ideas

5. *Unauthorized borrowing of private property* Using the words or sentence structure of a source and citing the source—but following it too closely and not including actual words from the source within quotation marks

6. *Trespassing over boundaries* Failing to indicate in your paper where ideas from a source end and your ideas take over (9i)

7. *Writing under the influence* Being too tired, lazy, or late to meet an imminent deadline and turning to any of the six previous sins in desperation

Consequences Obviously, these "sins" vary in their severity and in the intention to deceive. The types of plagiarism described in items 4 through 6 in the Key Points box sometimes occur unintentionally, but they may be perceived as plagiarism nevertheless. You have to work hard at avoiding them, especially since the consequences of plagiarism can be severe, ranging from an F on a paper or an F in a course to disciplinary measures or expulsion from college. In the world at large, it can lead to lawsuits and ruined careers. Those are reasons enough to work hard at resisting the temptation to plagiarize.

LANGUAGE AND CULTURE
Ownership Rights across Cultures

The Western view takes seriously the ownership of words and text. It respects both the individual as author (and authority) and the originality of the individual's ideas. Copyright laws define and protect the boundaries of intellectual property. However, even the Western world acknowledges that authors imitate and borrow from others' work, as Harold Bloom notes in *The Anxiety of Influence.* In some cultures, memorization and the use of classic texts are common in all walks of life. And worldwide, the ownership of language, texts, music, and videos is being called into question by the democratic, interactive nature of the Internet. In short, therefore, plagiarism is not something universal and easy to define. In Western academic culture, basic ground rules exist for the "fair use" of another writer's writing without payment, but easy access to music and media sources poses interesting questions about intellectual property and the opportunities to create and remix culture.

TECH NOTE
A Web Site on Plagiarism

For more on the topic of plagiarism, use the link to the excellent Georgetown University Web site *What Is Plagiarism?*

Online Study Center   **Research** More on avoiding plagiarism

9b How to avoid even the suspicion of plagiarism

Research and clear documentation open a channel of communication between you and your audience. Readers learn what your views are and what has influenced those views. They will assume that anything not documented is your original idea and your wording.

Remember that citing any words and ideas that you use from your sources plays out to your advantage. Citing accurately reveals a writer who has done enough research to enter ongoing conversations in the academic world. In addition, citations show readers how hard you have worked, how much research you have done, and how the points you make are supported by experts. So be proud to cite your sources.

KEY POINTS
How to Avoid Plagiarizing

- Start your research early enough to avoid panic mode.

- Make a record of each source so that you have all the information you need for appropriate documentation.

- Set up a working annotated bibliography.

- Take notes from the sources, with a systematic method of indicating quotation, paraphrase, and your own comments. For example, use quotation marks around quoted words, phrases, sentences, and passages; introduce a paraphrase with a tag, such as "Laird makes the point that . . ."; in your notes about a source, write your own comments in a different color. Then, later, you will see immediately which ideas are yours and which come from your source.

- Always acknowledge and document the source of any passage, phrase, or idea that you have used or summarized from someone else's work.

- Never use exactly the same sequence of ideas and organization of argument as your source.

- When you use a single key word from your source or three or more words in sequence from your source, use the appropriate format for quoting and documenting.

- Be aware that substituting synonyms for a few words in the source or moving a few words around is not enough to counter a charge of plagiarism.

- Don't use in your paper passages that have been written or rewritten by a friend or a tutor.

- Never even consider buying, downloading, or "borrowing" a paper or a section of a paper that you turn in as your own work.

9c Keeping track of sources

The first step toward avoiding plagiarism is keeping track of what your sources are and which ideas come from your sources and which from you. You will find that one of the frustrating moments for you as a researcher occurs when you find a note about an interesting point you read—but cannot remember where you found the passage or who wrote it or whether your notes represent an author's exact words. Avoid this frustration by keeping track as you go along.

Use the Bookmarks or Favorites feature.   Many browsers have a Bookmarks or Favorites feature that allows you to compile and save a list of useful sites you have visited. You can then easily revisit these sites by simply clicking on the bookmark. Bookmarks can be deleted later when you no longer need them. If you work on a networked computer in a lab where you cannot save your work on the hard drive, export your bookmarks to your own computer or CD, or use a free online bookmark service such as Furl at <http://www.furl.net>.

Record URL and date of access.   Note that bookmarking will not always last with a long, nonpersistent URL, such as URLs of online subscription services. To be safe, record the URL of the home page. In addition, use the Copy and Paste features to copy the complete URL on your hard drive, flash drive, or CD, along with the date on which you access the source. As a last resort, copy the URL by hand, but take care to get it exactly right: every letter, symbol, and punctuation mark is important.

Use any bibliographic software available.   Programs such as EndNote and RefWorks allow you to save source citations directly from online databases into your personal database file, where you can keep and add to the sources you find, along with your own comments and notes. The software also formats the source citations in the style you need—MLA, APA, and many more—for your list of works cited, with all the features and punctuation marks in the correct places.

Highlight, copy, and paste.   As you read material on the Web, highlight a passage you find, copy it, and then paste it into your own file. Make sure that you indicate clearly in your new document that you have included a direct quotation. Use quotation marks and/or a bigger or colored font along with an author/page citation, as in the following example:

> Novelist John Lanchester has made a telling point about our image of self by having his narrator declare that we **"wouldn't care so much what people thought of us if we knew how seldom they did"**(62).

Save as much information as you can about the original document in your working bibliography (9d).

Make photocopies of sources. Photocopying print articles allows you to devote research time to locating relevant sources and taking notes from reference works and books; you can take the copies of articles with you and use them when you are unable to be in the library.

Make copies of Web sources. When you print a useful Web page, the URL and your date of access will be included. Web sites can be volatile, changing frequently; a download date does not allow for access to a site that has changed. Save a copy of a source and include it in your paper if the site is volatile.

9d Setting up a working bibliography

From the first steps of your research, keep accurate records of each source in a working bibliography. Record enough information so that you will be able to make up a list of references in whichever style of documentation you choose, though not all the points of information you record will be necessary for every style of documentation.

Important: **Essential information for an online source is the URL and the date on which you access the material. Always make a note of that information.**

Sort your sources into four categories: print books, print articles, Web sources, and online database sources. The table on source essentials summarizes what you should record. Download or print our online templates provided for each category to prompt you to record the information you need for every source.

Source Essentials: What to Record

	Print Book	Print Article	Web Source	Online Database Source
Author(s), editor(s), translator(s), OR name of company or government agency	✓	✓	✓ (if available on site)	✓
Title and subtitle	✓	✓	✓	✓
Print publication information	✓	✓	✓ (if available on site)	✓
Volume/edition/issue	✓	✓		
Call number	✓	✓		
Page numbers of document	✓	✓	✓ Only for PDF documents. Include number of paragraphs only if numbers appear on screen.	✓ Only for PDF documents. Otherwise include start page if given.
Name of Web site			✓	✓ Name of database and service
Other essential information to include	Place: Publisher, date	**Scholarly article:** Include volume number, issue number, date of publication, inclusive page numbers. **Article in a book:** Include title, editor, place, publisher, year of publication, inclusive page numbers of the article.	**Web site:** Include name of sponsor, date of online publication or update, URL, and date of access. **Article in online journal:** Include volume number. Always include URL and your date of access. **E-mail message or discussion list posting:** Include name of sender, subject line, date of posting, name of list, and your date of access to the list.	**Article in a database:** Include volume number, issue number, date of print publication, and name and location of library. Also include URL of home page of database or persistent URL of article and your date of access.

 *Online Study Center* **Research** Templates for recording sources

 KEY POINTS

Helpful Hints for Recording Source Information

Print book Photocopy the title page and the copyright page, where much of the information is available.

Print article Photocopy the table of contents of the periodical or anthology.

Web source Save, e-mail yourself a copy, or print out the Web source. Set your computer so that the URL appears on the printout along with the date of access. Use the Copy and Paste functions to copy the URL accurately into your own document.

Online database source Save, e-mail yourself a copy, print out the online database source, or use bibliographic software to record sources you find and then format them for you (9c).

Keep your list of sources in a form that you can work with to organize them alphabetically, add and reject sources, and add summaries and notes. Note cards and computer files have the advantage over sheets of paper or a research journal. They don't tie you to page order.

Here is a sample bibliographical record for an article accessed in an online subscription database.

> Laird, Ellen. "Internet Plagiarism: We All
> Pay the Price." *Chronicle of Higher Education*
> 13 July 2001 : 5. *Academic Search Premier.*
> EBSCO. City U of New York Lib. 9 Jan. 2006
> < http://search.epnet.com/login.aspx?direct
> =true&db=aph&an=5459407>.

 TECH NOTE

Annotated Bibliographies

For information on how to prepare an annotated bibliography, along with examples, go to the Purdue Online Writing Lab.

9e Annotating and making notes

Printing and saving from online sources make a source text available for you to annotate. You can interact with the author's ideas, asking questions, writing comments, and jotting down your own ideas. Here is a passage from the article by Ellen Laird on plagiarism (see the bibliographical information on page 133). As Laird, a college professor, discusses the case of Chip, a student who has plagiarized, she is considering her own role and her student's explanation. The passage shows the annotations that student Juana Mere made as she gave the article a critical reading.

But what if her instructions weren't as clear as she thought?
To save face with myself, I must assume that Chip understood that downloading an essay and submitting it as his own was an *Look up* egregious act. Why, then, did he do it? *Can she ever really know?*

Chip explained he had been "mentally perturbed" the weekend *Sour* *But it's* before the paper was due and that the essay he had written failed to *like a* *specula-* meet his high standards. But I sensed that Chip felt he had made a *very* *tion on* choice akin to having a pizza delivered. He had procrastinated on an *gene* *her part* assignment due the next day, had no time left in which to prepare *excu* his work from scratch, and had to get on to those pressing matters *Is this* that shape the world of an 18-year-old. He dialed his Internet service *conde-* provider, ordered takeout, and had it delivered.
scending? Nice analogy   Good quotation

Annotating is useful for comments, observations, and questions. You also will need to make notes when you do not have a copy that you can write on or when you want to summarize, paraphrase, and make detailed connections to other ideas and other sources. Write notes on the computer, on legal pads, in notebooks, or on index cards—whatever works best for you. Index cards—each card with a heading and only one note—offer flexibility: you can shuffle and reorder them to fit the organization of your paper. In your notes, always include the author's name, a short version of the title of the work, and any relevant page number(s) when you summarize, paraphrase, or quote, as shown in 9f. Include full source information in your working bibliography (9d). Then when you write your paper, you will have at your fingertips all the information necessary for a citation.

9f Summarizing and paraphrasing

Summary   Summaries are useful for giving readers basic information about the work you are discussing. To summarize a source or a passage in a source, select only the main points as the author presents them, without your own commentary or interpretation. Be brief, and use your own words at all times. To ensure that you use your own words, do not have the original source in front of you as you write. Read, understand, and then put the passage away before writing your summary. If you find that you must include some particularly apt words from the original source, put them in quotation marks.

Use summaries in your research paper to let readers know the gist of the most important sources you find. When you include a summary in a paper, introduce the author or the work to indicate where your summary begins. At the end of the summary, give the page numbers you are summarizing. Do not include page numbers if you are summarizing the complete work or summarizing an online source; instead, indicate where your summary ends and your own ideas return (see 9i). When you write your paper, provide full documentation of the source in your list of works cited at the end.

After reading the article by Laird on plagiarism, Mere decided to write a research paper on Internet plagiarism. She wrote this sixty-five-word summary of an article of 1,635 words in a computer file headed "College plagiarism." (She could also have used an index card.) The heading of the summary (Laird) refers directly to the first word on the bibliography record on page 133.

Laird   Summary

"Internet plagiarism"

College professor Ellen Laird explores the possible reasons why a student might have plagiarized a whole essay. She concludes that Chip, otherwise a good student, knew what he was doing, but taking material from the Internet while at home might not have seemed unethical. Laird connects his behavior to our contemporary culture and laments that teaching will have to change to counteract opportunities for plagiarism.

Paraphrase   When you need more details than a summary provides, paraphrasing offers a tool. Use paraphrase more often than you use quotation. A paraphrase uses your words and your interpretations of and comments on the ideas you find in your sources. Many instructors feel that if you cannot paraphrase information, then you probably do not understand it. So paraphrase serves the purpose of showing that you have absorbed your source material.

A paraphrase is similar in length to the original material— maybe somewhat longer. In a paraphrase, present the author's argument and logic, but be very careful not to use the author's exact words or sentence structure.

KEY POINTS

How to Paraphrase

- Keep the source out of sight as you write a paraphrase so that you will not be tempted to copy the sentence patterns or phrases of the original.

- Do not substitute synonyms for some or most of the words in an author's passage.

- Use your own sentence structure as well as your own words. Your writing will still be regarded as plagiarized if it resembles the original in sentence structure as well as in wording.

- Do not comment or interpret: just tell readers the ideas that the author of your source presents.

- Check your text against the original source to avoid inadvertent plagiarism.

- Cite the author (and page number if a print source) as the source of the ideas, introduce and integrate the paraphrase, and provide full documentation. If the source does not name an author, cite the title.

When Mere was making notes for her paper on Internet plagiarism, she decided to paraphrase one of the key paragraphs from Laird's article, one that she had previously annotated (9e).

ORIGINAL SOURCE

> Chip explained that he had been "mentally perturbed" the weekend before the paper was due and that the essay he had written failed to meet his high standards. But I sensed that Chip felt that he had made a choice akin to having a pizza delivered. He had procrastinated on an assignment due the next day, had no time left in which to prepare his work from scratch, and had to get on to those pressing matters that shape the world of an 18-year-old. He dialed his Internet service provider, ordered takeout, and had it delivered.
>
> —Ellen Laird, "Internet Plagiarism: We All Pay the Price"

You can use common words and expressions such as "made a choice" or "due the next day." But if you use more unusual expressions from the source ("a choice akin to having pizza delivered"; "pressing matters"; "dialed his Internet service provider"), you need to enclose them in quotation marks. In Mere's first attempt at paraphrase, she does not quote, but her words and structure resemble the original too closely.

PARAPHRASE TOO SIMILAR TO THE ORIGINAL

Laird   Paraphrase, p. 5, ninth paragraph

Laird knew that Chip was mentally perturbed before he wrote his paper and his high standards prevented him from writing his own essay. But she felt that what he did was like having a pizza takeout. He had procrastinated so long that he could not write an essay from scratch and wanted to enjoy his life. So he ordered a takeout essay from his ISP (5).

Mere gives the name of the author and the page number of the source material (given in the online version) using the MLA style of documentation. Documentation, however, is not a guarantee against plagiarism. Mere's wording and sentence structure follow the original too closely. When classmates and her instructor pointed this out, she revised the paraphrase by keeping the ideas of the original, using different wording and sentence structure, and quoting what she regarded as a unique phrase.

REVISED PARAPHRASE

Laird   Paraphrase, p. 5, ninth paragraph

Laird's student Chip might have felt psychologically stressed and that might have affected his attitude to the paper he wrote, forcing him to reject it as not good enough to hand in for a grade. Laird, however, sees his transgression not so much as one of high moral principles as of expediency. He chose the easiest way out. He had left the assignment until the last minute. He had no time to do the work. He wanted to go out and have fun. So what did he do? He went on the Web, found an essay, and "ordered takeout" (5).

9g Quoting

Readers should immediately realize why you are quoting a particular passage and what the quotation contributes to the ideas you want to convey. They should also learn who said the words you are quoting and, if the source is a print source, on which page of the original work the quotation appears. Then they can look up the author's name in the list of works cited at the end of your paper and find out exactly where you found the quotation.

The Modern Language Association (MLA) format for citing a quotation from an article by one author is illustrated in this chapter and in Part 3. See Part 4 for examples of citations of other types of sources in other styles. For punctuation with quotation marks, see also chapter 49.

Deciding what and when to quote   Quote when you use the words of a well-known authority or when the words are particularly striking. Quote only when the original words express the exact point you want to make and express it succinctly and well. Otherwise, paraphrase. When you consider quoting, ask yourself: Which point of mine does the quotation illustrate? Why am I considering quoting this particular passage? Why should this particular passage be quoted rather than paraphrased? What do I need to tell my readers about the author of the quotation?

Quoting the exact words of the original   To understand how to deal with quotations in your paper, consider the following beginning of a newspaper article that a student used as she was working on a paper on the ethics of marketing to children.

> Think your talkative, trendy, Web-surfing 13-year-old might have a future in sales? She might already be in business. New forms of peer-to-peer, buzz-marketing campaigns—ignited and fanned by firms—are growing fast.
>
> In a practice still widely unregulated, marketers enlist youths they see as having real sway over friends. The goal? Solicit the help of these influential kids in broadening sales in exchange for products and the promise of a role in deciding what the marketplace will offer.
>
> Review a not-yet-released CD, score free concert tickets. Talk up a movie at a party, earn a DVD. The stakes are high: The 12-to-19 set reportedly spends about $170 billion a year.
>
> Marketers insist their efforts are transparent, that kids' reactions are unscripted, and that word of mouth, done right, is inherently authentic.
>
> At its first conference this week, the new Word of Mouth Marketing Association (WOMMA) will invite input on an evolving code of ethics aimed, in part, at protecting children.
>
> But opponents call the industry's youth-targeted component the odious next step in the commercialization of childhood, one that eyes ever-younger age groups, bribing them in a bid to cement brand loyalty and prompting them to wring friends for useful market data.
>
> "Some of the forms that [buzz marketing] takes have to do with recruiting kids to be marketers and encouraging them to keep

their identities as marketers secret," says David Walsh, president and founder of the National Institute on Media and the Family (NIMF) in Minneapolis. "So kids end up being junior ad people, and they're encouraged not to share this [even] with their friends."

Teens, he says, also often endanger themselves by sharing too much personal information, opening themselves to different kinds of exploitation. NIMF points out that at one marketer-facilitated online community, kids can create their own Old Spice "Girls of the Red Zone" calendar. And that signing up for membership at Soul-Kool.com, one of a handful of buzz-marketing firms that double as online communities, requires entering an instant-messenger address.

—Clayton Collins, "Marketers Tap Chatty Young Teens, and Hit a Hot Button," *Christian Science Monitor* 30 March 2005: 11

Any words you use from a source must be included in quotation marks (unless they are long quotations) and quoted exactly as they appear in the original, with the same punctuation marks and capital letters. Do not change pronouns or tenses to fit your own purpose, unless you enclose changes in square brackets (see the examples on p. 141.).

NOT EXACT QUOTATION
Collins reports that marketers think "that word of mouth is authentic when it is done correctly."

EXACT QUOTATION, WITHOUT CITATION
"Marketers," Collins reports, think that "word of mouth, done right, is inherently authentic."

EXACT QUOTATION, WITH CITATION
"Marketers," Collins reports, think that "word of mouth, done right, is inherently authentic" (11).

Note that if your quotation includes a question mark or exclamation point, you must include it within the quotation. Your sentence period then comes after your citation.

Collins asks, "Think your talkative, trendy, Web-surfing 13-year-old might have a future in sales?" (11).

Quoting part of a sentence You can make sure that quotations make a point and are not just dropped into your paper if you integrate parts of quoted sentences into your own sentences. When it is obvious that parts of the quoted sentence have been omitted, you do not need to use ellipsis dots.

> According to Collins, David Walsh believes that teenagers "endanger themselves by sharing too much personal information, opening themselves to different kinds of exploitation."

Not rigging the evidence   It should go without saying that quoting means quoting an author's ideas without omitting or adding any of your own contextual material that substantially changes the author's intent. For example, it would distort the author's views and rig the evidence the wrong way to write this, even though what is quoted is there in the original article:

> Clayton Collins sees "talkative, trendy" teenagers as having a bright "future in sales" (11).

Omitting words in the middle of a quotation   If you omit as irrelevant to your purpose any words from the middle of a quotation, signal the omission with an ellipsis mark, three dots separated by spaces. See 51g.

> Collins points out that "signing up for membership at Soul-Kool.com . . . requires entering an instant-messenger address."

In MLA style, if your source passage itself uses ellipses, place the dots within square brackets to indicate that your ellipsis mark is not part of the original text: [. . .].

Omitting words at the beginning of a quotation   If you omit as irrelevant to your purpose any words from the beginning of a quotation, *do not* use an ellipsis.

NO   **Collins reports that WOMMA's conference ". . . will invite input on an evolving code of ethics aimed, in part, at protecting children."**

YES   **Collins reports that WOMMA's conference "will invite input on an evolving code of ethics aimed, in part, at protecting children."**

Omitting words at the end of a quotation   If you omit the end of the source's sentence at the end of your own sentence, and your sentence is not followed by a page citation, signal the omission with three ellipsis dots following the sentence period—four dots in all— and then the closing quotation marks.

> Alarmed, Collins establishes the role of youths in "broadening sales. . . ."

When you include a page citation for the print source within your sentence, place it after the ellipsis dots and the closing quotation marks and before the final sentence period.

> Alarmed, Collins establishes the role of youths in "broadening sales . . ." (11).

Also use three dots after the period if you omit a complete sentence (or more). Use a line of dots for an omitted line of poetry (51g).

Adding or changing words   If you add any comments or explanations in your own words, or if you change a word in the quotation to fit it grammatically into your sentence, enclose the added or changed material in square brackets (51e). Generally, however, it is preferable to rephrase your sentence because bracketed words and phrases make sentences difficult to read.

AWKWARD   **Collins reports that the "practice [is] still widely unregulated [in which] marketers enlist youths they see as having real sway over friends."**

REVISED   **Collins reports that marketers freely "enlist youths they see as having real sway over friends."**

Quoting longer passages   If you quote more than three lines of poetry or four typed lines of prose, do not use quotation marks. Instead, begin the quotation on a new line and indent the quotation one inch or ten spaces from the left margin in MLA style, or indent it five spaces from the left margin if you are using APA or *Chicago* style. Double-space throughout. Do not indent from the right margin. You can establish the context for a long quotation and integrate it effectively into your text if you state the point that you want to make and name the author of the quotation in your introductory statement.

Author mentioned in introductory statement

> Despite his impartial detachment, Collins gives short shrift to marketers and waxes eloquent when introducing the National Institute on Media and the Family (NIMF):

No quotation marks around indented quotation

Quotation indented one inch or 10 spaces (MLA)

> But opponents call the industry's youth-targeted component the odious next step in the commercialization of childhood, one that eyes ever-younger age groups, bribing them in a bid to cement brand loyalty and prompting them to wring friends for useful market data. (11)

Page citation (only for a print source) after period

Note: After a long indented quotation, put the period before the parenthetical citation.

Avoiding a string of quotations Use quotations, especially long ones, sparingly and only when they bolster your argument. Readers do not want to read snippets from the works of other writers. They want your analysis of your sources, and they are interested in the conclusions you draw from your research.

Fitting a quotation into your sentence When you quote, use the exact words of the original, and make sure that those exact words do not disrupt the flow of your sentence and send it in another direction.

A BAD FIT
> It's obvious that Walsh finds the recruiting tactics duplicitous since they "encouraging them to keep their identities as marketers secret."

A BETTER FIT
> It's obvious that Walsh finds the recruiting tactics toward teenagers duplicitous since they encourage the youngsters "to keep their identities as marketers secret."

A BAD FIT
> Citing another insidious tactic of buzz-marketers, Collins adds "And that signing up for membership at Soul-Kool.com, one of a handful of buzz-marketing firms that double as online communities, requires entering an instant-messenger address."

A BETTER FIT
> Citing another insidious tactic of buzz-marketers, Collins adds "that signing up for a membership at Soul-Kool.com, one of a handful of buzz-marketing firms that double as online communities, requires entering an instant-messenger address."

KEY POINTS
Using Quotations: A Checklist

Examine a draft of your paper, and ask these questions about each quotation you have included.

☐ Why do you want to include this quotation? How does it support a point you have made?

☐ What is particularly remarkable about this quotation? Would a paraphrase be better?

☐ Does what you have enclosed in quotation marks exactly match the words and punctuation of the original?

☐ Have you told your readers the name of the author of the quotation?

☐ Have you included the page number of the quotation from a print source?

☐ How have you integrated the quotation into your own passage? Will readers know whom you are quoting and why?

☐ What verb have you used to introduce the quotation?

☐ Are there any places where you string quotations together, one after another? If so, revise. Look for quotation marks closing and then immediately opening again. Also look for phrases such as "X goes on to say . . ."; "X also says . . ."; "X then says . . . ."

☐ Have you indented quotations longer than four lines of type and omitted quotation marks?

☐ Have you used long quotations sparingly?

9h What to cite

When you refer to a source in your work, carefully cite and document it. Systematically provide information about the author, title, publication data, page numbers, Internet address, dates—whatever is available (9d shows the information you need to collect). You provide such documentation so that your readers can locate the sources and read them for further information. (See Parts 3 and 4 for guides to specific systems of documentation.) You also document sources so that there will be no question about which words and ideas are yours and which belong to other people.

KEY POINTS

What to Cite

1. Cite all facts, statistics, and pieces of information. However, citation is not necessary for facts regarded as common knowledge, such as the dates of the Civil War; facts available in many sources, such as authors' birth and death dates and

(Continued)

(Continued)

> chronological events; or allusions to folktales that have been handed down through the ages. When you are in doubt about whether a fact is common knowledge, cite your source.
>
> 2. Cite exact words from your source, enclosed in quotation marks.
>
> 3. Cite somebody else's ideas and opinions, even if you restate them in your own words in a summary or paraphrase.
>
> 4. Cite each sentence in a long paraphrase (if it is not clear that all the sentences paraphrase the same original source).

Note how James Stalker, in his article "Official English or English Only," does not quote directly but still cites Anderson as the source of the specialized facts mentioned in the following passage:

> By 1745 there were approximately 45,000 German speakers in the colonies, and by 1790 there were some 200,000, nine per cent of the population (Anderson 80).

9i Indicating the boundaries of a citation

Naming an author or title in your text tells readers that you are citing ideas from a source, and citing a page number at the end of a summary or paraphrase lets them know where your citation ends. However, for one-page print articles and for Internet sources, a page citation is not necessary, so indicating where your comments about a source end is harder to do. You always need to indicate clearly where your summary or paraphrase ends and where your own comments take over. Convey the shift to readers by commenting on the source in a way that clearly announces a statement of your own views. Use expressions such as *it follows that, X's explanation shows that, as a result, evidently, obviously,* or *clearly* to signal the shift.

UNCLEAR CITATION BOUNDARY

According to a Sony Web site, <u>Mozart Makes You Smarter</u>, the company has decided to release a recording on the strength of research indicating that listening to Mozart improves IQ. The products show the ingenuity of commercial enterprise while taking the researchers' conclusions in new directions.

[Does only the first sentence refer to material on the Web page, or do both sentences?]

REVISED CITATION, WITH SOURCE BOUNDARY INDICATED

According to a Sony Web site, <u>Mozart Makes You Smarter</u>, the company has decided to release a recording on the strength of research indicating that listening to Mozart improves IQ. Clearly, Sony's plan demonstrates the ingenuity of commercial enterprise, but it cannot reflect what the researchers intended when they published their conclusions.

Another way to indicate the end of your citation is to include the author's or authors' name(s) at the end of the citation instead of (or even in addition to) introducing the citation with the name.

UNCLEAR CITATION BOUNDARY

For people who hate shopping, Web shopping may be the perfect solution. Jerome and Taylor's exploration of "holiday hell" reminds us that we get more choice from online vendors than we do when we browse at our local mall because the online sellers, unlike mall owners, do not have to rent space to display their goods. In addition, one can buy almost anything online, from CDs, cell phones, and books to cars and real estate.

REVISED CITATION, WITH SOURCE BOUNDARY INDICATED

For people who hate shopping, Web shopping may be the perfect solution. An article exploring the "holiday hell" of shopping reminds us that we get more choice from online vendors than we do when we browse at our local mall because the online sellers, unlike mall owners, do not have to rent space to display their goods (Jerome and Taylor). In addition, one can buy almost anything online, from CDs, cell phones, and books to cars and real estate.

Chapter **10**

Writing the Research Paper

10a Writing research paper drafts

WHAT NOT TO DO

- Do not expect to complete a polished draft at one sitting.
- Do not write the title and the first sentence and then panic because you feel you have nothing left to say.
- Do not constantly imagine your instructor's response to what you write.

- Do not worry about coherence—a draft by its nature is something that you work on repeatedly and revise for readers' eyes.
- Do not necessarily begin at the beginning; do not think you must first write a dynamite introduction.

WHAT TO DO

- Wait until you have a block of time available before you begin writing a draft of your paper.
- Turn off your cell phone, close the door, and tell yourself you will not emerge from the room until you have written about six pages.
- Promise yourself a reward when you meet your target—a refrigerator break or a trip to a nearby ice cream store, for instance.
- Assemble your copy of the assignment, your thesis statement, all your copies of sources, your research notebook and any other notes, your working bibliography, and your proposal or outline.
- Write the parts you know most about first.
- Write as much as you can as fast as you can. If you only vaguely remember a reference in your sources, just write what you can remember—but keep writing, and don't worry about gaps:

  As so and so (who was it? Jackson?) has observed, malls are taking the place of city centers (check page reference).

- Write the beginning—the introduction—only after you have some ideas on paper that you feel you can introduce.
- Write at least something on each one of the points in your outline. Start off by asking yourself: What do I know about this point, and how does it support my thesis? Write your answer to that in your own words without worrying about who said what in which source. You can check your notes and fill in the gaps later.
- Write until you feel you have put down on the page or screen your main points and you have made reference to most of your source material.

Try not to go back over your draft and start tinkering and changing—at least not yet. Congratulate yourself on having made a start and take a break. Put your draft in a drawer and do not look at it for a while. In the meantime, you can follow up on research leads, find new sources, discuss your draft with your instructor or with a tutor at your campus writing center, and continue writing ideas in your research notebook.

10b Getting the most from your sources

Let readers know about the sources that support your point effectively. Don't mention an author of an influential book or long, important article just once and in parentheses. Let readers know why this source adds so much weight to your case. Tell about the expert's credentials, affiliations, and experience. Tell readers what the author does in the work you are citing. A summary of the work along with a paraphrase of important points may also be useful to provide context for the author's remarks and opinions. Show readers that they should be impressed by the expert opinions and facts you present.

10c Putting yourself in your paper and synthesizing

Large amounts of information are no substitute for a thesis with relevant support. Your paper should *synthesize* your sources, not just tell about them, one after the other. When you synthesize, you connect the ideas in individual sources to create a larger picture, to inform yourself about the topic, and to establish your own ideas on the topic. So leave plenty of time to read through your notes, think about what you have read, connect with the material, form responses to it, take into account new ideas and opposing arguments, and find connections among the facts and the ideas your sources offer. Avoid sitting down to write a paper at the last minute, surrounded by library books or stacks of photocopies. In this scenario, you might be tempted to lift material, and you will produce a lifeless paper. Remember that the paper is ultimately your work, not a collection of other people's words, and that your identity and opinions as the writer should be evident.

10d Organizing your essay with ideas, not sources

Let your ideas, not your sources, drive your paper. Resist the temptation to organize your paper in the following way:

1. What points Smith makes
2. What points Jones makes
3. What points Fuentes makes
4. What points Jackson and Hayes make in opposition
5. What I think

That organization is driven by your sources, with the bulk of the paper dealing with the views of Smith, Jones, and the rest. Instead, let your thesis and its points of supporting evidence determine the organization:

1. First point of support: what ideas I have to support my thesis and what evidence Fuentes and Jones provide
2. Second point of support: what ideas I have to support my thesis and what evidence Smith and Fuentes provide
3. Third point of support: what ideas I have to support my thesis and what evidence Jones provides
4. Opposing viewpoints of Jackson and Hayes
5. Common ground and refutation of those viewpoints
6. Synthesis

To avoid producing an essay that reads like a serial listing of summaries or references ("Crabbe says this," "Tyger says that," "Tyger also says this"), spend time reviewing your notes and synthesizing what you find into a coherent and convincing statement of what you know and believe.

- Make lists of good ideas your sources raise about your topic.
- Look for the connections among those ideas: comparisons and contrasts.
- Find links in content, examples, and statistics.
- Note connections between the information in your sources and what you know from your own experience.

If you do this, you will take control of your material instead of letting it take control of you.

10e Introducing and integrating source material

When you provide a summary, paraphrase, or quotation to support one of the points in your paper, set up the context. Don't drop in the material as if it came from nowhere. Think about how to introduce and integrate the material into the structure of your paper.

If you quote a complete sentence, or if you paraphrase or summarize a section of another work, prepare readers for your summary, paraphrase, or quotation by mentioning the author's name in an introductory phrase. In your first reference to the work, give the author's full name. To further orient readers, you can also provide the title of the work or a brief statement of the author's expertise or credentials and thesis. Here are some useful ways to introduce source material:

X has pointed out that	According to X,
X has made it clear that	As X insists,
X explains that	In 2003, X, the vice president of
X suggests that	the corporation, declared

The introductory verbs *say* and *write* are clear and direct. For occasional variety, though, use verbs that offer shades of meaning, such as *acknowledge, agree, argue, ask, assert, believe, claim, comment, contend, declare, deny, emphasize, insist, note, observe, point out, propose,* or *speculate*.

10f Using visuals

In a research paper, consider where tables and charts could present visual data concisely and clearly. Images may also help you strengthen an argument (see 4l). Use visuals to illustrate and enhance a point or to present information clearly and economically. Do not use visuals merely to fill up space or to look trendy (more on this in chapter 21).

If you look at the sample papers in 4m and chapters 13 and 16, you'll see how the visuals used there work well to highlight specific information, to convey quantitative information to number-phobic readers, or to capture the essence of an argument and thus make a point convincingly.

Finding appropriate visuals Several of the major search engines, including Google, AltaVista, and Yahoo!, offer specific image searches, and by using the advanced search forms there, you will be able to narrow your search to certain types of images. Another useful source is Flickr, which is now owned by Yahoo!. Flickr is a depository for photos only, and people can put their photos in this database independent of any Web site. This is, therefore, a complementary site providing access to a large volume of amateur photos.

Searching for images can often be difficult and frustrating because many "hits" may not be of interest to you. Image searches use keywords or tags attached to the image, and often these are not very accurate or do not describe the image the same way you would describe it. So rather than doing a general image search, it may be more productive to look for images at the Web sites where you find relevant textual information in the first place. Many Web sites, including government sites like the U.S. Bureau of the Census or nonprofit organizations like Public Agenda, make great efforts to present the information on their sites in visually attractive form. In addition, the National Telecommunications and Information Administration is a good source for tables and charts analyzing Internet use; and the College Board and the UCLA Higher Education Research Institute provide annual studies of first-year students.

Online Study Center   **Research** Finding appropriate visuals

10g Documenting to fit the discipline

Documentation is an integral part of a research paper. Conventions vary from discipline to discipline and from style manual to style manual—as illustrated by the inclusion of MLA, APA, CSE, and *Chicago* styles in Parts 3 and 4—but the various styles of documentation are not entirely arbitrary. The styles tend to reflect what the disciplines value and what readers need to know.

In the humanities, for instance, many research findings offer scholarly interpretation and analysis of texts, so they may be relevant for years, decades, or centuries. Publication dates in the MLA (Modern Language Association) style, therefore, occur only in the works-cited list and are not included in the in-text citation. Such a practice also serves to minimalize interruptions to the text.

The endnote/footnote system of the *Chicago Manual of Style* and the Council of Science Editors (CSE) citation-sequence and citation-name systems go further, requiring only a small superscript number in the text to send readers to the list of sources.

The APA and the CSE name-year style include the date of the work cited right there in the text citation, emphasizing that timeliness of research is an issue in the sciences and social sciences. In addition, abbreviations used in all three CSE styles (chapter 17) reflect the fact that scientists are expected to be aware of the major sources in their field.

See 5f for more on research in the humanities, sciences, and social sciences.

Samples of Entries in MLA List of Works Cited

Print Books, Parts of Books, and Pamphlets (12c)

Print Articles in Periodicals (12d)

Works in Online Library Subscription Databases (12e)

Web Sources (12f)

(Continued)

Visual, Performance, Multimedia, and Miscellaneous Sources: Live, Print, and Online (12g)

For research papers and shorter documented essays, always provide detailed information about any books, articles, Web sites, or other sources that you cite. Many composition and literature courses ask you to follow the guidelines of the Modern Language Association (MLA) as recommended in the *MLA Handbook for Writers of Research Papers,* 6th edition (New York: MLA, 2003), and on the MLA Web site at <http://www.mla.org>. Chapters 11 through 13 provide many examples to help you with your citations.

Your college may provide free access to bibliographic software that helps compile citations and bibliographies in any documentation style. Ask a librarian if a program such as EndNote, RefWorks, or NoodleBib is available. With these programs, you enter details in specific fields, and the program then formats your book or journal citations into a bibliography according to MLA, APA, or another documentation style. Some will also transfer the bibliographical references for titles found during a literature search directly into the user's Web-based account (9c). However, whether you use such a program or do the formatting yourself, you still have to find—and type—the information necessary for citations not directly transferred. The examples in the following chapters will help you find the information to include and the format to use.

Chapter **11**

Citing Sources in Your Text, MLA Style

When you refer to, comment on, paraphrase, or quote another author's material, you have to indicate that you have done so by inserting what is called a citation. All you need is the name of the author(s) and the page number(s) where you found the material. You can put the author's name in your own text to introduce the material, with the page number in parentheses at the end of the sentence; or, especially for a source you have cited previously, you can put both author and page number in parentheses at the end of the sentence in which you cite the material. Then all more detailed information about your sources goes into a works-cited list at the end of your paper (chapter 12).

Sections 11a–11c show you examples and variations on the basic principle of citation—for instance, what to do when no author is named or when you cite an online source that has no page numbers.

11a Two basic features of MLA style

KEY POINTS
Two Basic Features of MLA Style

1. *In your paper,* include an author/page citation for each source: the **last name(s)** of the author (or authors)—or title if no author is known—and **page number(s)** where the information is located, unless the source is online or only one page long. See 11c for examples.

2. *At the end of your paper,* include a list of all the sources you refer to in the paper, alphabetized by author's last name or by title if the author is not known. Begin the list on a new page, and title it "Works Cited." See chapter 12.

Illustrations of the Basic Features

In-Text Citation	Entry in List of Works Cited
Book:	
The renowned scholar of language, David Crystal, has promoted the idea of "dialect democracy" (168).	Crystal, David. The Stories of English. Woodstock: Overlook, 2004.

(Continued)

MLA (Modern Language Association)

Illustrations of the Basic Features (continued)

In-Text Citation	Entry in List of Works Cited
or	
A renowned scholar of language has promoted the idea of "dialect democracy" (Crystal 168).	
Print article:	
Barry Gewen questions the role of an art critic if "anything goes" in art (29).	Gewen, Barry. "State of the Art." New York Times Book Review 11 Dec. 2005: 28–32.
or	
The role of an art critic is questioned if "anything goes" in art (Gewen 29).	
Article in online database:	
Barry Gewen questions the role of an art critic if "anything goes" in art.	Gewen, Barry. "State of the Art." New York Times Book Review 11 Dec. 2005: 28– . Academic Universe: News. LexisNexis. City U of New York Lib. 14 Dec. 2005 <http://web.lexis-nexis.com>.
A model of nonviolent protest against the war is as simple as refusing to attend a White House dinner (Olds).	Olds, Sharon. "No Thanks, Mrs. Bush." Nation 10 Oct. 2005: 5–6. Academic Search Premier. EBSCO. City U of New York Lib. 13 Dec. 2005 <http://search.epnet.com/login.aspx?direct=true&db=aph&an=18335004>.
Web document with no author:	
Researchers have explored the link between the social rank of chimpanzees and their mating privileges ("Jane Goodall's").	"Jane Goodall's Wild Chimpanzees." Nature. Educational Broadcasting Corporation. 14 Dec. 2005: <http://www.pbs.org/wnet/nature/goodall/index.html>.

11b FAQs about MLA in-text citations

Frequently Asked Questions	Short Answer	Examples
What information do I put into the body of my essay?	Give only the name of the author(s) (if available) and the page number (for a print source of more than one page). Include the page numbers in parentheses, never in your own text.	11c

Frequently Asked Questions	**Short Answer**	**Examples**
Where do I supply that information?	Usually name the author as you introduce the information, and put the page number(s) in parentheses. Alternatively, put both author and page number in parentheses at the end of the sentence containing the citation.	11c, A, B
How do I refer to an author?	In your text, use both names (and maybe a brief identification of position or credentials) for the first mention. Use only the last name for subsequent references and within parentheses. If you name the author in your text, you will not need parentheses for a work with no page numbers.	11c, A, B
What if no author or editor is named for a source?	Give the title of the work or, in a parenthetical citation, an abbreviation containing the word of the title alphabetized in the works-cited list so that readers can find the source immediately. See 8e on finding the author of an online source.	11c, I, J
How do I give page numbers?	Do not use "p." or "pp." Give inclusive page numbers for information that spans pages: 35–36; 257–58; 305–06; 299–300. (Omit a shared first digit in numbers over 100.)	11c, A–F
Is a page number always necessary?	No. Omit page numbers for a reference to a whole work, to a work only one page long, or to an online or multimedia work with no visible page numbers.	11c, G, H, J, K

See the samples in 11c to answer other questions.

MLA **(Modern Language Association)**

11c MLA sample author/page citations in text

A. One author, named in your introductory text   Naming the author as you introduce the source material allows you to supply information about the author's credentials as an expert and so increases the credibility of your source for readers. Another advantage of naming your source in your text is that readers then know that everything between the mention of the author and the cited page number is a reference to your source material.

For the first mention of an author, use the full name and any relevant credentials. After that, use only the last name. Generally, use the present tense to cite an author. (See 12c, item 1, for the entry in a works-cited list.)

> ┌────── author and credentials ──────┐
> National Book Award winner Paul Fussell points out that even people
> in low-paying jobs show "all but universal pride in a uniform of any
> kind" (5).
> ╲ page number

When a quotation ends the sentence, as above, close the quotation marks before the parentheses, and place the sentence period after the parentheses. (Note that this rule differs from the one for undocumented writing, which calls for a period before the closing quotation marks.)

When a quotation includes a question mark or an exclamation point, also include a period after the citation:

> Fussell reminds us of our equating uniforms with seriousness of
> purpose when he begins a chapter by asking, "Would you get on an
> airplane with two pilots who are wearing cut-off jeans?" (85).

For a quotation longer than four lines, see 9g.

B. Author not mentioned in your introductory text   If you have referred to an author previously or if you are citing statistics, you do not need to mention the author while introducing the reference. In that case, include the author's last name in the parentheses before the page number, with no comma between them.

> The army retreated from Boston in disarray, making the victors
> realize that they had defeated the "greatest military power on earth"
> author and page
> ┌── number ──┐
> (McCullough 76).

See 9g, page 141, for the punctuation of a citation after a long quotation.

C. Two or more authors For a work with two or three authors, include all the names, either in your text sentence or in parentheses.

> (Lakoff and Johnson 42)
> (Hare, Moran, and Koepke 226–28)

For a work with four or more authors, use only the first author's last name followed by "et al." (*Et alii* means "and others.") See 12c, item 2.

> Some researchers have established a close link between success at work and the pleasure derived from community service (Bellah et al. 196–99).

D. Author with more than one work cited You can include the author and title of the work in your text sentence.

> Alice Walker, in her book In Search of Our Mothers' Gardens, describes revisiting her past to discover more about Flannery O'Connor (43–59).

If you do not mention the author in your text, include in your parenthetical reference the author's last name, followed by a comma, an abbreviated form of the title, and the page number.

> comma
> O'Connor's house still stands and is looked after by a caretaker (Walker,
> abbreviated title ⌐page number
> In Search 57).

E. Work in an edited anthology Cite the author of the included or reprinted work (not the editor of the anthology) and the page number in the anthology. The entry in the works-cited list will include the title of the article, its inclusive page numbers, and full bibliographical details for the anthology: title, editor(s), place of publication, publisher, and date. See 12c, items 5 and 6, for examples.

> Des Pres asserts that "heroism is not necessarily a romantic notion" (20).

F. Work quoted in another source Use "qtd. in" (for "quoted in") in your parenthetical citation, followed by the last name of the author of the source in which you find the reference (the indirect source) and the page number where you find the quotation. List the author of the indirect source you use in your list of works cited. In the following example, the indirect source Douthat would be included in the list of works cited, not Mansfield. See 12d, item 22, for the entry in the works-cited list.

> Harvey Mansfield of Harvard University has attributed grade inflation to "the prevalence in American education of the notion of self-esteem" (qtd. in Douthat 96).

G. Reference to an entire work and not to one specific page
If you are referring not to a quotation or idea on one specific page, but rather to an idea that is central to the work as a whole, use the author's name alone. Include the work in your works-cited list.

> We can learn from diaries about people's everyday lives and the worlds they create (Mallon).

H. One-page work   If an article is only one page long, cite the author's name alone; include the page number in your works-cited list (12d, item 22).

I. Author or editor not named   If no author is named for a source, refer to the book (underlined) or article (within quotation marks) by its title. Within a parenthetical citation, shorten the title to the first word alphabetized in the works-cited list (12c, item 8).

> According to The Chicago Manual of Style, writers should always "break or bend" rules when necessary (xiii).

> Writers should always "break or bend" rules when necessary (Chicago xiii).

If you need help in determining the author of an Internet source, see 8d and 8e. For a Web site with no author indicated, use the name of the site.

For an unsigned entry in an encyclopedia or dictionary, give the title of the entry; a page number is not necessary for an alphabetized work. Begin the entry in the works-cited list with the title of the alphabetized entry (12c, item 7).

> Drypoint differs from etching in that it does not use acid ("Etching").

J. Electronic and Internet sources   Electronic database material and Internet sources, which appear on a screen, have no stable page numbers that apply across systems or when printed, unless they are in PDF files. If your source as it appears on the screen includes no visible numbered pages or numbered paragraphs, provide information about the author in your text rather than in a parenthetical citation. See 12f, item 46, for the following work in a list of works cited.

> In the online journal 21st Century, science writer Stephen Hart
> describes how researchers Edward Taub and Thomas Ebert conclude
> that for musicians, practicing "remaps the brain."
>> No page citation: online source has no numbered pages or paragraphs.

With no page number to indicate the end of a citation, be careful to define where your citation ends and your own commentary takes over. Section 9h shows how to define the boundaries of a citation.

To document an online source with no author, give the title of the Web page or the posting, either in full or abbreviated to begin with the first word you alphabetize (see 12f, item 38). See 8e for help in finding an author's name.

> A list of frequently asked questions about documentation and up-to-
> date instructions on how to cite online sources in MLA style can be
> found on the association's Web site (MLA).

If possible, locate online material by the internal headings of the source (for example, *introduction, chapter, section*). Give paragraph numbers only if they are supplied in the source and you see the numbers on the screen (use the abbreviation "par." or "pars."). And then include the total number of numbered paragraphs in your works-cited list (see 12f, item 45).

> Hatchuel discusses how film editing "can change points of view and
> turn objectivity into subjectivity" (par. 6).

> Film editing provides us with different perceptions of reality (Hatchuel,
> par. 6).

K. Multimedia and other nonprint sources   For radio or TV programs, interviews, live performances, films, computer software, recordings, and other nonprint sources, include only the title or author (or, in some cases, the interviewer, interviewee, director, performer, or producer, and so on, corresponding to the first element of the information you provide in the entry in your list of works cited— see 12g, item 59, for examples of documenting the source below).

The musical <u>Mirette</u> weaves together music, song, and a warmly inspiring story to make a magical theatrical experience.

This season, playwright Elizabeth Diggs has given us a delightfully inspiring story of courage on the high-wire.

L. Work by a corporation, government agency, or some other organization Cite the organization as the author, making sure it corresponds with the alphabetized entry in your works-cited list (shown in 12f, item 39). Use the complete name in your text or a shortened form in parentheses. The following examples cite a Web site, so page numbers are not included.

     ─── full name ───

The United States Department of Education has projected an increase in college enrollment of 11% between 2003 and 2013.

An increase in college enrollment of 11% between 2003 and 2013 has

    ─── short name ───

been projected (US Dept. of Educ.).

M. Two authors with the same last name Include each author's first initial, or the whole first name if the authors' initials are the same.

A writer can be seen as both "author" and "secretary," and the two roles can be seen as competitive (F. Smith 19).

N. Multivolume work Indicate the volume number, followed by a colon, a space, and the page number. List the number of volumes in your works-cited list. (See 12c, item 11.)

Barr and Feigenbaum note that "the concept of translation from one language to another by machine is older than the computer itself" (1: 233).

O. More than one work cited in your sentence Use semicolons to separate two or more sources in the same citation. Avoid making a parenthetical citation so long that it disrupts the flow of your text.

The links between a name and ancestry have occupied many writers and researchers (Waters 65; Antin 188).

If sources refer to different points in your sentence, cite each one after the point it supports.

P. Lecture, speech, or personal communication such as a letter, an interview, an e-mail, or a conversation In your text, give the name of the lecturer or person you communicated with. In your works-cited list, list the type of communication after the author or title. (See 12e, item 51, and 12g, item 62.)

> According to Roberta Bernstein, professor of art history at the
> University of Albany, the most challenging thing about contemporary
> art is understanding that it is meant to be challenging. This may mean
> that the artist wants to make us uncomfortable with our familiar ideas
> or present us with reconceived notions of beauty.

Q. Literary works: Fiction, poetry, and drama For well-known works published in several different editions, include information so readers may locate material in whatever edition they are using. In your works-cited list, include the edition you used.

FOR A NOVEL Give the chapter or section number in addition to the page number in the edition you used: (104; ch. 3).

FOR A POEM Give line numbers, not page numbers: (lines 62–73). Subsequent line references can omit the word *lines.* Include up to three lines of poetry sequentially in your text, separated by a slash with a space on each side (/) (see 51f). For four or more lines of poetry, begin on a new line, indent the whole passage one inch from the left, double-space throughout, and omit quotation marks from the beginning and end of the passage (see 10f).

FOR CLASSIC POEMS, SUCH AS THE *ILIAD* Give the book or part number, followed by the line numbers, not page numbers: (8.21–25).

FOR A PLAY For dialogue, set the quotation off from your text, indented one inch with no quotation marks, and write the name of the character speaking in all capital letters, followed by a period. Indent subsequent lines of the same speech another quarter inch (three spaces). For a classic play, one published in several different editions (such as plays by William Shakespeare or Oscar Wilde), omit page numbers and cite in parentheses the act, scene, and line numbers of the quotation, in Arabic numerals. In your works-cited list, list the bibliographical details of the edition you use.

MLA (Modern Language Association)

Shakespeare's lovers in <u>A Midsummer Night's Dream</u> appeal to contemporary audiences accustomed to the sense of loss in love songs:

> LYSANDER. How now, my love! Why is your cheek so pale?
> How chance the roses there do fade so fast?
> HERMIA. Belike for want of rain, which I could well
> Beteem them from the tempest of mine eyes.
> (1.1.133–36)

For a new play available in only one published edition, cite author and page numbers as you do for other MLA citations.

FOR SHAKESPEARE, CHAUCER, AND OTHER LITERARY WORKS Abbreviate titles cited in parentheses, such as the following: *Tmp.* for *The Tempest*; *2H4* for *Henry IV, Part 2*; *MND* for *A Midsummer Night's Dream*; *GP* for the *General Prologue*; *PrT* for *The Prioress's Tale*; *Aen.* for *Aeneid*; *Beo.* for *Beowulf*; *Prel.* for Wordsworth's *Prelude*.

R. The Bible and other sacred texts In a parenthetical citation, give the title of the sacred text (underlined), along with the book (abbreviated), chapter, and verse. Note, though, that in a reference to a sacred text that is not directing readers to a specific citation in the list of works cited, the title of the sacred text is not underlined, as in the example that follows (see also 52a on underlining).

> Of the many passages in the Bible that refer to lying, none is more apt today than the one that says that a wicked person "is snared by the
>
> specific citation underlined
> transgression of his lips" (<u>Holy Bible</u>, Prov. 12.13).
> name of book (Proverbs) abbreviated

See 12c, item 18, for this entry and others in a list of works cited.

S. Two or more sequential references to the same work If you rely on several quotations from the same page within one of your paragraphs, one parenthetical reference after the last quotation is enough, but make sure that no quotations from other works intervene. If you are paraphrasing from and referring to one work several times in a paragraph, mention the author in your introductory phrase; cite the page number at the end of a paraphrase and again if you paraphrase from a different page. Make it clear to a reader where the paraphrase ends and your own comments take over (9h).

T. A long quotation   Indent a quotation of four or more lines one inch or ten spaces, without enclosing the quotation in quotation marks. See page 141 for an example.

U. A footnote or footnotes   To cite a footnote in a work, give the page number followed by "n" or "nn" (as in 65n). For a footnote in an annotated edition of the Bible, give the edition (with any "The" omitted from your citation), book, chapter, and verse(s), followed by "n" or "nn" (<u>New Oxford Annotated Bible</u>, Gen. 35.1–4n). See 12c, item 18, for this entry in a works-cited list.

V. Historical or legal document   Cite any article and section number of a familiar historical document, such as the Constitution, in parentheses in your text (US Const., art. 2, sec. 4), with no entry in the works-cited list. Underline the name of a court case (<u>Roe v. Wade</u>), but do not underline laws and acts. List cases and acts in your works-cited list (see 12g, item 63).

11d MLA explanatory footnotes and endnotes

With the MLA parenthetical style of documentation, use a footnote (at the bottom of the page) or an endnote (on a separate numbered page at the end of the paper before the works-cited list) only for notes giving supplementary information that clarifies or expands a point. You might use a note to refer to several supplementary bibliographical sources or to provide a comment that is interesting but not essential to your argument. Indicate a note with a raised number (superscript) in your text, after the word or sentence your note refers to. Begin the first line of each note one-half inch (or five spaces) from the left margin. Do not indent subsequent lines of the same note. Double-space endnotes. Single-space within each footnote, but double-space between notes.

NOTE NUMBER IN TEXT

Ethics have become an important part of many writing classes.[1]

CONTENT ENDNOTE

five spaces _____ raised number followed by space
⟵⟶[1]For additional discussion of ethics in the classroom, see Stotsky 799–806; Knoblauch 15–21; Bizzell 663–67; Friend 560–66.

The *MLA Handbook* also describes a system of footnotes or endnotes as an alternative to parenthetical documentation of references. This style is similar to the footnote and endnote style described in *The Chicago Manual of Style* (see chapter 18).

Chapter **12**

The MLA List of Works Cited

The references you make in your text to sources are brief—usually only the author's last name and a page number—so they allow readers to continue reading without interruption. For complete information about the source, readers can use your brief in-text citation as a guide to the full bibliographical reference in the list of works cited at the end of your paper.

12a How to format and organize the MLA list

Here are the basics for formatting and organizing your list.

KEY POINTS
Guidelines for the MLA List of Works Cited

1. *What to list*   List only works you actually cited in the text of your paper, not works you read but did not mention, unless your instructor requires you to include all the works you consulted as well as those mentioned in your text.

2. *Format of the list*   Begin the list on a new numbered page after the last page of the paper or any endnotes. Center the heading (Works Cited) without quotation marks, underlining, or a period. Double-space throughout the list.

3. *Organization*   Do not number the entries. List works alphabetically by author's last name (12b). List works with no stated author by the first main word of the title (12c, item 8, and 12d, item 26)

4. *Indentation*   To help readers find a source and to differentiate one entry from another, indent all lines of each entry, except

the first, one-half inch (or five spaces). A word processor can provide these "hanging indents" (20a, item 4).

5. *Periods*   Separate the main parts of an entry—author, title, publishing information, online information—with a period, followed by one space.

6. *Capitals*   Capitalize the first letter of all words in titles of books and articles except *a, an, the*, coordinating conjunctions, *to* in an infinitive, and prepositions (such as *in, to, for, with, without, against*) unless they begin or end the title or subtitle.

7. *Underlining or italics*   Underline the titles of books and the names of journals and magazines as in the examples in this chapter. You may use italics instead if your instructor approves and if your printer makes a clear distinction from regular type.

8. *Page numbers*   Give inclusive page numbers for print articles and sections of books. Do not use "p." ("pp.") or the word *page* (or *pages*) before page numbers in any reference. For page citations over 100 and sharing the same first number, use only the last two digits for the second number (for instance, 683–89, but 798–805). For an unpaginated work, write "n. pag." Do not include page numbers for online works unless they are PDF documents in which the page numbers appear on the screen. For what to do about page numbers in works in online databases, see 12e.

9. *URLs*   Remove any automatically inserted hyperlinks from a URL (go to Insert/Hyperlink to do this). Then you will be able to enclose the URL in angle brackets, followed by a period. Break a URL for a new line only after a slash. Never insert a hyphen into a URL.

TECH NOTE

Posting Your Paper Online

For an online list of works cited, do not use indentation, which HTML does not support well. Instead, keep all lines flush left and follow each entry with a line space. In addition, use italics in place of underlining for the titles of books or journals because underlining is a signal for a hypertext link.

12b How to list authors in the MLA list of works cited

Name of author(s)   Put the last name first for a single author or the first author: *Fussell, Paul.* For two or more authors, reverse the names of only the first author: *Engleberg, Isa, and Ann Raimes.*

Alphabetical order   Alphabetize entries in the list by authors' last names. Note the following:

- Alphabetize by the exact letters in the spelling: *MacKay* precedes *McHam.*

- Let a shorter name precede a longer name beginning with the same letters: *Linden, Ronald* precedes *Lindenmayer, Arnold.*

- With last names using a prefix such as *le, du, di, del,* and *des,* alphabetize by the prefix: *Le Beau, Bryan F.*

- When *de* occurs with French names of one syllable, alphabetize under *D: De Jean, Denise.* Otherwise, alphabetize by last name: *Maupassant, Guy de.*

- Alphabetize by the first element of a hyphenated name: *Sackville-West, Vita.*

- Alphabetize by the last name when the author uses two names without a hyphen: *Thomas, Elizabeth Marshall.*

Author not known   For a work with no author named, alphabetize by the first word in the title of the work other than *A, An,* or *The* (see 12c, item 8, and 12d, item 26).

Several works by the same author(s)   For all entries after the first, replace the name(s) of the author(s) with three hyphens followed by a period, and alphabetize according to the first significant word in the title. If an author serves as an editor or translator, put a comma after the three hyphens, followed by the appropriate abbreviation ("ed." or "trans."). If, however, the author has coauthors, repeat all authors' names in full and put the coauthored entry after all the single-name entries for the author.

Goleman, Daniel. <u>Destructive Emotions: A Scientific Dialogue with the Dalai Lama.</u> New York: Bantam-Dell, 2003.

---. <u>Working with Emotional Intelligence.</u> New York: Bantam, 2000.

Goleman, Daniel, Paul Kaufman, and Michael L. Ray. "The Art of Creativity." <u>Psychology Today</u> Mar.–Apr. 1992: 40–47.

Authors with the same last name   Alphabetize by first names: *Smith, Adam* precedes *Smith, Frank.*

12c   Sample MLA entries: Print books, parts of books, and pamphlets

1. Book with one author   See Source Shot 1 (p. 170) for an example.

2. Book with two or more authors   Use authors' names in the order in which they appear in the book. Separate the names with commas. Reverse the order of only the first author's name.

                        second author's name
           comma   not reversed
Lakoff, George, and Mark Johnson. <u>Metaphors We Live By</u>. Chicago:
     U of Chicago P, 1980.

For a work with four or more authors, either list all the names or use only the first author's name followed by "et al." (Latin for "and others").

Bellah, Robert N., et al. <u>Habits of the Heart: Individualism and Commitment
     in American Life</u>. Berkeley: U of California P, 1985.

3. Edited book   Use the abbreviation "ed." or "eds.," preceded by a comma, after the name(s) of the editor or editors.

Gates, Henry Louis, Jr., ed. <u>Classic Slave Narratives</u>. New York: NAL, 1987.

For a work with four or more editors, use only the name of the first, followed by a comma and "et al."

4. Author and editor   When an editor has prepared an author's work for publication, list the book under the author's name if you cite the author's work. Then, in your listing, include the name(s) of the editor or editors after the title, introduced by "Ed." for one or more editors. "Ed." stands for "edited by" in the following entry.

                                              name
  ┌ author of letters ┐   ┌─ of editor ─┐
Bishop, Elizabeth. <u>One Art: Letters</u>. Ed. Robert Giroux. New York: Farrar,
     1994.

MLA

(Modern Language Association)

SOURCE SHOT 1

Listing a Book (MLA)

Find the necessary information for documenting a book on its title page. If the date is not on the title page, look on the copyright page. Include the following:

❶ **Name of author(s)** Last name, first name, followed by a period

❷ **Title of Book: Subtitle** Underlined, with capitals for main words (see p. 167), followed by a period

❸ **Place of publication** The first city mentioned on the title page—not the state, but country or Canadian province if needed—followed by a colon

❹ **Name of publisher** In short form: *Houghton,* not *Houghton Mifflin;* *Basic,* not *Basic Books; Abrams,* not *Harry N. Abrams.* Omit abbreviations such as *Co.* and *Inc.*: *Simon,* not *Simon & Schuster, Inc.* For university presses, use the abbreviations "U" and "P" with no periods: *Columbia UP, U of Chicago P,* and so on.

❺ **Year of publication** Separated from the publisher's name with a comma; look for ©. Put a period at the end.

Items 1–19 give examples and provide information on variations.

Listing a Book with One Author (MLA)

First name
comma ╱ period   ❷ Title: underlined   ❸ Place of
❶ Last name ╱ ╱   ——— and capitalized ———   publication
Fussell, Paul. Uniforms: Why We Are What We Wear. Boston:
period   colon
❹ Publisher ❺ Year
⟵ Houghton, 2002.
Indented   comma period
½ inch

If you cite a section written by the editor, such as a chapter introduction or a note, list the source under the name of the editor.

name
┌— of editor —┐ editor   author of letters
Giroux, Robert, ed. One Art: Letters. By Elizabeth Bishop. New York: Farrar, 1994.

MLA (Modern Language Association)

Title Page

2 Title

★
UNIFORMS

2 Subtitle

Why We Are
What We Wear

1 Author

PAUL FUSSELL

4 Name of publisher

Houghton Mifflin Company
BOSTON NEW YORK
2002

3 City of publication (the first one mentioned)

5 Year of publication

Copyright Page

5 Copyright date

Copyright © 2002 by Paul Fussell
All rights reserved

information about permission to reproduce selections
his book, write Permissions, Houghton Mifflin Company,
1 5 Park Avenue South, New York, New York 10003.

Visit our Web site: www.houghtonmifflinbooks.com.

Library of Congress Cataloging-in-Publication Data
is available.
ISBN 0-618-06746-9

Printed in the United States of America

Book design by Victoria Hartman

QUM 10 9 8 7 6 5 4 3 2 1

thor is grateful for permission to quote from the following works:
ria," from *The Poems of Lincoln Kirstein*, by Lincoln Kirstein.
ght © 1987 by Lincoln Kirstein. Reprinted with the permission of
bner, an imprint of Simon & Schuster Adult Publishing Group.
a View to a Death, by Anthony Powell. Copyright © by Anthony
Powell. Reprinted by permission of Heinemann.

5. One work in an anthology (original or reprinted)   For a work included in an anthology, first list the author and title of the included work. Follow this with the title of the anthology, the name of the editor(s), publication information (place, publisher, date) for the anthology, and then, after the period, the pages in the anthology covered by the work you refer to.

author of article
or chapter —   means
"edited by"
Des Pres, Terrence. "Poetry and Politics." <u>The Writer in Our World</u>. Ed.

     name of editor
     of anthology
    Reginald Gibbons. Boston: Atlantic Monthly, 1986. 17–29.
                      inclusive page numbers of article or chapter

Alvarez, Julia. "Grounds for Fiction." <u>The Riverside Reader</u>. 8th ed.

    Ed. Joseph Trimmer and Maxine Hairston. Boston: Houghton, 2005.

    125–39.

If the work in the anthology is a reprint of a previously published scholarly article, supply the complete information for both the original publication and the reprint in the anthology.

Gates, Henry Louis, Jr. "The Fire Last Time." <u>New Republic</u> 1 June 1992:

    37–43. Rpt. in <u>Contemporary Literary Criticism</u>. Ed. Jeffrey W. Hunter.

    Vol. 127. Detroit: Gale, 2000. 113–19.

6. More than one work in an anthology, cross-referenced If you refer to more than one work from the same anthology, list the anthology separately, and also list each essay with a cross-reference to the anthology. Alphabetize in the usual way, as in the following three examples.

                title of article
author of article   in anthology   editor of anthology
Des Pres, Terrence. "Poetry and Politics." Gibbons 17–29.
                        page numbers of article

    editor of
  anthology   title of anthology
Gibbons, Reginald, ed. <u>The Writer in Our World</u>. Boston: Atlantic

    Monthly, 1986.

    author
  of article   title of article in anthology   editor of anthology
Walcott, Derek. "A Colonial's-Eye View of America." Gibbons 73–77.
                    page numbers of article

7. Entry in a reference book For a well-known reference book, such as a dictionary or encyclopedia, give only the edition number and the year of publication. When entries are arranged alphabetically, omit volume and page numbers.

Kahn, David. "Cryptology." <u>Encyclopedia Americana</u>. Internatl. ed. 2001.

"Etching." <u>The Columbia Encyclopedia</u>. 6th ed. 2000.

For works that are not widely known, also give details of editors, volumes, place of publication, and publisher.

8. Book or pamphlet with no author named Put the title first. Do not consider the words *A, An,* and *The* when alphabetizing the entries. The following entry would be alphabetized under C.

<u>The Chicago Manual of Style</u>. 15th ed. Chicago: U of Chicago P, 2003.

9. Book written by a corporation, organization, or government agency Alphabetize by the name of the corporate author or branch of government. If the publisher is the same as the author, include the name again as publisher.

Hoover's Inc. <u>Hoover's Handbook of World Business</u>. Austin: Hoover's, 2005.

If no individual author is named for a government publication, begin the entry with the name of the federal, state, or local government, followed by the agency. See item 39 for an online government publication.

United States. National Commission on Terrorist Attacks upon the US. <u>The 9/11 Commission Report</u>. New York: Norton, 2004.

10. Translated book After the title, include "Trans." followed by the name of the translator, first name first.

Grass, Günter. <u>Novemberland: Selected Poems, 1956–1993</u>. Trans. Michael Hamburger. San Diego: Harcourt, 1996.

11. Multivolume work If you refer to more than one volume of a multivolume work, indicate the number of volumes (abbreviated "vols.") after the title.

Barr, Avon, and Edward A. Feigenbaum, eds. <u>The Handbook of Artificial Intelligence</u>. 4 vols. Reading: Addison, 1981–86.

If you refer to only one volume of a work, limit the information in the entry to that one volume.

Richardson, John. <u>A Life of Picasso</u>. Vol. 2. New York: Random, 1996.

12. Book in a series Give the name of the series after the book title.

Connor, Ulla. <u>Contrastive Rhetoric: Cross-Cultural Aspects of Second Language Writing</u>. Cambridge Applied Linguistics Ser. New York: Cambridge UP, 1996.

13. Book published under a publisher's imprint State the names of both the imprint (the publisher within a larger publishing enterprise) and the larger publishing house, separated by a hyphen.

Atwood, Margaret. <u>Negotiation with the Dead: A Writer on Writing</u>. New York: Anchor-Doubleday, 2003.

14. Foreword, preface, introduction, or afterword List the name of the author of the book element cited, followed by the name of the element, with no quotation marks. Give the title of the work; then use "By" to introduce the name of the author of the book (first name first). After the publication information, give inclusive page numbers for the book element cited.

Remnick, David. Introduction. <u>Politics</u>. By Hendrik Hertzberg. New York: Penguin, 2004. xvii–xxiv.

15. Republished book For a paperback edition of a hardcover book, give the original date of publication. Then cite information about the current publication.

King, Stephen. <u>On Writing</u>. 2000. New York: Pocket, 2002.

16. Edition after the first After the title, give the edition number, using the abbreviation "ed."

Raimes, Ann. <u>Keys for Writers</u>. 5th ed. Boston: Houghton, 2008.

17. Book title including a title Do not underline a book title that is part of the source title. (However, if the title of a short work, such as a poem or short story, is part of the source title, enclose it in quotation marks.)

Hays, Kevin J., ed. The Critical Response to Herman Melville's
    book title not underlined
        Moby Dick. Westport: Greenwood, 1994.

18. The Bible and other sacred texts   Take the information from
the title page and give the usual bibliographical details for a book.
Also include the edition and the name of a translator or editor where
appropriate. When no date of publication is given, use *n.d.* Ignore
any *The* in the title for alphabetizing purposes in the list: Put *The Holy
Bible* under *H*.

Enuma Elish. Ed. Leonard W. King. Escondido: Book Tree, 1998.

The Holy Bible. King James Version. Peabody: Hendrickson, 2003.

The Koran. Trans. George Sales. London: Warne, n.d.

The New Oxford Annotated Bible. 3rd ed. Ed. Michael D. Coogan. Oxford,
    Eng.: Oxford UP, 2001.

19. Dissertation   Cite a published dissertation as you would a
book, with place of publication, publisher, and date, but also include
dissertation information after the title (for example, "Diss. U of
California, 1998.").

    If the dissertation is published by University Microfilms Inter-
national (UMI), underline the title and include "Ann Arbor: UMI,"
the year, and the order number at the end of the entry.

Diaz-Greenberg, Rosario. The Emergence of Voice in Latino High School
    Students. Diss. U of San Francisco, 1996. Ann Arbor: UMI, 1996.
    9611612.

For an unpublished dissertation, follow the title (in quotation marks)
with "Diss." and the university and year.

Hidalgo, Stephen Paul. "Vietnam War Poetry: A Genre of Witness." Diss. U of
    Notre Dame, 1995.

If you cite an abstract published in *Dissertation Abstracts International*,
give the relevant volume number and page number.

Hidalgo, Stephen Paul. "Vietnam War Poetry: A Genre of Witness." Diss. U of
    Notre Dame, 1995. DAI 56 (1995): 0931A.

SOURCE SHOT 2

Listing a Periodical Article (MLA)

Include the following when listing a periodical article:

❶ **Name of author(s)** Last name, first name, followed by a period

❷ **"Title of Article: Subtitle."** In quotation marks

❸ **Name of journal or periodical** Omitting any *A, An,* or *The,* and underlined, with no period following, and including **volume** and **issue** number where necessary (items 20 and 21)

❹ **Date of publication** Whatever is available and necessary for type of periodical—items 20–29—year in parentheses (items 20 and 21) or day, month, year, in that order, with all months except May, June, and July abbreviated. Follow the date with a colon.

❺ **Page number or range of pages** (such as 24–27; 365–72). End with a period. For newspapers, see items 23 and 24.

See items 20–29 for examples.

12d Sample MLA entries: Print articles in periodicals

The conventions for listing print articles (or older articles preserved on microform) depend on whether the articles appear in newspapers, popular magazines, or scholarly journals. For distinguishing scholarly journals from other periodicals, see 8b.

20. Article in a scholarly journal, continuously paged by volume
For journals with consecutive pagination through several issues of a volume (for example, the first issue of volume 1 ends with page 174, and the second issue of volume 1 begins with page 175), give the volume number, the year in parentheses, and page numbers. See Source Shot 2 above for an example.

Listing an Article in a Scholarly Journal

3 Volume number — Volume 66

Not needed in citation for this journal — Number 5

4 Year of publication — May 2004

3 Name of journal

College English

5 Page numbers (journal is continuously paged)

485 Drafting U.S. Literacy
2 Title of article
Deborah Brandt
1 Author

503 Meaning Finds a Way: Chaos (Theory) and Composition
Bonnie Lenore Kyburz

1 Last name First name
2 Title of article, in quotation marks
3 Name of journal, underlined
3 Volume number

Brandt, Deborah. "Drafting U.S. Literacy." College English 66 (2004):
period
4 Year   colon

485–502.
5 Inclusive page numbers

21. Article in a scholarly journal, paged by issue For journals in which each issue begins with page 1, include the issue number after the volume number, separated from the volume number by a period, or include the issue number alone if no volume number is given.

Ginat, Rami. "The Soviet Union and the Syrian Ba'th Regime: From Hesitation to Rapprochment." Middle Eastern Studies 36.2 (2000): 150–71.

22. Article in a magazine Do not include *The* in the name of a magazine: *Atlantic*, not *The Atlantic*. For a magazine published every week or biweekly, give the complete date (day, month, and year, in that order, with no commas between them). For a monthly or bimonthly magazine, give only the month and year, as in the following first example. In either case, do not include volume and issue numbers.

If the article is on only one page, give that page number. If the article covers two or more consecutive pages, list inclusive page numbers.

Douthat, Ross. "The Truth about Harvard." Atlantic Mar. 2005: 95–99.
Tyrangiel, Josh. "Barrel of Monkeys." Time 20 Feb. 2006: 62.

23. Article in a newspaper After the newspaper title (omit the word *The*), give the date, followed by any edition given at the top of the first page (*late ed., natl. ed.*). For a newspaper that uses letters to designate sections, give the letter before the page number: "A23." For a numbered section, write, for example, "sec. 2: 23." See 12f, item 47, for the online version of the entry for the following article.

Franklin, Deborah. "Vitamin E Fails to Deliver on Early Promise." New York
     Times 2 Aug. 2005, late ed.: F5.

24. Article that skips pages When an article does not appear on consecutive pages (the one by Spencer Reiss begins on pages 136–141, then skips ten pages and continues on pages 151–152), give only the first page number followed by a plus sign.

Reiss, Spencer. "The Dotcom King and the Rooftop Solar Revolution." Wired
     20 July 2005: 136+.

25. Review Begin with the name of the reviewer and the title of the review article if these are available. After "Rev. of," provide the title and author of the work reviewed, followed by publication information for the review.

Weintraub, Arlene. "Men in White." Rev. of World as Laboratory: Experiments
     with Mice, Mazes, and Men, by Rebecca Lemov. Business Week 5 Dec.
     2005: 108–09.

26. Unsigned editorial or article Begin with the title. For an editorial, include the label "Editorial" after the title. In alphabetizing, ignore an initial *A, An,* or *The.*

"Resident Evil." New Republic 19 Dec. 2005: 7.
"Spark the Revolution." Editorial. Wall Street Journal 27 Dec. 2005: A20.

27. Letter to the editor Write "Letter" or "Reply to letter of . . . " after the name of the author (or after the title, if there is one).

Nichol, Christina J. Letter. <u>Harper's</u> Jan. 2006: 6.

28. Abstract in an abstracts journal   For abstracts of articles, provide exact information for the original work, and add information about your source for the abstract: the title of the abstract journal, volume number, year, and item number or page number. (For dissertation abstracts, see 12c, item 19.)

Van Dyke, Jan. "Gender and Success in the American Dance World."
<u>Women's Studies International Forum</u> 19 (1996): 535–43. <u>Studies on Women Abstracts</u> 15 (1997): item 97W/081.

29. Article on microform (microfilm and microfiche)   To cite sources that are neither in hard copy nor in electronic form, provide as much print publication information as is available along with the name of the microfilm or microfiche and any identifying features. Many newspaper and magazine articles published before 1980 are available only in microfiche or microfilm, so you will need to use this medium for historical research. However, be aware that such collections may be incomplete and difficult to read and duplicate clearly.

"War with Japan." Editorial. <u>New York Times</u> 8 Dec. 1941: 22.
<u>UMI University Microfilm</u>.

12e Sample MLA entries: Works in online library subscription databases

Libraries subscribe to large information services (such as *InfoTrac, FirstSearch, EBSCO, SilverPlatter, Dialog, SIRS,* and *LexisNexis*) to gain access to extensive databases of online articles, as well as to specialized databases (such as *ERIC, Contemporary Literary Criticism,* and *PsycINFO*). You can use these databases to locate abstracts and full texts of thousands of articles.

The URLs used to access databases are useful only to those accessing them through a subscribing organization such as a college library or a public library. In addition, database URLs tend not to remain stable, changing day by day, so providing a URL at the end of your citation will not be helpful to your readers unless you know it will be persistent. Cite articles in library databases by providing the information in Source Shot 3 on pages 180–81.

SOURCE SHOT 3

Listing an Article from a Library Database (MLA)

❶ **Name of author(s)** Last name, first name, followed by a period

❷ **"Title of Article: Any Subtitle."** In quotation marks

❸ **Print information for the article Name of journal** underlined, plus date of publication, plus page numbers of the print document if given or shown on the screen or the starting page, followed by a hyphen and a space, for example, 26– . Use page numbers from a printout only if you cite a PDF document.

❹ **Name of the database** Underlined, for example, Academic Search Premier, and followed by a period

❺ **Name of service providing database** For example, *EBSCO, LexisNexis, InfoTrac,* plus a period

❻ **Name of library system** With city and state if necessary, abbreviated to "Lib."

❼ **Your date of access** Day month year, as shown on your printout of the work, with a period at the end

❽ **<URL>** Enclosed in angle brackets, followed by a period, with hyperlinks removed (Tools/AutoCorrect/AutoFormat or Insert/Hyperlink/Remove). Note the specific advice given in the *MLA Handbook for Writers of Research Papers*: "If possible, conclude with the URL of the specific document" (that is, with any persistent URL shown on the screen, provided it is not too long or complicated), but if the database provides no persistent or short URL, give the URL "of the service's home page" (229).

See items 30–34 for examples.

❶ Author   ❷ Title of article   ❸ Print publication information   starting page of article

Gray, Katti. "The Whistle Blower." <u>Essence</u> Feb. 2001: 148– . <u>Academic</u>

❹ Database   ❺ Service   ❻ Library   ❼ Date of access

<u>Search Premier</u>. EBSCO. City U of New York Lib. 2 Aug. 2005

<http://search.epnet.com/

—— ❽ EBSCO database provides a persistent URL ——
login.aspx?direct=true&db=aph&an=4011390>.

       period

MLA (Modern Language Association)

Listing an Article from an EBSCO Database

⑧ URL not persistent— and long!

⑥ Name of library system

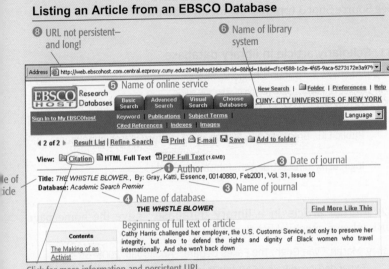

Click for more information and persistent URL.
See Citation Link screen

Citation Link Screen in EBSCO

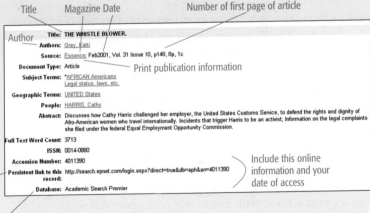

Database

30. Magazine article in a library database
See Source Shot 3 (pp. 180–81) for an example.

31. Scholarly article in library database

Lowe, Michelle S. "Britain's Regional Shopping Centres: New Urban Forms?"
    volume number for print version of scholarly article
    Urban Studies 37.2 (2000): 261–. MasterFile Premier. EBSCO. Brooklyn

                        persistent URL
    Public Lib., Brooklyn, NY. 20 Feb. 2005 <http://search.epnet.com/

    login.aspx?direct=true&db=f5h&an=2832704>.

32. Journal article in a library database
Give the home page URL when a specific URL is not persistent.

Bailey, Martin. "Van Gogh: The Fakes Debate." Apollo Jan. 2005: 55– .
    Expanded Academic ASAP. InfoTrac. University at Albany Lib., Albany,
    NY. 22 Feb. 2005 <http://www.galegroup.com>.

33. Newspaper article in a library database

Weeks, Linton. "History Repeating Itself; Instead of Describing Our Country's
    Past, Two Famous Scholars Find Themselves Examining Their Own."
    Washington Post 24 Mar. 2002: F01– . Academic Universe: News.

                      URL of home page
    LexisNexis. City U of New York Lib.3 Aug. 2005 <http://

    web.lexis-nexis.com>.

34. Abstract in a specialized library database
If the URL is not persistent or is impossibly long, give the URL of the home page of the subscription service, with any details of the path followed.

Kofman, Eleonora. "Gendered Global Migrations: Diversity and Stratification."
    International Feminist Journal of Politics 6 (2004): 643–65. Abstract.
    Sociological Abstracts. CSA Illumina. City U of New York Lib. 28 Feb.
    2005 <http://www.csa.com>. Path: Gender and migration.

35. Article in a database with no visible URL   If a library or service provider links directly to a licensed database without displaying the URL of the accessed database, give the name of the database, the name of the service or library, and your date of access. Specify any path or keywords that you used to access the source.

"Parthenon." <u>The Columbia Encyclopedia</u>. 6th ed. 2000. America Online.

12 Apr. 2003. Keywords: Reference; Encyclopedias; Encyclopedia.com;

Bartleby.com; Columbia Encyclopedia 6th ed.

12f   Sample MLA entries: Web sources

With whatever system of documentation you use, the basic question is, "What information do readers need to access the same Web site and find the same information I found?" Source Shot 4 shows you how to provide and format Web site information in an MLA list of works cited. For listing works from online databases, with corresponding print sources, see 12e. Sometimes you have to search a Web site to find the information you need, such as date and sponsor. But they may not always be available. (You'll find 8d and 8e helpful as you look for the information.) Always save or make a copy of a Web source as details may change over time.

36. Authored document on Web site   Web sites often comprise many pages, each with its own URL. To cite a specific document rather than the whole site, provide the URL for the specific page. Source Shot 4 on pages 184–85 shows an example.

37. Web site document, no author   For a Web site document for which no author is named, begin with the title. Continue with the details of site, date, sponsor, date of access, and URL.

If you follow a specific path to reach the document, it may be helpful to readers to supply details of the path:

MLA

(Modern Language Association)

SOURCE SHOT 4

Listing Web Sources (MLA)

Include these five basic items if they are available:

❶ **Name of author(s)** Last name, first, middle initial *or* corporation, institution, or government agency. Begin with the title if you find no author credited on the site. Put a period at the end.

❷ **"Title of Document."** In quotation marks plus any **print publication information**, if available. Give page numbers *only* for print documents in PDF format. Otherwise, give no page numbers.

❸ **Site information** Name of Web site (underlined) plus date of posting or update plus **sponsor** (if available). A Webmaster is not the sponsor of the site (see 8e).

❹ **Your date of access** Day month (abbrev.) year, with no period after the year. Make a copy of the Web page as soon as you find it; the date will appear on your printout.

❺ **<URL>** Enclosed in angle brackets, followed by a period; hyperlinks removed (Tools/AutoCorrect/AutoFormat). Line split only after a slash. No spaces or hyphens inserted.

See examples in items 36–51.

```
        ┌── ❶ Author ──┐ ┌────────── ❷ Title ──────────┐      ❸ Site
                                                              information
Coren, Michael. "The Science Debate behind Climate Change." CNN.com
        Date of                           ❹ Date of
   ┌──── update ────┐ ┌─── Sponsor ───┐ ┌── access ──┐
   10 Feb. 2006. Cable News Network. 13 Apr. 2006 <http://

   ──────────────── ❺ URL ────────────
   www.cnn.com/2005/TECH/science/04/08/earth.science/index

   ┌──┐
   .html>.
```

"Archaelogists Enter King Tut's Tomb." The History Channel 26 Nov. 1992. History.com. 3 Aug. 2006 <http://www.historychannel.com>. Path: This Day in History; November 26.

38. Entire Web site or professional site, no author named

Federal Relations and Information Policy. 6 Dec. 2005. Assn. of Research Libraries. 21 Dec. 2005 <http://www.arl.org/info/frn/copy/copytoc.html>.

Listing an Authored Web Site Document

③ Site information: name of site   **⑤** URL

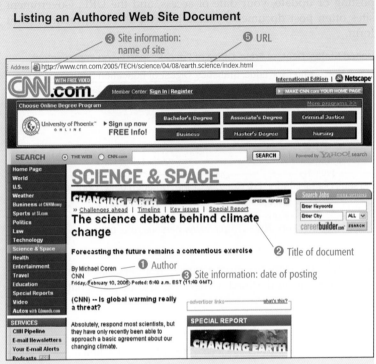

Address http://www.cnn.com/2005/TECH/science/04/08/earth.science/index.html

SCIENCE & SPACE

CHANGING EARTH

» Challenges ahead | Timeline | Key issues | Special Report

The science debate behind climate change

Forecasting the future remains a contentious exercise   **②** Title of document

By Michael Coren   **①** Author
CNN   **③** Site information: date of posting
Friday, February 10, 2006 Posted: 6:49 a.m. EST (11:49 GMT)

(CNN) -- Is global warming really a threat?

Absolutely, respond most scientists, but they have only recently been able to approach a basic agreement about our changing climate.

Bottom of Web page: **③** Site information: Sponsor (Cable News Network)

                          date of
    ┌───── title of site ─────┐   ┌─ update ─┐   ┌───── sponsor ─────┐
    MLA: Modern Language Association. 27 Jan. 2006. Mod. Lang. Assn. of Amer.

        date of
    ┌─ access ─┐
    17 Feb. 2006 <http://www.mla.org>.

39. Government publication online Begin with the government and agency and title of the work. Follow this with the date of electronic posting or update, your date of access, and the URL. Government sites often post documents online before publishing them in print form.

United States. Dept. of Educ. Office of Educ. Research and Improvement.
　　Natl. Center for Educ. Statistics. Digest of Education Statistics, 2003.
　　30 Dec. 2004. 18 Feb. 2006 <http://nces.ed.gov/programs/digest/d03>.

40. Scholarly project online

title of scholarly project — editor — date of electronic publication — sponsor
Perseus Digital Library. Ed. Gregory Crane. Updated daily. Dept. of Classics,

date of access
　　Tufts U. 1 Feb. 2003 <http://www.perseus.tufts.edu>.

41. Personal Web site/home page If a personal Web page has a title, supply it, underlined. Otherwise, use the designation "Home page."

date of update
Gilpatrick, Eleanor. Home page. Feb. 2006. 9 Feb. 2006 <http://
　　www.gilpatrickart.com>.

42. Course page For a course home page, give the name of the instructor and the course, the words *Course home page,* the dates of the course, the department and the institution, and then your access date and the URL.

Parry, Katherine. History of the English Language. Course home page.
　　Feb. 2006. Dept. of English, Hunter Coll. 20 Feb. 2006
　　<http://bb.hunter.cuny.edu>.

43. Online book or part of book Give whatever is available of the following: author, title, editor or translator, and any print publication information, as shown in items 1–18. Follow this with the available electronic publication information: title of site or database, date of electronic posting, sponsor, your date of access to the site, and the URL.

author ⌐⎯⎯⎯⎯⎯⎤ ⌐⎯⎯⎯ title of work ⎯⎯⎯⎤ ⌐⎯ print publication information ⎯⎤
Darwin, Charles. The Voyage of the Beagle. New York: Collier, 1909.

⌐⎯ title of database ⎯⎤ date of electronic ⌐ publication ⎤ ⌐⎯⎯⎯ name of sponsor of site ⎯⎯⎤
Oxford Text Archive. 27 Jan. 2005. Arts and Humanities Data

date of ⌐ access ⎤ URL enclosed ⌐⎯ in angle brackets ⎯⎤
Service. 22 Dec. 2005 <http://ota.ahds.ac.uk>.

44. Online poem

author ⌐⎯⎯⎯⎤ title of ⌐ poem ⎤ print ⌐ source ⎤ print publication ⌐⎯⎯⎯ information ⎯⎯⎯⎤
Levine, Philip. "What Work Is." What Work Is. New York: Knopf, 1991.

⌐⎯⎯ title of database ⎯⎯⎤ date of electronic ⌐ updating ⎤ sponsor ⌐⎯ of site ⎯⎤
Internet Poetry Archive. 4 Apr. 2000. U of North Carolina P.

date of ⌐ access ⎤ URL enclosed ⌐⎯⎯⎯⎯⎯ in angle brackets ⎯⎯⎯⎯⎯⎤
19 Dec. 2005 <http://www.ibiblio.org/ipa/levine/work.html>.

45. Article in an online scholarly journal   Give the author, title of article, title of journal, volume and issue numbers, and date of issue. Include page number or the number of paragraphs only if pages or paragraphs are numbered in the source, as they are for the first example below. End with date of access and URL.

author ⌐⎯⎯⎯⎤ ⌐⎯⎯⎯⎯⎯⎯⎯ title of article ⎯⎯⎯⎯⎯⎯⎯⎤
Hatchuel, Sarah. "Leading the Gaze: From Showing to Telling in Kenneth

name of ⌐⎯ online journal ⎯⎤ volume and issue numbers
Branagh's Henry V and Hamlet." Early Modern Literary Studies 6.1

date of online   number of paragraphs   date of
publication   (numbered in the text)   access
(2000): 22 pars. 21 Dec. 2005 <http://www.shu.ac.uk/emls/06–1/
hatchbra.htm>.

┌── author ──┐ ┌───────────── title of article ─────────────┐ ┌
Hart, Stephen. "Overtures to a New Discipline: Neuromusicology." <u>21st</u>

 volume and date of
 title of online journal issue numbers access
 ┌───────┐
 <u>Century</u> 1.4 (July 1996). 22 Dec. 2005 <http://www.columbia.edu/cu/
 └ date of ┘ └────── no numbered pages or paragraphs ──────┘
 electronic publication
 21stC/issue-1.4/mbmmusic.html>.

46. Article in an online magazine The first date is the date of
posting or update; the second is your date of access.

Gross, Daniel. "One Word: Logistics." <u>Slate</u> 20 Jan. 2006. 23 Jan. 2006
 <http://www.Slate.com/id/2134513/?nav=tap3>.

47. Article in an online newspaper Give author, title of article,
name of newspaper (underlined) and date, name of online site
(underlined), your date of access, and the URL of the article.

Franklin, Deborah. "Vitamin E Fails to Deliver on Early Promise." <u>New York</u>
 <u>Times on the Web</u> 2 Aug. 2005. 1 Aug. 2006 <http://
 www.nytimes.com/2005/08/02/science/02cons.html>.

48. Online review, editorial, letter, or abstract After author and
title, identify the type of text: "Letter," "Editorial," "Abstract," or
"Rev. of . . . by . . ." (see 12d, items 25–28). Continue with details of
the electronic source.

Raimes, Ann. Rev. of <u>Dog World: And the Humans Who Live There</u> by Alfred
 Gingold. <u>Amazon.com</u>. 18 Feb. 2005. <http://www.amazon.com>.

**49. Entry in an online encyclopedia, dictionary, or other refer-
ence work** When entries are not individually authored, begin with
the title of the entry. Give the latest date of posting. Provide details of
the sponsor, your date of access, and the URL.

 title of title of date of electronic date of
 article database updating sponsor access
"Atheism." <u>Wikipedia</u>. 27 Dec. 2005. Wikipedia Foundation. 3 Jan. 2006
 <http://en.wikipedia.org/wiki/Atheism>.

"Vicarious." <u>Cambridge Advanced Learner's Dictionary</u>. 2004. Cambridge UP. 6
Jan. 2006 <http://dictionary.cambridge.org/
define.asp?key=88182&dict=CALD>.

50. Online posting on a discussion list, blog, Usenet, etc.   Give
the author's name, the document title (as written in the subject line),
the label "Online posting," and the date of posting. Follow this with
the name of the forum in the discussion list or of the Web log (blog),
date of access, and URL or address of the list.

Tubbs, Brian. "Washington and Lincoln—Both Great Men." Online posting.

      ┌── name of forum ──┐

    21 Feb. 2005. American Revolution. 21 Feb. 2005 <http://
boards.historychannel.com/forum.jspa?forumID=90>.

Brattina, Tiffany. "The Life of a Salesman." Online posting. 16 Mar. 2004.

      name of

    ┌── blog ──┐

    Luna Dreams. 22 Feb. 2005 <http://blogs.setonhill.edu/
TiffanyBrattina/002755.html>.

For a Usenet newsgroup, give the name and address of the group,
beginning with the prefix *news:*

Zimmer, Ben. "Eggcorn Database." Online posting. 19 Feb. 2005. 21
Feb. 2005 <news:alt.usage.english>.

To make it easy for readers to find a posting, refer whenever possible
to one stored in Web archives.

Schwalm, David. "Re: Value of an Education." Online posting. 15 Feb. 2005.

      name of

    ┌── archive ──┐

    WPA-L Archives. 21 Feb. 2005. <http://lists.asu.edu/
archives.wpa-l.html>.

To cite a forwarded document in an online posting, include the
author, title, and date, followed by "Fwd. by" and the name of the

person forwarding the document. End with "Online posting," the date of the forwarding, the name of the discussion group, date of access, and address of the discussion list.

Gold, Tami. "Update on PSC-CUNY Contract." 16 Feb. 2005. Fwd. by Ken
　　Sherrill. Online posting. 17 Feb. 2005. Hunter-L. 20 Feb. 2005
　　<http://hunter.listserv.cuny.edu>.

51. Personal e-mail message　Provide the subject line heading.

Bernstein, Roberta. "Challenges." E-mail to the author. 12 Feb. 2006.

12g　Sample MLA entries: Visual, performance, multimedia, and miscellaneous sources (live, print, and online)

Document online visual, performance, and multimedia sources as you would sources that are not online, with the addition of electronic publishing information (site name and date) as well as your date of access and the URL. Items 52, 55, 56, 57, and 60 include citations of online works.

52. Work of art, slide, or photograph　List the name of the artist; the title of the work (underlined); the name of the museum, gallery, site, or owner; and the location. You can also include the date the work was created.

Christo. The Gates. Central Park, New York. Feb. 2005.
Duchamp, Marcel. Bicycle Wheel. 1951. Museum of Mod. Art, New York.
　　22 Feb. 2005 <http://www.moma.org/collection/depts/paint_sculpt/
　　blowups/paint_sculpt_020.html>.
Johns, Jasper. Racing Thoughts. Whitney Museum of Amer. Art, New York.

For a photograph in a book, give complete publication information, including the number of the page where the photograph appears.

Johns, Jasper. Racing Thoughts. Whitney Museum of Amer. Art, New York.
　　The American Century: Art and Culture 1950–2000. By Lisa Phillips.
　　New York: Norton, 1999. 311.

For a slide in a collection, include the slide number (Slide 17).

53. Cartoon   After the cartoonist's name and the title (if any) of the cartoon, add the label "Cartoon." Follow this with the usual information about the source, and give the page number for a print source.

Shanahan, Danny. "The Lawyer Fairy." Cartoon. New Yorker 7 Feb. 2005: 49.

54. Advertisement or placard   For an advertisement, give the name of the product or company, followed by the label "Advertisement" and any publication information. (If a print page is not numbered, write "n. pag.".)

Xerox. Advertisement. Fortune 7 Feb. 2005: 1.

For a placard such as a label on a museum wall, provide the label "Placard" after the name of the work. Also give the museum and the dates of the show.

Rauschenberg, Robert. Collection. Placard. New York: Metropolitan Museum
     of Art, 20 Dec. 2005–2 Apr. 2006.

55. Map or chart   Underline the title of the map or chart, and include the designation after the title.

Auvergne/Limousin. Map. Paris: Michelin, 1996.
Pearl Harbor. Multimedia attack map. Nationalgeographic.com. 19 Feb. 2005
     <http://plasma.nationalgeographic.com/pearlharbor>.

56. Film or video   List the title, director, performers, and any other pertinent information. End with the name of the distributor and the year of distribution.

Million Dollar Baby. Dir. Clint Eastwood. Perf. Hilary Swank. Warner, 2004.
Office Ninja. Dir. Matthew Johnston. iFilm, 2004. 19 Feb. 2005
     <http://www.ifilm.com/ifilmdetail/2659387>.

When you cite a videocassette or DVD, include pertinent details and the date of the original film, the medium, the name of the distributor of the DVD or cassette, and the year of the new release.

Casablanca. Dir. Michael Curtiz. Perf. Humphrey Bogart and Ingrid Bergman.
     1943. DVD. MGM, 1998.

57. Television or radio program Give the title of the program episode; the title of the program; any pertinent information about performers, writer, narrator, or director; the network; and the local station and date of broadcast.

"My Big Break." This American Life. Narr. Ira Glass. WBEZ, Chicago. 21 Jan.
    2005. 22 Feb. 2005 <http://www.thislife.org>.

"Seeds of Destruction." Slavery and the Making of America. Narr. Morgan
    Freeman. Thirteen, WNET. WLIW, New York. 22 Feb. 2005.

58. Sound recording List the composer or author, the title of the work, the names of artists, the production company, and the date. If the medium is not a compact disc, indicate the medium, such as "Audiocassette," before the name of the production company.

Turner, Alex, and Arctic Monkeys. Whatever People Say I Am, That's What I'm
    Not. Domino, 2006.

Walker, Alice. Interview with Kay Bonetti. Audiocassette. Columbia: American
    Audio Prose Library, 1981.

59. Live performance Give the title of the play, the author, pertinent information about the director or performers, the theater, the location, and the date of performance. If you are citing an individual's role in the work, begin your citation with the person's name.

Diggs, Elizabeth. Mirette. Dir. Drew Scott Harris. Perf. Robert Cuccioli. Saint
    Peter's Theatre, New York. 17 Dec. 2005.

Mirette. Book by Elizabeth Diggs. Dir. Drew Scott Harris. Perf. Robert
    Cuccioli. Saint Peter's Theatre, New York. 17 Dec. 2005.

60. Interview For a personal interview, include the type of interview (telephone, e-mail, personal, etc.).

Gingold, Toby. Telephone interview. 4 Mar. 2005.

For a published interview, give the name of the person interviewed, followed by the word "Interview" or "Interview with . . .". Include information about the print publication.

Parker, Dorothy. Interview with Marion Capron. <u>Writers at Work:</u> The Paris
Review <u>Interviews</u>. London: Secker and Warburg, 1958. 66–75.

For a broadcast or online interview, provide information about the
source and date of the interview.

Gladwell, Malcolm. Interview with Leonard Lopate. <u>The Leonard Lopate
Show: Think without Thinking</u>. WNYC, New York. 18 Feb. 2005.
Gladwell, Malcolm. Interview with Leonard Lopate. <u>The Leonard Lopate
Show: Think without Thinking</u>. WNYC, New York. 18 Feb. 2005. 4 Jan.
2006 <http://www.wnyc.org/shows/lopate/episodes/0218005>.

For a sound recording of an interview, see item 58.

61. Lecture or speech   Give the author and title, if known. For a
presentation with no title, include a label such as "Lecture" or
"Address" after the name of the speaker. Also give the name of any
organizing sponsor, the venue, and the date.

Gourevitch, Philip. Lecture. Hunter College, New York. 28 Feb. 2006.

62. Letter or personal communication   For a letter that you
received, include the phrase "Letter to the author" after the name of
the letter writer. Describe the type of any other personal communication ("Telephone call," for example). (See also 12f, item 48, for letters published online.)

Rogan, Helen. Letter to the author. 3 Feb. 2005.

Cite a published letter in a collection as you would cite a work in an
anthology. After the name of the author, include any title the editor
gives the letter and the date. Add the page numbers for the letter at
the end of the citation.

Bishop, Elizabeth. "To Robert Lowell." 26 Nov. 1951. <u>One Art: Letters</u>. Ed.
Robert Giroux. New York: Farrar, 1994. 224–26.

63. Legal or historical source   For a legal case, give the name of the
case with no underlining or quotation marks, the number of the case,
the name of the court deciding the case, and the date of the decision.

Roe v. Wade. No. 70–18. Supreme Ct. of the US. 22 Jan. 1973.

If you mention the case in your text, underline it.

Chief Justice Burger, in Roe v. Wade, noted that . . .

Give the Public Law number of an act, its date, and the cataloging number for its Statutes at Large.

USA Patriot Act. Pub. L. 107-56. 26 Oct. 2001. Stat. 115.272.

Well-known historical documents should not be included in your works-cited list (see 42c, item U).

64. CD-ROM or DVD   Cite material from a CD-ROM or DVD in the same way you cite an article in a book, but after the title of the CD or DVD, add the medium of publication and any version or release number.

Flanner, Janet. "Führer I." New Yorker 29 Feb. 1934: 20–24. The Complete
   New Yorker. DVD-ROM. New York: Random, 2005.
Keats, John. "To Autumn." Columbia Granger's World of Poetry. CD-ROM. Rel.
   3. New York: Columbia UP, 1999.

Chapter **13**

A Student's Research Paper, MLA Style

Here is Lindsay Camp's documented paper written in her required first-year composition course. She developed her argument (see chapter 4) about the need for both safety and equality because she was herself planning to become a police officer. Features of Camp's argument strategies are pointed out with blue annotations. Red annotations call attention to her use of MLA format conventions. If your instructor requires a separate title page, see 3f or ask for guidelines.

$\frac{1}{2}''$

1"

Camp 1

1"

Lindsay Camp

Professor Raimes

English 120, section 129

5 December 2003

Safety First: Women and Men in Police and Fire Departments

If any of us were caught in a fire, we would almost
certainly prefer to see a man rather than a woman coming to
carry us down a ladder out of the flames and smoke--though
we would certainty be grateful to either. In an interview, a
firefighter made precisely that point about perceptions of size
and strength (Mignone). However, because society is
increasingly conscious of discrimination based on gender,
police and fire departments have implemented quotas to hire
more women. In many cases, though, in order to meet the
quotas they have used different physical standards for women
and men, so women who want equality have been treated
unequally, men have experienced reverse discrimination, and
public safety has been threatened. To meet standards of both
safety and equality, women and men should pass the same
physical tests.

In order to become police officers, candidates have
to pass a series of exams and evaluations, among them
psychological tests (Wexler) and a physical fitness test, which
"assumes that being physically fit is a good predictor of job
success for fire and police department personnel" (Rafilson,

Margin annotations (left):

No extra space below title

Emotional appeal to engage readers

Cites an interview

Points out that progress has created its own problems

Cites whole work (no page number)

Margin annotations (right):

Title centered, not underlined

Double-spaced throughout

Establishes domain of enquiry

Thesis (claim): solution to problem

Online source (no page number)

Camp 2

"Legislative"). In most departments around the country, this test consists of sit-ups, a mile-and-a-half run, bench press repetitions, and a flexibility test (Rafilson, Police Officer 39). Women are encouraged to apply, but in the tests they are judged by lower standards than men.

Author and title for author with more than one work cited

Table 1 Minimum Fitness Standards for Entry to the Academy

Female Candidates

Age Group	20–29	30–39
Sit-ups (1 minute)	35	27
Sit & Reach (inches)	20	19
Push-ups	18	14
1.5-Mile Run (minutes)	14:55	15:26

Male Candidates

Age Group	20–29	30–39
Sit-ups (1 minute)	40	36
Sit & Reach (inches)	17.5	16.5
Push-ups	33	27
1.5-Mile Run (minutes)	12:18	12:51

Source: Rafilson, Police Officer 47.

Provides data visually in a table

Comments on table and explains data

Table 1 shows that women are given from 2 minutes and 37 seconds to 3 minutes and 15 seconds extra to run a mile-and-a-half. That could mean the difference between catching a suspect and not catching a suspect. Men have to complete 13 to 15 more push-ups than women because women generally do not have the same amount of upper body strength as men.

Uses data to appeal to logic

Camp 3

But police officers may need to climb fences, lift heavy items, or carry injured people; certainly firefighters may need to carry injured people and heavy hoses.

Recognizing that the physical fitness tests are flawed, police and fire departments have been turning to a different test, called a physical agility exam, in which the candidate must complete an obstacle course. For the New York Police Department's agility exam, candidates are required to wear a 10.5 lb utility belt as they run out of a patrol car, climb a six-foot wall, run up four flights of stairs, drag a 160 lb dummy 30 feet, run back down four flights of stairs, climb a four-foot wall, and run back to the patrol car (Rafilson, Police Officer 40–42). Such tasks are seen as relevant to what a police officer actually encounters while on duty. All candidates must complete every part of the obstacle course in the same amount of time in order to pass the exam, regardless of sex, age, or weight. The obstacles in the course and the time allotted may vary between departments, but there is no partiality given based on ethnicity, gender, or age. Women may need to be provided with preparation and training for the test, as an article in The Police Chief points out (Polisar and Milgram), but they should still be required to take and pass it.

More and more police and fire departments are now using the physical agility test instead of the fitness test. According to Dr. Fred M. Rafilson, the fitness model was

Gives page numbers for print source

Cites online source-- no page number

Gives author's credentials

Camp 4

Fig. 1: From Robie Liscomb, "Preparing Women for Firefighting in B.C."

popular because it "allows fire departments to hire more women because passing standards are adjusted based on a person's age, sex, and weight," but, as he says, a "woman can pass a fitness model test for the fire service and still not be able to perform essential job functions that require a great deal of upper body and leg strength" ("Legislative"). Some programs have been established to help prepare women for the new tests. The program at the University of Victoria in British Columbia, Canada, culminates in having women carry "65-pound pumps and heavy fire hoses across the infield of the warm-up track" (Liscomb). Figure 1 shows a participant in action.

Uses a visual to strengthen the argument that women can perform heavy physical work

Camp 5

Many see upper body strength as crucial. Firefighters are very much like a family, trust each other like brothers, and in a fire emergency may have to make life and death decisions. They need to know that the person next to them can handle all of the duties of the job. Thomas P. Butler, a spokesperson for the Uniformed Firefighters Association, the firefighters' union, points out that ''this is a job where one firefighter's life and safety depends on another. It is important that we attract the best and the brightest" (qtd. in Baker). Any person who cannot perform the tasks of a firefighter poses "a direct threat to human life and safety" (Rafilson, "Legislative") and does not belong on the job.

Frances Heidensohn's thorough study of women in law enforcement in the U.S.A. and in Britain does, however, point out that many women have "questioned the relevance and purpose of the physical standards as . . . irrelevant to policing" (170). Women in the police force testified that while they had been tested on doing a "body drag," they never had seen it done or had to do this on the job. And, of course, we all can recognize that having different (and lower) standards for women does allow more women to be hired as career officers and helps departments with affirmative action requirements.

Those who put themselves on the line on the job, however, still question the wisdom of different testing criteria for men and women. Douglass Mignone, a first lieutenant of

Cites a one-page work where quotation appears-- no page number necessary in citation

Considers opposing views

Establishes common ground ("we all")

Refers to introduction and uses evidence from interview to refute the opposing views

Camp 6

the Purchase Fire Department and a New York City Fire

Ethical appeal

Department applicant, for example, makes the case for equal

safety requirements and training:

Indents a long quotation

> If you were in a burning building and had the choice
>
> between my girlfriend Sinead, a five-foot-five, 130 lb

Emotional appeal

> woman, or myself, a six-foot-two, 200 lb man, to get
>
> you out alive, who would you choose? I have no
>
> problem with women being firefighters as long as they
>
> meet the same requirements and undergo the same
>
> training as myself.

This view is the consensus among male police officers and

male firefighters, but not that of the general public. The general

idea of safety seems to be slipping past the newspapers and

television. There are no activists standing outside City Hall

crying, "What about our safety?" "Make physical requirements

equal" (Rafilson, "Legislative"). There will be no activists, no

protests, and no media until someone dies or until there is a

Transition from safety to equality

tragedy.

Added to the issue of safety is the issue of equality. In

1964, Congress prohibited discrimination based on race, color,

Broadens the picture to legislation

sex, national origin, or religion under the Civil Rights Act of 1964

(Brooks 26). In 1991, Congress passed the 1991 Civil Rights Act,

which made it "an unlawful employment practice" to adjust any

Cites work in which quotation appears

tests or scores "on the basis of race, color, religion, sex, or

national origin" (qtd. in Rafilson, "Legislative").

Camp 7

Title VII under this Act claims that the employer accused of "disparate impact" would have to prove business necessity. This has left police and fire departments all over the country confused and asking themselves what to do and whom to hire next. Are police and fire departments going to claim that the physiological differences between men and women make different physical standards a business necessity? According to Special Agent Michael E. Brooks:

> The challenge comes when a male cannot meet the male standard but can meet the female standard. Such an action amounts to express disparate treatment of the male. Disparate treatment, like disparate impact, is only permissible under the business necessity justification. The administrator who uses different physical selection standards for female applicants would, therefore, have to show what business necessity justifies such a practice. (31)

Controversy and confusion abound, and male applicants are filing lawsuits claiming reverse discrimination. The Edmonton Fire Department has a "diversity" policy in which the 12 positions that were available did not go to the top 12 applicants but to women and minorities (Champion). Two groups of rejected applicants filed complaints with the Alberta Human Rights Commission claiming that "the City of Edmonton exercised race and gender bias in denying them employment"

Question draws readers into issue

Provides specific factual details

Camp 8

(Champion). Such practices make it clear that reforms are necessary.

Reminds readers of main point

The process of applying to be hired in a police or fire department must be clear to all and equitable to all. Only those with the highest scores on the written exam should be eligible to take the physical agility test. Then only the candidates who pass the physical should qualify for further testing and employment. Men who fail any of the tests should not be hired--nor should women. If police and fire departments lower standards for anyone, they are putting the general public's safety on the line as well as their fellow officers'. Peter Horne, an assistant professor at Meramec Community College, puts it succinctly: "Females and males should take the same physical agility test. Then it would not matter whether a recruit is 5'8" or 5'4", or a male or female, but only whether he/she possesses the physical capability to do the job" (33–34). The

Ends on a strong note

cost to safety is much too great for women to be held to lower requirements than men.

MLA (Modern Language Association)

Camp 9

Works Cited

Baker, Al. "Fire Department Looks to Diversify the Ranks." <u>New York Times</u> 3 Apr. 2002: B3. <u>Academic Universe: News</u>. LexisNexis. City U of New York Lib. 25 Oct. 2003 <http://web.lexis-nexis.com/>.

Brooks, Michael E. "Law Enforcement Physical Fitness Standard and Title VII." <u>FBI Law Enforcement Bulletin</u> May 2001: 26–33.

Champion, Chris. "Male Honkies Need Not Apply." <u>Western Report</u> 7 Aug. 1996: 24– . <u>Academic Search Premier</u>. EBSCO. City U of New York Lib. 27 Oct. 2003 <http://search.epnet.com/direct.asp?an=9607267865&db=aph>.

Heidensohn, Frances. <u>Women in Control? The Role of Women in Law Enforcement</u>. New York: Oxford UP, 1992.

Horne, Peter. <u>Women in Law Enforcement</u>. 2nd ed. Springfield: Thomas, 1980.

Liscomb, Robie. "Preparing Women for Firefighting in B.C." <u>The Ring</u> 6 Feb. 1998. University of Victoria Sport and Fitness Centre. 28 Oct. 2003 <http://communications.uvic.ca/ring/98feb06/firefighting.html>.

Mignone, Douglass. Telephone interview. 19 Oct. 2003.

Polisar, Joseph, and Donna Milgram. "Recruiting, Integrating and Retaining Women Police Officers: Strategies That Work." <u>The Police Chief</u> Oct. 1998. <u>IWITTS in the News</u>. Institute

1"

Entries organized alphabetically

Article spans consecutive pages.

EBSCO provides persistent URL.

1"

Published work on Web site

Title centered, not underlined

Article from a subscription database with URL of home page

Database gives first page number only.

Camp 10

for Women in Trades, Technology, and Science.

27 Oct. 2003 <http://www.iwitts.com/html/

the_police_chief.htm>.

Rafilson, Fred M. "Legislative Impact on Fire Service Physical

Fitness Testing." Fire Engineering Apr. 1995: 83– .

Academic Search Premier. EBSCO. City U of New York

Lib. 23 Oct. 2003 <http://search.epnet.com/

direct.asp?an=9505024136&db=aph>.

---. Police Officer. 15th ed. United States: Arco, 2000.

Wexler, Ann Kathryn. Gender and Ethnicity as Predictors of

Psychological Qualification for Police Officer Candidates.

Diss. California School of Professional Psychology, 1996.

Ann Arbor: UMI, 1996. 9625522.

Second
entry for
author

List includes
only sources
actually
cited in the
paper.

APA

(American Psychological Association)

In Part 4 you will find descriptions of documentation styles other than the MLA system. Chapters 14 and 15 focus on the style recommended for the social sciences by the *Publication Manual of the American Psychological Association,* 5th ed. (Washington, DC: Amer. Psychological Assn., 2001), and on the APA Web site. A student's paper written in APA styles is in chapter 16. Chapter 17 describes the citation-sequence and the citation-name styles recommended by the Council of Science Editors (CSE). Chapters 18 and 19 illustrate the endnote and footnote style recommended in *The Chicago Manual of Style,* 15th ed. (Chicago: U of Chicago P, 2003), for writing in the humanities; it is sometimes used as an alternative to MLA style.

Chapter **14**

Citing Sources in Your Text, APA Style

14a Two basic features of APA style

KEY POINTS
Two Basic Features of APA Style

1. *In the text of your paper,* include at least two pieces of information each time you cite a source:

    the last name(s) of the author (or authors)

    the year of publication

2. *At the end of your paper,* include on a new numbered page a list entitled "References," double-spaced and arranged alphabetically by authors' last names, followed by the initials of first and other names, the date in parentheses, and other bibliographical information. See chapter 15 for the information to include in an APA-style reference list.

Illustrations of the basic features

In-Text Citation	Entry in List of References
Book:	
The speed at which we live is seen as cause for concern and derision (Gleick, 1999).	Gleick, J. (1999). *Faster: The acceleration of just about everything.* New York: Pantheon.
The renowned scholar of language, David Crystal, has promoted the idea of "dialect democracy" (2004, p. 168). [Page number included for quotation]	Crystal, D. (2004). *The stories of English.* Woodstock, NY: Overlook Press.
Print Article:	
Ambition is seen as an impulse that "requires an enormous investment of emotional capital" (Kluger, 2005, p. 59). [Page number included for quotation] or Kluger (2005, p. 59) sees ambition as an impulse that "requires an enormous investment of emotional capital."	(Kluger, J. (2005, November 14). Ambition: Why some people are most likely to succeed. *Time, 166,* 48–54, 57, 59.
Article in Online Database:	
Research has shown that cross-cultural identification does not begin before eight years of age (Sousa, Neto, & Mullet, 2005).	Sousa, R. M., Neto, F., & Mullet, E. (2005). Can music change ethnic attitudes among children? *Psychology of Music, 33,* 304–316. Retrieved December 15, 2005, from Sage Psychology, CSA database.
Document on Web Site:	
Contributing to global warming in the past century is a considerable rise in sea levels (Coren, 2006). [See Source Shot 4 on p. 185.]	(Coren, M. (2006, February 10). *The science debate behind climate change.* Retrieved April 13, 2006, from http://www.cnn.com/2005/TECH/science/04/08/earth.science/index.html

14b APA author/year style for in-text citations

A. One author If you mention the author's last name in your own text, include the year in parentheses directly after the author's name.

author   year
Wilson (1994) has described in detail his fascination with insects.

(See 15c, item 1, to see how this work appears in a reference list.)

If you do not name the author in your own text, include both the name and the year, separated by a comma, in parentheses.

> The army retreated from Boston in disarray, making the rebels realize that they had achieved a great victory (McCullough, 2001).
>   author   comma   year

If you use a direct quotation or a paraphrase, include in parentheses the abbreviation "p." or "pp." followed by a space and the page number(s). Use commas to separate items within parentheses.

> Memories are built "around a small collection of dominating images" (Wilson, 1994, p. 5).
>   comma   comma   page number
>   with a quotation

B. More than one author   For a work by two authors, name both in the order in which their names appear on the work. Within parentheses, use an ampersand (&) between the names, in place of *and*. Use the word *and* for a reference made in your text.

> Kanazawa and Still (2000) in their analysis of a large set of data show that the statistical likelihood of being divorced increases if one is male and a secondary school teacher or college professor.

> Analysis of a large set of data shows that the statistical likelihood of being divorced increases if one is male and a secondary school teacher or college professor (Kanazawa & Still, 2000).
>
>   ampersand in parentheses

(See 15d, item 13, to see how this work appears in a reference list.)

For a work with three to five authors or editors, identify all of them the first time you mention the work. In later references, use only the first author's name followed by "et al." (for "and others") in place of the other names.

> Jordan, Kaplan, Miller, Stiver, and Surrey (1991) have examined the idea of *self*.

> Increasingly, the self is viewed as connected to other human beings (Jordan et al., 1991).

(15c, item 2, shows how this work appears in a reference list.)

For six or more authors, use the name of the first author followed by "et al." both for the first mention and in a parenthetical citation.

However, include the names of the first six authors on your reference list, using "et al." to indicate only authors beyond the first six.

C. Author with more than one work published in one year Identify each work with a lowercase letter after the date: (Zamel, 1997a, 1997b). Separate the dates with a comma. In the reference list, repeat the author's name in each entry, and alphabetize by the title. See 15b for how to order such entries in the list of references.

D. Work in an anthology In your text, refer to the author of the work, not to the editor of the anthology. In the reference list, give the author's name, title of the work, and bibliographical details about the anthology, such as the editor, title, publisher, and date (15c, item 4).

> Seegmiller (1993) has provided an incisive analysis of the relationship between pregnancy and culture.

E. Work cited in another source Give the author or title of the work in which you find the reference, preceded by "as cited in" to indicate that you are referring to a citation in that work. List that secondary source in your list of references. In the following example, *Smith* will appear in the list of references with details of the source; *Britton* will not.

> The words we use simply appear, as Britton says, "at the point of utterance" (as cited in Smith, 1982, p. 108).

F. An entire work or an idea in a work Use only an author and a year to refer to a complete work; for a paraphrase or a comment on a specific idea, a page number is not required but is recommended.

G. No author named In your text, use the complete title if it is short (capitalizing major words) or a few words for the title in parentheses, along with the year of publication.

> According to *Weather* (1999), one way to estimate the Fahrenheit temperature is to count the number of times a cricket chirps in 14 seconds and add 40.

> Increasing evidence shows that glucosamine relieves the symptoms of arthritis *(The PDR Family Guide, 1999)*.

(See 15c, item 5, for how to list the latter work.)

H. Internet or electronic source   Give author, if available, or title, followed by the year of electronic publication or of the most recent update. To locate a quotation in a source with no page or paragraph numbers visible on the screen, give the section heading, and indicate the paragraph within the section, such as "Conclusion section, para. 2."

Be wary of citing e-mail messages (personal, bulletin board, discussion list, or Usenet group) as these are not peer reviewed or easily retrievable. If you need to refer to an e-mail message, cite from an archived list whenever possible (see the example in 15e, item 30); otherwise, cite the message in your text as a personal communication (see 14b, item O), but do not include it in your list of references.

I. Entire Web site   Give the complete URL in the text of your paper. Do not list the site in your list of references.

> Research on the "Mozart effect" has generated an institute with a Web site providing links to research studies (http://www.mindinst.org).

J. Multimedia or nonprint source   For a film, television or radio broadcast, recording, live performance, or other nonprint source, include in your citation the name of the originator or main contributor (such as the writer, interviewer, director, performer, or producer) or an abbreviated title if the originator is not identified, along with the year of production—for example, "(Berman & Pulcini, 2003)." (See 15f, item 34, for how to list this work.)

K. Work by a corporation or government organization   In the initial citation, use the organization's full name; in subsequent references, use an abbreviation, if one exists.

> first mention:
> ┌— full name —┐
> The trends in college costs are published annually by the College Board. In 2005–2006, tuition increases slowed at public colleges (CB, 2005).

(15c, item 6, shows how to list this work.)

L. Two authors with the same last name   Include the authors' initials, even if the publication dates of their works differ.

> F. Smith (1982) first described a writer as playing the two competitive roles of author and secretary.

(For the order of entries in the list of references, see 15b.)

M. Multivolume work   In your citation, give the publication date of the volume you are citing: (Barr & Feigenbaum, 1982). If you refer to more than one volume, give inclusive dates for all the volumes you cite: (Barr & Feigenbaum, 1981–1986). (See 15c, item 8, for how to list this work.)

N. More than one work in a citation   List the sources in alphabetical order, separated by semicolons. List works by the same author chronologically (earliest source first) or by the letters *a, b,* and so on if the works were published in the same year.

> Criticisms of large-scale educational testing abound (Crouse &
> Trusheim, 1988; Nairn, 1978, 1980; Raimes, 1990a,1990b; Sacks, 2003).

O. Personal communication, such as a conversation, a letter, an e-mail, or an unarchived electronic discussion group   Mention these only in your paper; do not include them in your list of references. Give the last name and initial(s) of the author of the communication and the exact date of posting.

> According to V. Sand, Executive Director of the Atwater Kent Museum
> of Philadelphia, "Museums are essential to the educational fabric of the
> United States. They engage our spirit, help us understand the natural
> world, and frame our identities. They help us see our lives as having value
> within the continuum of human experience" (personal communication,
> February 7, 2006).

For archived postings, see 15e, item 30.

P. A classical or religious work   If the date of publication of a classical work is not known, use in your citation "n.d." for "no date." If you use a translation, give the year of the translation, preceded by "trans." You do not need a reference list entry for the Bible or ancient classical works. Just give information about book, chapter, verse, and line numbers in your text, and identify the version you use: Gen. 35: 1–4 (Revised Standard Version).

Q. Long quotation   If you quote more than forty words of prose, do not enclose the quotation in quotation marks. Start the quotation on a new line, and indent the whole quotation half an inch or five spaces from the left margin. Double-space the quotation. See page 242 for an example. Any necessary parenthetical citation should come after the final period of the quotation.

14c Notes, tables, and figures

Notes In APA style, you can use content notes to amplify information in your text. Number notes consecutively with superscript numerals. After the list of references, attach a separate page containing your numbered notes and headed "Footnotes." Use notes sparingly; include all important information in your text, not in footnotes.

Tables Place all tables at the end of your paper, after the references and any notes. Number each table and provide an italicized caption.

Figures After the references and any notes or tables, provide a separate page listing the figure captions, and place this page before the figures.

 **Online Study Center** **Research** Figures in APA style

 Chapter **15**

The APA List of References

15a How to format and organize the APA list

The APA *Publication Manual* and Web site provide guidelines for submitting professional papers for publication, and many instructors ask students to follow those guidelines to prepare them for advanced work. This section follows APA guidelines. Check with your instructor, however, as to any specific course requirements for the reference list.

KEY POINTS
Guidelines for the APA List of References

- **What to list** List only the works you cited (quoted, summarized, paraphrased, or commented on) in the text of your paper, not every source you examined.
- **Format** Start the list on a new numbered page after the last page of text or notes. Center the heading "References," without quotation marks, not underlined or italicized, and with no

period following it. Double-space throughout the list, with no additional space between entries. Place any tables and charts after the "References" list.

■ **Conventions of the list** List the works alphabetically by last names of primary authors. Do not number the entries. Begin each entry with the author's name, last name first, followed by an initial or initials. Give any authors' names after the first in the same inverted form, separated by commas. Use "et al." only to indicate authors beyond the first six. List works with no author by title, alphabetized by the first main word.

■ **Date** Put the year in parentheses after the authors' names. For journals, magazines, and newspapers, also include month and day, but do not abbreviate the names of the months.

■ **Periods** Use a period and one space to separate the main parts of each entry.

■ **Indentation** Use hanging indents. (Begin the first line of each entry at the left margin; indent subsequent lines one-half inch.)

■ **Capitals** In titles of books, reports, articles, and Web documents, capitalize only the first word of the title or subtitle and any proper names.

■ **Italics** Italicize the titles of books, but do not italicize or use quotation marks around the titles of articles. Italicize the names of newspapers, reports, and Web documents. For magazines and journals, italicize the publication name, the volume number, and the comma.

■ **Page numbers** Give inclusive page numbers for print articles, online PDF articles, and sections of books, using complete page spans ("251–259"). Use the abbreviation "p." or "pp." only for newspaper articles and sections of books (such as chapters or anthologized articles). Use document sections in place of page numbers for online HTML articles.

■ **Online sources** Include whatever is available of the following: author(s), date of work, title of work, any print publication information, and identification of the type of source in square brackets (for example, "[letter to the editor]"). For an online library subscription service, end with the name of the service and the document number (as in items 21 and 22). For a Web

(Continued)

(Continued)

site, always include the date of access and the URL of the actual document, not simply the home page (as in items 23–26). Split a URL across lines only after a slash or before a period. Do *not* underline the URL as a hyperlink unless you are posting the paper online (see 24a), and do *not* put a period after the URL at the end of your entry. Provide page numbers only for documents accessed as PDF files.

15b How to list authors in the APA reference list

Name of author(s)   Put the last name first, followed by a comma and then the initials.

> Gould, S. J.

Reverse the names of all authors listed, except the editors of an anthology or a reference work (15c, item 4). Use an ampersand (&), not the word *and*, before the last author's name. For listing multiple authors, see 15c, item 2.

Alphabetical order   Alphabetize letter by letter. Treat *Mac* and *Mc* literally, by letter.

> MacKay, M.   D'Agostino, S.
> McCarthy, T.   De Cesare, P.
> McKay, K.   DeCurtis, A.

A shorter name precedes a longer name beginning with the same letters, whatever the first initial: *Black, T.* precedes *Blackman, R.*

For a work with no known author, list by the first word in the title other than *A, An,* or *The.*

Alphabetize numerals according to their spelling: 5 ("five") will precede 2 ("two").

Individual author(s) not known   If the author is a group, such as a corporation, agency, or institution, give its name, alphabetized by the first important word (15c, item 6). Use full names, not abbreviations. If no author or group is named, alphabetize by the first main word of the title (15c, item 5).

Several works by the same author   List the author's name in each entry. Arrange entries chronologically from past to present. Entries published in the same year should be arranged alphabetically by title and distinguished with lowercase letters after the date (*a, b,* and so on). Note that entries for one author precede entries by that author but written with coauthors.

Goleman, D. (1996a, July 16). Forget money; nothing can buy happiness, some researchers say. *The New York Times,* p. C1.

Goleman, D. (1996b). *Vital lies, simple truths.* New York: Simon & Schuster.

Goleman, D. (2000). *Working with emotional intelligence.* New York: Bantam.

Goleman, D., Kaufman, P., & Ray, M. L. (1992, March–April). The art of creativity. *Psychology Today, 25,* 40–47.

Authors with the same last name   List alphabetically by first initial: Smith, *A.* precedes Smith, *F.*

15c Sample APA entries: Print books and parts of books

1. Book with one author   Give the last name first, followed by the initials. See Source Shot 5 (p. 218) for an example.

2. Book with two or more authors   List all authors' names in the order in which they appear on the book's title page. Reverse the order of each name: last first, followed by initials. Use "et al." only in place of names of authors beyond the first six. Separate all names with commas, and insert an ampersand (&) before the last name.

```
                                              ampersand
├──────────────── all names reversed ────────────┤
Jordan, J. V., Kaplan, A. G., Miller, J. B., Stiver, I. P., & Surrey, J. L. (1991).

indented
5 spaces
   └──→Women's growth in connection: Writings from the Stone Center.
       New York: Guilford Press.
```

3. Edited book   Use "Ed." or "Eds." for one or more editors, in parentheses.

Denmark, F., & Paludi, M. (Eds.). (1993). *Psychology of women: A handbook of issues and theories.* Westport, CT: Greenwood Press.

APA

(American Psychological Association)

SOURCE SHOT 5

Listing a Book (APA)

On the title page and copyright page of the book, you'll find the information you need for an entry in the list of references.

❶ **Author(s)** Last name, initials (see 15c, item 2 for when to use "et al.")

❷ **(Year of publication)** In parentheses; the most recent copyright © date or "n.d." if no date is supplied

❸ *Title of book: Any subtitle* In italics, with capital letters only for the first word of the title and subtitle and proper names

❹ **Place of publication** City and state (abbreviated), but state omitted for a major city, such as New York or San Francisco, or when state is shown in name of publisher, as in "University of Illinois Press"

❺ **Publisher** In a short but intelligible form, including *University* and *Press* but omitting *Co.* and *Inc.*

See items 1–12 for examples.

initials   periods
❶ Last name / ❷ Year in parentheses
/comma / / period ❸ Title italicized
Wilson, E. O. (1994). *Naturalist*. Washington, DC: Island Press.
                    ❹ Place of publication colon ❺ Publisher final period

4. Work in an edited collection or reference book List the author, date of publication of the edited book, and title of the work. Follow this with "In" and the names of the editors (not inverted), the title of the book, and the inclusive page numbers (preceded by "pp.") of the work in parentheses. End with the place of publication and the publisher. If you cite more than one article in an edited work, include full bibliographical details in each entry.

names of editors
┌──── not reversed ────┐
Seegmiller, B. (1993). Pregnancy. In F. Denmark & M. Paludi (Eds.),
    Psychology of women: A handbook of issues and theories
    (pp. 437–474). Westport, CT: Greenwood Press.

For a reference book with unsigned entries, begin with the title of the entry and include the page number(s).

APA (American Psychological Association)

Title Page

❸ Title

NATURALIST

EDWARD O. WILSON

❶ Author

❺ Publisher

ISLAND PRESS / Shearwater Books
Washington, D.C. · Covelo, California

❹ Place of publication

Copyright Page

A Shearwater Book
published by Island Press

❷ Year of publication

Copyright © 1994 by Island Press
Illustrations copyright © 1994 by Laura Simonds Southworth

The excerpt from "Daybreak in Alabama" is from
Selected Poems by Langston Hughes, copyright © 1948
by Alfred A. Knopf Inc., and renewed 1976
by The Executors of the Estate of Langston Hughes.
Reprinted by permission of the publisher.

All rights reserved under International and Pan-American
Copyright Conventions. No part of this book may be
reproduced in any form or by any means without permission
in writing from the publisher: Island Press, 1718 Connecticut
Avenue, N.W., Suite 300, Washington, DC 20009.
SHEARWATER BOOKS is a trademark of
The Center for Resource Economics.

LIBRARY OF CONGRESS
CATALOGING-IN-PUBLICATION DATA
Wilson, Edward Osborne, 1929–
Naturalist / Edward O. Wilson.
p.   cm.
Includes index.
ISBN 1-55963-288-7 (cloth)
1. Wilson, Edward Osborne, 1929–   2. Naturalists—
United States—Biography.   I. Title.
QH31.W64A3   1994
508'.092—dc20   94-13111
[B]   CIP

Printed on recycled, acid-free paper
Manufactured in the United States of America
10 9 8 7 6 5 4 3 2 1

Antarctica. (2000). In *The Columbia encyclopedia* (6th ed., pp. 116–118). New
York: Columbia University Press.

5. Book or pamphlet with no author identified   Put the title
first. Ignore *A, An,* and *The* when alphabetizing. Alphabetize the following under *P.*

The PDR family guide to natural medicines and healing therapies. (1999).
New York: Three Rivers-Random House.

**6. Book or pamphlet by a corporation or government or other
organization**   Give the name of the corporate author first. If the
publisher is the same as the author, write "Author" for the name of
the publisher.

College Board. (2005). *Trends in college pricing 2005.* New York: Author.

If no author is named for a government publication, begin with the name of the federal, state, or local government, followed by the agency.

United States. Department of Homeland Security. (2004). *Preparing for disaster for people with disabilities and other special needs.* Washington, DC: FEMA.

7. Translated book   In parentheses after the title of the work, give the initials and last name of the translator, followed by a comma and "Trans."

                                        name of translator not reversed

Jung, C. G. (1960). *On the nature of the psyche* (R. F. C. Hull, Trans.). Princeton, NJ: Princeton University Press.

8. Multivolume work   Give the number of volumes after the title, in parentheses. The date should indicate the range of years of publication, when appropriate.

Barr, A., & Feigenbaum, E. A. (1981–1986). *The handbook of artificial intelligence* (Vols. 1–4). Reading, MA: Addison-Wesley.

9. Foreword, preface, introduction, or afterword   List the name of the author of the book element cited. Follow the date with the name of the element, the title of the book, and, in parentheses, the page number or numbers on which the element appears, preceded by *p.* or *pp.*

Weiss, B. (Ed.). (1982). Introduction. *American education and the European immigrant, 1840–1940* (pp. xi–xxviii). Urbana: University of Illinois Press.

10. Revised, republished, or reprinted work   For a revised edition of a book, give the edition number after the title.

Raimes, A. (2006). *Pocket keys for writers* (2nd ed.). Boston: Houghton Mifflin.

For a republished work, give the most recent date of publication after the author's name and at the end in parentheses add "Original work published" and the date. In your text citation, give both dates: (Smith, 1793/1976).

Smith, A. (1976). *An inquiry into the nature and causes of the wealth of nations.* Chicago: University of Chicago Press. (Original work published 1793)

APA (American Psychological Association)

For a reprint, begin the details in the parentheses with "Reprinted from," followed by the title, author, date, place, and publisher of the original work.

11. Technical report Give the report number ("Rep. No.") after the title.

Morgan, R., & Maneckshana, B. (2000). *AP students in college: An investigation of their course-taking patterns and college majors* (Rep. No. SR-2000-09). Princeton, NJ: Educational Testing Service.

12. Dissertation or abstract For a manuscript source, give the university and year of the dissertation and the volume and page numbers of *DAI*.

Salzberg, A. (1992). Behavioral phenomena of homeless women in San Diego County (Doctoral dissertation, United States International University, 1992). *Dissertation Abstracts International, 52,* 4482.

For a microfilm source, also include in parentheses at the end of the entry the university microfilm number. For a CD-ROM source, include "CD-ROM" after the title. Then name the electronic source of the information and the *DAI* number.

For an abstract published in a collection of abstracts, put "[Abstract]" after the title of the work and before the name of the source. For an online abstract, see 15e, item 23.

15d Sample APA entries: Print articles in periodicals

13. Article in a scholarly journal: pages numbered consecutively through each volume Give only the volume number and year for journals with consecutive pagination through a volume (for example, the first issue of volume 1 ends on page 174, and the second issue of volume 1 begins on page 175). Italicize the volume number and the following comma as well as the title of the journal. See 8b on recognizing a scholarly journal.

no quotation marks around article title

Kanazawa, S., & Still, M. C. (2000). Teaching may be hazardous to your

journal title, volume number, and commas italicized

marriage. *Evolution and Human Behavior, 21,* 185–190.

no "p." or "pp." before page numbers

SOURCE SHOT 6

Listing a Periodical Article (APA)

When listing a print periodical article, include the following:

❶ **Author(s)** Last name, initials (see also 15b on how to list authors)

❷ **(Date of publication of article)** In parentheses: year, month (not abbreviated), day, according to type of periodical (items 13–20)

❸ **Title of article: Any subtitle** No quotation marks; capitals only for first word of title, subtitle, and proper names

❹ *Name of journal or magazine, volume number,* or *name of newspaper* All italicized

❺ **Inclusive range of page numbers** All digits included (167–168). Do not use *p.* or *pp.* (except with pages of newspaper articles).

See items 13–20 for examples.

❶ Author   ❹ Magazine
    ❷ Date   ❸ Title   and volume
Stix, G. (2006, February). Owning the stuff of life. *Scientific American, 294,*
         ❺ Page numbers
    76–83.

14. Article in a scholarly journal: each issue paged separately
For journals in which each issue begins with page 1, include the issue number—in parentheses but not in italics—immediately after the volume number.

Ginat, R. (2000). The Soviet Union and the Syrian Ba'th regime: From
     hesitation to *rapprochement. Middle Eastern Studies, 36*(2),
     150–171.   issue number not in italics

15. Article in a magazine Include the year and month and any exact date of publication in parentheses. Do not abbreviate months. Italicize the name of the magazine, the volume number, and the comma that follows; then give the page number or numbers. See Source Shot 6 above for an example.

16. Article in a newspaper In parentheses, include the month and day of the newspaper after the year. Give the section letter or num-

Table of Contents

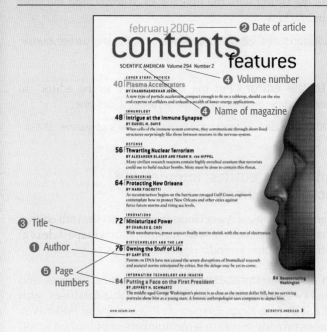

february 2006 — ❷ Date of article

contents
features

SCIENTIFIC AMERICAN Volume 294 Number 2

COVER STORY: PHYSICS
40 | **Plasma Accelerators**
BY CHANDRASHEKHAR JOSHI
A new type of particle accelerator, compact enough to fit on a tabletop, should cut the size
and expense of colliders and unleash a wealth of lower-energy applications.

IMMUNOLOGY
48 | **Intrigue at the Immune Synapse**
BY DANIEL M. DAVIS
When cells of the immune system converse, they communicate through short-lived
structures surprisingly like those between neurons in the nervous system.

DEFENSE
56 | **Thwarting Nuclear Terrorism**
BY ALEXANDER GLASER AND FRANK N. von HIPPEL
Many civilian research reactors contain highly enriched uranium that terrorists
could use to build nuclear bombs. More must be done to contain this threat.

ENGINEERING
64 | **Protecting New Orleans**
BY MARK FISCHETTI
As reconstruction begins on the hurricane-ravaged Gulf Coast, engineers
contemplate how to protect New Orleans and other cities against
fierce future storms and rising sea levels.

INNOVATIONS
72 | **Miniaturized Power**
BY CHARLES Q. CHOI
With nanobatteries, power sources finally start to shrink with the rest of electronics.

BIOTECHNOLOGY AND THE LAW
76 | **Owning the Stuff of Life**
BY GARY STIX
Patents on DNA have not caused the severe disruptions of biomedical research
and societal norms anticipated by critics. But the deluge may be yet to come.

INFORMATION TECHNOLOGY AND IMAGING
84 | **Putting a Face on the First President**
BY JEFFREY H. SCHWARTZ
The middle-aged George Washington's picture is as close as the nearest dollar bill, but no surviving
portraits show him as a young man. A forensic anthropologist uses computers to depict him.

84 Reconstructing Washington

www.sciam.com
SCIENTIFIC AMERICAN **3**

❹ Volume number

❹ Name of magazine

❸ Title

❶ Author

❺ Page numbers

ber before the page, where applicable. Use *p.* and *pp.* with page numbers. Do not omit *The* from the title of a newspaper or a magazine. For articles with no author, begin with the title.

Blakeslee, S. (2006, January 10). Cells that read minds. *The New York Times*, pp. F1, F4.

17. Article that skips pages When an article appears on discontinuous pages, give all the page numbers, separated by commas, as in item 16 above.

18. Review After the title of the review article, add in brackets a description of the work reviewed and identify the medium: book, film, or video, for example.

Madrick, J. (2006, January 12). The way to a fair deal [review of the book *The moral consequences of economic growth*]. *The New York Review of Books*, *53*, 37–40.

19. Unsigned editorial or article For a work with no author named, begin the listing with the title; for an editorial, add the label "Editorial" in brackets.

Spark the revolution [Editorial]. (2005, December 27). *The Wall Street Journal*, p. A20.

20. Letter to the editor Put the label "Letter to the editor" in brackets after the date or the title of the letter, if it has one.

Nichol, C. J. (2006, January). [Letter to the editor]. *Harper's Magazine, 312*, 6.

15e Sample APA entries: Internet and electronic sources

The American Psychological Association supplements the fifth edition of its *Publication Manual* with a Web site (http://www.apastyle.org) offering citation examples, periodic updates, and tips.

21. Work in an online database Many universities, libraries, and organizational Web sites subscribe to large searchable databases, such as *InfoTrac, EBSCO, LexisNexis, FirstSearch, PsycINFO,* and *WilsonWeb.* These databases provide access to large numbers of published scholarly abstracts and full-text articles.

See Source Shot 7 on pages 226–27 for an example.

22. Newspaper article retrieved from database or Web site Newspaper articles, as well as journal articles, are often available from several sources, in several databases and in a variety of formats, such as in a university online subscription database. Do not insert a period when the entry ends with a URL.

Wade, N. (2000, May 9). Scientists decode Down syndrome chromosome. *The New York Times,* p. F4. Retrieved January 2, 2006, from LexisNexis Academic Universe database.

Eisenberg, A. (2005, February 24). For simpler robots, a step forward. *The New York Times*. Retrieved January 3, 2006, from http://www.nytimes.com

no period at end of URL

23. Online abstract, review, editorial, or letter For an abstract retrieved from a database or from a Web site, begin the retrieval statement with the words "Abstract retrieved" followed by the date and the name of the database or by the URL of the Web site, with no period at the end.

Frith, H., & Gleeson, K. (2004). Clothing and embodiment: Men managing body image and appearance. *Psychology of Men & Masculinity, 5,* 40–48. Abstract retrieved January 5, 2006, from http://content.apa .org/journals/men/5/1/40.html

For an online review, editorial, or letter, provide the appropriate term in the retrieval statement.

24. Online article with a print source If information such as page numbers or figures is missing (as in HTML versions) or if the document may have additions or alterations, give full retrieval information.

Jones, C. C., & Meredith, W. (2000, June). Developmental paths of psychological health from early adolescence to later adulthood. *Psychology and Aging, 15,* 351–360. Retrieved January 6, 2006, from http://content.apa.org/journals/pag/15/2/351.html

However, if you access an article in PDF format (with page numbers visible and charts exactly the same as in the print version), cite it exactly as if you had read it in print, with the addition of "[Electronic version]" after the title of the article.

Campos, G. P. (2004, September). What are cultural models for? Child-rearing practices in historical perspective [Electronic version]. *Culture & Psychology, 10,* 279–291.

25. Article in an online journal with no print source

Holtzworth-Munroe, A. (2000, June). Domestic violence: Combining scientific inquiry and advocacy. *Prevention & Treatment, 3,* Article 22. Retrieved January 2, 2006, from http://journals.apa.org/prevention/volume3/ pre0030022c.html

26. Authored document on Web site

Delisio, E. (2002, June 24). No Child Left Behind: What it means to you. *Education World.* Retrieved January 5, 2006, from http://www.educationworld.com/a_issues/issues273.shtml

APA

(American Psychological Association)

SOURCE SHOT 7

Listing a Work in an Electronic Database (APA)

To cite a work in an electronic database, provide as much of the following information as you can find:

❶ **Author(s)** Last name, initials

❷ **(Date of work)** In parentheses, including whatever is necessary (items 13–16) and available of year, month (not abbreviated), day ("n.d." if no date is available)

❸ **Title of work: Subtitle** No quotation marks; capitals only for first word of title and subtitle and for proper names

❹ **Print publication information** *Name of periodical* (italicized) with *volume number* for journals and magazines (volume number and surrounding commas italicized) and inclusive *page numbers* if given on screen

❺ **Retrieval statement** "Retrieved" followed by your date of access (month day, year,) "from" followed by name of database

See examples and variations in items 21–23.

```
┌─────── ❶ Authors ───────┐  ❷ Date  ┌────────── ❸ Title ──────────┐
Goldstein, B. S. C., & Harris, K. C. (2000). Consultant practices in two
```

```
┌──────────────────────────────┐  ┌── ❹ Print publication information ──
heterogeneous Latino schools. The School Psychology Review, 29,
page numbers
┌──┐         ┌────────── ❺ Retrieval statement ──────────
368–377. Retrieved January 25, 2006, from WilsonWeb Education
                                          comma
┌──────────────────┐
Full Text database.
                    final period
```

27. Document on Web site, no author

Freedom of Information Act. (2005, June 1). *Federal Relations and Information Policy.* Retrieved January 3, 2006, from http://www.arl .org/info/frn/gov/foia/index.html#overview

28. Entire Web site, no author   Italicize the title of the Web page. Alphabetize by the first major word of the title.

Online Database

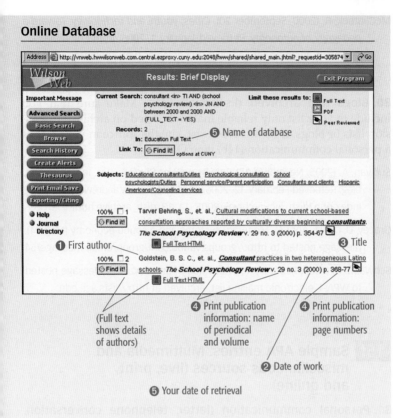

① First author

③ Title

(Full text shows details of authors)

④ Print publication information: name of periodical and volume

④ Print publication information: page numbers

② Date of work

⑤ Name of database

⑤ Your date of retrieval

NPR/Kaiser/Kennedy School Education Survey. (1999). Retrieved January 5, 2006, from http://www.npr.org/programs/specials/poll/education/ education.results.html

29. Document on a university or government site Italicize the title of the document. In the retrieval statement, give the name of the university or government agency (and the department or division if it is named). Follow this with a colon and the URL.

APA

(American Psychological Association)

McClintock, R. (2000, September 20). *Cities, youth, and technology: Toward a pedagogy of autonomy*. Retrieved January 1, 2006, from Columbia University, Institute for Learning Technologies Web site: http://www.ilt .columbia.edu/publications/cities/cyt.html

30. Blogs and archived discussion lists Make sure that you include in your list only reliable material posted on archived discussion lists or blogs. If no archives exist, cite the source in your text as a personal communication (14b, item O).

Sullivan, A. (2005, November 17). Department of tough issues. In *Daily Dish* blog. Retrieved February 12, 2006, from http://www.andrewsullivan.com/ index.php?dish_inc=archives/2005_11_13_dish_archive.html

Gracey, D. (2001, April 6). Monetary systems and a sound economy [Msg 54]. Message posted to http://groups.yahoo.com/group/email/message/54

Schwalm, D. (2005, February 15). Re: Value of an education. Message posted to WPA–L electronic mailing list, archived at http://lists.asu.edu

15f Sample APA entries: Multimedia and miscellaneous sources (live, print, and online)

31. Personal communication (letter, telephone conversation, interview, personal e-mail) Cite only in the body of your text as "personal communication." Do not include these communications in your list of references (see 14b, item O).

32. Conference paper

Szenher, M. (2005, September). Visual homing with learned goal distance information. Paper presented at the 3rd International Symposium on Autonomous Minirobots for Research and Edutainment, Fukui, Japan.

33. Poster session

Szenher, M. (2005, September). Visual homing in natural environments. Poster session presented at the annual meeting of Towards Autonomous Robotic Systems, London, U.K.

APA

(American Psychological Association)

34. Film   Identify the medium (motion picture, videocassette, DVD, etc.) in brackets after the title. Give the country where a film was released, or give the city for other formats.

Berman, S. S., & Pulcini, R. (Directors). (2003). *American splendor* [Motion picture]. United States: Fine Line Features.

Jacquet, L. (Director). (2005). *The march of the penguins* [DVD]. Burbank, CA: Warner Home Video.

35. Television or Radio Program

Gazit, C. (Writer). (2004). The Seeds of Destruction [Television series episode]. In D. J. James (Producer), *Slavery and the Making of America.* New York: WNET.

36. CD-ROM or DVD   Identify the medium in square brackets after the title.

Jones, M. (2005). *Who is Mike Jones?* [CD-ROM]. Houston, TX: Swishahouse.

World of warcraft [CD-ROM]. (2004). Irvine, CA: Blizzard Entertainment.

37. Computer software   Do not use italics for the name of the software.

Scilab (Version 3.1.1) [Computer software]. (2005). France: Institut National de Recherche en Informatique et en Automatique. Retrieved from http://www.scilab.org

Chapter **16**

A Student's Research Paper, APA Style

The paper that follows was written by Katelyn Davies when she was a junior at Trinity University, San Antonio, Texas, majoring in communication. She wrote the paper in June 2005 for Dr. Aaron Delwiche's course "Games for the Web: Ethnography of Massively Multiplayer Games" in the Communication department. The assignment was designed to introduce the students to quantitative and qualitative research methods within the limitations of the research setting, as expressed by the instructor:

> Time was too short to pursue in-depth ethnographic research, and sample sizes were too small to extrapolate with confidence to the broader gaming community. For many of the students, it was the first time that they had undertaken a research project of this scope. Nevertheless, this work reflects the efforts of a new generation of scholars grappling with the social significance of this vital medium. (Delwiche: http://www.trinity.edu/adelwich/mmo/students.html)

Davies concentrated on the game *World of Warcraft,* playing it herself to study her own reactions in comparison to what she discovered in her research survey. Her avatar in the game (the physical representation of her character on screen in the game) was Llandellyse, as shown in the attached image. Her paper is excerpted here, with annotations pointing out issues of formatting (red) and organization (blue). For her complete, interesting, and well-documented study, go to the Online Study Center.

An online avatar

World of Warcraft® provided courtesy of Blizzard Entertainment, Inc.

Addiction to Virtual Worlds 1

5 spaces

1" margin

APA (American Psychological Association)

Running head: ADDICTION TO VIRTUAL WORLDS

Capitals here

Addiction to Virtual Worlds: An Enticing Hobby,

or a Social Problem?

Katelyn Davies

Trinity University, San Antonio, TX

Midway on page: centered title, writer's name, and writer's affiliation

This is formal APA submission style. Your instructor may prefer your course name and number and date here.

APA

(American Psychological Association)

Heading
centered

Abstract

This paper investigates Massively Multi-Player Online Role Playing Games (MMORPGs) in society and the effects they have on players and their real-life responsibilities. While some scholars and media professionals have expressed concern regarding the addictive aspects of these games, players compare their habits and motivations for playing to other hobbies that provide escape and an enjoyable experience. The author conducted in-depth interviews and questionnaires with gamers in order to examine the social, psychological, and emotional needs that players satisfy in virtual worlds, such as *World of Warcraft*. The attractions and motivations that compel gamers to participate in virtual worlds are examined with respect to symptoms and behaviors that illustrate an addiction. A disparity between levels of experience in players and their reactions to addictive aspects of the game suggests a learning curve where more experienced players learn to recognize and disregard those factors in the game that may facilitate "addictive" behaviors.

Length:
151 words
(aim for
100–175)

Passive
voice
common in
accounts
of research

Summary
of results
of study

Addiction to Virtual Worlds   3

Addiction to Virtual Worlds: An Enticing Hobby,

or a Social Problem?

Title centered, not underlined

MMORPGs such as *World of Warcraft* have instigated concern in scholars and the press about the usage patterns and habits of the players. Often, doctors cite extreme cases of neglect of oneself and others in order to bring attention to this social phenomenon of popularity and addiction (Orzack, as cited in Steinkuehler, 2004). Indeed, certain factors and attributes that can promote or amplify addictive behaviors are present in these games, and are also cited as reasons for playing. The amount of time players spend in virtual worlds and the real life consequences of playing are seen by some as indicators of a new and dangerous addiction. However, players themselves compare their playing habits to any other hobby or activity that pleases and excites its user. Where can the line be drawn between addiction and proclivity? Does the fact that MMORPGs entice people and keep them playing necessarily mean that these games facilitate addictive behavior and negligence towards responsibilities? Doesn't it make a difference that these games often satisfy some important emotional, social, and psychological needs of players? We can surmise that MMORPGs provide players with valuable relationships, interactions, and learning experiences that do not necessarily detract from the real life counterparts of these fulfillments. However, why is it that players often choose to satisfy

Annotations (margin labels):

1" margin

Indirect citation (14b, item E)

Research questions

Hypothesis

Addiction to Virtual Worlds   4

these needs or desires in virtual worlds? From data collected in research, game play, and interviews, the answer is that a) they *can,* and b) it's *fun.* As simplified as this answer may seem, the nature of the game and the virtual environment promote (mostly) consistent and enjoyable ways for players to satisfy emotional, social, and psychological needs and desires. An attachment can be formed to friends made, avatars created, or environments explored, but the attachment and enjoyment that results from game play should not warrant the same concern that scholars assert toward gambling and narcotic addiction. True, some players allow their habits to negatively affect their responsibilities and obligations, but these players do not represent the majority. My research indicates that the more experience players have with these environments, the easier it is for them to manage both their virtual and real life responsibilities and recreations.

Literature Review

The Psychology of Addiction

Psychologists have studied certain aspects of psychological makeup that may amplify people's susceptibility toward addiction. Apparently, some of these personal qualities are especially catered to by the Internet and online games. Findings by Gabel et al. (1999) state that novelty seeking, or the need for "new, exciting, challenging, or varied experiences," is highly correlated with the misuse and abuse of substances (p. 103).

Margin notes: Indicates results of research and confirmation of hypothesis | Subhead italicized | Begins detailing relevant background material | "et al." for 5 authors (14b, item B) | No extra space around headings | Year in parentheses | Page number for a quotation

Introduces game that is focus of study

World of Warcraft and other MMORPGs present players with a variety of different quests to fulfill, areas to explore, monsters to kill, and people to meet. Shyness has also been a personality trait associated with Internet addiction. The Internet provides a simplified medium for communication that erects a shield between users, thus allowing people with insecure social skills to interact more comfortably and openly (Chak & Leung, 2004).

Ampersand within parentheses

[The Literature Review continues for about four pages, with the subheads *Attractions and Motivations* (focusing on Yee's research) and *Immersion, Engagement, and Flow* (focusing on McMahan's work).]

Main heading centered

Method

The purpose of this project was to determine the qualities of virtual environments that lead players to form attachments and addictive behaviors. Why are players so eager to satisfy their psychological, social, and emotional needs in virtual worlds? What aspects of MMORPGs encourage addiction in players, and how do players respond to the attachment that can result from extensive game play?

In order to answer these questions, open-ended questionnaires were distributed and in-depth interviews were conducted. The content of both methods was generally similar, although the interview allowed for a more interactive setting where responses could incite reactions and further probing where needed. Questions referred to time invested in

Passive voice for description of method

gaming; habits of game play such as grouping and reward reinforcement; characteristics of relationships with others; motivations such as shyness and escape; novelty seeking; mastery and control; and indications of flow, immersion, and engagement. The interview questions can be found in the appendix at the end of this paper.

Participants and Procedure

Subhead
italicized

The questionnaires and in-depth interviews were conducted with college students, game developers, and experienced gamers. The range of experience in MMORPGs varied from five months to eight years; a few gamers admitted to playing seven days of the week, while most said 3–5 days, depending on other time obligations and workload. The final sample for this study was acquired from college students (5 participants) and gamers on forums online (4 participants). I posted a thread on multiple MMORPG forums, requesting responses from gamers about playing habits and motivations and asking them to state a preference of method—a survey sent through e-mail, or an interview in-game or on AOL Instant Messenger. Most of my responses from students were in interview form through AOL Instant Messenger, whereas forum responses were conducted via open-ended questionnaires sent through e-mail. While I requested subjects on multiple forums, one forum in particular was much more willing to assist in research, and my thread stayed on the

Details of
participants

Addiction to Virtual Worlds   7

first page for a few days, resulting in replies and private messages of interest and encouragement. One interviewee informed me that older players, with an average age of about 28, mostly visited the forum. Their experience in virtual worlds may have contributed to their willingness to help. In addition to interviews and surveys, weblogs and sites of interest were consulted to obtain insight into more player habits and discussions of MMORPG addiction. After the in-depth interviews and questionnaires were conducted, the responses were coded according to which concept discussed in the literature review the response referred to. Each participant was assigned an arbitrary alias in order to ensure confidentiality; these pseudonyms are referred to in the Results section after quotations (axe, bear, jester, etc.).

Results and Discussion

The results from research indicate a definitive player's perspective on the characteristics of play behavior, habits, and investment. The names of the correspondents were created randomly in order to protect the identities of the project participants. The most common game attraction in responses referred to the network of relationships formed and maintained in the game.

> *My friends are pretty much the reason I keep coming back for more—if it wasn't for them I'd have gotten bored ages ago.—axe*

Provides direct evidence from interview responses

APA

(American Psychological Association)

The idea that grouping in MMORPGs is almost necessary once a certain level of difficulty in the game is reached is evident in most players' preference to playing in groups, membership in a guild, or at least some experience in group play. Groups and guilds often establish specific times to hold meetings or complete quests and dungeons, and dedication to a group or guild is an important aspect of membership.

> *When I was in a guild . . . we would have scheduled events that most people were expected to attend. . . . There were consequences for those who missed too many events.* —jester
>
> *I'll start a dungeon, and you won't want to get up in the middle of the dungeon because a) your party will f _ _ _ ing hate you forever if you bail on them in a dungeon, and b) sometimes it takes a lot of effort to get a decent party for a dungeon.* —koala

This obligation to fulfill certain roles in groups, along with simply being present for events, can increase a player's time investment as well as provide him/her with a necessary reason for playing. If social relationships are an important aspect of game play, then fulfilling commitments to online friends is a necessary activity. The difficulty of forming valuable groups with strangers to complete certain quests, dungeons, or instances was expressed by multiple players.

APA (American Psychological Association)

Addiction to Virtual Worlds   9

I prefer to stick with my friends in groups—by and large
I don't like to look for pick-up groups. —axe
[I usually group with the] same people. I almost never
group with strangers, as they can be self-centered and
extremely immature as a rule. —bear

[The Results section continues for about five pages as Davies uses quotations from her survey responses to make connections with and comment on the important concepts in the literature review. Davies then analyzes the limitations of her research.]

This research has some limitations. First, the sample involved is extremely small and cannot be representative of the entire gaming community in any way; nine interviews from two main sources cannot be generalized to the 1.5 million subscribers to *World of Warcraft* alone, not to mention the plethora of other MMORPGs available. Similarly, the time allotted to conduct this research was much shorter than the amount of time necessary to receive quantifiable data from a multitude of sources. Another problem lies in the ability of potentially addicted players to accurately recognize and portray their gaming habits and behaviors. Whereas a player may say his/her "hobby" is under control, sources close to the subject may beg to differ. I attempted to tackle this problem in one question of the survey, which asked, "If I asked your roommates if your time responses were accurate, would

Discusses limitations of the study and suggests follow-up

they agree with you?" My responses to this question were overwhelmingly positive, which may suggest a problem, but at the same time, heavy players willingly offered up answers of extensive playing times. If more time could be dedicated, a brief interview with a source close to the respondent could clear up any discrepancies in behaviors reported by players.

Another problem may lie in my lack of attention to the extreme cases often cited by doctors and researchers investigating this topic. These cases of addiction and neglect are not hard to find; in fact, an entire forum exists for loved ones of addicted players and "cured" players who once had a serious addiction. The extremes do exist, and serious problems can result from extensive game play. However, my reasons for not focusing on these data lie in the fact that previous researchers used these extremes to imply a norm, and they assumed that an addiction would necessarily lead to dangerous consequences for players and their loved ones. While reviewing the thoughts of players on this topic, I recognized an obvious frustration with these assumptions and the existence of an in-group vs. out-group perspective. Gamers, especially those who were able to control their playing, were exhausted with and annoyed at doctors and journalists who freely applied such a negative label without much experience in the game and with the gaming community.

APA (American Psychological Association)

[Discussion now takes up the term "addiction," which Davies deliberately did not use in her research in order to avoid "the bias of a preliminary negative assumption." She then moves to her Conclusion section.]

Conclusion

These multiple factors of addiction and symbols of addictive behavior express the ability of games to entice some players into the virtual worlds and keep them there, always wanting more. However, some players experience a few of these aspects and are aware of the rest, but do not allow them to influence their behaviors or habits of game play. It seems as if the more experienced players have caught on to the addictive aspects of the games and allowed themselves to play without being heavily influenced by these qualities of MMORPGs. Although they may play for extended periods of time (some cited seven days a week), they also claim that their responsibilities and obligations in the real world are not negatively influenced by game play. Specific questions were integrated into the survey that were directly taken from Dr. Greenfield's Virtual Addiction Test (1999). When asked about concerns from friends or family members, most experienced players stated that if, or when, these concerns were stated, they scaled down their playing time appropriately.

Others gauged their amount of time spent playing depending on the amount of work and other real world obligations they had at the time. Most did not lose sleep, were

Supports hypothesis

Addiction to Virtual Worlds   12

not preoccupied with the game when not playing, and
explicitly expressed their priorities of work before play. While
many players, experienced and new alike, expressed playing as
a form of escape, they compared this escape to any activity a
person would take to relieve stress or relax, such as watching
television, going out to a bar, or exercising. Rheingold (1993,
p. 152) cites Pavel Curtis, the creator of LambdaMOO, in his
discussion of the addictive nature of MUDs:

> These are very enticing places for a segment of the
> community. And it's not like the kinds of addictions
> we've dealt with as a society in the past. If they're out of
> control, I think that's a problem. But if someone is
> spending a large portion of their time being social with
> people who live thousands of miles away, you can't say
> they've turned inward. They aren't shunning society.
> They're actively seeking it. They're probably doing it
> more actively than anyone around them. It's a whole
> new ballgame.

This concept of communication and relationship-seeking
activities in players can still be applied today to MMORPGs.

[The Conclusion section continues for a few more pages,
describing the responses of less experienced players and
relating the desire for procrastination and escape to the general frustrations of college life, not necessarily tied to games.
Davies finds in her research "a *desire* to play more than a
need."]

Gives author, date, and page of work in which Curtis quotation was found

Long quotation indented five spaces

Interview Questions

- How long have you been playing MMORPGs?
- On average, how many days of the week do you play MMORPGs/*World of Warcraft*?
- How much time do you usually spend online during each gaming session?
- Do you often find that you intend to play for a certain amount of time, but end up spending considerably more time playing than originally planned?
- If I asked your roommates if your time responses were accurate, would they agree with you?
- How many different characters do you play?
- What are the levels of each of these characters?
- Why do you play?
- Do you find yourself extending your play time after a minor setback or when you're close to completing a quest/leveling up/acquiring a desired item, etc., in order to get that one last thing?

[The list continues for a total of 33 questions.]

APA (American Psychological Association)

Addiction to Virtual Worlds   14

References

Adams, E. (2002, July). *Stop calling games "addictive"!* Retrieved April 23, 2005, from www.gamasutra.com/features/ 20020727/adams_01.htm

Chak, K., & Leung, L. (2004). Shyness and locus of control as predictors of Internet addiction and Internet use [Electronic version]. *CyberPsychology & Behavior, 7*(5), 559–570.

Chou, T., & Ting, C. (2003). The role of flow experience in cyber-game addiction. *CyberPsychology & Behavior, 6*(6), 663–676.

Eysenck, H. J. (1997). Addiction, personality and motivation [Electronic version]. *Human Psychopharmacology, 12,* S79–S87.

Gabel, S., Stallings, M., Schmitz, S., Young, S., & Fulker, D. (1999). Personality dimensions and substance misuse: Relationships in adolescents, mothers and fathers [Electronic version]. *The American Journal of Addictions, 8,* 101–113.

Greenfield, D. (1999). *Virtual addiction: Help for netheads, cyberfreaks and those who love them.* Oakland, CA: New Harbinger Publications.

McMahan, A. (2003). Immersion, engagement, and presence: A method for analyzing 3-D video games. In M. Wolf and B. Perron (Eds.), *The video game theory reader* (pp. 67–86). Oxford, UK: Routledge.

New page for references, double-spaced

Year in parentheses after authors

Hanging indents

Last names first (15c, item 2)

Alphabetical organization

URL split after a slash

Italics extend through volume number and commas

Names of editors not reversed

Addiction to Virtual Worlds   15

Rheingold, H. (1993). *The virtual community: Homesteading on the electronic frontier.* New York: Harper Perennial.

Steinkuehler, C. (2004). American Psychological Association joins the fray. In *TerraNova.* Retrieved April 23, 2005, from http://terranova.blogs.com/terra_nova/2004/06/onlinevideogame.html

Tobold. (2005, February 25). WoW Journal-Day 15. In *Tobold's MMORPG Blog.* Retrieved May 4, 2005, from http://tobolds.blogspot.com/2005_02_01_tobolds_archive.html

Yee, N. (2002). Ariadne: Understanding MMORPG addiction. Retrieved April 12, 2005, from http://www.nickyee.com/hub/addiction/home.html

No period after URL

Retrieved from a blog (15e, item 30)

Commas after date and year

CSE

(Council of Science Editors)

Chapter **17**

The CSE Style of Documentation in the Sciences

This chapter describes the documentation style recommended for all scientific disciplines by the Council of Science Editors (CSE), previously the Council of Biology Editors, in *Scientific Style and Format: The CSE Manual for Authors, Editors, and Publishers*, 7th ed. (New York: Cambridge University Press, 2006). This new edition describes three systems of documentation for citing the elements necessary to "ensure retrievability of the cited documents" (p. xii). One is a name-year system similar to APA style, in which the in-text citation includes author(s) and year of publication. Another is a citation-sequence system that numbers and lists sources in the order in which they are cited in the paper. The third is a citation-name system that also gives numbers to citations but organizes and numbers the list of references alphabetically by author or title, so citation numbers in the text are not sequential.

This last option is the one used in *The CSE Manual* itself. Because the name-year system is so similar to APA and because citations for the citation-sequence and citation-name systems differ only in the numbering, this chapter concentrates on examples of entries for those last two citation systems.

17a Two basic features of CSE citation styles

Always check with your instructors about documentation style guidelines. Some may not specify one particular style but will ask you to select one and use it consistently.

KEY POINTS
Two Basic Features of CSE Citation-Sequence or Citation-Name Style

1. *In the text of your paper,* number each reference with a super-script number in a smaller size than the type for the text, or place the reference number on the line within parentheses. Place punctuation *after* the superscript number (new to 7th edition).

2. *At the end of your paper,* list the references by number. For the *citation-sequence system,* arrange and number the references in your list in the order in which you cite them in your paper. The first citation that appears in your paper will be 1, and the first reference in your list (also number 1) will give information about that first citation. Therefore, an author's name beginning with Z could be number 1 and listed first if it is the first source to be cited in your paper.

    For the *citation-name system,* arrange and number the references in your list alphabetically by author (or title when no author is known). The first citation number in your paper will then match the alphabetical placement. The citation numbered 1 in your text could appear anywhere in your text but the reference will appear first in your alphabetical list of references, probably among the As or Bs. An author's name beginning with Z is therefore likely to appear near the end of your list and to be numbered accordingly, wherever the citation appears in your paper.

    For either system, begin the list on a new page and title it "References."

CSE

(Council of Science Editors)

Example of documenting a periodical article

In-Text Number Citation	Numbered Entry in List of References
The mutation may prevent degradation of unknown substrates leading to their accumulation in Lewy bodies in neuronal cells[6].	6. De Silva HR, Khan NL, Wood NW. The genetics of Parkinson's disease. Curr Opin Genet Dev. 2000; 10(3):292–298

17b CSE in-text citations (citation-sequence and citation-name styles)

Use superscript numbers to refer readers to the list of references at the end of your paper.

superscript number
One summary of studies of the life span of the fruit fly[1] has shown . . .

Refer to more than one entry in the reference list as follows:

Two studies of the life span of the fruit fly[1,2] have shown that . . .

Several studies of the life span of the fruit fly[1–4] have shown that . . .

Studies of the fruit fly are plentiful[1–4], but the most revealing is . . .

17c How to list CSE references (citation-sequence and citation-name systems)

KEY POINTS

Setting Up the CSE List of Cited References

1. After the last page of your paper, attach the list of references, headed "References" or "Cited References."

2. Arrange and number the works either (1) consecutively in the order in which you mention them in your paper or (2) alphabetically. Invert all authors' names, and use the initials of first and middle names. Use no punctuation between last names and initials, and leave no space between initials.

3. Begin each entry with the note number followed by a period and a space. Do not indent the first line of each entry; indent subsequent lines to align beneath the first letter on the previous line.

4. Do not italicize, underline, or use quotation marks for the titles of articles, books, or journals and other periodicals.

5. Capitalize only the first word of a book or article title, and capitalize any proper nouns.

6. Abbreviate titles of journals and organizations.

7. Use a period between major divisions of each entry.

8. Use a semicolon and a space between the name of the publisher (not abbreviated in the new 7th edition) and the publication date of a book. Use a semicolon with no space between the date and the volume number of a journal.

9. For books, you may give the total number of pages, followed by a space and "p." For journal articles, give inclusive page spans, using all the digits: 135–136.

10. For online sources, provide author, title, print publication information, date and place of online publication, your date of access, and the URL.

17d Examples of entries in a CSE citation-sequence or citation-name system

1. Whole book, with one author

title not underlined,
no punctuation ┌──────── only first word capitalized ────────┐
1. Finch CE. Longevity, senescence and the genome. Chicago:
initials with no periods between

┌────────── publisher ──────────┐ semicolon number of pages in book
The University of Chicago Press; 1990. 922 p. (optional)

2. Part of a book

Include inclusive page numbers for the excerpt, specific reference, or quotation.

2. Thomas L. The medusa and the snail. New York: Viking Press; 1979. On cloning a human being; p. 51–56.

3. Book with two or more authors

List all the authors.

  all authors'
 ┌─ names inverted ─┐
3. Ferrini AF, Ferrini RL. Health in the later years. 2nd ed. Dubuque (IA):
  Brown & Benchmark; 1993. 470 p.
     semicolon after publisher

4. Book with editor(s)

4. Aluja M, Norrbom AL, editors. Fruit flies (tephritidae): Phylogeny and
  evolution of behavior. Boca Raton (FL): CRC Press; 2000. 984 p.

5. Article in a scholarly journal

      no spaces in information about journal
5. Kowald A, Kirkwood TB. Explaining fruit fly longevity. Science. 1993;260:
           volume number

 1664–1665.
   complete page span

In a journal paginated by issue, include the issue number in parentheses after the volume number.

6. Newspaper or magazine article

Give the full name of the newspaper, the edition, the date, and the first page and column number of the article.

6. Pollack A. Custom-made microbes, at your service. The New York Times
  (Late Ed.). 2006 Jan 17;Sect F:1 (col. 5).

7. Article with no author identified Begin with the title of the article.

8. Audiovisual materials Begin the entry with the title, followed by the medium, such as *CD-ROM* or *DVD*, in brackets. Then include the author (if known), producer, place, publisher, and date. Include a description, such as number of disks or cassettes, length, color or black and white, and accompanying material. End with a statement of availability, if necessary.

8. AIDS in Africa: living with a time bomb [videocassette]. Princeton (NJ):
  Films for the Humanities and Sciences; 1991. 33 min, sound, color, 1/2 in.

9. Electronic journal article with a print source Cite as for a print journal article, and include the type of medium in brackets after the journal title. Include any document number, the accession date "[cited (year, month, date)]," and an availability statement with the URL.

9. Jones CC, Meredith W. Developmental paths of psychological health from early adolescence to later adulthood. Psych Aging [Internet]. 2000 [cited 2006 Jan 18];15(2):351–360. Available from: http://www.psycinfo.com

10. Electronic journal article with no print source If no print source is available, provide an estimate of the length of the document in pages, paragraphs, or screens. Place the information in square brackets, such as "[about 3 p.]," "[15 paragraphs]," or "[about 6 screens]."

10. Holtzworth-Munroe A. Domestic violence: Combining scientific inquiry and advocacy. Prev Treatment [Internet]. 2000 Jun 2 [cited 2006 Jan 20];3 [about 6 p.]. Available from: http://journals.apa.org/prevention/volume3/pre0030022c.html

11. Article in an electronic database After author, title, and print publication information, give the name of the database, the designation in square brackets "[database on the Internet]," any date of posting or modification, or the copyright date. Follow this with the date of access, the approximate length of the article, the URL, and any accession number.

11. Mayor S. New treatment improves symptoms of Parkinson's disease. BMJ. 2002;324(7344):997. In: PubMedCentral [database on the Internet]; c2002 [cited 2006 Jan 19]. [about 1 screen]. Available from: http://www.pubmedcentral.gov/articlerender.fcgi?tool=pmcentrez&artid=1122999

12. Web page Give author (if available) and title of page followed by "[Internet]." Follow this with any available information about place of home page publication and sponsor, and then include date of publication or copyright date, along with any update. End with your date of citation and the URL.

12. Anemia and iron therapy [Internet]. Hinsdale (IL): Medtext, Inc.; c1995-2006 [cited 2006 Jan 20]. Available from: http://www.hdcn.com/ch/rbc/

13. Posting to a discussion list After the author's name and the subject line of the message, give information about the discussion list, including name of list; place and sponsor, if available; year, date, and time of posting; date of citation; and approximate length of the posting. End with an availability statement of the address of the discussion list or the archive.

13. Bishawi AH. Summary: hemangioendothelioma of the larynx. In: MEDLIB-L [discussion list on the Internet]. [Buffalo (NY): State University of NY]; 2002 May 6, 11:25am [cited 2006 Jan 19]. [about 4 screens]. Available from: MEDLIBL@listserv.acsu.buffalo.edu; item 087177.

17e A student's list of references (CSE)

The following list of references for a paper on "Research Findings and Disputes about Fruit Fly Longevity" shows the CSE citation-sequence numbering system (in which Kowald's article is the first to be cited in the paper). Note the use of abbreviations and punctuation.

Fruit fly longevity 17

Cited References

1. Kowald A, Kirkwood TB. Explaining fruit fly longevity. Science. 1993;260:1664–1665.

2. Finch CE. Longevity, senescence and the genome. Chicago: The University of Chicago Press; 1990. 922 p.

3. Carey JR, Liedo P, Orozco D, Vaupel JW. Slowing of mortality rates at older ages in large medfly cohorts. Science. 1992;258:457.

4. Skrecky D. Fly longevity database. In Cryonet [discussion list on the Internet]. 1997 Jun 22. [cited 2006 Feb 21]. [about 12 screens]. Available from: http://www.cryonet.org/cgi-bin/dsp.cgi?msg=8339

For the citation-name system, the references would be ordered alphabetically and numbered (in the text as well as in the list) as follows, with the rest of each list entry remaining the same:

1. Carey

2. Finch

3. Kowald

4. Skrecky

Chapter **18**

Chicago Manual of Style: Endnotes, Footnotes, and Bibliography

Chicago

(Chicago Manual of Style)

As an alternative to an author/year citation style similar to the APA system, *The Chicago Manual of Style,* 15th ed. (Chicago: University of Chicago Press, 2003), describes a system in which sources are documented in footnotes or endnotes. This system is used widely in the humanities, especially in history and art history.

Use endnotes, not footnotes, for material you publish online. For a *Chicago*-style paper, include an unnumbered title page, and number the first page of your text as page "2."

18a Two basic features of *Chicago* endnotes and footnotes

KEY POINTS

Two Basic Features of *Chicago* Endnotes and Footnotes

1. Place a superscript numeral at the end of the quotation or the sentence in which you mention source material; place the number after all punctuation marks except a dash.

2. List all endnotes—single-spaced, but double-spaced between notes, unless your instructor prefers double-spaced throughout—on a separate numbered page at the end of the paper, and number the notes sequentially, as they appear in your paper. Your word processing program will automatically place footnotes at the bottom of each page (Insert/Footnote). See 20a.

Example of an endnote or footnote for a book

In-Text Citation with Numeral	Numbered Endnote or Footnote
For footnote (source at bottom of page): Mondrian planned his compositions with colored tape.[3]	3. H. Harvard Arnason and Marla F. Prather, *History of Modern Art* (New York: Abrams, 1998), 393.
For endnote (mentioning source): According to Arnason and Prather, Mondrian planned his compositions with colored tape.[3]	

18b *Chicago* in-text citations, notes, and bibliography

In-text citation Use the following format, and number your notes sequentially.

George Eliot thought that *Eliot* was a "good, mouth-filling, easy to pronounce word."[1]

If you use endnotes and not footnotes, mention the source in your text so that readers do not have to go to the end to find the source. If you include at the end of your paper a bibliography listing all the sources cited in your notes (see 18h), then the note citation can be concise. If no bibliography is attached, give full information about a source the first time you include it in your notes.

First note for a source when a full bibliography is included   A bibliography includes full publication details, so in a short note, only the author's last name, a shortened form of the title, and the page number (if a specific reference is made) are necessary. Indent the first line of the note.

author's last name   short title   page number for a specific reference or a quotation
1. Crompton, *George Eliot*, 123.

Entry in bibliography (first line not indented)

Crompton, Margaret. *George Eliot: The Woman.* London: Cox and Wyman, 1960.

Full first note for a source when no bibliography is included

author's name   title italic, all important
— in normal order —   — words capitalized —
1. Margaret Crompton, *George Eliot: The Woman* (London: Cox and

comma   page number
Wyman, 1960), 123.

Note referring to the immediately preceding source   In a reference to the immediately preceding source, you may use "Ibid." (Latin *ibidem*, meaning "in the same place") instead of repeating the author's name and the title of the work. All the details except the page number must be the same as in the previous citation. If the page number is the same, too, omit it following "Ibid."

2. Ibid., 127.

However, avoid a series of "ibid." notes. These are likely to irritate your reader. Instead, place page references within your text: *As Crompton points out (127),* . . .

Any subsequent reference to a previously cited source   For a reference to a source cited in a previous note, but not in the immediately preceding note, give only the author and page number. However, if you cite more than one work by the same author, include a short title to identify the source.

6. Crompton, 124.

18c How to format *Chicago* endnotes and footnotes

KEY POINTS
Guidelines for *Chicago* Endnotes and Footnotes

1. In the list of endnotes, place each number on the line (not as a superscript), followed by a period and one space. For footnotes, word processing software will often automatically make the number a superscript number—just be consistent with whatever format you use.

2. Indent the first line of each entry three or five spaces. Single-space within a note and double-space between notes, unless your instructor prefers double-spacing throughout.

3. Use the author's full name, not inverted, followed by a comma and the title of the work. Put quotation marks around article titles, and italicize titles of books and periodicals.

4. Capitalize all words in the titles of books, periodicals, and articles except *a, an, the,* coordinating conjunctions, *to* in an infinitive, and prepositions. Capitalize any word that begins or ends a title or subtitle.

5. Follow a book title with publishing information in parentheses (city—and state if necessary: name of publisher, year) followed by a comma and the page number(s), with no "p." or "pp." Follow an article title with the name of the periodical and pertinent publication information (volume, issue, date, page numbers where appropriate). Do not abbreviate months.

6. Separate major parts of the citation with commas, not periods.

7. For online sources, provide the URL, and for time-sensitive material, end with the date on which you last accessed the source.

18d *Chicago* print books and parts of books

Note the indented first line, the full name of the author, the commas separating major sections of the note, and the publication details in parentheses (City: Publisher, year of publication). If you quote or refer to a specific page of the source, provide the page number following the publication details and a comma, as in item 1. For a general reference or a reference to the work as a whole, end the note after the closing parenthesis, as in item 2.

1. Book with one author

1. Robert A. Caro, *Master of the Senate: The Years of Lyndon Johnson* (New York: Knopf, 2002), 8.

2. Book with two or three authors

2. George Lakoff and Mark Johnson, *Metaphors We Live By* (Chicago: University of Chicago Press, 1980).

3. Book with four to ten authors
For a book with multiple authors, use the name of only the first author followed by "and others" in a note; in a bibliography, include the first six names and use "et al." for the rest.

3. Randolph Quirk and others, *A Comprehensive Grammar of the English Language* (London: Longman, 1985).

4. Book with no author identified

4. *The Chicago Manual of Style,* 15th ed. (Chicago: University of Chicago Press, 2003).

5. Book with editor or translator

5. John Updike, ed., *The Best American Short Stories of the Century* (Boston: Houghton Mifflin, 1999).

For a translated work, give the author, title, and then the name of the translator after "trans."

6. Author's work quoted in another work

6. E. M. Forster, *Two Cheers for Democracy* (New York: Harcourt, Brace and World, 1942), 242, quoted in Phyllis Rose, *Woman of Letters, A Life of Virginia Woolf* (New York: Oxford University Press, 1978), 219.

Note, however, that *The Chicago Manual of Style* recommends that a reference be found in and cited from the original work.

7. Government document

7. U.S. Department of Education, National Center for Education Statistics, *The Condition of Education, 2005* (Washington, DC: GPO, 2005).

8. Scriptures, Greek and Latin works, classic works of literature
Provide the reference in the text or in a note. For the Bible, include the book (in abbreviated form, chapter, and verse, not a page number), and the version used (not italicized).

8. 1 Cor. 7:1–5. (New Revised Standard Version).

You do not need to include the Bible in your bibliography.

For Greek and Roman works and for classic plays in English, locate by the number of book, section, and line or by act, scene, and line. Cite a classic poem by book, canto, stanza, and line, whichever is appropriate. Specify the edition used only in the first reference in a note.

9. Part of an edited volume or anthology (essay or chapter)

9. Terrence Des Pres, "Poetry and Politics," in *The Writer in Our World*, ed. Reginald Gibbons (Boston: Atlantic Monthly Press, 1986), 17–29.

18e *Chicago* print articles in periodicals

10. Article in a scholarly journal, continuously paged through issues of a volume
If journal volumes are paged continuously through issues (for example, if issue 1 ends on page 188 and issue 2 of the same volume begins with page 189), give only the volume number and year, not the issue number. If you refer to a specific page, put a colon after the year in parentheses and then add the page number or numbers. To cite an abstract, include the word *abstract* before the name of the journal. For more on scholarly journals, see 8b.

10. Douglas Hesse, "The Place of Creative Nonfiction," *College English* 65 (2003): 238.

11. Article in a scholarly journal, each issue paged separately
When each issue of a journal is paged separately, with each issue beginning on page 1, include "no." for number after the volume number, and follow it with the issue number.

11. Rami Ginat, "The Soviet Union and the Syrian Ba'th Regime: From Hesitation to *Rapprochement,*" *Middle Eastern Studies* 36, no. 2 (2000): 160.

12. Article in a magazine   Include the month for monthly magazines and the complete date for weekly magazines (month, day, year). Cite only a specific page number in a note (after a comma), not the range of pages. Provide the range of pages of the whole article in any bibliographical citation.

12. Andrew Sullivan, "We Don't Need a New King George," *Time,* January 23, 2006, 74.

13. Article in a newspaper   Include the complete date, the edition (if relevant), and the section number. Do not include an initial *The* in the name of a newspaper. A page number is not necessary as a newspaper may appear in several editions. You may, however, give the edition and any section number.

13. Michiko Kakutani, "Bending the Truth in a Million Little Ways," *New York Times,* late edition, sec. E, January 17, 2006.

If the city is not part of the newspaper title, include it in parentheses: *Times* (London).

14. Editorial, no author identified   When no author is identified, begin the note with the title of the article.

14. "Spark the Revolution," *Wall Street Journal,* December 27, 2005, sec. A.

15. Letter to the editor

15. Christina J. Nichol, letter to the editor, *Harper's,* January 2006, 6.

16. Review of book, play, or movie

16. Anne Hollander, "Men in Tights," review of *Why We Are What We Wear,* by Paul Fussell, *New Republic,* February 10, 2003, 34.

18f *Chicago* online, media, and other sources

17. Online reference work   Cite an online dictionary or an encyclopedia in a note, but do not include it in a bibliography. Because reference works are frequently updated, you need to give the date on which you access the material. Precede the title of the article with the initials *s.v.* (Latin for *sub verbo*—"under the word").

17. *Columbia Encyclopedia,* 6th ed., s.v. "Bloomsbury group," http://www.bartleby.com/65/bl/Bloomsbury.html (accessed January 5, 2006).

18. Online book   Include your date of access only for time-sensitive material or material that may be revised for different editions.

18. Mary Wollstonecraft Shelley, *Frankenstein, or, The Modern Prometheus* (London: Dent, 1912), http://ota.ahds.ac.uk.

19. Article obtained through an online database   After any available print information, give the URL of the entry page of the service and other retrieval information, and (only if the material is time-sensitive or may exist in varying editions) the date you accessed the material. Give a page number only if it is indicated on the screen.

19. Geoffrey Bent, "Vermeer's Hapless Peer," *North American Review* 282 (1997), http://www.infotrac.galegroup.com.

20. Article in an online journal

20. Sarah Hatchuel, "Leading the Gaze: From Showing to Telling in Kenneth Branagh's *Henry V* and *Hamlet,*" *Early Modern Literary Studies* 6 no. 1 (2000), http://www.shu.ac.uk.emls/06-1/hatchba.htm.

21. Article in an online magazine   Cite as for a print publication, but add the URL.

21. Daniel Gross, "One Word: Logistics," *Slate,* January 20, 2006, http://www.Slate.com/id/2134513/?nav=tap3.

22. Article in an online newspaper   Cite as for a print publication, but add the URL. See item 13 above.

22. John Johnson Jr., "Shining a Light on the Dark Planet," *Latimes.com,* January 15, 2006, http://www.latimes.com/news/printedition/asection/ la-sci-pluto15jan15,1,3860080.story?ctrack=1&cset=true.

23. Government publication online

23. U.S. Department of Education, National Center for Education Statistics, *Digest of Education Statistics, 2004,* October 12, 2005, http://nces.ed.gov/pubsearch/pubsinfo.asp?pubid=2006005.

24. Web page or document from a Web site   Give the author of the content (if known), the title of the document, the owner or sponsor of the site, the URL, and your date of access if the material is frequently updated.

> 24. "MLA Style," Modern Language Association, http://www.mla.org (accessed May 20, 2006).

25. Personal home page   If a page does not have a title, use a descriptive phrase such as "home page."

> 25. Eleanor Gilpatrick, home page, http://www.gilpatrickart.com.

26. E-mail communication

> 26. George Kane, e-mail message to the author, January 7, 2006.

27. Posting on an electronic discussion list or blog   Whenever possible, cite a URL for archived material. Otherwise, end the note after the date.

> 27. David Schwalm, e-mail to WPA-L mailing list, February 15, 2005, http://lists.asu.edu/archives.wpa-l.html.

28. CD-ROM, DVD, e-book   Indicate the medium.

> 28. Ann Raimes, *Digital Keys 4.0* (Boston: Houghton Mifflin, 2005), CD-ROM.

29. Interview   Treat a published interview like an article or a book chapter, including the phrase "interview with." For unpublished interviews, include the type of interview and the date.

> 29. Douglass Mignone, telephone interview with the author, October 19, 2003.

30. Lecture or speech   Give location and date.

> 30. Peter Kwong, "Chinese America: The Untold Story of America's Oldest New Community" (lecture, Asian Research Institute, New York, February 10, 2006).

31. Film, slide, videocassette, audiocassette, or DVD   End the note with an indication of the type of medium, such as *film, slide, videocassette, DVD*. For online multimedia, include the type of medium, such as *MP3 audio file*.

31. *Citizen Kane,* produced, written, and directed by Orson Welles, 119 min., RKO, 1941, film.

18g *Chicago* bibliography guidelines

Check whether your instructor wants you to include a bibliography of works cited (or a bibliography of works consulted) in addition to notes. The bibliography form differs from the note form in several ways:

NOTE FORM

note number indented   publication details in parentheses

7. Peter C. Sutton, *Pieter de Hooch, 1629–1684* (New Haven, CT: Yale University Press, 1988), 57.

                        page number of exact citation

Note that commas are used to separate the major parts of the note.

BIBLIOGRAPHY FORM

no number, no indent in first line

Sutton, Peter C. *Pieter de Hooch, 1629–1684.* New Haven, CT: Yale University Press, 1988.

    indented after first line

Note that periods separate the major parts of the entry.

Bibliography Guidelines

- Begin a bibliography on a new, numbered page after the endnotes.
- List entries alphabetically, by authors' last names.
- Include authors' full names, the first author's inverted.
- Indent all lines three or five spaces except the first line of each entry.
- Single-space entries and double-space between entries, or double-space the whole list.
- Separate the major parts of each entry with a period and one space.
- If you include a bibliography, you can use the short form for notes (18b).

Chapter **19**

An Excerpt from a Student's Research Paper, *Chicago* Style

Chicago (Chicago Manual of Style)

Eva Hardcastle's class had been discussing slang and Standard English, and she chose to expand the discussion by doing research on slang dictionaries. She was instructed not to include a bibliography, so her endnotes include the full citation for each source. She single-spaced her notes, with a double space between notes, as her instructor required. Some instructors may prefer double-spacing throughout.

In the following excerpt, annotations in red comment on formatting; those in blue point out Hardcastle's argument strategies. Go to the Online Study Center for the complete essay.

Online Study Center   **Research** Student *Chicago* essay

Title page

SLANG DICTIONARIES:

MIRRORING OUR FLEXIBLE USE OF LANGUAGE

EVA HARDCASTLE

ENGLISH 218

PROFESSOR MARINO

APRIL 22, 2006

First page of essay

2

Page numbering begins after title page

More information in note

The reference section of every library contains one or more slang dictionaries.[1] At first it is puzzling to consider why there are slang dictionaries and how they are used. People who use slang do not get it out of a slang dictionary, do not check the spelling of slang, and do not look up the meaning of an unfamiliar slang expression they may hear used by a friend or coworker. Close examination of slang dictionaries, however, suggests that these works reflect the flexible ways people shift back and forth between informal and formal speech. On one hand, we often communicate in a standardized way, so we can be clearly understood and can successfully fit into the larger society. On the other hand, we often talk in many diverse and free-style ways, so we can express our individuality and belong to various subgroups within society. Slang dictionaries convey the message that both types of speech have validity and historical interest.

States thesis

Slang exists largely in relation to what it is not—it is not Standard English. James Stalker makes this point as he summarizes colleagues' attempts to date the beginning of slang:

> Lighter (1994) maintains that we cannot really label words as being slang before c. 1660, the Restoration period, because "standard" English did not exist before that time, hence the concept of slang could not exist

Quotation indented at left

Second page

3

Quotation cited in a note

before that time, although cant, criminal jargon, could. Partridge (1954) seems to agree. Slang arose as a response to Standard.[2]

In-group slang is informal, irreverent, and edgy, while Standard English is formal, respectful, and mainstream. Slang dictionaries make these distinctions clear, neatly translating slang into Standard English and highlighting the difference between the two in a nonjudgmental way.

Specific examples to illustrate a point

These dictionaries let a reader know, for instance, that in Australia *narky* means "upset," that in the Royal Air Force *pukka gen* means "trustworthy information," or that in England in 1811 *Pompkin* meant "A man or woman of Boston in America; from the number of pumpkins raised and eaten by the people of that country."[3] With slang words and their definitions each presented in this straightforward, neutral manner, it is easy to see both as valid ways of expressing oneself. Which you use depends on your choices, aims, priorities, audience, time period, and context.[4]

First page of notes

NOTES

First line of each note indented

1. Examples include Eric Partridge, *A Dictionary of Slang and Unconventional English,* 7th ed., ed. Paul Beale (London: Routledge and Kegan Paul, 1984); Harold Wentworth and Stewart Berg Flexner, *Dictionary of American Slang* (New York: Crowell, 1975); Jonathan Lighter, *Random House Historical Dictionary of American Slang,* 2 vols. (New York: Random House, 1994–97).

Complete bibliographical information contained in notes: no separate bibliography needed

2. James C. Stalker, "Slang Is Not Novel," paper presented at a meeting of the American Association for Applied Linguistics, Long Beach, California, 1995, 8, ERIC, ED 392 251.

3. Pete Alfano, "Australian for Olympics," *Fort Worth Star Telegram,* Sports, 10 September 2000; Eric Partridge, *A Dictionary of Slang and Unconventional English,* 5th ed. (New York: Macmillan, 1961), 1103; Francis Grose, *Lexicon Balatronicum: A Dictionary of the Vulgar Tongue: A Dictionary of Buckish Slang, University Wit, and Pickpocket Eloquence* (London: Jones, 1811; reprint, Chicago: Follett, 1971).

4. This concept is discussed in Harvey Daniels, *Famous Last Words: The American Language Crisis Reconsidered* (Carbondale: Southern Illinois University Press, 1983), 68. In his chapter "Nine Ideas about Language," Idea 5 is, "Speakers of all languages employ a range of styles and a set of subdialects or jargons."

5. Tom McArthur, *The English Languages* (Cambridge, U.K.: Cambridge University Press, 1998), xiv. See also Tom McArthur, *Living Words: Language, Lexicography, and the Knowledge Revolution* (Exeter: University of Exeter Press, 1998), 37. Here McArthur calls the pro-diversity group "permissivists."

6. Kenneth Cmiel, *Democratic Eloquence: The Fight over Popular Speech in Nineteenth-Century America* (New York: William Morrow, 1990), 127–8.

Same source as in note 6

7. Ibid., 90.

8. Quoted in Cmiel, 224.

Page numbers at bottom of page when page has a heading

Readers have expectations as to what a particular type of document will look like. Think, for example, of what you would expect in the following: a college essay on paper or on the screen, a business letter, an e-mail message, a memo, an advertisement, a Web site or blog, a brochure, a résumé, or information displayed on presentation software.

With ongoing technological expansion, the design of documents and the presentation of information have become more complex as well as more visual. Just consider the expectations of text that Internet-savvy teenagers hold compared with those of their older family members. Straight text (in words) has been joined by pictures, photographs, tables, graphs, music, and film to convey information and emotion, often more immediately and dramatically than words alone. Printed text is supplemented by multimedia displays.

Online readers have the complex task of analyzing and evaluating the new media. They also use the texts of the new media interactively—changing photographs, adding or deleting illustrations or sound, and inserting their own contributions to a Web site, as in wikis. To the ancient art of rhetoric (the art of effective communication and persuasion in words) we now add the component of visual rhetoric, in daily life and increasingly in college and the workplace. An important question to ask when you consider how to present your project to your audience, therefore, is this: What is the best way to meet my readers' or listeners' expectations, engage their attention, and make my points with the most impact?

Chapter **20**

Document Design

20a Using Word for document design

As a college student in the twenty-first century, you're probably quite at ease with using the functions of a word processing program to add, delete, and move material, and to check your spelling. But you may not know how much help a word processor can provide for the conventions of academic writing. Most of the formatting functions that your instructor may insist on are readily available with a click.

This section outlines the features of Word that are useful in academic writing. WordPerfect provides similar functions, as does a free alternative to Word, Open Office.

1. Setting up the page and previewing it before printing
Before you start your document, go to File/Page Setup to set page size, paper orientation, margins, layout for headers and footers, and so on. When you have written your document, Print Preview shows what each page will look like, before you actually print. The following screenshot shows Word 2003; other versions of Word may vary, as will individual settings.

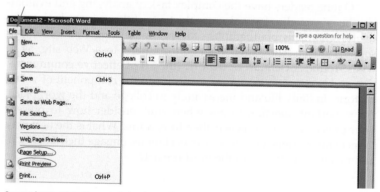

Screenshot reprinted by permission from Microsoft.

2. Adding a header or footer on every page When you open the View menu, you will see the Header and Footer option. The toolbar (p. 271) allows you to (a) include a page number along with any text, such as your name or a short running head; (b) include the date and time; and (c) toggle between the choice of headers or footers. Headers and footers will adjust automatically to any changes in the pagination of your document. You type the information once only, and it appears in the place you specify on every page, however much material you add or delete.

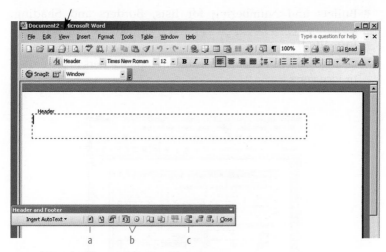

Screenshot reprinted by permission from Microsoft.

In addition, use the View menu to show toolbars on your screen. The Drawing and Reviewing toolbars are useful for college and business writing.

3. **Inserting text features and visuals** The Insert menu provides access to useful functions. Here you can insert into your text a page number, a footnote, or a hyperlink to a URL, though you can also set up Word to hyperlink all the URLs automatically (Tools/AutoFormat). You can insert Comments into your own or someone else's document, a useful feature for writing collaboratively and giving feedback. It is also possible to insert into your text a picture, caption, diagram, or chart. For presentation of data, the chart feature is particularly useful and easy to use: you simply type your data into a data grid and then choose from a wide variety of charts, such as bar, line, pie, doughnut, scatter, and pyramid. One click—and your chart appears (see 21b; Figures 2 and 5 show a graph and a chart made in Word).

4. **Formatting a document** The Format menu takes you to the following features:

- Font: for changing typeface, style, and size as well as using superscripts, useful for *Chicago Manual of Style* citations; see also 20b
- Paragraph: options for line spacing and indenting (see the screen capture on page 272 for how to set the special command for the hanging indents used in an MLA list of works cited)

- Bullets and Numbering for lists, Borders and Shading, Columns, Tabs, Dropped Capitals (just highlight the text to be formatted)

- Change Case: for changing text from capital letters to lowercase, or vice versa

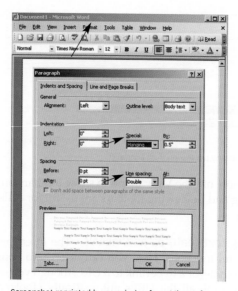

Screenshot reprinted by permission from Microsoft.

5. Using Word tools for checking, correcting, and changing The Tools menu gives you access to a word count, to spelling and grammar checkers and a thesaurus, and to AutoCorrect and AutoFormat functions (such as turning off the automatic hyperlinks when you do not need them underlined for an MLA list of works cited). Note that you can set a grammar checker to look for specific features, such as "Punctuation with quotes" and "Passive sentences": from the Tools menu, go to Options/Spelling and Grammar/Check Grammar with Spelling/Settings. In the Tools menu you will also find the Track Changes feature, a useful tool for adding editing suggestions to your own or somebody else's text.

6. Inserting a table When you click on Table/Insert Table, you can then select the numbers of columns and rows you want.

Screenshot reprinted by permission from Microsoft.

20b Typefaces

What's in a typeface? A lot. It's not just what you write but also how it looks when it's read. Fitting the typeface to the content of a public document can be seen as an aesthetic challenge, as it was for the choice of the simple and legible Gotham typeface for the Freedom Tower cornerstone at the site of the former World Trade Center. The silver-leaf letters, with strokes of uniform width with no decorative

touches, have been described by David Dunlap in the *New York Times* as conjuring "the exuberant, modernist, midcentury optimism of New York even as they augur the glass and stainless-steel tower to come." That's what's in a typeface. The cornerstone, according to Dunlap, looks "neutral enough so that viewers could impose their own meanings" on a site of profound historical and emotional impact.

Of course, you are designing the presentation of an essay, not of a historic monument. However, you can still make a choice that emphasizes simplicity and legibility.

The business text *Contemporary Business Communication,* 6th edition, by Scot Ober (Boston: Houghton, 2006) recommends the following typefaces in business correspondence, and the advice extends to college essays in hard copy:

> Times Roman for the body of the text (This is a *serif* font, with little strokes—serifs—at the top and bottom of individual characters: ₸imes Roman.)

> **Arial** or some other *sans serif* font for captions and headings (The word *sans* is French for "without"; a sans serif font does not have the little strokes at the top and bottom of the characters.)

Avoid ornamental fonts such as **Dom Casual** and *Brush Script*. They are distracting and hard to read.

Note that if you are designing a Web page or an online communication, your readers' computer settings determine which fonts can be displayed. The simpler the font you choose, the more likely readers are to see the font of your choice.

For the body of your text in a college essay or a business communication, stick to 10- to 12-point type. Use larger type only for headings and subheadings in business, technical, or Web documents (chapters 23, 24, and 28). Never increase or decrease font size in order to achieve a required page length. You will convey desperation, and you will certainly not fool your instructor.

Note: MLA and APA guidelines do not recommend typeface changes or bold type for titles and headings.

20c Color

Color printers and online publication have made the production of documents an exciting enterprise for both writers and readers. You can include graphs and illustrations in color, and you can highlight headings or parts of your text by using a different color typeface.

However, simplicity and readability should prevail. Use color only when its use will enhance your message. Certainly, in the design of business reports, newsletters, brochures, and Web pages, color can play an important and eye-catching role. But for college essays, the leading style manuals ignore and implicitly discourage the use of color. Also keep in mind that many people may not have a color printer, and printing color charts on a black-and-white printer may lead to parts that are difficult to distinguish.

20d Headings and columns

Headings divide text into helpful chunks and give readers a sense of your document's structure. Main divisions are marked by first-level headings, subdivisions by second-level and third-level headings. In the heading structure of chapter 20, for example, the main heading is "Document Design," and the subheadings include "Using Word for document design," "Typefaces," "Color," "Headings and columns," and "Lists."

For headings, bear in mind the following recommendations:

- If you use subheadings, use at least two—not just one.
- Whenever possible, use the Style feature from the Format menu to determine the level of heading you need: heading 1, 2, 3, and so on.
- Style manuals, such as the one for APA style, recommend specific formats for typeface and position on the page for levels of headings. Follow these recommended formats. See chapter 16 for an APA paper with headings.
- Keep headings clear, brief, and parallel in grammatical form (for instance, all commands: "Set Up Sales Strategies"; all beginning with -*ing* words: "Setting Up Sales Strategies"; or all noun-plus-modifier phrases: "Sales Strategies").

Columns, as well as headings, are useful for preparing newsletters and brochures (see the example in 25b). In Word, go to Format/ Columns to choose the number of columns and the width. Your text will be automatically formatted.

20e Lists

Lists are particularly useful in business reports, proposals, and memos. They direct readers' attention to the outlined points or steps.

Decide whether to use numbers, dashes, or bullets to set off the items in a list (20a, item 4). Introduce the list with a sentence ending in a colon (see 20d for an example). Items in the list should be parallel in grammatical form: all commands, all *-ing* phrases, or all noun phrases, for example (see 40j). Listed items should not end with a period unless they are complete sentences.

Chapter **21**

Visuals

The technology of scanners, photocopiers, digital cameras, and downloaded Web images provides the means of making documents more functional and more attractive by allowing the inclusion of visual material. Frequently, when you are dealing with arguments using complicated data, the best way to get information across to readers is to display it visually.

For a college paper, you can download visuals from the Web (with a source acknowledgment) to strengthen an argument or to present data clearly and efficiently. Alternatively, computers make it easy for you to take data from your own research and present the data as a table, graph, or chart (20a).

KEY POINTS
On Using Visuals

1. Decide which type of visual presentation best fits your data, and determine where to place your visuals; these are usually best within your text. However, APA style for papers to be printed requires visuals in an appendix. See 28d and 28e on using PowerPoint for an oral presentation.

2. Whenever you place a visual in your text, introduce it and discuss it fully before readers come across it. Do not just make a perfunctory comment like "The results are significant, as seen in Figure 1." Rather, say something like "Figure 1 shows an increase in the number of accidents since 1997." In your discussion, indicate where the visual appears ("In

the table below" or "In the pie chart on page 8"), and carefully interpret or analyze the visual for readers, using it as an aid that supports your points, not as something that can stand alone.

3. When you include a visual in an online document, make sure the image file is not so large that it will take a long time for readers to download.

4. Give each visual a title, number each visual if you use more than one of the same type, and credit the source.

5. Do not include visuals simply to fill space or make your document look colorful. Every visual addition should enhance your content and provide an interesting and relevant illustration.

21a Tables

Tables are useful for presenting data in columns and rows. They can be created easily with word processing programs using figures from large sets of data, as the table below was (see 20a, item 6).

TABLE 1   Internet Use from Any Location by Individuals Age 3 and Older, September 2001 and October 2003, and Living in a Home with Internet Broadband, Age 3 and Older, October 2003

Educational Attainment	Internet Users (Percent)		Lives in a Broadband Household (Percent)
	Sept. 2001	Oct. 2003	Oct. 2003
Less than high school	13.7	15.5	5.9
High school diploma/GED	41.1	44.5	14.5
Some college	63.5	68.6	23.7
Bachelor's degree	82.2	84.9	34.9
Beyond bachelor's degree	85.0	88.0	38.0

Source: *A Nation Online: Entering the Broadband Age,* September 2004. From Appendix, Table 1. U.S. Dept. of Commerce, National Telecommunications and Information Administration. Data from *U.S. Bureau of the Census, Current Population Survey* supplements, September 2001 and October 2003, based on a survey of 57,000 households.

21b Graphs and charts

Graphs and charts are useful for presenting data and comparisons of data. Many software products allow you to produce graphs easily, and even standard word processing software gives you several ways to present your numbers in visual form. In Microsoft Office you can create graphs and charts in Word or Excel. In Word, for example, go to Insert/Picture/Chart, and in the Chart screen go to Chart/Chart Type. You will be able to select a type of chart, such as a pie chart or a bar chart, and enter your own details, such as title, labels for the vertical and horizontal axes of a bar chart, numbers, and data labels.

Simple line graph Use a line graph to show changes over time. Figure 1 has a clear caption and is self-explanatory.

FIGURE 1   **Freshmen Keeping Up-to-Date with Political Affairs**

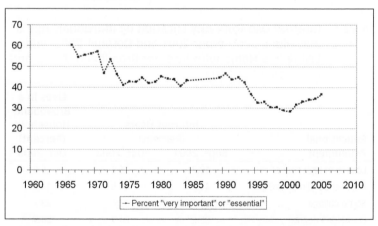

Source: Data are excerpted from Sylvia Hurtado and John H. Pryor, *The American Freshman: National Norms for Fall 2005,* Los Angeles, Higher Education Research Institute, University of California, 2006 at <http://www.gseis.ucla.edu/heri/heri/html>, slide 14; sample size varies over the years; for 2005 data are based on the responses of 26,710 first-time, full-time freshmen at 385 4-year colleges and universities.

Comparative line graph Line graphs such as Figure 2 are especially useful for comparing data over time.

FIGURE 2 Changes in Childbearing in Five Nations

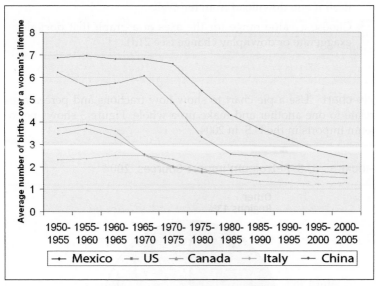

Source: Data from the Population Division of the Department of Economic and Social Affairs of the United Nations Secretariat, World Population Prospects: The 2004 Revision and World Urbanization Prospects: The 2003 Revision, <http://esa.un.org/unpp>

KEY POINTS

Using Graphs and Charts

- Use a graph or chart only to help make a point.
- Set up a graph or chart so that it is self-contained and self-explanatory.
- Make sure that the items on the time axis of a line graph are proportionately spaced.
- Always provide a clear caption.

(Continued)

(Continued)

- Use precise wording for labels.
- Always give details about the source of the data or the chart itself if you download from the Web.
- Choose a value range for the axes of a graph that does not exaggerate or downplay change (see 21d).

Pie chart   Use a pie chart to show how fractions and percentages relate to one another and make up a whole. Figure 3 shows petroleum imports in the U.S. in 2004.

FIGURE 3   **U.S. Petroleum Import Sources, 2004**

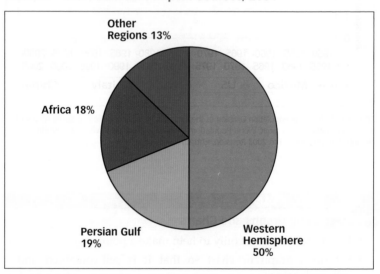

Source: United States, National Energy Information Center, Department of Energy, June 2005, <http://www.eia.doe.gov/neic/brochure/gas04/gasoline.htm>

Bar chart   A bar chart is useful to show comparisons and correlations and to highlight differences among groups. The bar chart in Figure 4 presents clear data for grade inflation over time at a variety of institutions.

FIGURE 4 **Grade Inflation among Students Entering Different Types of Institutions (Percentage Earning A Averages)**

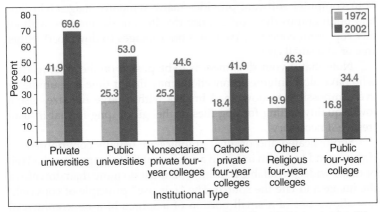

Source: L. J. Sax et al., *The American Freshman: National Norms for Fall 2002,* Los Angeles, Higher Education Research Institute, UCLA, 2003 at <http://www.gseis.ucla.edu/heri/norms.charts.pdf>. Data are from 282,549 students at 437 higher education institutions.

A bar chart can also be presented horizontally, which makes it easier to attach labels to the bars. Figure 5 was produced in MS Office using the data from Table 1.

FIGURE 5 **Internet Use from Any Location by Individuals Age 3 and Older, September 2001 and October 2003, and Living in a Home with Internet Broadband, Age 3 and Older, October 2003**

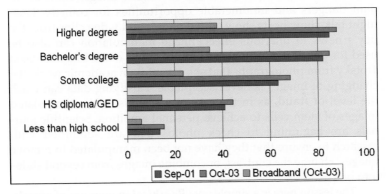

21c Images and copyright issues

Your computer software provides many standard images (clip art) and photographs that you can use free in your documents, without any copyright concerns. Web sites offer images to download, either free or at a small cost.

Note that if your document is to be posted on the Web, readers who have slow Internet connections may find it time-consuming or even impossible to download images with a large file size. Use a lower-quality setting for .jpg files or the .gif or .png format instead (resave if necessary).

Sophisticated and original graphics are usually copyrighted, so if you intend to use an image in a document that you post on the Web or make widely available in print, you must do more than download the image and cite the source. The "fair use" principle of copyright law allows use of a small portion of a source in a noncommercial work, but you need to write to the originator for permission to use an image or text.

For a college paper intended for your classmates and instructor alone and not posted publicly on the Web, you may want to include an illustration you find on the Web, such as a graph, a map, a photograph of an author or artist, a work of art, or an illustration from an online encyclopedia. You can do so without getting permission, but you must cite the source in your paper.

21d Honesty in visuals

With the ability to use software programs such as Photoshop to crop, combine, juxtapose, erase, and enhance images come attendant dangers and innumerable opportunities for comedy. Late-night talk-show hosts show edited photos and video clips from the day's news to hilarious effect. Image manipulation can also be used for political effect (such as Josef Stalin's order to delete Leon Trotsky from photographs that show Lenin). In academic work, the changing of images is never acceptable. Falsifying data can reach the level of fraud, as in the case of a scientist who manipulated images of stem cells to achieve personal ambition. Scientific journals are beginning to check photos that are submitted with research to ensure that they have not been manipulated to remove images, change the contrast, or combine images from several slides into one.

The lesson here is a simple one: *Be ethical in your use of visuals.*

Charts and graphs can also be manipulated—not by changing the original data but simply by selectively plotting the axes of a graph. Take care when choosing the value range for the axes to avoid exaggerating or downplaying changes over time. For example, for comparative data on population projections ranging between a 50% and 60% increase, a vertical axis of 0 to 100% will show the lines as almost flat, indicating little change over time, while a vertical axis of 40% to 70% will emphasize and maybe exaggerate the small projected increase—one that could be attributable solely to a sampling fluctuation.

Chapter **22**

Online Communication Forums

22a E-mail in academic and business settings

Communicating online to professors or supervisors in academic or business contexts is different from writing personal e-mail. Observe the following conventions.

Length and readability Be brief, and state your main points clearly at the start. One screen holds about 250 words, and online readers do not want to scroll repeatedly to find out what you are saying. Keep paragraphs short and manageable so that readers can take in the information at a glance. Use numbered or bulleted lists to present a sequence of points as brief items that can be readily seen and absorbed. Avoid multiple colors, fonts, and graphics unless you are certain your readers can receive and read these features.

Capitals Avoid using all capital letters in an e-mail message. To readers, it looks as if you are SHOUTING. But do use capitals when appropriate, especially for "I."

URLs Pay attention to accuracy of punctuation and capital letters. Both matter; one slip can invalidate an address and cause you great frustration. Whenever possible, to avoid having to write out a long URL, simply copy that URL from a document and paste it into your own document (Select/Copy/Paste). If you need to spread an address over two lines, break it after a slash (MLA style) or before a dot, and do not insert any spaces, hyphens, or line breaks.

Accuracy   Use a spelling checker and edit your e-mail before sending if you are writing to people you do not know well and if you want them to take your ideas seriously.

Subject heading   Subscribers to a list and regular e-mail correspondents are likely to receive a great deal of mail every day. Be clear and concise when composing a subject heading so that readers will know at a glance what your message is about.

Flames   Sometimes a writer fires off a message full of anger and name-calling. Such a message is called a *flame.* Avoid flaming. If someone flames you, do not get drawn into battle.

Signing off   Always put your actual name (not just <cutiepie3 @aol.com>) at the end of your online message. You can also construct a "signature file," which will appear automatically at the end of every message you send. Find out how to do this from the Help or Tools menu of your e-mail program.

The danger of attachments   Attachments can harbor computer viruses, so always be cautious about opening any attachments to an e-mail message. Open attachments only from known senders, and keep your own antivirus software up-to-date so that you will not spread a virus.

Spam   Make sure you add your instructor or business associates to your safe list so that their messages are not classified as spam.

22b E-mail discussion lists, discussion boards, and online communities

E-mail discussion lists, discussion boards on the Web and within course sites such as Blackboard, and online communities provide a forum for a virtual community of people sharing an interest in a topic. Thousands of these forums exist—some public, some private—providing opportunities for you to find information and to enter discussions with others and make your own contributions. Since many of the groups and forums may not be moderated or refereed in any way, you must always be careful about evaluating the reliability of a source of information. However, any discussion group can be valuable not only for the information it provides but also for the ideas that emerge as participants discuss an issue and tease out its complexities. As a general rule, e-mail lists to which it is necessary to first subscribe or register tend to be more substantive and professional than lists or boards with no access control.

E-mail discussion lists The administrators of even a public list may screen potential subscribers carefully, even though generally there is no fee for subscribing. (To participate in an e-mail list, you need only an e-mail address and a mail program.) Private lists and professionally moderated lists, especially those with a technical focus, can be reliable sources of factual information and informed opinion. When you join an online discussion group, all the messages posted are sent automatically to the e-mail accounts of all those who have registered as "subscribers." Subscribing simply means registering, not paying a fee. Lists are managed by specific software programs, such as LISTSERV, Listproc, and Majordomo, which have similar but not identical procedures.

Caution: Discussion lists often sell e-mail addresses, so you may get huge amounts of spam. Be careful about giving out your e-mail address. If there is a box you can check to prohibit giving out your address, be sure to check it.

Finding discussion lists Use the following directories to find the public lists that are available:

- CataList, the official catalog of LISTSERV® lists. As of June 26, 2006, it contained 82,104 public lists out of a total of 451,439 LISTSERV lists.
- Topica/LISZT, a catalog of e-mail lists of all types
- Yahoo! Groups

Online Study Center   **Design/Media** Discussion lists

KEY POINTS

Guidelines for Participating in Online Discussion Lists

1. If a Web interface is available for an e-mail discussion list, use it. Subscription management and posting, each with its own address, will be all in one place and therefore easier to manage.

2. If you do subscribe via e-mail, remember that a list has two addresses: the *posting* address (to send messages to all subscribers) and the *subscription* address (to send commands about managing your subscription). To differentiate between them, think of the difference between sending a letter to the editor of a printed newspaper for publication and sending a note to the circulation manager about a vacation suspension of your subscription. Use the subscription address (not the posting address) to subscribe to a list, suspend your subscription, unsubscribe from a list, or make other changes to your subscription details. The wording you use must be exact. Follow the list's directions for the commands, and save a copy.

3. Lurk before you post! Spend time reading and browsing in the Web archives in order to learn the conventions and the types of topics before you start sending messages to everyone on the list.

4. Manage the volume of mail. A mailing list may generate thirty, one hundred, or more messages a day, so after a few days away, you may feel overwhelmed. Use the options the list provides to select—for example—Nomail, Digest, or Index. Nomail temporarily suspends the sending of messages to your mailbox; Digest allows you to get only one bundle of mail every day; Index simply lists the messages once a day, and you retrieve the ones you want to read. However, not all options are available for all lists. You can also use filters to put messages into a special folder so that you can read them when you are ready.

5. Pay close attention to who the actual recipient is—the whole list or the person who posted the original message. Make sure you know who will actually receive your message. If you want to reply to only the individual sender of a message, do not send your message to the whole list; choose "Reply," not "Reply All." (Don't complain to Manuel about Bob's views

and then by mistake send your reply to the whole list, including Bob!) However, some lists automatically send a message to everyone. Find out the policy of your list.

6. Do not quote the whole original message. Select only a short passage, the one you immediately refer or reply to.

7. Avoid sending a message like "I agree" to the many subscribers to the list. Make your postings substantive and considerate so that subscribers find them worth reading.

8. Do not forward a posting from one list to another unless you ask the sender for permission or unless the posting is a general informational announcement.

Discussion boards and online communities Now sharing many features with discussion lists, discussion boards are Web pages to which you can post messages directly, but messages are not sent to your e-mail inbox. Sometimes you post spontaneously; in other instances, you have to register first. Discussion boards, such as those hosted by the *New York Times* on a variety of topics (at <http://www.nytimes.com/pages/readersopinions/index.html>), are included in many online magazine and media Web sites and in course management software, such as Blackboard, which provide a forum for students' discussions. Many sponsors, including Blackboard, have established "communities," which set up a site for those with similar interests to communicate online. In these public venues, follow the e-mail advice in 22a.

22c Other forums: Blogs, wikis, and virtual classrooms

Blogs Blogs are publicly posted observations on a topic initiated by the author or authorized group; they cover a range from personal diaries, family photos, and stories about pets to statements of political/religious/cultural views and observations of social issues. Typically open to everyone, they have been called the soapbox of the electronic age; they can be initiated with little technical expertise, thus making contributing to the Web truly democratic.

More and more, blogs are becoming comments on the state of our society at a particular point and place in the world, and they broaden from the personal not only in content but also by including images and links to other sites. To some extent, they have become a challenge for traditional media, a new avenue for an "independent" press. Blogs provide an opportunity to learn how others are thinking and to express your own views for a special audience or for anyone who happens to read your entries. Blogs can be set up so that groups as well as individuals can have posting and discussion rights, so they are useful and affordable discussion venues for student course sites and clubs (for a student's blog for a course, see 1d). Because blogs are often spontaneous, personal, unedited, and frequently written (often daily), they may not be reliable sources of information for researchers. But they serve as a corrective to a self-censoring press, and from them you can learn about how people view current issues and react to actions taken by individuals, political parties, and governments. Several providers, such as Blogger and Seedwiki, offer free server space for blogs.

Wikis *Wiki* is a Hawaiian term meaning "quick." Wikis are Web texts with open access to anyone, demanding no technical expertise and allowing information to be instantaneously corrected and changed. Pages are created as a team or community effort. Some college instructors use wikis in their courses as a venue for student-instructor discussion, but a wiki accomplishes little more than a discussion board on a course site.

One of the best-known wikis is one you are probably familiar with, the collaborative encyclopedia *Wikipedia*. In collaborative writing situations such as a report assigned to a group of students or a team of employees, wikis can be a fast way to work together on generating and editing text. The disadvantage is that changes are made without indicating who made the changes and what the changes were.

Virtual classrooms Course management systems such as Blackboard provide virtual classrooms, cyberspaces in which a whole class or a group of students can log in at the same time and communicate in real time in chat rooms. Virtual classrooms exist at different levels of sophistication:

- no more than a chat room, but typically archiving all entries
- adding a "whiteboard," a display/draw space that can be used by both instructor and student (upon permission)
- adding an audio channel to allow verbal exchange

- adding two-way video (including live feed from instructor to students, and vice versa)

Virtual classrooms are used for serious instruction in distance learning, with some providing videoconferencing tools for group projects and opportunities for online discussions.

Note: Whether you participate in discussion lists, communities, blogs, wikis, or virtual classrooms, remember that all are public forums, with their own inherent conventions different from those of personal e-mail or a private journal. When you post messages, pay attention to the conventions listed in 22a and avoid chat room abbreviations (CUL8R, etc.) and the use of emoticons.

Chapter **23**

Web Site Design

A great deal of online help is available for the mechanics of finding a server for a site (many schools offer space for student Web pages, as do many Internet service providers) and for the actual creation of a site (use MS Word and save a file as "Web page" for instance). With so much technical help accessible, you don't need to worry too much about HTML and coding. Instead, you can focus on adapting what you know about writing for the page: the important rhetorical considerations of purpose, audience, voice, structure, interaction of text and images, and the design of your document.

23a Planning a Web site

Purpose   Determine the message you want your site to convey and what you want your audience to learn from your site or do as a result of viewing it. Do you want to inform, persuade, entertain—or all three?

Audience   Try to form a clear idea of the main audience you want to reach: friends and family, fellow students, colleagues, members of a club or community, or the general public? Consider what their expectations will be. For a professional or academic audience, choose fonts and colors that are sober rather than flashy. If you know that many do not have broadband access, that will make a difference in the speed of downloading any video or audio clips you may want to include on the site.

Voice and tone Visitors to your Web site take away an impression of you or the institution you represent, so make sure that the content, language, and images work well to keep any readers who visit your site interested and engaged. Some sites and some audiences enjoy extremes, but for a professional site, play it safe and avoid rants, insults, jargon, terminal cuteness, and flat attempts at humor.

Structure Web sites typically consist of several pages and many internal and external links. Your viewers need directions on finding their way and not getting lost. On each page, include a link to the home page on a navigational bar at the top or bottom or in a sidebar. Also consider including an "About" page to explain the purpose of the site. Refer to the structure of sites you like and find easy to navigate to help you devise the structure for your site. Make a site map (see an example in 23b).

Interaction of text and images Plan the look of each page so that images supplement and complement the text and the site's purpose and draw the audience into the content. In other than personal sites designed for family and friends, avoid using images and animations to add peripheral glitz and clutter. Remember the need to acknowledge text or images from another source, and request permission to use them; the Web is a highly public forum.

Design and presentation Design and presentation of your work are extremely important in a Web site as it is open to so many more potential readers than a paper text, even one widely distributed. See 23c for tips on Web site design.

23b Making a site map

Draw a flowchart that shows how the different parts of your site will relate to each other. In the *Refugee Resettlement Program* Web site (shown in 23e), the structure is simple. The home page clearly links to the other pages within the site. Here is a map of that site:

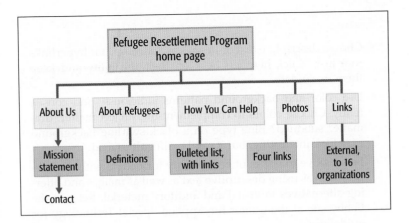

23c Tips for Web site design

KEY POINTS

Web Site Design Guidelines

- Keep pages short and simple—as a general rule, no more than two to three screens, with no fancy fonts.

- To test your page, set your own monitor to a resolution not higher than 800 × 600, and make sure all the text is visible on your screen without horizontal scrolling.

- Keep sentences short and direct.

- Break text into short passages. Use lists to help readers scan quickly.

- Use headings, and provide internal links to the headings. Use a larger point size for the type in headings.

- Use visuals—such as pictures, diagrams, photographs, graphs, clip art, or animations—to enhance and illustrate ideas. Save photos as .jpeg and graphs as .gif files. Pay attention to the file size of such add-ons. It is often possible to reduce the file size significantly with only a minimal loss of image quality. Position visuals so that they relate clearly to the written text.

(Continued)

(Continued)

- Choose descriptive text or images as "anchors" for hyperlinks (not just "Click here"). Check on their reliability and keep them up-to-date.

- Use color and background patterns judiciously and consistently. Choose colors to complement the subject matter: dramatic? subdued? Blue type on a black swirling background may look interesting, but it can be difficult to read.

- Be sensitive to issues of accessibility for people with disabilities, such as using descriptive text as well as images and offering alternatives to visual and auditory material. Refer to the Bobby site at the Center for Applied Special Technology for guidelines.

- Keep the site uncluttered for ease of navigation.

- Include relevant navigational links from each page of your site to other pages, such as the home page. Consider the use of a navigation bar that appears on each page of your site. Update your site regularly to maintain the links to external URLs.

- Include your own e-mail address for comments and questions about your site. State the date of the last page update.

- For text and graphics that you download to use in your own site, ask for permission and acknowledge the fact that you received permission to use the material. Be aware that you may have to pay a fee to use copyrighted material. Also, provide full documentation for your sources (see 21c).

23d Getting feedback

Before you launch the site, get as much feedback as you can from classmates or colleagues. Ask for feedback on the following:

- the ease of use and of getting to individual pages and back to where you started
- the length of time it takes graphics to appear
- page length and width (no horizontal scrolling and little vertical scrolling)
- the legibility and relevance of images (no animations or flashing icons just for effect)

- the sense that everything on the site serves a purpose
- grammatical and mechanical errors (there shouldn't be any!)

> **TECH NOTE**
>
> **Getting Help with Web Site Design**
>
> A useful resource is Jennifer Nierderst, *Learning Web Design: A Beginner's Guide to HTML, Graphics, and Beyond,* 2nd edition (Cambridge: O'Reilly, 2003).

Online Study Center   **Design/Media** Web site design

23e A community Web site: A student's project

The Soling Program at Syracuse University focuses on experiential learning and community involvement (for more on community service writing, see 5d). The program offers a course in Web Design for Novices in which students work with community organizations to design Web sites. In the fall of 2005, Daniel Sauve worked with the Refugee Resettlement Program sponsored by the Interreligious Council of Central New York and by the United Way to develop an informational site containing an appeal for help. Two pages from the site shown next illustrate features of good Web site design.

- The purpose of the site is clear, and the content is succinct and accessible.
- The home page provides a good introduction to the whole site, with no distractions and no vertical scrolling necessary.
- Text does not fill the width of the screen, and no horizontal scrolling is necessary.
- The navigation bar appears on the left side of each page.
- Clicking on the title (Refugee Resettlement Program) on each page takes one back to the home page.
- The logos of the two sponsors, linked to their sites, appear on each page, providing instant access to information about the organizations and their purpose.
- The tone is objective, direct, and clear throughout, avoiding hype.
- The content of a hyperlink is made clear in the wording of the text for the link.
- The consistent use of color and the heading format unify the whole site.

Home Page of Site

A United Way
Organization

The Refugee Resettlement Program of the InterReligious Council Central New York (RRP-IRC-CNY) fosters inter-religious and intercultural understanding between refugees and asylees of many different religions and cultures and residents of the Central New York, Ithaca, Binghamton and Albany areas. In partnership with Church World Service, Episcopal Migration Ministries, local faith communities and civic groups, we assist refugees from around the world begin their new lives in America. More...

"How You Can Help" Page

Refugee Resettlement Program

How You Can Help Refugees

About Us

About Refugees

How You Can Help

Photos

Links

- Invite us to speak to a group about refugees and asylees.
- As a part of a civic group or religious congregation, sponsor a refugee, refugee family, or an asylee.
- Stay informed about world refugee and immigration needs and policies
- Donate household furnishings and goods for newly arrived refugees
- Volunteer your time to help a refugee family or asylee with their life in America.
- Encourage your elected officials to support policies that assist refugees and immigrants.
- Assemble Personal Care Kits
- Assemble Household Care Kits

A United Way
Organization

Chapter **24**

Academic Writing Online and E-Portfolios

You may be required to submit an essay for a course online rather than in hard copy. Your instructor may ask you to e-mail him or her an attachment, or in a hybrid or a synchronous distance-learning course, you may be required to submit your essays in a dropbox or post them on a class online discussion board for the instructor and other students to read and comment on. Alternatively, you may have your own e-portfolio or Web site where you display your work. In any of these cases, keep in mind the following general guidelines, and ask your instructor for instructions specific to the course, format, and type of posting.

24a Guidelines for posting academic writing online

Recent versions of word processing programs can automatically convert a document and save it as an HTML file for the Web. In Word, for example, you simply produce your document in the usual way but then, when you save it, go to "Save As" and change "Save as type" from "Word" to "Web page." The HTML commands are done for you, automatically. In addition, Netscape Composer provides an HTML editor that tends to be more efficient in display speed.

KEY POINTS
Posting an Essay or a Research Paper Online

1. *Structure* Set up a structure with sections and subsections (called "fragments"), all with headings, that allows each section to be accessed directly—for example, from your table of contents (see item 2 below) and from any other part of your paper as well. So instead of saying diffusely, "See above" or "See below," you can provide a specific link allowing readers to jump directly to this part (see item 3).

2. *Links to sections from a table of contents* Provide a table of contents, with an internal link anchored to each fragment, marked with a "bookmark" or "target," and give each bookmark

(Continued)

(Continued)

(MS IE) or target (Netscape) a name. Readers can then click on and go directly to any section they are interested in.

3. *Internal hyperlinks*   Use internal hyperlinks (Insert/Hyperlink) to connect readers directly to relevant sections of your text, content notes, and visuals. Also provide a link from a source cited in the body of your paper to the entry in your list of works cited.

4. *External hyperlinks*   Use external hyperlinks to connect to Web documents from references in the body of your paper and from your list of works cited. Useful for the works-cited list, Word has a function that will automatically convert any string starting with <http://> into a hyperlink (go to Tools/Auto Correct/AutoFormat and Autoformat As You Type, and then check Replace Internet and Network Paths with Hyperlinks).

5. *No paragraph indentation*   Do not indent for a new paragraph. Instead, leave a line space between paragraphs.

6. *Attribution of sources*   Make sure that the link you give to an online article in a database is a persistent link, not a link that works for only a few hours or days. It is often difficult to determine at first glance whether a link is persistent or not. Some databases are explicit; others are not. Double-check your links after a few days to see whether the links are still working. Some sites (such as Thomas at Library of Congress at <http://thomas.loc.gov>) and EBSCO databases provide persistent links).

7. *List of works cited or list of references.*   Give a complete list, with visible hyperlinked URLs, even if you provide some external links to the sources from the body of your paper. If a reader prints your paper, the exact references will then still be available.

 *Online Study Center*   **Design/Media** Student online research paper

24b Preparing an e-portfolio

Increasingly, individual instructors as well as collegewide programs require or strongly encourage students to construct an e-portfolio. They provide space on a server where students can store writing samples, a résumé, information about their experience, and relevant images. Students can also reflect on their work as they present it to Web readers. The specific charges or tasks vary with the course. While an English instructor will probably focus on writing samples, a social science instructor may ask students to locate primary sources about a specific research topic (like the environment or laws and court cases related to civil unions). In education, e-portfolios have become quite common to document a student's progress through a course of study—for example, to file lesson plans, lesson evaluations, and so on.

TECH NOTE

E-Portfolios in Action

For examples of college programs that assign e-portfolios, see the following:

- Penn State includes instructions on building e-portfolios and examples of students' e-portfolios (including video and audio clips) that they used when applying for jobs.

- LaGuardia Community College in Queens, NY, includes a useful e-portfolio flowchart, instructions for developing a portfolio, resources, student samples, and advice about the language to use, the information to provide, and ways to avoid plagiarizing images and sounds you find on the Web. See <http://www.eportfolio.lagcc.cuny.edu>.

Whatever software your school may use to support e-portfolios, typically you will have control over the material that goes onto your pages of the (Web) server. In your private storage area, you'll be able to make material available to your instructors and/or other students for review so that these "reviewers" can add their comments to the material. Also, you may have the option of making a document (without the reviewer comments) available to a wider audience ("publish it to the Web") so that future employers or friends and family can also see the work. You can make different documents—aimed at different audiences—available for viewing at any time. One advantage to e-portfolios is that you have the flexibility to remix the materials for different purposes. In addition, you can include a variety of materials that you produce, such as HTML documents, graphics, images, sound, and film clips, rather than simply printed college essays that make up more conventional portfolios.

ePortfolio

Welcome   About me   Classes and Projects   Educational goals   Resume   Contact Info   My Links

About Me

The photo above was taken in fall 2004 by Gary Vollo, when I was interning in the Visual Arts Department at LaGuardia Community College. At the time I was ambushed by Gary with a camera while carrying a manikin from the drawing studio to be placed in storage. My pure smile shown in this photograph represents my personality.

I am Charles Mak, a current student at LaGuardia Community college. This is my senior year, and I am proud to be graduating in the fall. I was born in the United States; my parents are from Hong Kong. Besides speaking English, I speak Cantonese fluently.

I am currently majoring in Fine Arts at LaGuardia and transferring to Hunter College in fall 2005 for my Bachelors. I chose Fine Arts as my major because I always believed that art is prominent in society; we see it everywhere we go. Also, I've always been involved with art. In my early adolescence I spent a lot of time in arts and craft activities. I also copied comic book images out of interest. In my teenage years, I finally understood that art is a form of communication. Like words in a poem, elements of art transmit messages and they differ in their effect upon the receiver.

Entering this college was a major step for me; it introduced me to a whole different environment. Studying and working among diverse students with different backgrounds has improved my interpersonal skills. It has enlightened me and changed my perspective. Each culture has different ideals and approaches in thought. To experience how others feel about issues and approach problems is important in self-development. Attending LaGuardia Community College has given me the opportunity to develop myself and work on my weaknesses.

LaGuardia Community College

Permission to reprint granted by Charles Mak and the LaGuardia Center for Teaching and Learning, coordinators of the e-portfolio initiative at LaGuardia Community College, CUNY, available at <http://www.lagcc.cuny.edu/ctl>.

24c A student's e-portfolio

Charles Mak prepared an e-portfolio over the course of one semester when he was a student at LaGuardia Community College, City

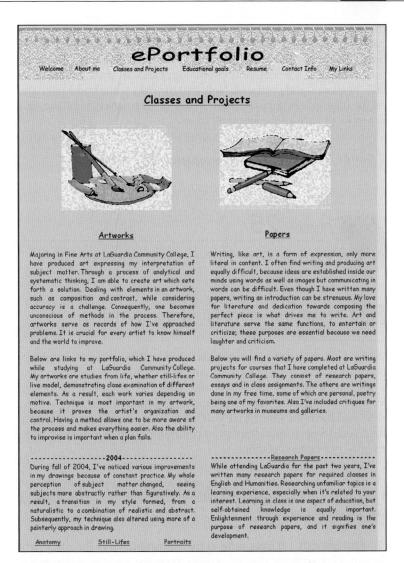

ePortfolio

Welcome   About me   Classes and Projects   Educational goals   Resume   Contact Info   My Links

Classes and Projects

Artworks

Majoring in Fine Arts at LaGuardia Community College, I have produced art expressing my interpretation of subject matter. Through a process of analytical and systematic thinking, I am able to create art which sets forth a solution. Dealing with elements in an artwork, such as composition and contrast, while considering accuracy is a challenge. Consequently, one becomes unconscious of methods in the process. Therefore, artworks serve as records of how I've approached problems. It is crucial for every artist to know himself and the world to improve.

Below are links to my portfolio, which I have produced while studying at LaGuardia Community College. My artworks are studies from life, whether still-lifes or live model, demonstrating close examination of different elements. As a result, each work varies depending on motive. Technique is most important in my artwork, because it proves the artist's organization and control. Having a method allows one to be more aware of the process and makes everything easier. Also the ability to improvise is important when a plan fails.

-------------------2004------------------
During fall of 2004, I've noticed various improvements in my drawings because of constant practice. My whole perception of subject matter changed, seeing subjects more abstractly rather than figuratively. As a result, a transition in my style formed, from a naturalistic to a combination of realistic and abstract. Subsequently, my technique also altered using more of a painterly approach in drawing.

Anatomy   Still-Lifes   Portraits

Papers

Writing, like art, is a form of expression, only more literal in content. I often find writing and producing art equally difficult, because ideas are established inside our minds using words as well as images but communicating in words can be difficult. Even though I have written many papers, writing an introduction can be strenuous. My love for literature and dedication towards composing the perfect piece is what drives me to write. Art and literature serve the same functions, to entertain or criticize; these purposes are essential because we need laughter and criticism.

Below you will find a variety of papers. Most are writing projects for courses that I have completed at LaGuardia Community College. They consist of research papers, essays and in class assignments. The others are writings done in my free time, some of which are personal, poetry being one of my favorites. Also I've included critiques for many artworks in museums and galleries.

--------------Research Papers--------------
While attending LaGuardia for the past two years, I've written many research papers for required classes in English and Humanities. Researching unfamiliar topics is a learning experience, especially when it's related to your interest. Learning in class is one aspect of education, but self-obtained knowledge is equally important. Enlightenment through experience and reading is the purpose of research papers, and it signifies one's development.

University of New York. Then a fine arts major, he is now majoring in studio art at Hunter College. The seven-part structure of the portfolio was provided by templates offered by his college; the actual appearance of the template, with its unifying color scheme throughout the site, is his own design. The screenshots show an excerpt from two pages—About Me and Classes and Projects—

the site, is his own design. The screenshots show an excerpt from two pages—About Me and Classes and Projects—both combining text and images and providing internal links to his research papers (on literature, biological sciences, and psychology) and art projects (anatomy, still-life works, and portraits). Note that the links to the home page and all the other pages appear across the top of each screen, allowing easy access to all parts of the site at all times.

 **Online Study Center**   **Design/Media** Student e-portfolio

 Chapter **25**

Flyers, Brochures, and Newsletters

25a Design principles for flyers, brochures, and newsletters

When you are producing material that will be printed or photocopied and then distributed to many people, take extra care to create a document that is attractive and effective. Attention to design increases the chance that your brochure, newsletter, or flyer will be read and have the effect that you intend. Some basic principles can help you design a successful print communication in academic, community, or business settings.

1. **Plan.** Consider the audience and the purpose of your document: Who will read the document? What is the most important message you are communicating?

2. **Experiment.** Leave time to try out variations in the document format. Play with the design—colors, typeface, images, white space, and so on—and get feedback from sample audience members.

3. **Value readability and clarity.** Consider the proportion of one element to another within your piece. Give priority to important information.

4. Be consistent. Keep consistency and coherence from page to page in matters of margins, typefaces, headings, captions, borders, column widths, and so forth. *Note*: If you are using a desktop publishing program, set up a grid or template to block out the consistent placement of headings, columns, margins, and boxed features for each document you are designing. The lines of a grid appear on your computer but will not appear when the document is printed.

5. Give careful consideration to the following design variables:

TYPE SIZE AND FONT Choose a readable type size. Serif fonts (the ones with little strokes at the top and bottom of each letter) are more readable and thus the best choice for the main body of a print document. For headlines and headings, use a limited number of other larger type sizes.

USE OF WHITE SPACE Allow for a generous amount of white space in your margins and borders and above and below headings. Adequate line spacing is important, too, to make the text easy to read.

END-OF-LINE ALIGNMENT Justified lines (lines are all the same length to create a squared off box of text) appear more formal, have a greater type density, and can create a lot of hyphenated words; lines that are ragged right create a less formal and more open look.

COLUMN WIDTH AND LINE LENGTH Shorter columns and shorter lines of type are easier to read.

RULES (PRINTED LINES) Horizontal and vertical rules of various thicknesses can be effective in setting off columns, headings, pull-out quotations, photos, and captions.

BOXES AND SIDEBARS Boxing a part of your document can give it extra emphasis or attention.

REVERSED TYPE With this technique, type appears white against a black or other colored background. However, reversed type becomes hard to read when the type is very small.

SCREENED BACKGROUNDS OR IMAGES If your document is to be printed with black ink and you want a certain section of your document to have a gray background, printers can create that effect by "screening" the section at a certain percentage, which you specify. Ink of any color can be screened.

BLEED IMAGES OR BLEED TYPE This effect makes an image or word appear to be running off the side of the page. It can be used to create a sense of an expanded design space.

25b Sample community brochure

Community Brochure Offering Volunteer Opportunities (Front)

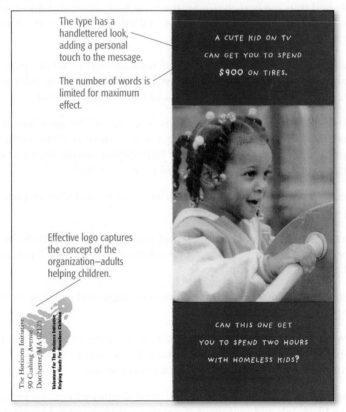

The type has a handlettered look, adding a personal touch to the message.

The number of words is limited for maximum effect.

A CUTE KID ON TV CAN GET YOU TO SPEND $900 ON TIRES.

Effective logo captures the concept of the organization—adults helping children.

The Horizons Initiative
90 Cushing Avenue
Dorchester, MA 02125

Volunteer for The Horizons Initiative
Helping Hands For Homeless Children

CAN THIS ONE GET YOU TO SPEND TWO HOURS WITH HOMELESS KIDS?

See the next page for the reverse side of this brochure.

Community Brochure Offering Volunteer Opportunities (Back)

Tan background sets off introduction.

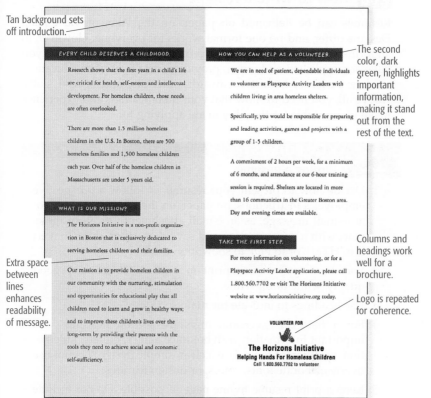

EVERY CHILD DESERVES A CHILDHOOD.

Research shows that the first years in a child's life are critical for health, self-esteem and intellectual development. For homeless children, those needs are often overlooked.

There are more than 1.5 million homeless children in the U.S. In Boston, there are 500 homeless families and 1,500 homeless children each year. Over half of the homeless children in Massachusetts are under 5 years old.

WHAT IS OUR MISSION?

The Horizons Initiative is a non-profit organization in Boston that is exclusively dedicated to serving homeless children and their families.

Extra space between lines enhances readability of message.

Our mission is to provide homeless children in our community with the nurturing, stimulation and opportunities for educational play that all children need to learn and grow in healthy ways; and to improve these children's lives over the long-term by providing their parents with the tools they need to achieve social and economic self-sufficiency.

HOW YOU CAN HELP AS A VOLUNTEER.

We are in need of patient, dependable individuals to volunteer as Playspace Activity Leaders with children living in area homeless shelters.

Specifically, you would be responsible for preparing and leading activities, games and projects with a group of 1-5 children.

A commitment of 2 hours per week, for a minimum of 6 months, and attendance at our 6-hour training session is required. Shelters are located in more than 16 communities in the Greater Boston area. Day and evening times are available.

TAKE THE FIRST STEP.

For more information on volunteering, or for a Playspace Activity Leader application, please call 1.800.560.7702 or visit The Horizons Initiative website at www.horizonsinitiative.org today.

VOLUNTEER FOR

The Horizons Initiative
Helping Hands For Homeless Children
Call 1.800.560.7702 to volunteer

The second color, dark green, highlights important information, making it stand out from the rest of the text.

Columns and headings work well for a brochure.

Logo is repeated for coherence.

Courtesy of The Horizons Initiative, Dorchester, Massachusetts.

Chapter **26**

Résumés and Letters of Application

Communication in the work world frequently revolves around technology: telephones, faxes, computers, e-mail, presentational software, and spreadsheets. In business, knowing how to prepare documents for the screen and the page is a valuable skill whether you are applying for a job or communicating with colleagues and clients.

26a How to write a résumé

Résumés can be delivered on paper, on the Web, or via e-mail. Designs differ, and no one format works for everyone. However, in all formats, you need to convey to a prospective employer what you have accomplished and when, providing details of your education, work experience, honors or awards, interests, and special skills. Above all, you need to show that your qualifications and experience make you suitable for the job you are applying for.

KEY POINTS
Writing a Résumé

1. Decide how to present your résumé, or follow a prospective employer's instructions: on paper, on the Web, in the body of an e-mail message, as an e-mail attachment—or all of these. Start with a paper version and save it as .rtf or .doc. Convert it to HTML or to PDF to show it on the Web.

2. For a hard-copy version, print on standard-size paper of good quality, white or off-white.

3. Use headings to indicate the main sections.

4. For a hard-copy version, highlight section headings and important information with boldface, italics, bullets, indentation, or different fonts. Use a clear, simple design. Do not use overly elaborate fonts, colors, or design features.

5. Keep a print résumé to one page, if possible. Do not include extraneous information to add length, but do not cram by using single-spacing between sections, a small font, or a tiny margin.

6. Include information and experience relevant to the job you are applying for. Use reverse chronological order (begin with your most recent work experience and education).

7. Proofread your résumé several times, and ask someone else to examine it carefully as well. Make sure it contains no errors. Avoid howlers such as "rabid typist" and "responsible for ruining a five-store chain."

8. Accompany your print résumé with a cover letter (26e), also carefully checked to avoid an error such as "Thank you for considering me. I look forward to hearing from you shorty."

Note: Microsoft Word provides résumé templates that set up headings for you—a useful guide.

26b Sample print or Web page résumé

Notice how Aurelia Gomez organized her résumé into clear divisions, using bold headings and a space between sections. This résumé presents the most recent job experience and education first and works backward.*

225 West 70th Street
New York, NY 10023
Phone: 212-555-3821
E-mail: agomez@nyu.edu

Aurelia Gomez

Objective:	Entry-level staff accounting position with a public accounting firm	Provides specific enough objective to be useful
Experience:	Summer 2005 — **Accounting Intern:** Coopers & Lybrand, NYC • Assisted in preparing corporate tax returns • Attended meetings with clients • Conducted research in corporate tax library and wrote research reports	Places work experience before education because applicant considers it to be her stronger qualification
	Sept. 2001– Nov. 2003 — **Payroll Specialist:** City of New York • Worked full-time in a civil service position in the Department of Administration • Used payroll and other accounting software on both DEC 1034 minicomputer and Pentium III • Represented 28-person work unit on the department's management-labor committee • Left job to pursue college degree full-time	Uses action words such as *assisted* and *conducted*; uses incomplete sentences to emphasize the action words and to conserve space
Education:	Jan. 2000– Present — Pursuing a 5-year bachelor of business administration degree (major in accounting) from the Stern School of Business, NYU • Expected graduation date: June 2006 • Attended part-time from 2001 until 2003 while holding down a full-time job • Have financed 100% of all college expenses through savings, work, and student loans • Plan to sit for the CPA exam in May 2007	Provides degree, institution, major, and graduation date Makes the major section headings parallel in format and in wording Formats the side headings for the dates in a column for ease of reading
Personal Data:	• Helped start the Minority Business Student Association at NYU and served as program director for two years; secured the publisher of *Black Enterprise* magazine as a banquet speaker • Have traveled extensively throughout South America • Am a member of the Accounting Society • Am willing to relocate	Provides additional data to enhance her credentials
References:	Available on request	Omits actual names and addresses of references

*Sample documents in 26b–27d are adapted from Scot Ober's *Contemporary Business Communication*, 6th ed. (Boston: Houghton, 2006). Used with permission.

26c A scannable electronic résumé

Companies often scan the print résumés they receive in order to establish a database of prospective employees. They can then use a keyword search to find suitable candidates from those in the database. You may also need to e-mail your résumé to a prospective employer. In either case, you need to be able to adapt a print or formatted résumé to make it easy for users to read and scan. You do not need to limit the length of either a scannable or an e-mail résumé.

KEY POINTS
Preparing a Scannable or an E-mail Résumé

- Check any prospective employer's Web site to find its emphasis and important keywords.

- Use nouns as résumé keywords to enable prospective employers to do effective keyword searches (use "educational programmer," for example, rather than "designed educational programs").

- To transform a formatted MS Word document, such as a résumé, into a plain text format suitable for scannable and electronic résumés, copy your document into Notepad (go to Start, then Accessories). Documents created in or pasted into Notepad are automatically stripped of formatting.

- Use a standard typeface (Times New Roman or Arial) and 10- to 12-point type, and for an e-mail document, use "plain text" or ASCII (a file name with a .txt extension).

- Avoid italics, underlining, and graphics.

- Avoid marked lists, or change bullets to + (plus signs) or to * (asterisks).

- Begin each major heading at the left margin.

- Do not include any decorative vertical or horizontal lines or borders.

- E-mail yourself or a friend a copy of your résumé (both as an attachment and within the body of a message) before you send one to an employer so that you can verify the formatting.

- If you feel that it is necessary, attach a note saying that a formatted version is available in hard copy, and send one as a backup.

26d Sample electronic résumé

Here is Aurelia Gomez's résumé adapted for e-mailing and scanning.

AURELIA GOMEZ

225 West 70 Street
New York, NY 10023
Phone: 212-555-3821
E-mail: agomez@nyu.edu

OBJECTIVE

Entry-level staff accounting position with a public accounting firm

EXPERIENCE

Summer 2005
Accounting Intern: Coopers & Lybrand, NYC
* Assisted in preparing corporate tax returns
* Attended meetings with clients
* Conducted research in corporate tax library and wrote
  research papers

Sept. 2001–Nov. 2003
Payroll Specialist: City of New York
* Full-time civil service position in the Department of
  administration
* Proficiency in payroll and other accounting software on DEC 1034
  minicomputer and Pentium III
* Representative for a 28-person work unit on the department's
  management-labor committee
* Reason for leaving job: To pursue college degree full-time

EDUCATION

Jan. 2000–Present
Pursuing a 5-year bachelor of business administration degree (major
in accounting) from the Stern School of Business, NYU
* Expected graduation date: June 2006
* Attended part-time from 2001 until 2003 while holding down a full-
  time job
* Have financed 100% of all college expenses through savings,
  work, and student loans
* Plan to sit for the CPA exam in May 2007

PERSONAL DATA

* Helped start the Minority Business Student Association at New
  York University and served as program director for two years;
  secured the publisher of BLACK ENTERPRISE magazine as a
  banquet speaker
* Have traveled extensively throughout South America
* Am a member of the Accounting Society
* Am willing to relocate

REFERENCES

Available upon request

NOTE

An attractive and fully formatted hard-copy version of this resume
is available upon request.

Begins with name at the top, followed immediately by address

Emphasizes, where possible, nouns as keywords

Uses only ASCII characters—one size with no special formatting; no rules, graphics, columns, or tables are used

Uses vertical line spaces (Enter key) and horizontal spacing (space bar) to show relationship of parts

Formats lists with asterisks instead of bullets

Runs longer than one page (acceptable for electronic résumés)

Includes notice of availability of a fully formatted version

26e Cover letter and sample

Accompany your print or e-mail résumé with a cover letter that explains what position you are applying for and why you are a good candidate. Find out as much as you can about the potential employer

---

February 13, 2006

Mr. David Norman, Partner
Ross, Russell & Weston
452 Fifth Avenue
New York, NY 10018

Dear Mr. Norman:

Subject: EDP Specialist Position (Reference No. 103-G)

My varied work experience in accounting and payroll services, coupled with my accounting degree, has prepared me for the position of EDP specialist that you advertised in the February 9 *New York Times*.

In addition to taking required courses in accounting and management information systems as part of my accounting major at New York University, I took an elective course in EDP auditing and control. The training I received in this course in applications, software, systems, and service-center records would enable me to immediately become a productive member of your EDP consulting staff.

My college training has been supplemented by an internship in a large accounting firm. In addition, my two years of experience as a payroll specialist for the city of New York have given me firsthand knowledge of the operation and needs of nonprofit agencies. This experience should help me to contribute to your large consulting practice with government agencies.

After you have reviewed my enclosed résumé, I would appreciate having the opportunity to discuss with you why I believe I have the right qualifications and personality to serve you and your clients. I can be reached by e-mail or phone after 3 p.m. daily.

Sincerely,

Aurelia Gomez

Aurelia Gomez
225 West 70th Street
New York, NY 10023
Phone: 212-555-3821
E-mail: agomez@nyu.edu

Enclosure

Addresses the letter to a specific person

Identifies the job position and source of advertising

Emphasizes a qualification that might distinguish her from other applicants

Relates her work experience to the specific needs of the employer

Provides a telephone number (may be done either in the body of the letter or in the last line of the address block)

and type of work; then, in your letter, emphasize the connections between your experience and the job requirements. (On page 308 is an example of a solicited application letter; it accompanies the résumé on page 305.) Let the employer see that you understand what type of person he or she is looking for. State when, where, and how you can be contacted. As you do with the résumé itself, proofread the letter carefully.

Once you have had an interview, write a short note to thank the interviewer and emphasize your interest in the position.

 Online Study Center **Across/Beyond College** Cover letters and résumés

 Chapter **27**

Business Letters and Memos

27a Features of a business letter

A good business letter usually has the following qualities:

1. It is brief.
2. It clearly conveys to the reader information and expectations for action or response.
3. It lets the reader know how he or she will benefit from or be affected by the proposal or suggestion.
4. It is polite.
5. It is written in relatively formal language.
6. It contains no errors.

27b Sample business letter

The sample letter uses a block format, with all parts aligned at the left. This format is commonly used with business stationery.

November 1, 2006 ↓ 4

> The arrows indicate how many lines to space down before typing the next part. For example, ↓ 4 after the date means to press Enter four times before typing the recipient's name.

Ms. Ella Shore, Professor
Department of Journalism
Burlington College
North Canyon Drive
South Burlington, VT 05403 ↓ 2

Dear Ms. Shore: ↓ 2

Subject: Newspaper Advertising

Thank you for thinking of Ben & Jerry's when you were planning the advertising for the back-to-school edition of your campus newspaper at Burlington College. We appreciate the wide acceptance your students and faculty give our products, and we are proud to be represented in the *Mountain Lark*. We are happy to purchase a quarter-page ad, as follows.

• The ad should include our standard logo and the words "Welcome to Ben & Jerry's." Please note the use of the ampersand instead of the word "and" in our name. Note also that "Jerry's" contains an apostrophe.

• We would prefer that our ad appear in the top right corner of a right-facing page, if possible.

Our logo is enclosed for you to duplicate. I am also enclosing a check for $375 to cover the cost of the ad. Best wishes as you publish this special edition of your newspaper. ↓ 2

Sincerely, ↓ 4

Joseph W. Dye

Joseph W. Dye
Sales Manager ↓ 2

rmt
Enclosures
c: Advertising Supervisor

> **Reference initials:** initials of the person who typed the letter (if other than the signer)
> **Notations:** indications of items being enclosed with the letter, copies of the letter being sent to another person, special-delivery instructions, and the like

30 Community Drive • South Burlington, Vermont • 05403-6828 • Tel: 802/846-1500 • www.benjerry.com

LANGUAGE AND CULTURE
Business Letters across Cultures

Basic features of business letters vary from culture to culture. Business letters in English avoid both flowery language and references to religion, elements that are viewed favorably in some other cultures. Do not assume that there are universal conventions. When writing cross-cultural business letters, follow these suggestions:

1. Use a formal style; address correspondents by title and family name.
2. If possible, learn about the writing conventions of your correspondent's culture.
3. Use clear language and summary to get your point across.
4. Avoid humor; it may fall flat and could offend.

27c Technical requirements of a business letter

Paper and page numbering   Use $8^1/_2'' \times 11''$ white unlined paper. If your letter is longer than one page, number the pages beginning with page 2 in the top right margin.

Spacing   Type single-spaced, on one side of the page only, and double-space between paragraphs. Double-space below the date, the inside address, and the salutation. Double-space between the last line of the letter and the closing. Quadruple-space between the closing and the typed name of the writer, and then double-space to *Enclosure* (or *Enc.*) or *c:* (indicating that you are enclosing materials or are sending a copy to another person). See also page 312.

Left and right margins   The sample letter in 27b uses a block format: the return address, inside address, salutation, paragraphs, closing, and signature begin at the left margin. The right margin should not be justified; it should be ragged (with lines of unequal length) to avoid awkward gaps in the spacing between words. A modified block format places the return address and date, closing, and signature on the right.

Return address   If you are not using business letterhead, give your address as the return address, followed by the date. Do not include your name with the address. (If you are using business letterhead on which an address is printed, you do not have to write a return address.)

Inside address The inside address gives the name, title, and complete address of the person you are writing to. With a word processing program and certain printers, you can use this part of the letter for addressing the envelope.

Salutation In the salutation, mention the recipient's name if you know it, with the appropriate title (*Dr., Professor, Mr., Ms.*), or just the recipient's title (*Dear Sales Manager*). If you are writing to a company or institution, use a more general term of address (*Dear Sir or Madam*) or the name of the company or institution (*Dear Gateway 2000*). Use a colon after the salutation in a business letter.

Closing phrase and signature Capitalize only the first word of a closing phrase, such as *Yours truly* or *Sincerely yours.* Type your name four lines below the closing phrase (omitting *Mr.* or *Ms.*). If you have a title (*Supervisor, Manager*), type it underneath your name. Between the closing phrase and your typed name, sign your name in ink.

Other information Indicate whether you have enclosed materials with the letter (*Enclosure* or *Enc.*) and to whom you have sent copies (*cc: Ms. Amy Ray*). The abbreviation *cc:* used to refer to *carbon copy* but now refers to *courtesy copy* or *computer copy.* You may, however, use a single *c:* followed by a name or names, to indicate who besides your addressee is receiving the letter.

The envelope Choose an envelope that fits your letter folded from bottom to top in thirds. Use your computer's addressing capability to place the name, title, and full address of the recipient in the middle of the envelope, and your own name and address in the top left-hand corner. Remember to include ZIP codes. Word processing programs include a function (Tools) that allows you to create labels for envelopes.

27d Basic features of a memo

A memo (from the Latin *memorandum,* meaning "to be remembered") is a message from one person to someone else within an organization. It can be sent on paper or by e-mail. A memo usually reports briefly on an action, raises a question, or asks permission to follow a course of action. It addresses a specific question or issue in a quick, focused way, conveying information in clear paragraphs or numbered points.

Begin a memo with headings such as *To, From, Date,* and *Subject;* such headings are frequently capitalized and in boldface type. In the first sentence, tell readers what your point is. Then briefly explain, giving reasons or details. Single-space the memo. If your message is long, divide it into short paragraphs, or include numbered or bulleted lists and headings (see 20d and 20e) to organize and draw attention to essential points. Many computer programs provide a standard template for memo format. The design and headings are provided; you just fill in what you want to say.

 **Online Study Center**   **Across/Beyond College**   Sample memo

 Chapter **28**

Oral and Multimedia Presentations

You may be asked to give oral presentations in writing courses, in other college courses, and in the business world. Usually you will do some writing as you prepare your talk, and you will deliver your oral report either from notes or from a manuscript text written especially for oral presentation.

28a Preparing an oral presentation

Consider the background and expectations of your audience. Jot down what you know about your listeners and what stance and tone will best convince them of the validity of your views. For example, what effect do you want to have on the members of your audience? Do you want to inform, persuade, move, or entertain them? What do you know about your listeners' age, gender, background, education, occupation, political affiliation, beliefs, and knowledge of your subject? What do listeners need to know? In a college class, your audience will be your classmates and instructor. You can often help build a sense of community with your audience by asking questions and using the inclusive pronoun *we.*

Making an effective oral presentation is largely a matter of having control over your material, deciding what you want to say, and knowing your subject matter well. Preparation and planning are essential.

KEY POINTS

Tips for Preparing an Oral Presentation

1. Select a topic you are committed to, and decide on a clear focus. If you are assigned a topic, concentrate on its key points.

2. Make a few strong points. Back them up with specific details. Have a few points that you can expand on and develop with interesting examples, quotations, and stories.

3. Include signposts and signal phrases to help your audience follow your ideas (*first, next, finally; the most important point is . . .*).

4. Structure your report clearly. Present the organizational framework of your talk along with illustrative materials in handouts, overhead transparencies, PowerPoint slides (28e), posters, charts, or other visuals (21).

5. Use short sentences, accessible words, memorable phrases, and natural language. In writing, you can use long sentences with one clause embedded in another, but these are difficult for listeners to follow.

6. Use repetition much more in an oral report than in a written report. Your audience will appreciate being reminded of the structure of the talk and of points you referred to previously.

7. Meet the requirements set for the presentation in terms of time available for preparation, length of presentation, and possible questions from the audience.

8. Prepare a strong ending that will have an impact on the audience. Make sure that you conclude. Do not simply stop or trail off.

28b Speaking from notes or manuscript

Speaking from notes   Speaking from notes allows you to be more spontaneous and to look your audience in the eye. Think of your presentation as a conversation. For this method, notes or a key-word outline must be clear and organized so that you feel secure about which points you will discuss and in what order. Here are a speaker's notes for a presentation of her views on paternity leave.

Paternity Leave
1. Children's needs
   Benefits
   Bonding
2. Issue of equity
   Equal treatment for men and women
   Cost

Your notes or outline should make reference to specific illustrations and quotations and contain structural signals so that the audience knows when you begin to address a new point. You can also use either slides prepared with your word processor or PowerPoint slides to guide the direction and structure of your presentation (28e). For a short presentation on a topic that you know very well, use notes with or without the visual aid of slides. Do not read aloud, though, especially in front of a small audience.

Speaking from a manuscript Writing out a complete speech may be necessary for a long formal presentation. Still, even if you do this, you should practice and prepare so that you do not have to labor over every word. Remember, too, to build in places to pause and make spontaneous comments. The advantages of speaking from a prepared manuscript are that you can time the presentation exactly and that you will never dry up and wonder what to say next. The disadvantage is that you have to read the text, and reading aloud is not easy, especially if you want to maintain eye contact with your audience. If you prefer to speak from a complete manuscript text, prepare the text for oral presentation as follows:

- Triple-space your text and use a large font.
- When you reach the bottom of a page, begin a new sentence on the next page. Do not start a sentence on one page and finish it on the next.
- Highlight key words in each paragraph so that you will be able to spot them easily.
- Underline words and phrases that you want to stress.
- Use slash marks (/ or //) to remind yourself to pause. Read in sense groups (parts of a sentence that are read as a unit—

a phrase or clause, for example—often indicated by a pause when spoken and by punctuation when written). Mark your text at the end of a sense group.

■ Number your pages so that you can keep them in the proper sequence.

28c Practicing and presenting

Whether you speak from notes or from a manuscript, practice is essential.

■ Practice not just once, but many times. Try tape-recording yourself, listening to the tape, and asking a friend for comments.

■ Speak at a normal speed and at a good volume. Speaking too quickly and too softly is a common mistake.

■ Imagine a full audience; use gestures, and practice looking up to make eye contact with people in the audience.

■ Beware of filler words and phrases like *OK, well, you know*, and *like*. Such repeated verbal tics annoy and distract an audience.

■ Do not punctuate pauses with "er" or "uhm."

It is natural to feel some anxiety before the actual presentation, but most people find that their jitters disappear as soon as they begin talking, especially when they are well prepared.

Look frequently at your listeners. Work the room so that you gaze directly at people in all sections of the audience. In *Secrets of Successful Speakers*, Lilly Walters points out that when you look at one person, all the people in a V behind that person will think you are looking at them. Bear in mind that no matter how well prepared a report is, listeners will not respond well if the presenter reads it too rapidly or in a monotone or without looking up and engaging the audience. If your topic is lighthearted, remember to smile.

Today presenters are not limited to using handouts or visuals printed on a page. Thanks to multimedia technology, they can use screens to present an interaction of words, drawings, photographs, animation, film, video, and audio to make a point.

TECH NOTE

An Introduction to Finding Images on the Web

This comprehensive Web site, constructed by librarian Heidi Abbey of the University of Connecticut Libraries, provides demystifying information on digital image formats; a primer on basic copyright issues; links to search engines; and best of all, links to several annotated image Web sites, including image resources for specific subjects.

Online Study Center   **Design/Media** Finding images online

In preparing a live or online multimedia presentation, consider the effectiveness of positioning images near your words and of conveying emotion and meaning through pictures. Imagine, for instance, how you might present an argument against genetic engineering of food crops to classmates or colleagues. In addition to your well-formed argument, you could show graphs of public opinion data on the issue, pictures of chemicals that are used on crops and of the way they are applied, and a movie clip of interviews with shoppers as they read labels and buy produce. If you use media imaginatively, you can do what writing teachers have long advised for printed essays: Show; don't just tell.

TECH NOTE

A Multimedia Project

"The City of Troy" is a multimedia project created by undergraduates at the University of Southern California for a course in Near Eastern and Mediterranean archeology.

Online Study Center   **Design/Media** Student multimedia project

28d Using PowerPoint

Using a multimedia tool like PowerPoint to prepare a presentation gives you access to organizing tools. As the name suggests, PowerPoint forces you to think of your main points and organize them. Preparing slides that illustrate the logic of your presentation helps you separate the main points from the supporting details, and the slides keep you focused as you give your presentation. Your audience follows your ideas not only because you have established a clear principle of organization but also because the slide on the presentation screen reminds people of where you are in your talk, what point you are addressing, and how that point fits into your total scheme. Presentation software also allows you to include sound, music, and movie clips to illustrate and drive home the points you want to make. However, be careful not to overdo these effects. PowerPoint features can easily become distracting "bells and whistles" to make up for lack of content. They should enhance your work, not dominate it.

A PowerPoint specialist has advised, "If you have something to show, use PowerPoint." *Show* is the important word. Do not expect your audience to read a lot of text. PowerPoint is not for writing paragraphs and essays for readers to digest. It's for getting and keeping the audience's attention with the main points and illustrative details. Displaying outlines, bulleted lists, tables, pie charts, and graphs is what PowerPoint does well.

Peter Norvig, a computer scientist and director of search quality at Google, cautions PowerPoint users to "use visual aids to convey visual information: photographs, charts, or diagrams. But do not use them to give the impression that the matter is solved, wrapped up in a few bullet points." For a wonderful object lesson of PowerPoint gone wrong, see Norvig's Web site spoofing the Gettysburg Address in PowerPoint!

Online Study Center   **Design/Media** PowerPoint slides

Style is important to readers. It affects their response to a piece of writing and influences their willingness to continue reading. Sometimes, even when good ideas are well organized, readers can suffer from the so-called MEGO reaction to a piece of writing—"My Eyes Glaze Over." Readers are bored by wordiness, flatness, inappropriate word choice, clichés, and sentences constructed without interesting variations. Working on style can help prevent that glazing over.

LANGUAGE AND CULTURE
Style across Cultures

It is impossible to identify one style as the best. What is considered good (or appropriate) style varies according to the writer's purpose and the expectations of the anticipated readers. Country, culture, region, ethnic heritage, language, gender, class—all can play a role in influencing what readers define as *style*. What may please readers in one language and culture in one setting in one part of the world may seem too flat or too adorned in another. The Japanese novelist Junichuro Tanizaki, for example, gives writers this advice: "Do not try to be too clear; leave some gaps in the meaning." Other cultures value clarity. Good style is relative.

With acknowledgment to Joseph Williams's *Style: Ten Lessons in Clarity and Grace*, 7th edition, chapters 29–33 examine five anti-MEGO strategies, called here the "Five C's of Style": cut, check for action, connect, commit, and choose the best words. Chapters 34–36 focus on developing sentence variety and offer stylistic options, a sample of a passage revised for style, and tips for writers.

THE FIVE C'S OF STYLE

Chapter **29**

The First C: Cut

You can improve most of your writing if you focus on stating your ideas succinctly. Examine your writing for unnecessary ideas, sentences, phrases, and individual words. Do not be tempted to pad your work to fill an assigned number of pages.

29a Cut repetition and wordiness.

Say something only once and in the best place.

▶ The Lilly Library ~~contains many rare books.~~

~~The books in the library are~~ carefully preserved, ⁵

       many rare books and manuscripts.
~~The library also houses a manuscript collection.~~

                              director of
▶ Steven Spielberg, ~~who has directed~~ the movie ~~that has been~~ described as the best war movie ever made, ~~is someone who~~ knows many politicians.

▶ California residents voted to abolish bilingual education. ~~The main reason for their voting to~~

                                because
    ~~abolish bilingual education was that~~ many children

    were being placed indiscriminately into programs
    and kept there too long.

If your draft says something like "As the first paragraph states" or "As previously stated," beware. Such phrases probably indicate that you have repeated yourself.

29b Cut formulaic phrases.

Writers sometimes use formulaic phrases in a first draft to keep the writing process going. In revision, these wordy phrases should come out or be replaced with shorter or more concise expressions.

Formulaic	Concise
at the present time at this point in time in this day and age in today's society	now
because of the fact that due to the fact that	because
are of the opinion that	believe
have the ability to	can
in spite of the fact that	although, despite
last but not least	finally
prior to	before
concerning the matter of	about

In the classic *Elements of Style,* authors Strunk and White rail against any use of the phrase "the fact that," seeing it as "especially debilitating." Their advice? Cut it out.

▶ Few people realize ~~the fact~~ that the computer controlling the *Eagle* lunar module in 1969 had less memory than a cheap wristwatch does today.

29c Cut references to your intentions.

Eliminate references to the organization of your text and your own planning, such as *In this essay, I intend to prove . . .* or *In the next few paragraphs, I hope to show . . .* or *In conclusion, I have demonstrated . . .* In a short essay, there's no need to announce a plan.

However, note that in writing for the social sciences or sciences, the main goal is usually to provide information in a set order. In those disciplines, therefore, you may acceptably state how you intend to structure your argument—for example, *This paper describes three approaches to treating depression.*

29d Cut redundant words and phrases.

Trim words that simply repeat an idea expressed by another word in the same phrase: *basic* essentials, *true* facts, circle *around*, cooperate *together*, *final* completion, return *again*, refer *back*, *advance* planning, consensus *of opinion*, *completely* unanimous, *free* gift. Also edit redundant pairs: *various and sundry*, *hopes and desires*, *each and every*.

▶ The task took ~~diligence and~~ perseverance.

▶ His surgeon _{has} ~~is a doctor with~~ a great deal of
clinical experience.

▶ _{Ninety-seven} ~~A total of 97~~ students completed the survey.

Chapter **30**

The Second C: Check for Action

The parts of a sentence that carry the weight of the meaning are the subject and the verb. Don't waste them. As a general rule, write vigorous sentences with vivid, expressive verbs. Avoid overusing the verb *be* (*be, am, is, are, was, were, being, been*), and use the active voice to have the subject of your sentence perform the action.

30a Ask "Who's doing what?" about subject and verb.

The subject (*approval*) and verb (*was*) in the following sentence tell readers very little:

WORDY   **The mayor's approval of the new law was due to
voters' suspicion of the concealment of campaign
funds by his deputy.**

This dull thud of a sentence revolves around the verb *was*. It contains three abstract nouns (*approval, suspicion,* and *concealment*) formed from verbs (*approve, suspect,* and *conceal*), as well as five prepositional phrases: *of the new law, due to voters' suspicion, of the concealment, of campaign funds,* and *by his deputy.*

Who's Doing What?

Subject	Verb
the mayor	approved
the voters	suspected
his deputy	had concealed

Always put verbs to work to make a stronger sentence.

REVISED   **The mayor approved the new law because voters suspected that his deputy had concealed campaign funds.**

30b   Use caution in beginning a sentence with *there* or *it*.

For a lean, direct style, rewrite sentences in which *there* or *it* occupies the subject position (as in *there is, there were, it is, it was*). Revise by using verbs that describe an action and subjects that perform the action.

WORDY   **There was a discussion of the health care system by the politicians.** [Who's doing what?]

REVISED   **The politicians discussed the health care system.**

WORDY   **There is a big gate guarding the entrance to the park.**

REVISED   **A big gate guards the entrance to the park.**

WORDY   **It is a fact that Arnold is proudly displaying a new tattoo.**

REVISED   **Arnold is proudly displaying a new tattoo.**

TECH NOTE

Searching for *There* and *It*

Use the Find function of your computer to find all instances in your draft of *it is, there is,* and *there are* in the initial position in a clause. If you find a filler subject with little purpose, revise.

30c Avoid unnecessary passive voice constructions.

The *passive voice* tells what is done to the grammatical subject of a clause ("The turkey *was cooked* too long"). Extensive use of the passive voice makes your style dull and wordy. When you can, replace it with active voice verbs, especially when you mention who or what is doing the action.

PASSIVE   **The problem will be discussed thoroughly by the committee.**

ACTIVE   **The committee will discuss the problem thoroughly.**

If you are studying in the social sciences or sciences, where readers are primarily interested in procedures and results, not in who developed or produced them, the frequent use of passive voice constructions may seem natural. For example, in lab reports and experiments, you will read *The rats were fed* instead of *The researchers fed the rats*. For other acceptable uses of the passive voice, see 31a and chapter 42.

Chapter 31

The Third C: Connect

In coherent pieces of writing, information that has been mentioned before is linked to new information in a smooth flow, not in a series of grasshopper-like jumps.

31a Use consistent subjects and topic chains for coherence.

Readers expect to be able to connect the ideas beginning a sentence with what they have already read. From one sentence to the next, avoid jarring and unnecessary shifts from one subject to another. Let your subjects form a topic chain.

JARRING   *Memoirs* **are becoming increasingly popular.** *Readers*
SHIFT   **of all ages are finding them appealing.**

TOPIC
CHAIN

Memoirs **are becoming increasingly popular.** *They* **appeal to readers of all ages.**

In the revised version, the subject of the second sentence, *they,* refers to the subject of the previous sentence, *memoirs*; the new information about "readers of all ages" comes at the end, where it receives more emphasis (31b).

Examine your writing for awkward topic switches. Note that preserving a connected topic chain may mean using the passive voice, as in the last sentence of the revision that follows (see also 42d).

FREQUENT
TOPIC
SWITCHES

I have lived all my life in Brooklyn, New York. *Park Slope* **is a neighborhood that has many different ethnic cultures.** *Harmony* **exists among the people, even though it does not in many other Brooklyn neighborhoods.** *Many articles in the press* **have praised the Slope for its ethnic variety.**

REVISED
WITH TOPIC
CHAIN

Many different ethnic cultures **flourish in Park Slope, Brooklyn, where I have lived all my life.** *These different cultures* **live together harmoniously, even though they do not in many other Brooklyn neighborhoods. In fact,** *the ethnic variety* **of the Slope has often been praised in the press.**

31b Put new information at the end of a sentence for emphasis.

If you form a topic chain of old information, new information will come at the end of a sentence. Make your sentences end on a strong and interesting note, one that you want to emphasize. This technique helps keep the flow of your ideas moving smoothly. Don't let a sentence trail off weakly.

WEAK
ENDING

Women often feel silenced by men, according to one researcher.

REVISED

According to one researcher, women often feel silenced by men.

31c Explore options for connecting ideas: Coordination, subordination, and transitions.

When you write sentences containing two or more clauses (34c), consider where you want to place the emphasis.

Coordination You give two or more clauses equal emphasis when you connect them with one of the following coordinating conjunctions: *and, but, or, nor, so, for,* or *yet.* (For more on coordination, see 31d, 34c, and 37d.)

> ─── independent clause ───┐ ┌─── independent clause ───
> ► **The bus trip was long, and the seats seemed more**
>
> **uncomfortable with every mile.**

> ─── independent clause ───┐ ┌─── independent clause ───┐
> ► **The bus trip was long, but we managed to enjoy it.**

Subordination When you use subordinating conjunctions such as *when, if,* or *because* to connect clauses, you give one idea more importance by putting it in the independent clause (34c and 38b).

> ► **We cannot now end our differences. At least we can help make the world safe for diversity.** [Two sentences with equal importance]

> ┌─────── dependent clause ───────┐ ┌───
> ► **If we cannot now end our differences, at least we**
> ─────── independent clause ───────┐
> **can help make the world safe for diversity.**
> —John F. Kennedy

[Two clauses connected by *if;* emphasis on the independent clause at the end of the sentence]

Transitional expressions Use words such as *however, therefore,* and *nevertheless* (known as *conjunctive adverbs*) and phrases such as *as a result, in addition,* and *on the other hand* to signal the logical connection between independent clauses (for a list of transitional expressions, see 2d). A transitional expression can move around in its own clause—yet another stylistic option for you to consider.

▶ He made a lot of money; *however*, his humble roots were always evident.

▶ He made a lot of money; his humble roots, *however*, were always evident.

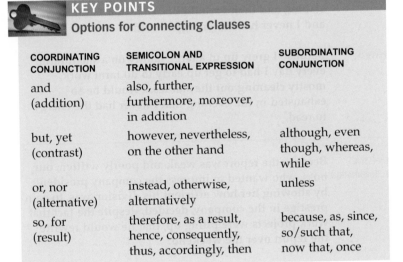

KEY POINTS
Options for Connecting Clauses

COORDINATING CONJUNCTION	SEMICOLON AND TRANSITIONAL EXPRESSION	SUBORDINATING CONJUNCTION
and (addition)	also, further, furthermore, moreover, in addition	
but, yet (contrast)	however, nevertheless, on the other hand	although, even though, whereas, while
or, nor (alternative)	instead, otherwise, alternatively	unless
so, for (result)	therefore, as a result, hence, consequently, thus, accordingly, then	because, as, since, so/such that, now that, once

The following examples illustrate some stylistic options open to you as you write and revise.

▶ Brillo pads work well. I don't give them as gifts.

▶ Brillo pads work well, *but* I don't give them as gifts.

▶ *Although* Brillo pads work well, I don't give them as gifts.

▶ Brillo pads work well; *however*, I don't give them as gifts.

▶ Brillo pads work well; I, *however*, don't give them as gifts.

Make your choice by deciding what you want to emphasize and seeing what structures you used in nearby sentences. If, for example, you used *however* in the immediately preceding sentence, choose some other option for expressing contrasting ideas. In addition, notice how subordinating a different idea can change your meaning and emphasis.

▶ *Although* I don't give Brillo pads as gifts, they work well.

Avoiding excessive coordination or subordination Too much of any one stylistic feature will become tedious to readers.

EXCESSIVE
COORDINATION
WITH *AND*

I grew up in a large family, and we lived on a small farm, and every day I had to get up early and do farm work, and I would spend a lot of time cleaning out the stables, and then I would be exhausted in the evening, and I never had the energy to read.

REVISED

Because I grew up in a large family on a small farm, every day I had to get up early to do farm work, mostly cleaning out the stables. I would be so exhausted in the evening that I never had the energy to read.

EXCESSIVE
SUBORDINATION

Because the report was weak and poorly written, our boss, who wanted to impress the company president by showing her how efficient his division was, to gain prestige in the company, decided, despite the fact that work projects were piling up, that he would rewrite the report over the weekend.

REVISED

Because the report was weak and poorly written, our boss decided to rewrite it over the weekend, even though work projects were piling up. He wanted to impress the company president by showing her how efficient his division was; that was his way of gaining prestige.

31d Perhaps begin a sentence with *and* or *but*.

Occasionally, writers choose to start a sentence with *and* or *but*, either for stylistic effect or to make a close connection to a previous, already long sentence:

▶ You can have wealth concentrated in the hands of a few, or democracy. But you cannot have both.

—Justice Louis Brandeis

People who consider *and* and *but* conjunctions to be used to join two or more independent clauses within a sentence may frown when they see these words starting a sentence. Nevertheless, examples of this usage can be found in literature from the tenth century onward. As with any other stylistic device, it is wise not to use *and* or *but* too often to begin a sentence. And, given the difference of opinion on this usage, check with your instructor, too.

31e Connect paragraphs.

Just as readers appreciate a smooth flow of information from sentence to sentence, they also look for transitions—word bridges—to move them from paragraph to paragraph. A new paragraph signals a shift in topic, but careful readers will look for transitional words and phrases that tell them *how* a new paragraph relates to the paragraph that precedes it. Provide your readers with steppingstones; don't ask them to leap over chasms.

KEY POINTS
A Checklist for Connecting Paragraphs

- [ ] Read your draft aloud. When you finish a paragraph, make a note of the point you made in the paragraph. Then, check your notes for the flow of ideas and logic.

- [ ] Refer to the main idea of the previous paragraph as you begin a new paragraph. After a paragraph on retirement, the next paragraph could begin like this, moving from the idea of retirement to saving: *Retirement is not the only reason for saving. Saving also provides a nest egg for the unexpected and the pleasurable.*

- [ ] Use adjectives like *this* and *these* to provide a link. After a paragraph discussing urban planning proposals, the next paragraph might begin like this: *These proposals will help. However, . . .*

- [ ] Use transition words such as *also, too, in addition, however, therefore,* and *as a result* to signal the logical connection between ideas (2d).

Chapter **32**

The Fourth C: Commit

E. B. White tells us that William Strunk, Jr., author of *The Elements of Style*, "scorned the vague, the tame, the colorless, the irresolute. He felt it was worse to be irresolute than to be wrong." This chapter focuses on ways to be detailed, colorful, bold, and resolute.

32a Commit to a personal presence.

Academic writing is certainly not the same as personal accounts of feelings, events, and opinions. But it is not writing from which you as the writer should fade from sight. The best academic writing reveals personal engagement with the topic and details of what the writer has observed and read, an unmistakable *you.* Always ask yourself: Where am I in this draft? What picture of me and my world do readers get from my piece of writing? Do they see clearly what I base my opinions on? If you use sources, readers should be able to perceive you in conversation with your sources; they should see not just a listing of what sources say but also your responses to and comments on those sources.

Showing a personal presence does not necessarily mean always using *I* or repeatedly saying "In my opinion." It means writing so that readers see you in what you write and recognize that you have integrated any research findings into your views on a topic. See 1b for more on a personal voice.

32b Commit to an appropriate and consistent tone.

Readers will expect the tone of your document to fit its purpose. The tone of your piece of writing reflects your attitude toward your subject matter and is closely connected to your audience's expectations and your purpose in writing. If you were, for example, writing about a topic such as compensation for posttraumatic stress disorder suffered by families of victims of the September 11, 2001, World Trade Center attack, anything other than a serious, respectful tone would be inappropriate.

For most academic writing, commit resolutely to an objective, serious tone. Avoid sarcasm, colloquial language, name-calling, or pedantic words and structures, even in the name of variety. Make sure you dedicate a special reading of a draft to examining your tone; if you are reading along and a word or sentence strikes you as unexpected and out of place, flag it for later correction. In formal college essays, watch out especially for sudden switches to a chatty and conversational tone, as in "Nutrition plays a large part in whether people *hang on to* their own teeth as they age." (You would revise *hang on to*, changing it to *retain*.) Since tone is really a function of how you anticipate your readers' expectations, ask a tutor or friend to read your document and note any lapses in consistency of tone.

32c Commit to a confident stance.

Your background reading, critical thinking, and drafting will help you discover and decide upon a perspective and thesis that seem correct to you (1e). Once you have made those decisions, commit to that point of view. When you are trying to persuade readers to accept your point of view, avoid the ambivalence and indecisiveness evident in words and phrases like *maybe, perhaps, it could be, it might seem,* and *it would appear.*

Hedging will not heighten readers' confidence in what you say:

> ▶ **Tough economic times did not stop me from bidding on eBay,~~but others might have had different experiences.~~**
> ⊙

Aim for language that reflects accountability and commitment: *as a result, consequently, of course, believe, need, demand, should, must.* It's important, however, to use the language of commitment only after thoroughly researching your topic and satisfying yourself that the evidence is convincing.

In addition, convey to readers an attitude of confidence in your own abilities and judgment. Make an ethical appeal to readers by stressing your evenhanded expertise (4f). Avoid apologies. One student ended a first draft this way:

TOO
APOLOGETIC

I hope I have conveyed something about our cultural differences. I would like my reader to note that this is just my view, even if a unique one. Room for errors and prejudices should be provided. The lack of a total overview, which would take more time and expertise, should also be taken into account.

If you really have not done an adequate job of making and supporting a point, try to gather more information to improve the draft instead of adding apologetic notes. The writer revised the ending after reading 2e on conclusions.

REVISED
VERSION

The stories I have told and the examples I have given come from my own experience; however, my multicultural background has emphasized that cultural differences do not have to separate people but can bring them closer together. A diverse, multicultural society holds many potential benefits for all its members.

Chapter **33**

The Fifth C: Choose the Best Words

Word choice, or *diction*, contributes a great deal to the effect your writing has on your readers. Do not give readers puzzles to solve.

33a Word choice checklist

KEY POINTS
Checklist for Word Choice

☐ Underline words whose meaning or spelling you want to check and words that you might want to replace. Then spend some time with a dictionary and a thesaurus. (33b)

☐ Look for words that might not convey exactly what you mean (*thrifty* vs. *stingy*, for example), and look for vague words. (33c)

☐ Check figurative language for appropriateness, think about where a simile (a comparison) might help convey your meaning, and find original substitutes for any clichés. (33e, 33g)

☐ Check for level of formality and for the appropriateness of any colloquial, regional, ethnic, or specialized work terms. (33d)

☐ Check for gender bias in your use of *he* and *she* and other words that show gender. (33f)

☐ Look for language that might exclude or offend (such as *normal* to mean people similar to you). Build community with your readers by eliminating disrespectful or stereotyping terms referring to race, place, age, politics, religion, abilities, or sexual orientation. (33f)

33b Use a dictionary and a thesaurus.

The dictionary in your word processor informs you about spelling, pronunciation, and definitions. Sometimes, though, you need more than that. Don't forget about the comprehensive dictionaries such as the *Oxford English Dictionary* (OED), available online in many libraries or in print form. In the OED you can explore the historical development of the meaning and usage of a word (its etymology), find synonyms and antonyms (words of similar and opposite meaning), and learn about grammatical functions and current usage. If you have no easy online access to the OED, invest in a good desk dictionary such as *The American Heritage Dictionary of the English Language*. There, people and places are included, the usage notes make fascinating reading, and the pictures provide instant access to meaning. If you can never remember which is which of the three orders of column capitals in Greek architecture (an affliction suffered by the author of this book), you do not have to try to rely on the written definitions: each definition (Doric, Ionic, and Corinthian) is accompanied by a color illustration.

Online Study Center **Style** Annotated dictionary entry

   Use a dictionary to learn or confirm the *denotation*—the basic meaning—of a word. Some words that appear similar are not interchangeable. For example, *respectable* has a meaning very different from *respectful; emigrant* and *immigrant* have different meanings; and so do *defuse* and *diffuse, uninterested* and *disinterested,* and *principal* and *principle.*
   A thesaurus is useful when you want to find alternatives to words that you know. Exercise caution, however, to make sure that the word you choose fits your context. Suppose you use the word *privacy* a few times and want an alternative in the sentence "She values

the privacy of her own home." You could consult a thesaurus but might find words such as *aloofness, seclusion,* and *isolation* listed.

The word *aloofness* would not work as a replacement for *privacy* in the example sentence, and the others do not capture the idea of *privacy.* You might, in the end, want to use two words to convey your meaning: *She values the* safety *and* seclusion *of her own home,* or you might stick with *privacy.*

Thesaurus programs attached to word processing programs typically offer lists of synonyms but little guidance on *connotation*—the meaning associated with a word beyond its literal definition. Using a thesaurus alone is not enough. Always check a word in a dictionary that provides examples of usage.

33c Use exact words and connotations.

When you write, use words that convey exactly the meaning you intend. Two words that have similar dictionary definitions (*denotation*) can also have additional positive or negative implications and emotional overtones (*connotation*). Readers will not get the impression you intend if you describe a person as *lazy* when the more positive *relaxed* is what you have in mind.

Select words with appropriate connotations. Hurricanes *devastate* neighborhoods; construction workers *demolish* buildings. Writing "Construction workers devastated the building" would be inappropriate. Note how the connotations of words can affect meaning:

VERSION 1 **The crowd consisted of young couples holding their children's hands, students in well-worn clothes, and activist politicians, all voicing support of their cause.**

VERSION 2 **The mob consisted of hard-faced workers dragging children by the hand, students in leather jackets and ragged jeans, and militant politicians, all howling about their cause.**

Some words do little more than fill space because they are so vague. The following oh-so-general words signal the need for revision: *area, aspect, certain, circumstance, factor, kind, manner, nature, seem, situation, thing.*

VAGUE **Our perceptions of women's roles differ as we enter new *areas*. The girl in Kincaid's story did many *things* that are commonly seen as women's work.**

REVISED **Our perceptions of women's roles differ as we learn more from what we *see, hear, read, and experience*. The girl in Kincaid's story did many *household chores* that are commonly seen as women's work. She washed the clothes, cooked, swept the floor, and set the table.**

Some words are abstract and general; other words are concrete and specific. Notice the increasing concreteness and specificity in this list: *tool, cutting instrument, knife, penknife. Tool* is a general term; *penknife* is more specific. If you do not move away from the general and abstract, you will give readers too much imaginative leeway. "Her grandmother was shocked by the clothing she bought" leaves a great deal to readers' imaginations. What kind of clothing do you mean: a low-necked dress, high-heeled platform shoes, and black fishnet stockings, or a conservative navy blue wool suit? Choose words that convey exact images and precise information.

33d Monitor the language of speech, region, and workplace.

The language of speech   In a formal college essay, avoid colloquial language and slang unless you are quoting someone's words. Don't enclose a slang expression in quotation marks to signal to readers that you know it is inappropriate. Instead, revise to reach an appropriate level of formality.

▶ The working conditions were ~~"gross."~~ *disgusting.*

▶ Organic farmers have ~~a rough time~~ *difficulty* protecting their crops.

▶ The jury returned the verdict that the ~~guy~~ *defendant* was guilty.

In formal writing, avoid colloquial words and expressions, such as *folks, guy, OK, okay, pretty good, hassle, kind of interesting/nice, too big of a deal, a lot of, lots of, a ways away, no-brainer.*

Note that the synonyms of the italicized words listed below convey different eras, attitudes, and degrees of formality:

child: kid, offspring, progeny

friend: dog, peeps, buddy, mate, brother/sister, comrade

jail: slammer, cooler, prison, correctional institution

angry: pissed off, ticked off, furious, mad, fuming, wrathful

computer expert: geek, hacker, techie, programmer

threatening: spooky, scary, eerie, menacing

fine: rad, phat, dope, fly, cool, first-rate, excellent

Some of these words—*kid, slammer, ticked off, geek, spooky, rad*—are so informal that they would rarely if ever be appropriate in formal academic writing or business letters, though they would raise no eyebrows in most journalism, advertising, or e-mail. Overuse of formal words—*progeny, comrade, wrathful*—on the other hand, could produce a tone that suggests a stuffy, pedantic attitude (see 33g).

Regional and ethnic language   Use regional and ethnic dialects in your writing only when you are quoting someone directly (*"Your car needs fixed," the mechanic grunted.*) or you know that readers will understand why you are using a nonstandard phrase.

▶ I bought ~~me~~ **myself** a camcorder.

▶ He vowed that he wouldn't pay them ~~no never mind.~~ **any attention.**

▶ They**~~'re~~ have been** here three years already.

▶ She used to ~~could~~ **be able to** run two miles, but now she's out of shape.

LANGUAGE AND CULTURE
Dialect and Dialogue in Formal Writing

Note how Paule Marshall uses Standard English for the narrative thread of her story while reproducing the father's Barbadian dialect and idioms in the dialogue, thus combining the formal and the informal, the academic and the personal into a rich whole:

> She should have leaped up and pirouetted and joined his happiness. But a strange uneasiness kept her seated with her

knees drawn tight against her chest. She asked cautiously, "You mean we're rich?"

"We ain rich but we got land."

"Is it a lot?"

"Two acres almost. I know the piece of ground good. You could throw down I-don-know-what on it and it would grow. And we gon have a house there—just like the white people own. A house to end all house!"

"Are you gonna tell Mother?"

His smile faltered and failed; his eyes closed in a kind of weariness.

—Paule Marshall, *Brown Girl, Brownstones*

The language of the workplace   People engaged in most areas of specialized work and study use technical words that outsiders perceive as jargon. A sportswriter writing about baseball will refer to *balks, ERAs, brushbacks,* and *cutters.* A linguist writing about language for an audience of linguists will use terms like *phonemics, sociolinguistics, semantics, kinesics,* and *suprasegmentals.* If you know that your audience is familiar with the technical vocabulary of a field, specialized language is acceptable. Try to avoid jargon when writing for a more general audience; if you must use technical terms, provide definitions that will make sense to your audience.

33e Use figurative language for effect, but don't overuse it.

Figures of speech can enhance your writing and add to imaginative descriptions. Particularly useful are similes and metaphors. A simile is a comparison in which both sides are stated explicitly and linked by the words *like* or *as.* A metaphor is an implied comparison in which the two sides are indirectly compared. When figurative language is overused, however, it can become tedious and contrived.

Simile: an explicit comparison with both sides stated

▶ America is *not like a blanket*—one piece of unbroken cloth, the same color, the same texture, the same size. America is more *like a quilt*—many pieces, many colors, many sizes, all woven and held together by a common thread.

—Rev. Jesse Jackson

▶ He was reading, leaning so far back in the chair that it was balanced on its two hind legs *like a dancing dog.*

—Barbara Kingsolver

Metaphor: an implied comparison, without *like* or *as*

▶ A foolish consistency is the hobgoblin of little minds.

—Ralph Waldo Emerson

▶ Some television programs are so much chewing gum for the eyes.

—John Mason Brown

Mixed metaphors Take care not to mix metaphors.

▶ As she walked onto the tennis court, she was ready to sink or swim. [Swimming on a tennis court?]

▶ He is a snake in the grass with his head in the clouds. [The two metaphors clash.]

▶ He was a whirlwind of activity, trumpeting defiance whenever anyone crossed swords with any of his ideas. [The three metaphors—*whirlwind, trumpet, crossed swords*—obscure rather than illuminate.]

For more on figurative language in literature, see 5b.

33f Avoid biased and exclusionary language.

You cannot avoid writing from perspectives and backgrounds that you know about, but you can avoid divisive terms that reinforce stereotypes or belittle other people. Be sensitive to differences. Consider the feelings of members of the opposite sex, minorities (now sometimes called "world majorities"), and special-interest groups. Do not emphasize differences by separating society into *we* (people like you) and *they* or *these people* (people different from you). Use *we* only to be truly inclusive of yourself and all your readers. Be aware, too, of terms that are likely to offend. You don't have to be excessive in your zeal to be PC (politically correct), using *underachieve* for *fail*, or *vertically challenged* for *short*, but do your best to avoid alienating readers.

Gender The writer of the following sentence edited to avoid gender bias in the perception of women's roles and achievements.

> Andrea
> ▶ ~~Mrs. John~~ Harrison, ~~married to a real estate tycoon and~~
> ~~herself the bubbly, blonde~~ chief executive of a successful
> computer company, has expanded the business overseas.

Choice of words can reveal gender bias, too.

Avoid	Use
actress	actor
chairman	chairperson
female astronaut	astronaut
forefathers	ancestors
foreman	supervisor
mailman	mail carrier
male nurse	nurse
man, mankind (meaning any human being)	person, people, our species, human beings, humanity, humankind
manmade	synthetic
policeman, policewoman	police officer
salesman	sales representative, salesclerk
veterans and their wives	veterans and their spouses

When using pronouns, too, avoid the stereotyping that occurs by
assigning gender roles to professions. See 44e.

or she
▶ Before a surgeon can operate, he must know every detail of
the patient's history.

Often it is best to avoid the phrase "he or she" by recasting the sentence or using plural nouns and pronouns.

> ▶ Before operating, a surgeon must know every detail of the
> patient's history.

> ▶ Before *surgeons* can operate, *they* must know every detail of
> the patient's history.

See 44e for more on gender, the use of the phrase *he or she*, and the
use of plural pronouns.

Race   Mention a person's race only when it is relevant. If you write, "Attending the meeting were three doctors and an Asian computer programmer," you reveal more about your own stereotypes than you do about the meeting. In general, use the names that people prefer for their racial or ethnic affiliation. The *Columbia Guide to Standard American English* advises: "It is good manners (and therefore good usage) to call people only by the names they wish to be called." Consider, for example, that *black* and *African American* are preferred terms; *American Indian*, or better still, the particular group (*Sioux*, etc.) is sometimes preferred to *Native American*; *Asian* is always preferred to *Oriental*.

Place   Avoid stereotyping people according to where they come from. Some British people may be stiff and formal, but not all are. Not all Germans eat sausage and drink beer; not all North Americans carry cameras and wear plaid shorts.

Be careful, too, with the way you refer to countries and continents. The Americas include both North and South America, so you need to make the distinction. England, Scotland, Wales, and Northern Ireland make up Great Britain, or the United Kingdom. In addition, shifts in world politics and national borders have resulted in the renaming of many countries. Always consult a current atlas, almanac, or Web reference site.

Age   Avoid derogatory or condescending terms associated with age. Refer to a person's age or condition neutrally, if at all: not "a well-preserved little old lady" but "a woman in her eighties" or just "a woman."

Politics   Words referring to politics are full of connotations. Consider, for instance, the positive and negative connotations of *liberal* and *conservative* in various election campaigns. Take care when you use words like *radical, left-wing, right-wing*, and *moderate*. How do you want readers to interpret them? Are you identifying with one group and implicitly criticizing other groups?

Religion   An older edition of an encyclopedia referred to "devout Catholics" and "fanatical Muslims." A newer edition refers to both Catholics and Muslims as "devout," thus eliminating bias of a sweeping generalization. Examine your use of the following: words that sound derogatory or exclusionary, such as *cult* or *fundamentalist*; expressions, such as *these people*, that emphasize difference; and even the word *we* when it implies that all your readers share your beliefs.

Health and abilities   Avoid expressions such as *confined to a wheelchair* and *AIDS victim* so as not to focus on difference and disability. Instead, write *someone who uses a wheelchair* and *person with AIDS,* but only if the context makes it necessary to include that information. Do not unnecessarily draw attention to a disability or an illness.

Sexual orientation   Mention a person's sexual orientation only if the information is relevant in context. To write that someone accused of stock market fraud was "defended by a homosexual lawyer" would be to provide gratuitous information. The sexual orientation of the attorney might be more relevant in a case involving discrimination against homosexuals. Since you may not know the sexual orientation of your readers, do not assume it is the same as your own.

The word *normal*   Be especially careful about using the word *normal* when referring to your own health, ability, or sexual orientation. Some readers might justifiably find that usage offensive.

33g   Avoid tired expressions (clichés) and pretentious language.

Avoid clichés.   *Clichés* are tired, overly familiar expressions, those anyone can complete: as cool as a _____. Common clichés are *hit the nail on the head, crystal clear, better late than never,* and *easier said than done.* They never contribute anything fresh or original. Avoid or eliminate them as you revise your early drafts.

▶ ~~Last but not least,~~ the article recommends the TeleZapper.
   Finally,

▶ My main ambition in life is not to make a fortune, since I know that ~~as they say, "money is the root of all evil."~~
   having money does not guarantee a good life.

▶ For Baldwin, the problem never ~~reared its ugly head~~ until one dreadful night in New Jersey.
   arose

Distinguish the formal from the stuffy. *Formal* does not mean stuffy and pretentious. Writing in a formal situation does not require you to use obscure words and long sentences. In fact, convoluted writing is not a sign of brilliance or of a powerful mind. It is usually just a sign of bad writing. Pretentious language makes reading difficult, as the following example shows:

▶ **When a female of the species ascertains that a male with whom she is acquainted exhibits considerable desire to extend their acquaintance, that female customarily will first engage in protracted discussion with her close confidantes.**

Simplify your writing if you find sentences like that in your draft. Aim for clear, direct expression of ideas. Here are some words to watch out for:

Stuffy	Direct	Stuffy	Direct
ascertain	find out	optimal	best
commence	begin	prior to	before
deceased	dead	purchase	buy
endeavor	try	reside	live
finalize	finish	terminate	end
implement	carry out	utilize	use

Avoid euphemisms. *Euphemisms* are expressions that try to conceal a forthright meaning and make the concept seem more delicate, such as *change of life* for *menopause* or *downsized* for *fired*. Because euphemisms often sound evasive or are unclear, avoid them in favor of direct language. Similarly, avoid *doublespeak* (evasive expressions that seek to conceal the truth, such as *incendiary device* for *firebomb*, *combat situation* for *battle*, and *collateral damage* for *civilian casualties*). Examples of such language are easy to find in advertising, business, politics, and especially in war reporting. Do not equate formality with these indirect expressions.

▶ **The building's owners offered the inspectors many**
bribes
~~**financial incentives**~~ **to overlook code violations.**
    ^

STYLE IN ACTION

The more you write, the more you will strive for variety, rhythm, and specific effects. The next two chapters focus on using a variety of sentences and revising your work to improve style and sentence variety. In the concluding chapter are some tips to help you actively review your drafts for style.

Chapter **34**

Sentence Variety

34a Sentence length

Readers appreciate variety, so aim for a mix of long and short sentences. If your editing program can print out your text in a series of single numbered sentences, you will easily be able to examine the length and structure of each. Academic writing need not consist solely of long, heavyweight sentences. Short sentences interspersed among longer ones can have a dramatic effect.

This passage from a student memoir demonstrates the use of short sentences to great effect:

> When I started high school and Afros became the rage, I immediately decided to get one. Now at that time, I had a head full of long, thick, kinky hair, which my mother had cultivated for years. When she said to me, "Cut it or perm it," she never for one minute believed I would do either. I cut it. She fainted.
>
> ——Denise Dejean, student

34b Using statements, questions, commands, and exclamations

Declarative sentences make statements, *interrogative* sentences ask questions, *imperative* sentences give commands, and *exclamatory* sentences express surprise or some other strong emotion. Most of the sentences in your college writing will be declarative.

▶ **Winsor McCay's surrealist comic strip** *Little Nemo in Slumberland* **ran intermittently in newspapers from 1905 to 1927. It remains famous for its extraordinary beauty and artistry.**

34c Types of sentences

Vary the structure of your sentences throughout any piece of writing. Aim for a mix of simple, compound, complex, and compound-complex sentences.

A *simple sentence* contains one independent clause.

▶ **Kara raised her hand.**

A *compound sentence* contains two or more independent clauses connected with one or more coordinating conjunctions (*and, but, or, nor, so, for, yet*), or with a semicolon alone, or with a semicolon and a transitional expression (2d).

⌐ independent clause ¬   ⌐ independent clause ¬
▶ **She raised her hand, and the whole class was surprised.**

⌐ independent clause ¬   ⌐ independent clause ¬
▶ **She raised her hand, but nobody else responded.**

⌐ independent clause ¬   ⌐ independent clause ¬
▶ **She raised her hand; the whole class was surprised.**

⌐ independent clause ¬   ⌐ independent clause ¬
▶ **She raised her hand; as a result, the whole class was surprised.**

A *complex sentence* contains an independent clause and one or more dependent clauses.

⌐ dependent clause ¬   ⌐ independent clause ¬
▶ **When she raised her hand, the whole class was surprised.**

⌐ independent clause ¬   ⌐ dependent clause ¬
▶ **The whole class was surprised when she raised her hand.**

A *compound-complex sentence* contains at least two independent clauses and at least one dependent clause.

⌐ dependent clause ¬   ⌐ independent clause ¬
▶ **When she raised her hand, the whole class was surprised,**

⌐ independent clause ¬   ⌐ dependent clause ¬
and the professor waited eagerly as she began to speak.

In addition, be aware of *cumulative* and *periodic sentences.* Cumulative (or loose) sentences begin with the independent clause and add on to it. Periodic sentences begin with words and phrases that lead to the independent clause, giving emphasis to the end of the sentence. The cumulative sentence is the norm in English prose. Use a periodic sentence to make a specific impact.

CUMULATIVE   *The experienced hunter stood stock still for at least five minutes,* **sweat pouring from his brow, all senses alert, waiting to hear a twig snap.**

PERIODIC   **Sweat pouring from his brow, all senses alert, waiting to hear a twig snap,** *the experienced hunter stood stock still for at least five minutes.*

34d Inverted word order

Sometimes, inverted word order of verb followed by subject (v + s) will help you achieve coherence, consistent subjects, emphasis, or a smooth transition:

▶ Next to the river runs a superhighway.

▶ Never have I been so tired.

▶ Not only does the novel entertain, but it also raises our awareness of poverty.

▶ So eager was I to win that I set off before the starter's gun.

▶ Rarely has a poem achieved such a grasp on the times.

Using an occasional rhetorical question will also help drive a point home:

▶ How could anyone have thought that war was the answer?

34e Sentence beginnings

Consider using some of these variations to begin a sentence, but remember that beginning with the subject will always be clear and direct for readers. Any of the following beginnings repeated too often will seem like a stylistic tic and may annoy readers.

Begin with a dependent or condensed clause.

┌──────────────── dependent clause ────────────────┐
▶ **While my friends were waiting for the movie to begin, they ate three tubs of popcorn.**

┌────── clause condensed to a phrase ──────┐
▶ **While waiting for the movie to begin, my friends ate three tubs of popcorn.**

Begin with a participle or an adjective.

A sentence can begin with a participle or an adjective, but only if the word is in a phrase that refers to the subject of the independent clause. If the phrase does not refer to the subject, the result is a *dangling modifier* error (40c).

-ing participle
▶ **Waiting for the movie to begin, my friends ate popcorn.**

past participle
▶ **Forced to work late, they ordered a pepperoni pizza.**

adjective
▶ **Aware of the problems, they nevertheless decided to continue.**

Begin with a prepositional phrase.

┌─ prepositional phrase ─┐
▶ **With immense joy, we watched our team win the pennant.**

You can also occasionally use inverted word order after a prepositional phrase (34d, 43d).

┌── prepositional phrases ──┐ verb ┌── subject ──┐
▶ **At the end of my block stands a deserted building.**

Chapter **35**

Revising for Style: A Student's Drafts

When Mariana Gonzalez was asked in class to freewrite (see 1d) on the issue of banning smoking in bars as well as in restaurants, she produced the following draft:

> I think smoking is not a good idea in bars and restaurants, so it should be banned in New York. Some people may disagree with this, but it is not fair to people that they should have to breathe in the smoke that other

people breathe out. Bars and restaurants are public places. They are crowded and there are always some people among all the people there who smoke and do not go outside to smoke. I think those people should be made to go outside. If they stay inside they should not be allowed to smoke. All people should be allowed to be healthy. Smoking can kill you, even if you are not doing the smoking yourself, and should be banned.

Extensive discussion of style ensued in a peer group discussion in her class, during which her group members read and discussed her paragraph. They wrote her the following feedback:

You make a point, but I wonder if you need to make it so often. There's a lot of repetition.

Remember what the prof said about cutting.

It is all a bit general. I don't get any sense that you have a real place in mind. Could you tell about a restaurant or bar that *you* go to? Include real people, too, if you can.

Play up the point about secondhand smoke.

Are there too many instances of "should" and "I think"?

Try to paint a picture of a place. I can't see a time, a place, or *you* here anywhere.

Remember what the book says about being confident. I'd cut out "Some people may disagree with this."

Gonzalez then produced the following revision:

The Corner Bistro on West 4th Street in Manhattan is a crowded neighborhood bar and restaurant where Greenwich Village customers have been enjoying burgers and mugs of beer since the 1960s. They also used to enjoy, or suffer, what the Zagat Survey calls "side orders of cigarette smoke." It is a cleaner, safer environment since smoking has been banned in all Manhattan restaurants and bars. Some of the locals there, however, are outraged. One of them, shouting hoarsely above the noise, gestures with nicotine-stained fingers toward an unnamed enemy: "Who do they think they are, telling me I can't smoke in here? Soon they will be telling me I can't eat and drink in here. They talk about freedom *from* smoke. What about my freedom *to* smoke?" He storms outside to light up. The issue, though, is not just freedom. The issue is the proven danger of secondhand smoke. Out there he will no longer endanger the health of his fellow customers or of the restaurant employees.

Chapter **36**

Style Tips

As you write and revise, keep in mind the five C's of style, and aim for sentence variety. For a final quick review of your style, read your draft aloud and use these tips.

KEY POINTS
Tips for Style

1. *Be adaptable.* Consider the style your readers will expect. Don't work on developing a figurative style for short stories and then continue to use it in business communications or e-mail. Choose a style as you choose your clothes: the right outfit for the occasion.

2. *When in doubt, favor a plain style.* Be clear and straightforward. Don't search for the big words or the obscure turn of phrase. The following sentences, part of an e-mail message to the author of this book from an online service provider, are decidedly overdressed and stuffed with bureaucratic nothings: "It has been a pleasure assisting you. It is my hope that the information provided would be of great help with regards to your concern."

3. *Less is often better.* Details and descriptions are interesting, but don't overload your writing with adjectives and adverbs: *The perky little redheaded twin sat languidly in the comfortable overstuffed green-striped armchair and bit enthusiastically into a red and yellow fleshy, overripe peach.* Such prose is as overripe as the peach. Also avoid intensifying adverbs such as *very, really, extremely, terribly,* and *enormously.* Find a stronger word to use in place of the two words, such as *terrified* in place of *extremely scared.*

4. *Focus on rhythm, not rules.* Heed the advice of *The New York Times Manual of Style and Usage:* "One measure of skill is exceptions, not rules." And keep in mind this remark by novelist Ford Madox Ford: "Carefully examined, a good—an interesting—style will be found to consist in a constant succession of tiny, unobservable surprises." Ask yourself how you can provide pleasant surprises for your readers.

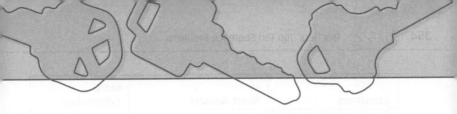

Chapter **37**

Troublespots and Terms

37a Students' frequently asked questions— and where to find answers

Questions	Short Answer	More Information
Can I begin a sentence with *and* or *but*?	Occasionally, yes	31d, p. 330
Can I begin a sentence with *because*?	Yes	38b, p. 363

(Continued)

Questions	Short Answer	More Information
How do I know whether to use *I* or *me* with *and*?	Use the "Drop the noun in the *and* phrase" test.	44a, p. 409
What is the difference between *who* and *whom*?	Use *whom* in formal writing as an object form.	44i, 46a: pp. 420, 429
When do I use *who*, *which*, or *that*?	Ask: person or thing? Consider *restrictive* vs. *nonrestrictive*.	46a, 46d: pp. 429, 433
When is it okay to use the phrase *he or she*?	To refer to a singular noun phrase—but limit the use, or use plural throughout.	44e, p. 417
Can I interchange *but* and *however*?	No. Meanings are similar; usage and punctuation differ.	39c, 47e: pp. 369, 444
When do I use *good* or *well, bad* or *badly*?	*Good* and *bad* modify nouns, not verbs, but can follow linking verbs.	45a, 45b, 45c: p. 422
What is the difference between a. *its* and *it's*?	*It's* stands for *it is* or *it has*.	48f, p. 453
b. *whose* and *who's*?	*Who's* stands for *who is* or *who has*.	Glossary of Usage, p. 529
c. *lie* and *lay*?	Use *lay* with a direct object. Learn all the forms.	41b, p. 383

37b Teachers' top ten sentence problems

Here are the problems that teachers often find and mark in their students' writing. Try to find these in your own writing before your instructor does. If you cannot immediately identify and explain an error in the middle column, read the section listed in the right column for more explanation and examples.

Type of Error	Example of Error	More Details and Examples
1. Fragment	She had an ambitious dream. *To become a CEO.*	38, p. 362
2. Run-on sentence or comma splice	The city is *lively the clubs* are open late. The city is *lively, the clubs* are open late.	39, p. 367
3. Sentence snarls	In the essay "Notes of a Native Son" by James Baldwin discusses his feelings about his father.	40, p. 369
4. Wrong verb form or tense	They have never *drank* Coke.	41a, 41d: pp. 378, 386
5. Tense shift	Foote *wrote* about Shiloh and *describes* its aftermath.	41h, p. 391
6. Lack of subject-verb agreement	The *owner have* gone bankrupt.	43, p. 398
7. Pronoun error	The coach rebuked my teammates and *I.* Nobody knows *whom* will be fired.	44a, 44i: pp. 409, 420
8. Pronoun case and reference	When I crossed the border, *they* searched my backpack.	44c, p. 413
9. Adjective/ adverb confusion	The Diamondbacks played *good* in spring training.	45a–45c, p. 422
10. Double negative	They *don't* have *no* luck.	45g, p. 426

Pages 594 and 595 show you some editing and correction marks that your instructor is likely to use.

37c What is Standard English?

Science fiction writer and editor Teresa Neilson Hayden, in *Making Book*, characterizes English as "a generous, expansive, and flexible language" but adds, "a less charitable description would characterize it as drunk and disorderly." The task of editing, she claims, is to try to impose "a degree of regularity on something that is inherently irregular." What can help you move away from irregularities in your writing is a set of conventions referred to as Standard English.

The American Heritage Dictionary, 4th edition, defines *Standard English* as "the variety of English that is generally acknowledged as

The Circle of World English (used with permission)

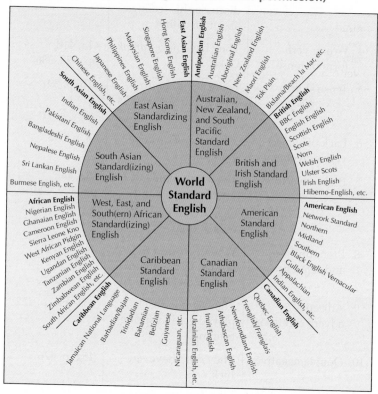

the model for the speech and writing of educated speakers." A Usage Note in the AHD, however, continues, "A form that is considered standard in one region may be nonstandard in another" and points out that *standard* and *nonstandard* are relative terms, depending largely on context.

In short, the concept of Standard English is complex. It is inextricably entwined with the region, race, class, education, and gender of both the speaker (or writer) and the listener (or reader). Standard English is far from monolithic (see the Circle of World English on p. 356). It is constantly being supplemented and challenged by other ways of writing, such as those coming from technology, the rap movement, the worlds of gender and sexual politics, popular culture, and conventions in use in different parts of the English-speaking world. (See also 59a.)

Nevertheless, Standard English, with all its quirks, irregularities, rules, and exceptions, is politically and sociologically branded as the language of those in power; its practices are what most readers expect in the academic and business worlds. However insightful and original your ideas may be, readers will soon become impatient if those ideas are not expressed in sentences that follow conventions determined by the history of the language and the prescriptive power of its educated users.

Attention to accuracy is important in the business world as well as in college. A recent study of 120 corporations found that one third of the employees of major companies had poor writing skills, leading an executive to say, "It's not that companies want to hire Tolstoy. But they need people who can write clearly."

To meet readers' expectations in academic and business settings, use the version of Standard English represented in this book.

37d What are the terms for the parts of a sentence?

To think about and discuss how sentences work, a shared vocabulary is useful. Here are some of the basic terms covering the parts of speech and the parts of a sentence. The Glossary of Grammatical Terms on page 543 provides further definitions and examples.

Parts of speech   Words are traditionally classified into eight categories called *parts of speech*. Note that the part of speech refers not to the word itself but to its function in a sentence. Some words can function as different parts of speech.

verb
▶ They respect the orchestra manager.

noun
▶ Respect is a large part of a business relationship.

NOUNS   Words that name a person, place, thing, or concept—*teacher, valley, furniture, Hinduism*—are called *nouns*. When you use a noun, determine the following: Is it a proper noun, requiring a capital letter? Does it have a plural form? If so, are you using the singular or plural form? See 53b and 60a for more on nouns.

PRONOUNS   A pronoun represents a noun or a noun phrase. In writing, a pronoun refers to its antecedent—that is, a noun or noun phrase appearing just before it in the text.

▶ My sister loves *her* new car, but *she* dented *it* last week.

Pronouns fall into seven types: personal (44a), possessive (43j, 44b), demonstrative (43j), intensive or reflexive (44h), relative (46a), interrogative (44i), and indefinite (43h). When you use a pronoun, determine the following: What word or words in the sentence does the pronoun refer to? Does the pronoun refer to a noun or pronoun that is singular or plural?

VERBS   Words that tell what a person, place, thing, or concept does or is—*smile, throw, think, seem, become, be*—are called *verbs*. Verbs change form, so when you use a verb, determine the following: What time does the verb refer to? What auxiliary or modal verbs are needed for an appropriate tense? Is the subject of the verb singular or plural? Is the verb in the active voice or passive voice? What are the five forms of the verb (*sing, sings, singing, sang, sung*), and are you using the correct form?

Main verbs often need auxiliary verbs (*be, do, have*) or modal auxiliaries (*will, would, can, could, shall, should, may, might, must*) to complete the meaning. For more on verbs, see chapters 41, 42, and 43.

ADJECTIVES   Words that describe nouns—*purple, beautiful, big*—are called *adjectives*. An adjective can precede a noun or follow a linking verb:

▶ Samantha is wearing *purple* boots.

▶ Her boots are *purple*.

Descriptive adjectives have comparative and superlative forms: *short, shorter, shortest* (45g). Also functioning as adjectives (before a noun) are *a, an,* and *the,* as well as possessives and demonstratives: *a* cabbage, *an* allegory, *their* poems, *this* book. For more on adjectives, see chapter 45.

ADVERBS Words that provide information about verbs, adjectives, adverbs, or clauses are called *adverbs*. Many but not all adverbs end in *-ly: quickly, efficiently.* Adverbs also provide information about how or when: *very, well, sometimes, often, soon, never.* Adverbs modify verbs, adjectives, other adverbs, or clauses.

> modifies verb   modifies adverb
> ▶ **Rafael dunked brilliantly. He played spectacularly well.**

> modifies adjective   modifies whole clause
> ▶ **He is a very energetic player. Undoubtedly, he is a genius.**

Conjunctive adverbs—such as *however, therefore, furthermore*—make connections between independent clauses. For more on conjunctive adverbs and other transitional expressions, see 2d, 45f, and 47e.

CONJUNCTIONS Words that connect words, phrases, and clauses are called *conjunctions*.

> ▶ **Martin loves ham *and* eggs.**

> ▶ **We bought a red table, a blue chair, *and* a gold mirror.**

> ▶ **The magazine was published, *and* his article won acclaim.**

The seven coordinating conjunctions—*and, but, or, nor, so, for, yet*—connect ideas of equal importance. Subordinating conjunctions—*because, if, when, although,* for instance (see the list in 38b)—make one clause dependent on another. Consider meaning and style (31c) when deciding whether to use a conjunction or a transition.

PREPOSITIONS Words used before nouns and pronouns to form phrases that usually do the work of an adjective or adverb are called *prepositions*.

> preposition   preposition
> ▶ **A bird with a red crest flew onto the feeder.**

Some common prepositions are *against, around, at, behind, between, except, for, from, in, into, like, on, over, regarding, to,* and *without.* Prepositional phrases are often idiomatic: *on occasion, in love.* To understand their use and meaning, consult a good dictionary. See also chapter 63.

INTERJECTIONS Words that express emotion and can stand alone—*Ha! Wow! Ugh! Ouch! Say!*—are called *interjections*. Interjections are not used frequently in academic writing. The more formal ones (such as *alas, oh*) are sometimes used in poetry:

> But she is in her grave, and, oh,
> The difference to me!
> —William Wordsworth

A sentence and its parts You have probably heard various definitions of a *sentence*, the common one being that "a sentence is a complete thought." Sometimes it is. Sometimes it is not, depending on what one expects by "complete." In fact, that definition is not particularly helpful. How complete is this thought?

▶ **He did not.**

You probably do not regard it as complete because it relies on text around it, on other sentences, to tell who he is and what it was he did not do, as in the following example.

▶ **Sarah was always competitive with her brother. She studied hard. He did not.**

Each of these sentences is grammatically complete, containing a subject and verb in an independent clause.

SUBJECT AND PREDICATE A sentence needs at the very least a *subject* (the person or thing doing or receiving the action) and a *predicate* (a comment or assertion about the subject). Only a command (such as "Run!") will not state the subject (*you*). A predicate must contain a complete verb, expressing action or state.

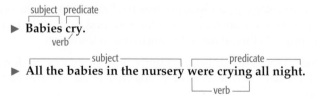

DIRECT AND INDIRECT OBJECT Some verbs are followed by a *direct object*, a word that receives the action of a verb.

> direct object
> ▶ **Many people wear glasses.** [A verb that is followed by a direct object is known as a *transitive verb. Intransitive verbs* such as *sit, happen, occur,* and *rise* are never followed by a direct object.]

Verbs such as *give, send,* and *offer* can be followed by both a direct and an *indirect object*. See 62c.

┌── indirect object ──┐ ┌──── direct object ────┐
▶ **He gave his leading lady one exquisite rose.**

COMPLEMENT Verbs such as *be, seem, look,* and *appear* are not action verbs but *linking verbs*. They are followed by a *subject complement* that renames or describes the subject.

subject complement
▶ **The singers in the choir look happy.**

An *object complement* renames or describes the direct object.

direct object ┌────── object complement ──────┐
▶ **We appointed a student the chairperson of the committee.**

PHRASE A *phrase* is a group of words that lacks a subject, a verb, or both. A phrase is only a part of a sentence. It cannot be punctuated as a sentence.

> an elegant evening gown
> singing in the rain
> on the corner
> worried by the news
> with her thoughts in turmoil
> to travel around the world

See 38a for more on phrase fragments.

CLAUSE Clauses can be independent or dependent. A sentence must contain a *main clause,* also called an *independent clause,* one that can stand alone. A clause introduced by a word such as *because, when, if,* or *although* is a *dependent clause.* Every independent clause and dependent clause needs its own subject and predicate.

┌──── independent clause ────┐
▶ **Her eyesight is deteriorating.**

independent
┌──── clause ────┐
┌──── dependent (subordinate) clause ────┐
▶ **Because her eyesight is deteriorating, she wears glasses.**

Dependent clauses can function as adverbs, adjectives, or nouns.

▶ ***When the sun shines,*** **the strawberries ripen.** [Adverb clause expressing time]

▶ **The berries *that we picked yesterday* were delicious.** [Adjective clause modifying *berries*]

▶ **The farmers know** *what they should do.* [Noun clause functioning as a direct object]

See 38b for more on dependent clause fragments.

Chapter **38**

Sentence Fragments

A *fragment* is a group of words incorrectly punctuated as if it were a complete sentence.

KEY POINTS

The Requirements of a Sentence

To be complete, a sentence must begin with a capital letter; end with a period, question mark, or exclamation point; and contain the following:

1. A subject

   It should
   ▶ **The film lasted three hours.** ~~Should~~ **have been edited.**

   A command has an understood *you* subject: [You] Arrive early.

2. A predicate that includes a complete verb

   sat
   ▶ **Kong on the Empire State Building striking airplanes down.**

   or

   struck
   ▶ **Kong on the Empire State Building** ~~striking~~ **airplanes down.**

3. An independent clause (a clause that can stand alone) with its own subject and predicate

   because
   ▶ **The audience dwindled**, ~~Because~~ **the film was so long.**

   [A clause introduced by *because* is a dependent, not an independent, clause. It needs to be attached to an independent clause.]

38a Identifying and correcting a phrase fragment

A *phrase* is a group of words that lacks a subject, a complete verb, or both. Do not punctuate a phrase as a complete sentence.

┌────── phrase fragment ──────┐
▶ He wanted to make a point. **To prove his competence.**

Methods of correcting a phrase fragment

1. Attach the phrase to a nearby independent clause. Remove the period and the capital letter.

   to
   ▶ He wanted to make a point, ~~To~~ prove his competence.

   on
   ▶ The officer parked illegally, ~~On~~ the corner, right in front of a hydrant.

   the
   ▶ A prize was awarded to Ed, ~~The~~ best worker in the company.

   [Use a comma before an explanatory tag, called an *appositive phrase*.]

2. Change the phrase to an independent clause with its own subject and verb.

   She is just
   ▶ Althea works every evening. ~~Just~~ trying to keep up with her boss's demands.

   he valued
   ▶ Nature held many attractions for Thoreau. First, the solitude.

3. Rewrite the passage.

   was so   elated   that he talked for hours.
   ▶ Ralph ~~talked for hours. Elated~~ by the company's success,

38b Identifying and correcting a dependent clause fragment

A *dependent clause* begins with a word that makes the clause subordinate. Unable to stand alone, a subordinate clause must be attached to an independent clause. Here are the words that introduce subordinate adverb clauses:

SUBORDINATING CONJUNCTIONS

time: when, whenever, until, till, before, after, while, once, as soon as, as long as

place: where, wherever

cause: because, as, since

condition: if, even if, unless, provided that

contrast: although, though, even though, whereas, while

comparison: than, as, as if, as though

purpose: so that, in order that

result: so . . . that, such . . . that

                                — fragment —

▶ **Lars wants to be a stand-up comic. Because he likes to make people laugh.**

Words introducing dependent (adjective or noun) clauses include *who, whom, whose, which, that, what, when,* and *whoever.*

Methods of correcting a dependent clause fragment

1. Connect the dependent clause to an independent clause.

   ▶ **Lars wants to be a stand-up comic/ ~~Because~~ he likes to make people laugh.** *(because)*

   ▶ **The family set out for a new country/ ~~In~~ which they could practice their culture and religion.** *(in)*

   ▶ **She made many promises to her family/ ~~That~~ she would write to them every day.** *(that)*

2. Delete the subordinating conjunction. The dependent clause then becomes an independent clause, which can stand alone.

   ▶ **Lars wants to be a stand-up comic. ~~Because he~~ likes to make people laugh.** *(He)*

Note: A subordinating conjunction at the beginning of a sentence does not always signal a fragment. A correctly punctuated sentence may begin with a subordinating conjunction introducing a dependent clause, as long as the sentence also contains an independent clause.

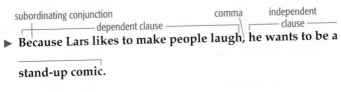

▶ Because Lars likes to make people laugh, he wants to be a

stand-up comic.

38c Identifying and correcting a fragment with a missing verb or verb part

Every sentence must contain a complete verb in an independent clause. A word group that is punctuated like a sentence but lacks a verb or has an incomplete verb is a *fragment*. A complete verb is a verb that shows tense (see 41a, 41c).

── fragment: incomplete verb ──
▶ Overcrowding is a problem. Too many people living in

one area.

── fragment: missing verb ──
▶ The candidate explained his proposal. A plan for off-street

parking.

Methods of correcting Supply all necessary verb forms, connect the fragment to the sentence before or after, or recast the sentence.

are
▶ Overcrowding is a problem. Too many people ʌliving in
one area.

with too
▶ Overcrowding is a problem⸴ ~~Too~~ many people living in
one area.

▶ The candidate explained his ~~proposal. A~~ plan for off-street
parking.

He emphasized a
▶ The candidate explained his proposal. ʌA plan for off-street
parking.

38d Identifying and correcting a fragment with a missing subject after *and, but*, or *or*

Unless it is a command with the implied subject *you*, a word group appearing without a subject is never a complete clause. Pay special attention to sentences beginning with *and, but*, or *or*.

▶ After an hour, the dancers changed partners. And adapted to

┌─── fragment ───┐

a different type of music.

Methods of correcting

1. Correct the fragment by removing the period and capital letter.

▶ After an hour, the dancers changed partners, ~~And~~ adapted to
and
a different type of music. [This forms what is known as a
compound predicate.]

2. Include an appropriate subject to form an independent clause.

▶ After an hour, the dancers changed partners. ~~And~~ adapted to
They
a different type of music.

3. Turn the fragment into an *-ing* participle phrase, and attach it to
the independent clause.

▶ After an hour, the dancers changed partners, ~~And~~ ~~adapted~~ to
adapting
a different type of music.

38e Using fragments intentionally

Advertisers and writers occasionally use fragments deliberately for a
crisp, immediate effect: "What a luxury should be." "Sleek lines."
"Efficient in rain, sleet, and snow." "A magnificent film." Novelists
and short story writers use fragments in dialogue to simulate the
immediacy and fragmentary nature of colloquial speech. Journalists
and nonfiction writers often use a fragment for a stylistic effect, to
make a point. In academic writing, too, writers sometimes use a
fragment intentionally to make an emphatic point.

> He [Dylan Thomas] lived twenty-four years after he began to be a
> poet. Twenty-four years of poetry, dwindling rapidly in the last
> decade.
> —Donald Hall, *Remembering Poets*

You will also find fragments used intentionally in question form.
This use is quite common in academic writing.

> The point of the expedition is to bring them back alive. But what
> then?
> —Carl Sagan, *Cosmos*

By all means, use fragments to achieve a specific effect. However,
edit fragments that serve no identifiable rhetorical purpose.

Chapter **39**

Run-ons and Comma Splices

39a Identifying run-on (or *fused*) sentences and comma splices

A writer who takes two independent clauses and rams them up against each other, end to end, creates the error of a *run-on sentence*, also known as a *fused sentence*.

RUN-ON ERROR

> ┌─────── independent clause ───────┐
> ▶ Blue jeans were originally made as tough work clothes
> ┌─────── independent clause ───────┐
> they became a fashion statement in the 1970s.

Inserting a comma between the two clauses adds a little more separation, but not enough. The result is a *comma splice*—another error.

COMMA SPLICE ERROR

> ▶ Blue jeans were originally made as tough work clothes, they became a fashion statement in the 1970s.

Note: As with fragments, you will find comma splices and run-ons used in advertising, journalism, and other writing for stylistic effect, often for emphasizing a contrast.

> ▶ W. [George W. Bush] and Hillary [Clinton] took radically
>   comma splice emphasizing contrast
> different paths. She clutched her husband's coattails,/he
>
> clutched his father's.
>   —Maureen Dowd, "From A to Y at Yale"

Readers of academic expository writing may prefer a period or semicolon or a recasting of the sentence instead of such use of a comma. Take the stylistic risk of using an intentional comma splice only if you are sure what effect you want to achieve and if you are sure readers will realize your intentions.

39b Correcting run-on sentences and comma splices

You can correct run-ons and comma splices in the following five ways. Select the one that works best for the sentence you are editing.

KEY POINTS

Options for Editing a Run-on or a Comma Splice

1. Separate the sentences. (Create two sentences by adding either a period or a semicolon when the two are closely related in meaning or by adding a question mark, if appropriate.)

   ▶ Blue jeans were originally made as tough work clothes. *They* became a fashion statement in the 1970s.

   ▶ Blue jeans were originally made as tough work clothes; *they* became a fashion statement in the 1970s.

2. Include a comma, but make sure it is followed by one of the seven coordinating conjunctions: *and, but, or, nor, so, for,* or *yet.*

   ▶ Blue jeans were originally made as tough work clothes, *but* they became a fashion statement in the 1970s.

3. Separate the sentences with a period or a semicolon, followed by a transitional expression such as *however* or *therefore,* followed by a comma (see 39c and 45f).

   ▶ Blue jeans were originally made as tough work clothes; *however,* they became a fashion statement in the 1970s.

4. Rewrite the sentences as one sentence by using a subordinating conjunction (see the list in 38b) to make one clause dependent on the other.

   ▶ *Although* blue jeans were originally made as tough work clothes, they became a fashion statement in the 1970s.

5. Condense or restructure the sentence.

   ▶ Blue jeans, *originally made* as tough work clothes, became a fashion statement in the 1970s.

39c Correcting run-ons and comma splices occurring with transitional expressions

Run-ons and comma splices often occur with transitional expressions such as *in addition, however, therefore, for example,* and *moreover* (see the list in 2d). When one of these expressions precedes the subject of its own clause, end the previous sentence with a period or a semicolon. Put a comma after the transitional expression, not before it.

CORRECTED
RUN-ON
ERROR

Martha cleaned her closets in addition she reorganized the kitchen. ⊙ ^In^ ^,^

CORRECTED
COMMA
SPLICE ERROR

The doctor prescribed some medicine however she did not alert the patient to the side effects. ^;^ ^,^

Note: You can use the coordinating conjunctions *and, but,* and *so* after a comma to connect two independent clauses, but *in addition, however,* and *therefore* do not follow the same punctuation pattern.

▶ The stock market was rising, so he decided to invest most of his savings.

▶ The stock market was rising; therefore, he decided to invest most of his savings.

Commas should both precede and follow a transitional expression that does not appear at the beginning of its own clause:

▶ The doctor prescribed some medicine. She did not, however, alert the patient to the side effects.

Chapter **40**

Sentence Snarls

Snarls, tangles, and knots are as difficult to deal with on a bad writing day as on a bad hair day, though they may not be as painful. Sentences with structural inconsistencies give readers trouble. They make readers work to untangle the meaning.

Always begin your editing by looking for the verb of a clause and matching it to its subject. This chapter points out how to avoid or edit common sentence snarls.

40a Fuzzy syntax

Revise sentences that begin in one way and then veer off the track, departing from the original structure. When you mix constructions, make faulty comparisons, or tangle your syntax (sentence structure), you confuse readers. Pay special attention to sentences beginning with *with, by -ing,* or *when -ing.*

MIXED
CONSTRUCTION
When wanting to take on a greater role in business might lead a woman to adopt new personality traits. [The reader gets to the verb *might lead* without knowing what the subject is. Fix mixed constructions by making sure you have a clear subject and verb that belong together.]

POSSIBLE
REVISIONS
When wanting to take on a greater role in business, a woman might adopt new personality traits. [This version provides a grammatical subject—*woman*—for the independent clause.]

Wanting to take on a greater role in business might lead a woman to adopt new personality traits. [This version deletes the preposition *when*. Now the *-ing* phrase functions as the subject of *might lead.*]

When you make comparisons, be sure to tell readers clearly what you are comparing to what. See also 44a, 44b, and 45i.

FAULTY
COMPARISON
Like Wallace Stevens, her job strikes readers as unexpected for a poet. [It is not her job that is like the poet Wallace Stevens; her job is like his job.]

REVISED
Like Wallace Stevens, she holds a job that strikes readers as unexpected for a poet.

Revise sentences that ramble on to such an extent that they become tangled. Make sure your sentences have clear subjects and verbs, and use coordination or subordination effectively. Cut and check for action (chapters 29 and 30).

TANGLED
SYNTAX

The way I feel about getting what you want is that when there is a particular position or item that you want to try to get to do your best and not give up because if you give up you have probably missed your chance of succeeding.

POSSIBLE
REVISION

To get what you want, keep trying.

40b Misplaced modifiers

A *modifier* is a word or phrase that describes or limits another word or phrase. Keep single words, phrases, and clauses next to or close to the sentence elements that they modify. That is, avoid *misplaced modifiers*.

> Next year, everyone in the company will ~~not~~ get a raise.
> [over the word *not* is written: **not**]

[The unrevised sentence says that nobody at all will get a raise. If you move the word *not*, the sentence now says that although not all workers will get a raise, some will.]

Take care with words such as *only*. Place *only, even, just, nearly, not, merely,* or *simply* immediately before the word it modifies.

> She ~~only~~ likes Tom. [Tom is the only one she likes.]
> [over the text is written: **only**]

The meaning of a sentence changes significantly as the position of *only* changes, so careful placement is important.

> ▶ *Only* the journalist began to investigate the forgery.
>   [and nobody else]

> ▶ The journalist *only* began to investigate the forgery.
>   [but did not finish]

> ▶ The journalist began to investigate *only* the forgery.
>   [and nothing else]

Place a phrase or clause close to the word it modifies.

MISPLACED

Sidel argues that young women's dreams will not always come true in her essay. [Will the dreams come true in Sidel's essay, or does Sidel argue in her essay?]

REVISED

In her essay, Sidel argues that young women's dreams will not always come true.

Consider the case for splitting an infinitive. You split an infinitive when you place a word or phrase between *to* and the verb. Avoid splitting an infinitive when the split is unnecessary or the result is clumsy, as in the following examples:

> to shine brightly.
> ► They waited for the sun ~~to brightly shine.~~

> to inform
> ► We want ~~to honestly and in confidence inform~~ you
> honestly and in confidence.
> of our plans.

Traditionally, a split infinitive was frowned upon, but it is now much more acceptable, as in the *Star Trek* motto "To boldly go where no man has gone before. . . ." Sometimes, splitting is necessary to avoid ambiguity.

> ► We had to stop them from talking *quickly.* [Were they talking too quickly? Did we have to stop them quickly? The meaning is ambiguous.]

> ► We had to *quickly stop* them from talking. [The split infinitive clearly says that we were the ones who had to do something quickly.]

40c Dangling modifiers

A word ending in *-ing* or *-ed* at the beginning of a sentence must provide information about the subject of the sentence. When this modifier is not grammatically linked to the noun or phrase it is intended to describe, it is said to be *dangling*.

DANGLING **Walking into the house, the telephone rang.**
[The sentence says the telephone was walking.]

DANGLING **Delighted with the team's victory, the parade route was decorated by the fans.** [The sentence says the parade route was delighted.]

You can fix a dangling modifier in the following ways:

Method 1 Retain the modifier, but make it modify the subject of the independent clause.

REVISED **Walking into the house, we heard the telephone ring.**

REVISED **Delighted with the team's victory, the fans decorated the parade route.**

Method 2 Change the modifier phrase into a clause with its own subject and verb.

REVISED **While we were walking into the house, the telephone rang.**

REVISED **Because the fans were delighted with the team's victory, they decorated the parade route.**

40d Shifts: From statements to commands, from indirect to direct quotation, and in point of view

Sudden shifts in your sentences can disconcert readers. (See also 41h on avoiding unnecessary shifts in verb tense.)

Do not shift abruptly from statements to commands.

▶ **The students in this university should do more to keep the**
  They should pick
place clean. ~~Pick~~ up the litter and treat the dorms like home.

Do not shift from indirect to direct quotation. (See 41h and 62d for more on tenses in indirect quotations.)

SHIFT **The client told us that he wanted to sign the lease and would we prepare the papers.**

REVISED **The client told us that he wanted to sign the lease and asked us to prepare the papers.**

SHIFT **She wanted to find out whether any interest had accumulated on her account and was she receiving any money.**

REVISED | She wanted to find out whether any interest had accumulated on her account and whether she was receiving any money.

Do not shift point of view in pronouns. Be consistent in using first, second, or third person pronouns. For example, if you begin by referring to *one*, do not switch to *you* or *we*. Also avoid shifting unnecessarily between third person singular and plural forms.

SHIFT | *One* needs a high salary to live in a city because *you* have to spend so much on rent and transportation.

POSSIBLE REVISIONS | *One* needs a high salary to live in a city because *one* has to spend so much on rent and transportation.

People need a high salary to live in a city because *they* have to spend so much on rent and transportation.

A high salary is necessary in a city because rent and transportation cost so much.

40e Mismatch of subject and predicate

To avoid confusing readers, never use a subject and predicate that do not make logical sense together. This error is known as *faulty predication.*

▶ ~~The decision to build~~ Building an elaborate extension onto the train station made all the trains arrive late. [The decision did not delay the trains; the building of the extension delayed them.]

▶ ~~The~~ Finding the solution to the problem is a hard task. [A solution is not a task.]

40f Definitions and reasons ("is when" and "is because")

When you write a definition of a term, use parallel structures on either side of the verb *be*. In formal writing, avoid defining a term by using *is when* or *is where* (or *was when, was where*).

FAULTY | A tiebreaker in tennis *is where* they play one final game to decide the set.

REVISED | A tiebreaker in tennis is the final deciding game of a tied set.

Writing about reasons, like writing definitions, has pitfalls. Avoid *the reason is because* in Standard English. Grammatically, an adverb clause beginning with *because* cannot follow the verb *be*. Instead, use *the reason is that,* or recast the sentence.

FAULTY **The reason Andy Roddick lost *is because* his net game isn't aggressive enough.**

POSSIBLE **The reason Roddick lost *is that* his net game isn't**
REVISIONS **aggressive enough.**

Roddick lost *because* his net game isn't aggressive enough.

Note that Standard English requires *the reason that* and not *the reason why*.

▶ **The TV commentator explained the reason ~~why~~ ^that^ Roddick lost.** [Another possibility here is to omit *that*.]

40g *Because* and *when* clauses as subject

A dependent adverb clause (37d) beginning with *because* or *when* cannot function as the subject of a sentence.

▶ ^Swimming^ **~~Just because she swims~~ every day does not mean she is healthy.** [The subject is now a noun phrase, *Swimming every day*, instead of a clause, *Because she swims every day*.]

▶ **When people eat too much fat ^, they^ increases their cholesterol.** [The dependent clause *When people eat too much fat* is now attached to an independent clause with its own subject, *they*.]

40h Omitted words and apostrophes

Include necessary words in compound structures. If you omit a verb form from a compound verb, the main verb form must fit into each part of the compound; otherwise, you must use the complete verb form (see 40j on parallelism).

▶ **He has always ^tried^ and will always try to preserve his father's good name in the community.** [*Try* fits only with *will*, not with *has*.]

Include necessary words in comparisons. (See also 45h.)

▶ The volleyball captain is as competitive$\overset{as}{\wedge}$or even more competitive than her teammates. [The comparative structures are *as competitive as* and *more competitive than*. Do not merge them.]

If you omit the verb in the second part of a comparison, ambiguity may occur.

▶ He liked baseball more than his son$\overset{did.}{\wedge}$[Omitting *did* implies he liked baseball more than he liked his son.]

Include apostrophes with words that need them.

▶ My mother's expectations differed from Jing-Mei's

mother$\overset{'s.}{\wedge}$

See also 45h and 48c.

40i Restated subject

Even when a phrase or clause separates the subject from the main verb of a sentence, do not restate the subject in pronoun form. (See also 62f.)

incorrect restated subject

▶ The nurse who took care of my father for many years ~~she~~ gave him comfort and advice.

When the subject is a whole clause, do not add an *it* subject.

▶ What may seem moral to some ~~it~~ is immoral to others.

40j Structures not parallel

The use of parallel structures helps produce cohesion and coherence in a text. Aim for parallelism in sentences and in longer passages. The structures can be clauses or phrases, as shown in the following passages from "Maintenance" by Naomi Shihab Nye.

PARALLEL STRUCTURES: CLAUSES

We saw one house *where walls and windows had been sheathed in various patterns of gloomy brocade*. We visited another *where the kitchen had been removed* because the owners only ate in restaurants.

PARALLEL STRUCTURES: VERB PHRASES

Sometimes I'd come home to find her *lounging* in the bamboo chair on the back porch, *eating* melon, or *lying* on the couch with a bowl of half-melted ice cream balanced on her chest.

Sentences become confusing when you string together phrases or clauses that lack parallelism.

NOT PARALLEL **He wants a new girlfriend, to get a house, and find a good job.**

PARALLEL **He wants a new girlfriend, a house, and a good job.**

Parallel structures with paired (correlative) conjunctions

When your sentence contains *correlative conjunctions*—pairs such as *either ... or, neither ... nor, not only ... but also, both ... and, whether ... or,* and *as ... as*—the structure after the second part of the pair should be exactly parallel in form to the structure after the first part.

▶ **He made up his mind *either* to paint the van *or* ^to^ sell it to another buyer.** [*To paint* follows *either*; therefore, *to sell* should follow *or*.]

▶ **She loves *both* swimming competitively *and* ~~to play~~ ^playing^ golf.** [An -*ing* form follows *both*; therefore, an -*ing* form should also follow *and*.]

▶ **The drive to Cuernavaca was *not only* too expensive *but also* ~~was~~ too tiring to do alone.** [*Too expensive* follows *not only*; therefore, *too tiring* should follow *but also*.]

Parallel structures in comparisons

When making comparisons with *as* or *than*, use parallel structures.

▶ ^To drive^ ~~Driving~~ to Cuernavaca is *as* expensive *as* to take the bus.

▶ ^Taking^ ~~To take~~ the bus is less comfortable *than* driving.

Chapter **41**

Verbs

A verb will fit into one or more of the following sentences:

a. They want to _____ .   It is going to _____.

b. They will _____ .   It might _____.

Identify a verb by checking that the *base form* (that is, the form listed as a dictionary entry) fits these sentences.

41a   Verb forms in Standard English

Although you might use a variety of verb forms when you speak, readers generally expect formal writing to conform to Standard English usage. All verbs except *be* have five forms.

Regular verbs   The five forms of regular verbs follow a predictable pattern. Once you know the base form, you can construct all the others:

1. base form: the form listed in a dictionary (*paint, help*)
2. *-s* form: the third person singular form of the present tense (*paints, helps*)
3. *-ing* form (the *present participle*): needs auxiliary verbs to function as a complete verb; can appear in a verbal phrase and as a noun (gerund) (*painting, helping*)
4. past tense form: functions as a complete verb, without auxiliary verbs (*painted, helped*)
5. past participle: sometimes called the *-ed* form; needs auxiliary verbs to function as a complete verb (*has painted, was helped*); can appear in a phrase (*the painted wall*)

Irregular verbs   Irregular verbs do not use *-ed* to form the past tense and the past participle. Here are the forms of some common irregular verbs.

Irregular Verbs

Base Form	Past Tense	Past Participle
arise	arose	arisen
be	was/were	been
bear	bore	born, borne
beat	beat	beaten
become	became	become
begin	began	begun
bend	bent	bent
bet	bet	bet, betted
bind	bound	bound
bite	bit	bitten
bleed	bled	bled
blow	blew	blown
break	broke	broken
bring	brought	brought
build	built	built
burst	burst	burst
buy	bought	bought
catch	caught	caught
choose	chose	chosen
cling	clung	clung
come	came	come
cost	cost	cost
creep	crept	crept
cut	cut	cut
deal	dealt	dealt
dig	dug	dug
do	did	done
draw	drew	drawn
drink	drank	drunk
drive	drove	driven

Base Form	Past Tense	Past Participle
eat	ate	eaten
fall	fell	fallen
feed	fed	fed
feel	felt	felt
fight	fought	fought
find	found	found
flee	fled	fled
fly	flew	flown
forbid	forbad(e)	forbidden
forget	forgot	forgotten
forgive	forgave	forgiven
freeze	froze	frozen
get	got	gotten, got
give	gave	given
go	went	gone
grind	ground	ground
grow	grew	grown
hang*	hung	hung
have	had	had
hear	heard	heard
hide	hid	hidden
hit	hit	hit
hold	held	held
hurt	hurt	hurt
keep	kept	kept
know	knew	known
lay	laid	laid (41b)
lead	led	led
leave	left	left
lend	lent	lent

Hang meaning "put to death" is regular: *hang, hanged, hanged.*

Base Form	Past Tense	Past Participle
let	let	let
lie	lay	lain (41b)
light	lit, lighted	lit, lighted
lose	lost	lost
make	made	made
mean	meant	meant
meet	met	met
put	put	put
quit	quit	quit
read	read	read
ride	rode	ridden
ring	rang	rung
rise	rose	risen (41b)
run	ran	run
say	said	said
see	saw	seen
seek	sought	sought
sell	sold	sold
send	sent	sent
set	set	set (41b)
shake	shook	shaken
shine	shone, shined	shone, shined
shoot	shot	shot
shrink	shrank	shrunk
shut	shut	shut
sing	sang	sung
sink	sank	sunk
sit	sat	sat (41b)
sleep	slept	slept
slide	slid	slid
slit	slit	slit
speak	spoke	spoken
spend	spent	spent
spin	spun	spun
spit	spit, spat	spit

Base Form	Past Tense	Past Participle
split	split	split
spread	spread	spread
spring	sprang	sprung
stand	stood	stood
steal	stole	stolen
stick	stuck	stuck
sting	stung	stung
stink	stank, stunk	stunk
strike	struck	struck, stricken
swear	swore	sworn
sweep	swept	swept
swim	swam	swum
swing	swung	swung
take	took	taken
teach	taught	taught
tear	tore	torn
tell	told	told
think	thought	thought
throw	threw	thrown
tread	trod	trodden, trod
understand	understood	understood
upset	upset	upset
wake	woke	waked, woken
wear	wore	worn
weave	wove	woven
weep	wept	wept
win	won	won
wind	wound	wound
wring	wrung	wrung
write	wrote	written

41b Verbs commonly confused

Give special attention to verbs that are similar in form but differ in meaning. Some of them can take a direct object; these are called *transitive verbs*. Others never take a direct object; these are called *intransitive verbs*. (See 62c.)

1. *rise:* to get up, to ascend (intransitive; irregular)

   raise: to lift, to cause to rise (transitive; regular)

Base	-s	-ing	Past Tense	Past Participle
rise	rises	rising	rose	risen
raise	raises	raising	raised	raised

   ▶ The sun *rose* at 5:55 a.m. today.

   ▶ She *raised* the blind and peeked out.

2. *sit:* to occupy a seat (intransitive; irregular)

   set: to put or place (transitive; irregular)

Base	-s	-ing	Past Tense	Past Participle
sit	sits	sitting	sat	sat
set	sets	setting	set	set

   ▶ He *sat* on the wooden chair.

   ▶ She *set* the vase on the middle shelf.

3. *lie:* to recline (intransitive; irregular)

   lay: to put or place (transitive; regular)

Base	-s	-ing	Past Tense	Past Participle
lie	lies	lying	lay	lain
lay	lays	laying	laid	laid

        lay
   ▶ I ~~laid~~ down for half an hour.

        lying
   ▶ I was ~~laying~~ down when you called.

        Lay
   ▶ ~~Lie~~ the map on the floor.

In addition, note the verb *lie* ("to say something untrue"), which is intransitive and regular.

Base	*-s*	*-ing*	Past Tense	Past Participle
lie	lies	lying	lied	lied

▶ He *lied* when he said he had won three trophies.

41c Auxiliary verbs

An auxiliary verb is used with a main verb and sometimes with other auxiliaries. The auxiliary verbs are *do, have,* and *be,* and the nine modal verbs are *will, would, can, could, shall, should, may, might,* and *must* (61b). Note the irregular forms of *do, have,* and *be.*

Base	Present Tense Forms	*-ing*	Past	Past Participle
do	do, does	doing	did	done
have	have, has	having	had	had
be	am, is, are	being	was, were	been

See 43a for agreement with present tense forms of *do, have,* and *be.*

 LANGUAGE AND CULTURE

Language and Dialect Variation with *Be*

In some languages (Chinese and Russian, for example), forms of *be* used as an auxiliary ("She *is* singing") or as a linking verb ("He *is* happy") can be omitted. In some spoken dialects of English (African American Vernacular, for example), subtle linguistic distinctions not possible in Standard English can be achieved: the omission of a form of *be* and the use of the base form in place of an inflected form (a form that shows number, person, mood, or tense) signal entirely different meanings.

Vernacular		Standard
He busy.	(temporarily)	He is busy now.
She be busy.	(habitually)	She is busy all the time.

Standard English always requires the inclusion of a form of *be.*

   are
▶ Latecomers always at a disadvantage.
     ^

Auxiliary verbs can be used in combination. Whatever the combination, the form of the main verb is determined by the auxiliary that precedes it.

Verb Forms Following Auxiliaries

Last Auxiliary and Its Forms	+ base	+ *ing*	+ past participle
do modals (can, could, will, would, shall, should, must, might, may)	did **run** might **go** would **fall**		
have			has/have/had **written** **should** have **seen** **would** have **gone**
be (active)		is **writing** were **singing** **might** be **driving** **has** been **running** **should** have been **thinking**	
be (passive)			are **grown** was **taken** **was** being **stolen** **would** be **eaten** **has** been **written** **might have** been **worn**

Pay careful attention to the tricky editing points here:

1. Make sure you use a past participle form after *have*. In speech, we run sounds together, and the pronunciation may be mistakenly carried over into writing.

   > have
   > ▶ He could ~~of~~ run faster.
   > ⌃

   > have
   > ▶ She should ~~of~~ left that job a long time ago.
   > ⌃

The contracted forms *could've, should've, would've,* and so on, are probably responsible for the nonstandard substitution of the word *of* in place of *have.* Watch out for this as you edit.

2. With modal verbs, *do,* and *have,* the verb form following is fixed. It is only with *be* that a conscious choice of active or passive voice comes into play.

▶ Laura *is taking* her driving test. [active]

▶ Laura *was taken* to the hospital last night. [passive]

ESL NOTE

What Comes before *Be, Been,* and *Being*

Be requires a modal auxiliary before it to form a complete verb (*could be jogging; will be closed*). *Been* requires *have, has,* or *had* (*have been driving; has been eaten*). *Being* must be preceded by *am, is, are, was,* or *were* to form a complete verb and must be followed by an adjective or a past participle: *You are being silly. He was being followed.*

41d Verb tenses

Tenses indicate time as perceived by the speaker or writer. The following examples show active voice verbs referring to past, present, and future time. For passive voice verbs, see chapter 42.

Past Time

Simple past	They *arrived* yesterday./They *did* not *arrive* today.
Past progressive	They *were leaving* when the phone rang.
Past perfect	Everyone *had left* when I called.
Past perfect progressive	We *had been sleeping* for an hour before you arrived.

Present Time

Simple present	He *eats* Wheaties every morning./ He *does* not *eat* eggs.
Present progressive	They *are working* today.
Present perfect	She *has* never *read* Melville.
Present perfect progressive	He *has been living* here for five years.

Future Time (using *will*)

Simple future	She *will arrive* soon.
Future progressive	They *will be playing* baseball at noon tomorrow.
Future perfect	He *will have finished* the project by Friday.
Future perfect progressive	By the year 2009, they *will have been running* the company for twenty-five years.

Other modal auxiliaries can substitute for *will* and thus change the meaning: *must arrive, might be playing, may have finished, should have been running.* (See also 61b.)

ESL NOTE

Verbs Not Using *-ing* Forms for Progressive Tenses

Use simple tenses, not progressive forms, with verbs expressing mental activity referring to the senses, preference, or thought, as well as with verbs of possession, appearance, and inclusion (for example, *smell, prefer, understand, own, seem, contain*).

▶ The fish in the showcase ~~is smelling~~ bad.
  _{smells}

▶ They ~~are possessing~~ different behavior patterns.
  _{possess}

41e Present tenses

Simple present Use the simple present tense for the following purposes:

1. To make a generalization

   ▶ Babies *sleep* a lot.

2. To indicate an activity that is permanent or happens habitually or repeatedly

   ▶ He *works* for Sony.

   ▶ We *turn* the clocks ahead every April.

3. To discuss literature and the arts even if the work was written in the past or the author is no longer alive

> In *Zami,* **Audre Lorde** *describes* how a librarian *introduces* her to the joys of reading.

When used in this way, the present tense is called the *literary present.* However, when you write a narrative of your own, use past tenses to tell about past actions.

>   walked   kissed
> **Then the candidate ~~walks~~ up to the crowd and ~~kisses~~ all the babies.**

ESL NOTE

No *Will* in Time Clause

In a dependent clause beginning with a conjunction such as *if, when, before, after, until,* or *as soon as,* do not use *will* to express future time. Use *will* only in the independent clause. Use the simple present in the dependent clause.

> **When they ~~will~~ arrive, the meeting will begin.**

Present progressive   Use the present progressive to indicate an action in progress at the moment of speaking or writing.

> **Publishers** *are getting* **nervous about plagiarism.**

Present perfect and present perfect progressive   Use the present perfect in the following instances:

1. To indicate that an action occurring at some unstated time in the past is related to present time

> **They** *have worked* **in New Mexico, so they know its laws.**

2. To indicate that an action beginning in the past continues to the present

> **She** *has worked* **for the same company since I** *have known* **her.**

If you state the exact time when something occurred, use the simple past tense, not the present perfect.

>   worked
> **They ~~have worked~~ in Arizona three years ago.**

3. To report research results in APA style

> **Feynmann** *has shown* **that science can be fun.**

Use the present perfect progressive when you indicate the length of time an action has been in progress up to the present time.

▶ Researchers *have been searching* for a cure for arthritis for many years. [This implies that they are still searching.]

41f Past tenses

Use past tenses consistently. Do not switch from past to present or future for no reason (see 41h).

Simple past   Use the simple past tense when you specify a past time or event.

▶ World War I soldiers *suffered* in the trenches.

When the sequence of past events is indicated with words like *before* or *after*, use the simple past for both events.

▶ She *knew* how to write her name before she went to school.

Past progressive   Use the past progressive for an activity in progress over time or at a specified point in the past.

▶ Abraham Lincoln *was attending* the theater when he was assassinated.

Past perfect   Use the past perfect or the past perfect progressive only when one past event was completed before another past event or stated past time.

▶ Ben *had cooked* the whole meal by the time Sam arrived. [Two events occurred: Ben cooked the meal; then Sam arrived.]

▶ He *had been cooking* for three hours when his sister finally offered to help. [An event in progress—cooking—was interrupted in the past.]

Make sure that the past tense form you choose expresses your exact meaning.

▶ When the student protesters marched into the building at noon, the administrators *were leaving*. [The administrators were in the process of leaving. They began to leave at, say, 11:57 a.m.]

▶ **When the student protesters marched into the building at noon, the administrators *had left*.** [There was no sign of the administrators. They had already left at 11 a.m.]

▶ **When the student protesters marched into the building at noon, the administrators *left*.** [The administrators saw the protesters and then left at 12:01 p.m.]

41g *-ed* endings: Past tense and past participle forms

Both the past tense form and the past participle of regular verbs end in *-ed*. This ending causes writers trouble because in speech the ending seems to be dropped—particularly when it blends into the next sound.

▶ **They wash$\overset{ed}{\wedge}$ two baskets of laundry last night.**

Standard English requires the *-ed* ending in the following instances.

1. To form the past tense of a regular verb

   ▶ **He ask$\overset{ed}{\wedge}$ to leave early.**

2. To form the expression *used to,* indicating past habit

   ▶ **Computers use$\overset{d}{\wedge}$ to be more expensive than they are now.**

3. To form the past participle of a regular verb after the auxiliary *has, have,* or *had* in the active voice or after forms of *be* (*am, is, are, was, were, be, being, been*) in the passive voice (see chapter 42)

   ▶ **The Kennedy family has work$\overset{ed}{\wedge}$ in politics for a long time.** [Active]

   ▶ **Their work will not be finish$\overset{ed}{\wedge}$ soon.** [Passive]

4. To form a past participle to serve as an adjective

   ▶ **The recipe calls for chop$\overset{ped}{\wedge}$ meat.**

   ▶ **The frighten$\overset{ed}{\wedge}$ soldier ran to his commanding officer.**

Note: The following *-ed* forms are used with *be*: *concerned, confused, depressed, divorced, embarrassed, married, prejudiced, satisfied, scared, supposed (to), surprised, used (to), worried.* Some can also be used with *get, seem, appear,* and *look.* Do not omit the *-d* ending.

▶ I was surprise to see how many awards he had won.

▶ The general was suppose to be in charge.

▶ Parents get worry when their children look depress.

Do not confuse the past tense form and the past participle of an irregular verb. A past tense form stands alone as a complete verb with no auxiliaries, but a past participle does not.

▶ The students drunk too much at the game.

▶ She done her best.

▶ The skiers should not have went alone.

▶ The bell was rang five times.

41h Unnecessary tense shifts

If you use tenses consistently throughout a piece of writing, you help readers understand what is happening and when. Check that your verbs consistently express present or past time, both within a sentence and from one sentence to the next. Avoid unnecessary tense shifts.

TENSE
SHIFTS

Selecting a jury *was* very difficult. The lawyers *ask* many questions to discover bias and prejudice; sometimes the prospective jurors *had* the idea they *are acting* in a play.

REVISED

Selecting a jury *was* very difficult. The lawyers *asked* many questions to discover bias and prejudice; sometimes the prospective jurors *had* the idea they *were acting* in a play.

When you write about events or ideas presented by another writer, use the literary present consistently (see 41e).

illustrates
► The author i̶l̶l̶u̶s̶t̶r̶a̶t̶e̶d̶ the images of women in two shows
using advertisements and dramas on TV. One way shows
women who advanced their careers by themselves, and the
other shows those who used beauty to gain recognition.

Tense shifts are appropriate in the following instances:

1. When you signal a time change with a time word or phrase

    signal for switch from past to present
    ► Harold *was* my late grandfather's name, and *now* it *is* mine.

2. When you follow a generalization (present tense) with a specific
   example of a past incident

    ┌──────────────── generalization ────────────────┐
    ► Some bilingual schools *offer* intensive instruction in English.

    ┌──────────────── specific example ────────────────┐
    My sister, for example, *went* to a bilingual school where she
    studied English for two hours every day.

41i Tenses in indirect quotations

An indirect quotation reports what someone said. It does not use
quotation marks, and it follows the tense of the introductory verb.
For example, when the verb introducing an indirect quotation is in a
present tense, the indirect quotation should preserve the tense of the
original direct quotation. See also 62d.

DIRECT   **"The client has signed the contract."**

            present   ┌────────── indirect quotation ──────────┐
INDIRECT   **The lawyer *says* that the client *has signed* the contract.**

When the introductory verb is in a past tense, use forms that express
past time in the indirect quotation.

DIRECT   **"The meetings are over and the buyer has signed the
            contract."**

            past   ┌────────── indirect quotation ──────────┐
INDIRECT   **The lawyer *told* us that the meetings *were* over and the**

            ┌────────────────────────────────────┐
            buyer *had signed* the contract.

In a passage of more than one sentence, preserve the sequence of tenses showing past time throughout the whole passage.

▶ Our lawyer, Larraine, told us that the meetings *were* over and the buyer *had signed* the contract. Larraine's firm *had reassigned* her to another case, so she *was leaving* the next day.

Note: Use a present tense after a past tense introductory verb only if the statement is a general statement that holds true in present time.

▶ Our lawyer *told* us she *is* happy with the progress of the case.

41j Verbs in conditional sentences, wishes, requests, demands, and recommendations

Conditions When *if* or *unless* is used to introduce a dependent clause, the sentence expresses a condition. Four types of conditional sentences are used: two refer to actual or possible situations, and two refer to speculative or hypothetical situations.

"If he doesn't go nuts first, he'll be the first person to ever write a novel on a cell phone."

KEY POINTS
Verb Tenses in Conditional Sentences

Meaning Expressed	*If* Clause	Independent Clause
1. Fact	Simple present	Simple present

▶ If mortgage rates *go* down, house sales *increase*.

(Continued)

(Continued)

Meaning Expressed	If Clause	Independent Clause
2. Prediction/ possibility	Simple present	*will, can, should, might* + base form

▶ If you *turn* left here, you *will end up* in Mississippi.

▶ If we *don't speak* ill of the dead, who *will*?

—Harold Bloom

3. Speculation about present or future	Simple past or subjunctive *were*	*would, could, should, might* + base form

▶ If he *had* a cell phone, he *would use* it. [But he does not have one.]

▶ If she *were* my lawyer, I *might win* the case. [But she is not.]

4. Speculation about past	Past perfect (*had* + past participle)	*would have, could have, should have, might have* + past participle

▶ If they *had saved* the diaries, they *could have sold* them. [But they did not save them.]

USE OF SUBJUNCTIVE *WERE* IN PLACE OF *WAS*   With speculative conditions about the present and future using the verb *be*, *were* is used in place of *was* in the dependent *if* clause. This use of *were* to indicate hypothetical situations involves what is called the *subjunctive mood*.

▶ If my aunt *were* sixty-five, she *could get* a discount air fare. [My aunt is sixty.]

BLENDING   Some blending of time and tenses can occur, as in the case of a condition that speculates about the past in relation to the effect on the present.

▶ If I *had bought* a new car instead of this old wreck, I *would feel* a lot safer today.

USE OF *WOULD* When writing Standard English, use *would* only in the independent clause, not in the conditional clause. However, *would* occurs frequently in the conditional clause in speech and in informal writing.

> ▶ If the fish fry committee ~~would show~~ ^{showed} more initiative, people might attend their events more regularly.

> ▶ If the driver ~~would have~~ ^{had} heard what the pedestrian said, he would have been angry.

***WOULD*, *COULD*, AND *MIGHT* WITH CONDITIONAL CLAUSE UNDERSTOOD** *Would, could,* and *might* are used in independent clauses when no conditional clause is present. These are situations that are contrary to fact, and the conditional clause is understood.

> ▶ I *would* never *advise* her to leave college without a degree. She *might come back* later and blame me for her lack of direction.

Wishes   Like some conditions, wishes deal with speculation. For a present wish—about something that has not happened and is therefore hypothetical and imaginary—use the past tense or subjunctive *were* in the dependent clause. For a wish about the past, use the past perfect: *had* + past participle.

A WISH ABOUT THE PRESENT

> ▶ I wish I *had* your attitude.

> ▶ I wish that Shakespeare *were* still alive.

A WISH ABOUT THE PAST

> ▶ Some union members wish that the strike *had* never *occurred*.

> ▶ He wishes that he *had bought* a lottery ticket.

Requests, demands, and recommendations   The subjunctive also appears after certain verbs, such as *request, command, insist, demand, move* (meaning "propose"), *propose,* and *urge*. In these cases, the verb in the dependent clause is the base form, regardless of the person and number of the subject.

> ▶ The dean suggested that students *be* allowed to vote.

▶ He insisted that she *submit* the report.

▶ I move that the treasurer *revise* the budget.

Some idiomatic expressions preserve the subjunctive in Standard English—for example, *far* be *it from me, if need* be, *as it* were.

Chapter **42**

Passive Voice

In the active voice, the grammatical subject is the doer of the action, and the sentence tells "who's doing what." The passive voice tells what "is done to" the subject of the sentence. The person or thing doing the action may or may not be mentioned but is always implied: "My car was repaired" (by somebody at the garage).

ACTIVE

┌─ subject ─┐   active voice verb   ┌─ direct object ─┐
▶ **Alice Walker**   **wrote**   *The Color Purple.*

PASSIVE

                           passive voice
┌──── subject ────┐   ┌── verb ──┐   ┌─ doer or agent ─┐
▶ *The Color Purple*   **was written**   **by Alice Walker.**

42a When to use the passive voice

Use the passive voice sparingly. A general rule is to use the passive voice only when the doer or agent in your sentence (the person or thing acting) is unknown or is unimportant or when you want to connect the topics of two clauses (see 31a and 42d).

▶ The pandas are rare. Two of them *will be returned* to the wild.

▶ He had a lot of people working for him, maybe sixty, and most of them liked him most of the time. Three of them *will be* seriously *considered* for his job.

—Ellen Goodman, "The Company Man"

However, in scientific writing, the passive voice is often preferred to indicate objective procedures. Scientists and engineers are interested in analyzing data and in performing studies that other researchers can replicate. The individual doing the experiment is therefore relatively unimportant and usually is not the subject of the sentence.

▶ **The experiment *was conducted* in a classroom. Participants *were instructed* to remove their watches prior to the experiment.**

ESL NOTE

Passive Voice with Transitive Verbs

Use the passive voice only with verbs that are transitive in English. Intransitive verbs such as *happen, occur,* and *try (to)* are not used in the passive voice.

▶ **The accident ~~was~~ happened yesterday.**

▶ **Morality is an issue that ~~was~~ ^{have} tried to explain ~~by many philosophers~~.**

42b How to form the passive voice

The complete verb of a passive voice sentence consists of a form of the verb *be* followed by a past participle.

```
                    verb: be +
   receiver         past participle   doer omitted or named after by
  ┌─ as subject ─┐ ┌──────────┐
▶ The windows    are cleaned   [by someone] every month.
```

▶ **The windows *were being cleaned* yesterday afternoon.**

▶ **The windows *will have been cleaned* by the end of the workday.**

Auxiliaries such as *would, can, could, should, may, might,* and *must* can also replace *will* when the meaning demands it.

▶ **The windows *might be cleaned* next month.**

42c Overuse of the passive voice

In the humanities, your writing will generally be clearer and stronger if you name the subject and use verbs in the active voice to explain who is doing what. If you overuse the passive voice, the effect will be heavy and impersonal (see 30a).

UNNECESSARY PASSIVE   **He *was alerted* to the danger of drugs by his doctor and *was persuaded* by her to enroll in a treatment program.**

REVISED   **His doctor alerted him to the danger of drugs and persuaded him to enroll in a treatment program.**

42d The passive voice as connector

In the following passage, notice how the passive voice preserves the topic chain of *I* subjects (see also 31a):

▶ **I remember to start with that day in Sacramento . . . when I first entered a classroom, able to understand some fifty stray English words. The third of four children, I *had been preceded* to a Roman Catholic school by an older brother and sister.**

—Richard Rodriguez, *Hunger of Memory*

Chapter **43**

Subject-Verb Agreement

In Standard English, a third person singular subject in the present tense takes a singular verb (with *-s*), and a plural subject takes a plural verb (with no *-s*).

Singular Subject	Plural Subject
A baby *cries*.	Babies *cry*.
He *loses*.	They *lose*.
His brother *plays* baseball.	His brothers *play* baseball.

43a Basic principles for an -s ending

When you use the present tense, subject and verb must agree in person (first, second, or third) and number (singular or plural). In English, the ending -s is added to both nouns and verbs, but for very different reasons.

1. An -s ending on a noun is a plural signal: *her brothers* (more than one).
2. An -s ending on a verb is a singular signal; -s is added to a third person singular verb in the present tense: *Her plumber wears gold jewelry.*

KEY POINTS
Two Key Points about Agreement

1. Follow the "one -s rule." Generally, you can put an -s on a noun to make it plural, or you can put an -s on a verb to make it singular. (But see the irregular forms *is* and *has* on p. 400.) An -s on both subject and verb is not Standard English.

   NO   **The articles explains the controversy.**
        [Violates the "one -s rule"]

   POSSIBLE   **The article explains the controversy.**
   REVISIONS
        The articles explain the controversy.

2. Do not omit a necessary -s.

   ▶ His supervisor wanṱ him to work the night shift.

   ▶ The book on my desk describḙ life in Tahiti.

   ▶ She *uses* her experience, *speaks* to the crowds, and *wiṋ* their confidence.

Most simple present verbs show agreement with an -s ending. The verb *be,* however, has three instead of two present tense forms. In addition, *be* is the only verb to show agreement in the past tense, where it has two forms: *were* and the third person singular *was.*

Subject-Verb Agreement

Base Form	like (regular)	have	be	do
Simple Present: Singular				
First person: I	like	have	am	do
Second person: you	like	have	are	do
Third person: he, she, it	likes	has	is	does
Simple Present: Plural				
First person: we	like	have	are	do
Second person: you	like	have	are	do
Third person: they	like	have	are	do

LANGUAGE AND CULTURE

Issues of Subject-Verb Agreement

Many languages make no change in the verb form to indicate number and person, and several spoken versions of English, such as African American Vernacular (AAV), Caribbean Creole, and London Cockney, do not observe the standard rules of agreement.

▶ **AAV: She *have* a lot of work experience.**

▶ **Cockney: He *don't* never wear that brown whistle.**
[The standard form is *doesn't;* other nonstandard forms in this sentence are *don't never* (a double negative) and *whistle* —short for *whistle and flute,* rhyming slang for *suit.*]

Use authentic forms like these when quoting direct speech; for your formal academic writing, though, follow the subject-verb agreement conventions of Standard English.

43b Words between the subject and verb

When words separate the subject and verb, find the verb and ask "Who?" or "What?" about it to determine the subject. Ignore any intervening words.

▶ **The general discussing the attacks looks tired.** [Who looks tired? The subject, *general,* is singular.]

▶ **Her collection of baseball cards is valuable.** [What is valuable? The subject, *collection*, is singular.]

▶ **The government's proposals about preserving the environment cause controversy.** [What things cause controversy? The subject, *proposals*, is plural.]

Do not be confused by intervening words ending in -*s*, such as *always* and *sometimes*. The -*s* ending still must appear on a present tense verb if the subject is singular.

▶ **His assistant always make^s^ mistakes.**

Phrases introduced by *as well as, along with,* and *in addition to* that come between the subject and the verb do not change the number of the verb.

▶ **His daughter, as well as his two sons, want^s^ him to move nearby.**

43c Agreement with a linking verb

Linking verbs such as *be, seem, look,* and *appear* are followed by a complement, and a subject complement should not be confused with a subject (see 37d). Make the verb agree with the subject stated before the linking verb, not with the noun complement that follows the verb.

plural | singular   singular | plural
┌─ subject ─┐ ┌ complement ┐   ┌─ subject ─┐ ┌ complement ┐
▶ **Rare books *are* her passion.**   ▶ **Her passion *is* rare books.**
    plural verb   singular verb

▶ **My favorite part of city life *is* the parties.**

▶ **Parties *are* my favorite part of city life.**

43d Subject after verb

When the subject follows the verb in the sentence, make the subject and verb agree.

1. Questions In a question, the auxiliary verb agrees with the subject.

▶ *Does* the editor agree to the changes?

▶ *Do* the editor and the production manager agree to them?

2. Initial *here* or *there* When a sentence begins with *here* or *there*, the verb agrees with the subject.

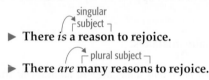

▶ There *is* a reason to rejoice.

▶ There *are* many reasons to rejoice.

However, avoid excessive use of an initial *there* (see 30b): *We have a reason to rejoice.*

ESL NOTE
Singular Verb after *It*

It does not follow the same pattern as *here* and *there*. The verb attached to an *it* subject is always singular.

▶ It *is* hundreds of miles away.

3. Inverted word order When a sentence begins not with the subject but with a phrase preceding the verb, the verb still agrees with the subject (see also 34d).

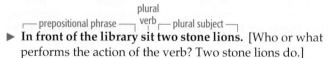

▶ In front of the library sit two stone lions. [Who or what performs the action of the verb? Two stone lions do.]

43e Tricky subjects with singular verbs

1. *Each* and *every* *Each* and *every* may seem to indicate more than one, but grammatically they are singular words. Use them with a singular verb, even if they are parts of a compound subject joined by *and* or *or* (43g).

▶ Each of the cakes *has* a different frosting.

▶ Every change in procedures *causes* problems.

▶ Every toy and game *has* to be put away.

▶ Each plate and glass *looks* new.

2. -ing or infinitive form as subject With a subject beginning with the *-ing* verb form (called a *gerund*) or with an infinitive, always use a singular verb form.

singular
subject
▶ Playing the piano in front of a crowd *causes* anxiety.

▶ To keep our air clean *takes* careful planning.

3. Singular nouns ending in -s Some nouns that end in *-s* (*news, economics, physics, politics, mathematics, statistics*) are not plural. Use them with a singular verb.

▶ The news *has* been bad lately.   ▶ Politics *is* dirty business.

4. Phrases of time, money, and weight When the subject is regarded as one unit, use a singular verb.

▶ Five hundred dollars *seems* too much to pay.

▶ Seven years *was* a long time to spend at college.

But

▶ Seven years *have* passed.

5. Uncountable nouns An uncountable noun (*furniture, jewelry, equipment, advice, happiness, honesty, information, knowledge*) encompasses all the items in its class. An uncountable noun does not have a plural form and is always followed by a singular verb (60b).

▶ That advice *makes* me nervous.

▶ The information found in the press *is* not always accurate.

6. *One of* *One of* is followed by a plural noun (the object of the preposition *of*) and a singular verb form. The verb agrees with the subject *one.*

▶ One of her friends *loves* to tango.

▶ One of the reasons for his difficulties *is* that he spends too much money.

For agreement with *one of* and *the only one of* followed by a relative clause, see 46c.

7. *The number of/a number of* The phrase *the number of* is followed by a plural noun (the object of the preposition *of*) and a singular verb form.

▶ The number of reasons *is* growing.

However, with the phrase *a number of,* meaning "several," use a plural verb.

▶ A number of reasons *are* listed in the letter.

8. The title of a long work or a word referred to as the word itself Use a singular verb with the title of a long, whole work or a word referred to as the word itself. Use a singular verb even if the title or word is plural in form. See also 52a and 52c.

▶ <u>Cats</u> *was* based on a poem by T. S. Eliot.

▶ In her story, the word <u>dudes</u> *appears* five times.

43f Collective nouns

Generally, use a singular verb with a collective noun (*class, government, family, jury, committee, group, couple, team*) if you are referring to the group as a whole.

▶ My family *goes* on vacation every year.

Use a plural verb if you wish to emphasize differences among individuals or if members of the group are thought of as individuals.

▶ His *family are* mostly artists and musicians.

▶ The *jury are* from every walk of life.

If that usage seems awkward, revise the sentence.

▶ His close *relatives are* mostly artists and musicians.

▶ The members of the *jury are* from every walk of life.

Some collective nouns, such as *police, poor, elderly,* and *young,* always take plural verbs.

▶ The *elderly deserve* our respect.

43g Subjects with *and, or,* or *nor*

With *and*　　When a subject consists of two or more parts joined by *and,* treat the subject as plural and use a plural verb.

┌──────── plural subject ────────┐   plural verb
▶ His instructor and his advisor *want* him to change his major.

However, if the parts of the compound subject refer to a single person or thing, use a singular verb.

┌──── singular subject (one person) ────┐   singular verb
▶ The restaurant's chef and owner *makes* good fajitas.

┌─singular subject─┐ singular verb
▶ Fish and chips *is* a popular dish in England, but it is
　no longer served wrapped in newspaper.

Also, use a singular verb with a subject beginning with *each* or *every.*

▶ Every claim and conclusion *was* evaluated.

With *or* or *nor*　　When the parts of a compound subject are joined by *or* or *nor,* the verb agrees with the part nearer to it.

▶ Her sister or her *parents plan* to visit her next week.

▶ Neither her parents nor her *sister drives* a station wagon.

43h Indefinite pronouns

Words that refer to nonspecific people or things (indefinite pronouns) can be tricky. Most of them take a singular verb. Usage may differ in speech and writing, so when you write, it is important to pay attention to Standard English usage.

Indefinite pronouns used with a singular verb

anybody	everybody	nothing
anyone	everyone	somebody
anything	everything	someone
each	nobody	something
either	no one	

▶ **Nobody** *knows* **the answer.**

▶ **Someone** *has* **been sitting on my chair.**

▶ **Everyone** *agrees* **on the author's intention.**

▶ **Everything about the results** *was* **questioned in the review.**

▶ **Each of the chairs** *costs* **more than $300.**

See 44d on the personal pronouns to use (*he? she? they?*) to refer to indefinite pronouns.

A note on *none* and *neither*

NONE Some writers prefer to use a singular verb after *none* (*of*), because *none* means "not one": *None of the contestants has smiled.* However, as *The American Heritage Dictionary* (4th ed.) points out, a singular or a plural verb is technically acceptable: *None of the authorities has* (or *have*) *greater tolerance on this point than H. W. Fowler.* Check to see if your instructor prefers the literal singular usage.

NEITHER The pronoun *neither* is, like *none*, technically singular: *The partners have made a decision; neither wants to change the product.* In informal writing, however, *neither* may occur with a plural verb, especially when followed by an *of* phrase: *Neither of the novels reveal a polished style.*

43i Quantity words

Some quantity words are singular; some are plural; some can be used to indicate either singular or plural, depending on the noun they refer to.

Words Expressing Quantity

With Singular Nouns and Verbs	With Plural Nouns and Verbs
much	many
(a) little	(a) few
a great deal (of)	several
less	fewer
another	both
every	all

See 64c for more on the difference between *few* and *a few*.

▶ Much *has* been accomplished.

▶ Much of the machinery *needs* to be repaired.

▶ Many *have* gained from the recent stock market rise.

▶ Few of his fans *are* buying his recent book.

You will see and hear *less* used in place of *fewer*, especially with numbers ("5 items or less"), but in formal writing, use *fewer* to refer to a plural word.

▶ More *movies* have been made this year than last, but *fewer* *have* made money.

The following quantity words can be used with either singular or plural nouns and verbs: *all, any, half (of), more, most, no, other, part (of), some*.

▶ You gave me *some information. More is* necessary.

▶ You gave me *some facts. More are* needed.

▶ *All the furniture is* old.

▶ *All the students look* healthy.

43j Agreement with *this, that, these, those, mine, ours,* etc.

Demonstratives agree in number with a noun: *this solution, these solutions; that problem, those problems.*

plural

▶ The mayor is planning changes. These will be controversial.

Singular	**Plural**
this	these
that	those

Possessives such as *mine, his, hers, ours, yours,* and *theirs* can refer to both singular and plural antecedents (see 44d).

singular
┌── subject ──┐   singular verb
▶ Her average is good, but *mine is* better.

plural
┌── subject ──┐   plural verb
▶ His grades are good, but *mine are* better.

43k Subject clauses beginning with *what* or other question words

When a clause introduced by *what* or other question words, such as *how, who,* and *why,* functions as the subject of an independent clause, use a third person singular verb in the independent clause.

┌────────── subject ──────────┐
▶ What they are proposing *concerns* us all.

┌────────── subject ──────────┐
▶ How the players train *makes* all the difference.

When the verb is followed by the linking verb *be* and a plural complement, some writers use a plural verb. However, some readers may object.

▶ What I need *are* black pants and an orange shirt.

You can avoid the issue by revising the sentence to eliminate the *what* clause.

▶ I need black pants and an orange shirt.

Chapter **44**

Pronouns

A pronoun is a word that substitutes for a noun, a noun phrase, or another pronoun (see 37d).

▶ Jack's hair is so long that *it* hangs over *his* collar.

44a Forms of personal pronouns (*I* or *me,* *he* or *him*?)

Personal pronouns change form to indicate person (first, second, or third), number (singular or plural), and function in a clause.

In a compound subject or compound object with *and*: *I* or *me*; *he* or *him*? To decide which pronoun form to use with a compound subject or compound object, mentally recast the sentence with only the pronoun in the subject or object position.

▶ ~~Him~~ He and his sister invited my cousin and ~~I~~ me to their party. [He invited me.]

KEY POINTS

Summary of Forms of Personal Pronouns

Person	Subject	Object	Possessive (+ Noun)	Possessive (Stands Alone)	Intensive and Reflexive
1st person singular	I	me	my	mine	myself
2nd person singular and plural	you	you	your	yours	yourself/ yourselves
3rd person singular	he	him	his	his	himself
	she	her	her	hers	herself
	it	it	its	its [rare]	itself

(Continued)

(Continued)

Person	Subject	Object	Possessive (+ Noun)	Possessive (Stands Alone)	Intensive and Reflexive
1st person plural	we	us	our	ours	ourselves
3rd person plural	they	them	their	theirs	themselves

▶ **Jenny and** ~~me~~ **went to the movies.** [If *Jenny* is dropped, you would say *I went to the movies*, not *Me went to the movies*. Here you need the subject form, *I*.]

She   I
▶ ~~Her~~ **and** ~~me~~ **have solved the problem.** [She has solved the problem. I have solved the problem.]

Sometimes people who are not sure of the use of *I* or *me* in the subject position get anxious and overcorrect from *me* to *I* in the object position, too—and make another error.

me
▶ **They told my brother and** ~~I~~ **to wait in line.** [If *my brother* is dropped, you would say, *They told me to wait in line.* Here you need the object form, *me*.]

After a preposition After a preposition, you need an object form.

me
▶ **Between you and** ~~I~~**, the company is in serious trouble.**

me
▶ **Rachid stared at my colleague and** ~~I~~**.** [He stared at my colleague. He stared at me.]

After a linking verb In formal academic writing, use the subject form of a personal pronoun after a linking verb, such as *be, seem, look,* or *appear.*

▶ **Was that Oprah Winfrey? It was** *she.* [Informal: "It was her."]

▶ **It was** *she* **who gave away cars.** [Many writers would revise this sentence to sound less formal: "She was the one who gave away cars."]

After a verb and before an infinitive   Use the object form of a personal pronoun after a verb and before an infinitive. When a sentence has only one object, this principle is easy to apply.

▶ **The dean wanted** *him* **to lead the procession.**

Difficulties occur with compound objects.

him and me

▶ **The dean wanted** ~~he and I~~ **to lead the procession.**

In appositive phrases and with *we* **or** *us* **before a noun**   When using a personal pronoun in an appositive phrase (a phrase that gives additional information about a preceding noun), determine whether the noun that the pronoun refers to functions as subject or as object in its own clause.

                  appositive
      ┌── direct object ──┐ ┌── phrase ──┐
▶ **The supervisor praised only two employees, Ramon and me.**

           appositive phrase
    ┌── subject ──┐ ┌──────────┐
▶ **Only two employees, Ramon and I, received a bonus.**

Similarly, when you consider whether to use *we* or *us* before a noun, use *us* when the pronoun is the direct object of a verb or preposition; use *we* when it is the subject.

     object of preposition
▶ **LL Cool J waved to** *us* **fans.**

   subject
▶ **We fans have decided to form a club.**

In comparisons   When writing comparisons with *than* and *as*, decide when to use the subject or object form of the personal pronoun by mentally completing the meaning of the comparison. (See also 45h.)

▶ **She is certainly not more intelligent than I.** [. . . than I am.]

▶ **Matt and Juanita work in the same office; Matt criticizes his boss more than she.** [. . . more than Juanita does.]

▶ **Matt and Juanita work in the same office; Matt criticizes his boss more than her.** [. . . more than he criticizes Juanita.]

44b Possessive forms of pronouns (*my* or *mine*, *her* or *hers*?)

Distinguish between the adjective form of the possessive personal pronoun and the pronoun itself, standing alone.

▶ **The large room with three windows is *her* office.**
[*Her* is an adjective.]

▶ **The office is *hers*.**
[*Hers*, the possessive pronoun, can stand alone.]

Note: The word *mine* does not follow the pattern of *hers, theirs, yours,* and *ours.* The form *mines* is not Standard English.

▶ **The little room on the left is *mine*.**

When a possessive pronoun functions as a subject, its antecedent determines singular or plural agreement for the verb. (See 43j.)

▶ **My shirt is cotton; hers *is* silk.** [Singular antecedent and singular verb.]

▶ **My gloves are black; hers *are* yellow.** [Plural antecedent and plural verb.]

Possessive pronoun before an *-ing* form   Generally, use a possessive personal pronoun before an *-ing* verb form used as a noun.

▶ **We would appreciate *your* participating in the auction.**

▶ **We were surprised at *their* winning the marathon.**

Sometimes the *-ing* form is a participle functioning as an adjective. In that case, the pronoun preceding the *-ing* form should be in the object form.

▶ **We saw *them* giving the runners foil wraps.**

No apostrophe with possessive personal pronouns   Even though possessive in meaning, the pronouns *yours, ours, theirs, his,* and *hers* should never be spelled with an apostrophe. Use an apostrophe only with the possessive form of a noun.

▶ That coat is *Maria's*.

▶ That is *her* coat.

▶ That coat is *hers*.

▶ These books are the *twins'*. (48c)

▶ These are *their* books.

▶ These books are *theirs*.

No apostrophe with *its* as a possessive pronoun   The word *it's* is not a pronoun; it is the contraction of *it is* or *it has*. An apostrophe is never used with *its*, the possessive form of the pronoun *it* (see also 48f).

▶ The paint has lost *its* gloss.

▶ *It's* not as glossy as it used to be. [It is not as glossy . . .]

Comparisons using possessive forms   Note how using *them* in place of *theirs* in the following sentence would change the meaning by comparing suitcases to roommates, not suitcases to suitcases.

▶ It's really hard to be roommates with people if your suit-cases are much better than *theirs*.

—J. D. Salinger, *The Catcher in the Rye*

Forgetting to use the appropriate possessive form in the next example, too, could create a misunderstanding: are you comparing a house to a person, or his house to her house?

▶ I like his house more than I like her.
                                     s.

44c   Pronoun reference to a clear antecedent

A pronoun substitutes for a noun, a noun phrase, or a pronoun already mentioned. The word or phrase that a pronoun refers to is known as the pronoun's *antecedent*. Antecedents should always be clear and explicit.

▶ Although the Canadian skater practiced daily with *her* trainers,

    she didn't win the championship.

State a specific antecedent.   Be sure to give a pronoun such as *they* or *it* an explicit antecedent.

NO SPECIFIC ANTECEDENT   **When Mr. Rivera applied for a loan, they outlined the procedures for him.** [The pronoun *they* lacks an explicit antecedent.]

REVISED   **When Mr. Rivera applied to bank officials for a loan, *they* outlined the procedures for him.**

When you use a pronoun, make sure it does not refer to a possessive noun or to a noun within a prepositional phrase.

▶ In ~~George Orwell's~~ "Shooting an Elephant," ~~he~~ *George Orwell* reports an incident that shows the evil effects of imperialism. [The pronoun *he* cannot refer to the possessive noun *Orwell's*.]

▶ ~~In the essay by Lance Morrow, it~~ *Lance Morrow's essay* points out the problems of choosing a name. [*It* refers to *essay*, which functions as the object of the preposition *in* and therefore cannot function as an antecedent.]

Avoid ambiguous pronoun reference.   Readers should never wonder what your pronouns refer to.

AMBIGUOUS   **My husband told my father that he should choose the baby's name.** [Does *he* refer to *husband* or *father*?]

REVISED   **My husband told my father to choose the baby's name.**

REVISED   **My husband wanted to choose the baby's name and told my father so.**

AMBIGUOUS   **He had to decide whether to move to California.**

This was not what he wanted to do. [Does *This* refer to making the decision or to moving to California?]

REVISED   **He had to decide whether to move to California. The decision was not one he wanted to make.**

REVISED   **He had to decide whether to move to California. Moving there was not something he wanted to do.**

44d Agreement of pronoun with its antecedent

A plural antecedent needs a plural pronoun; a singular antecedent needs a singular pronoun.

Make a demonstrative pronoun agree with its antecedent. The demonstrative pronouns *this* and *that* refer to singular nouns; *these* and *those* refer to plural nouns: *this/that house, these/those houses* (43i).

singular antecedent

▶ He published his autobiography two years ago. This was his first book.

plural antecedent

▶ One reviewer praised his honesty and directness. Those were qualities he had worked hard to develop.

Make a pronoun agree with a generalized (generic) antecedent. Generic nouns name a class or type of person or object, such as *a student* meaning "all students" or *a company* meaning "any company" or "all companies." Sometimes writers use *they* to refer to a singular generic noun, but the singular/plural mismatch annoys some readers.

singular antecedent   plural pronoun

MISMATCH ▶ When a student is educated, they can go far in the world.

singular antecedent   singular pronoun

REVISED BUT SOMEWHAT STILTED   When a student is educated, he or she can go far in the world.

plural antecedent   plural pronoun

BEST   When students are educated, they can go far in the world.

Increasingly, you see in advertising, journalism, and informal writing (and you will certainly hear this usage in speech, too) a plural pronoun referring to a singular antecedent, as in the following station wagon advertisement:

▶ One day *your child* turns sixteen, and you let *them* borrow the keys to the wagon.

However, in formal academic writing, many readers may still expect a pronoun to agree with its antecedent. Even though usage may be changing, you can avoid problems by making the antecedent plural.

> ► We should judge ~~a person~~ by who they are, not by the color
>   of their skin.

people

Make a pronoun agree with an indefinite pronoun. Indefinite pronouns, such as *everyone, somebody,* and *nothing* (43h), are singular in form and referred to with a singular pronoun. A singular antecedent traditionally needs a singular pronoun to refer to it, but which one: *he, she, he or she*? The *Oxford English Dictionary* points out that for centuries, *they* has often been used "in reference to a singular noun made universal by *every, any, no,* etc., or applicable to one of either sex (= 'he or she')." And R. W. Burchfield, the author of *The New Fowler's Modern English Usage,* adds this to the debate:

> All such "non-grammatical" constructions arise either because
> the notion of plurality resides in many of the indefinite pronouns
> or because of the absence in English of a common-gender third
> person singular pronoun (as distinct from *his* used to mean "his
> or her" or the clumsy use of *his or her* itself). (779)

Despite the increasingly widespread use of *they,* some readers may still object to it, so revising the sentence is a good idea.

SINGULAR PRONOUN	*Everyone* picked up *his* marbles and ran home to do *his* homework. [Sentence needs revision because of the gender bias.]
REVISED BUT CLUMSY	*Everyone* picked up *his or her* marbles and ran home to do *his or her* homework.
REVISED BUT SOME MAY OBJECT	*Everyone* picked up *their* marbles and ran home to do *their* homework. [The plural pronoun *their* refers to a singular antecedent.]
PROBABLY BEST	The *children* all picked up *their* marbles and ran home to do *their* homework.

Make a pronoun agree with the nearer antecedent when *or* or *nor* is used. When the elements of a compound antecedent are connected by *or* or *nor,* a pronoun agrees with the element that is nearer to it. If one part of the compound is singular and the other part is plural, put the plural antecedent closer to the pronoun and have the pronoun agree with it.

▶ **Either my tutor or my professor has left *his* wallet on the table.**

▶ **Neither Bill nor the campers could find *their* soap.**

Make a pronoun agree with a collective noun. Use a singular pronoun to refer to a collective noun (*class, family, jury, committee, couple, team*) if you are referring to the group as a whole.

▶ **The class revised *its* examination schedule.**

▶ **The committee has not yet completed *its* report.**

Use a plural pronoun if members of the group named by the collective noun are considered to be acting individually.

▶ **The committee began to cast *their* ballots in a formal vote.**

44e Gender bias

Personal pronouns For many years, the pronoun *he* was used routinely in generic references to unspecified individuals in certain roles or professions, such as student, teacher, doctor, lawyer, and banker; and *she* was used routinely in generic references to individuals in roles such as nurse, secretary, or typist. This usage is now considered biased language.

NOT
APPROPRIATE
When an accountant learns a foreign language, *he* gains access to an expanded job market.

To revise such sentences that make general statements about people, roles, and professions, use one of the following methods:

1. Use a plural antecedent plus *they* (see also 33f and 44d).

   ▶ **When accountants learn a foreign language, *they* gain access to an expanded job market.**

2. Avoid the issue by rewriting the sentence to eliminate the pronoun.

   ▶ **An accountant who learns a foreign language gains access to an expanded job market.**

3. Use a singular antecedent and the phrase *he or she.*

   ▶ **When an accountant learns a foreign language, *he or she* gains access to an expanded job market.**

The problem with option 3 is that awkward and repetitive structures can result when such a sentence is expanded.

   ▶ **When an accountant learns a foreign language, *he or she* gains access to an expanded job market once *he or she* has decided on *his or her* specialty.**

That's clumsy. Use the *he or she* option only when a sentence is relatively short and does not repeat the pronouns. On the whole, though, revision is usually the best.

See also pronoun agreement with indefinite pronouns (44d).

44f Consistent point of view

Always have a consistent perspective from which you are writing. Pronouns can help maintain consistency. Consider the person and number of the pronouns you use:

- Are you emphasizing the perspective of the first person (*I* or *we*)?

- Are you primarily addressing the reader as the second person (*you*)?

- Are you, as is most common in formal academic writing, writing about the third person (*he, she, it, one,* or *they*)?

Avoid confusing readers by switching from one perspective to another.

INCONSISTENT   ***The company*** **decided to promote only three mid-level managers. *You* had to have worked there for ten years to qualify.**

REVISED   *The company* decided to promote only three mid-level managers. *The employees* had to have worked there for ten years to qualify.

44g The use of the pronoun *you*

In formal writing, do not use the pronoun *you* when you mean "people generally." Use *you* only to address readers directly and to give instructions.

NOT
APPROPRIATE   **Credit card companies should educate students about how to handle credit. *You* should not have to find out the problems the hard way.** [This usage assumes readers are all students and addresses them directly. Some readers will not feel included in the group addressed as "you." A reader addressed directly in this way might think, "Who, me? I don't need to be educated about credit and I have no problems."]

APPROPRIATE   **Turn to the next page, where *you* will find an excerpt from Edith Wharton's novel that will help *you* appreciate the accuracy of the details in this film.**

Edit uses of *you* if you are making a generalization about a group or if using *you* entails a switch from the third person.

▶ While growing up, ~~you~~ teenagers face arguments with ~~your~~ their parents.

▶ It doesn't matter if young professionals are avid music admirers or comedy fans; ~~you~~ they can find anything ~~you~~ they want in the city.

44h Intensive and reflexive pronouns

Intensive pronouns emphasize a previously mentioned noun or pronoun. Reflexive pronouns identify a previously mentioned noun or pronoun as the person or thing receiving the action. See the Key Points box in 44a.

INTENSIVE   **The president *himself* appeared at the gates.**

REFLEXIVE   **He introduced *himself*.**

Do not use an intensive pronoun in place of a personal pronoun in a compound subject:

> ► Joe and ~~myself~~ will design the brochure.

Forms such as *hisself, theirself, a*nd *theirselves* occur in spoken dialects but are not Standard English.

44i *Who/whom, whoever/whomever*

In all formal writing situations, distinguish between the subject and object forms of the pronouns used to form questions (interrogative pronouns) or to introduce a dependent noun clause.

Subject	Object
who	whom (or, informally, *who*)
whoever	whomever

In questions In a question, ask yourself whether the pronoun is the subject of its clause or the object of the verb. Test the pronoun's function by rephrasing the question as a statement, substituting a personal pronoun for *who* or *whom*.

> ► **Who wrote that enthusiastic letter?** [*He* wrote that enthusiastic letter. Subject: use *who*.]

> ► **Whoever could have written it?** [*She* could have written it. Subject: use *whoever*.]

> ► **Who[m] were they describing?** [*They* were describing *him*. Object: *whom* (formal), though *who* is common in such contexts both in speech and in writing.]

When introducing a dependent clause with a pronoun, determine whether to use the subject or object form by examining the pronoun's function in the clause. Ignore expressions such as *I think* or *I know* when they follow the pronoun; they have no effect on the form of the pronoun.

▶ They want to know who runs the business.
subject of clause

▶ They want to know who I think runs the business.
subject of clause (who runs the business)

▶ They want to know whom the manager reports to.
object of *to* [the manager reports to him or her]

▶ I will hire whoever is qualified.
subject of clause

▶ I will hire whomever my boss recommends.
object of *recommends*

For uses of *who* and *whom* in relative clauses, see 46a.

Chapter **45**

Adjectives and Adverbs

Adjectives describe, or modify, nouns or pronouns. They do not add -s or change form to reflect number or gender. For the order of adjectives, see 62g.

▶ Analysts acknowledge the *beneficial* effects of TV.

▶ The director tried a *different* approach to a documentary.

▶ The depiction of rural life is *accurate*.

▶ The reporter keeps her desk *tidy*.

ESL NOTE

No Plural Form for Adjectives

Do not add -s to an adjective that modifies a plural noun.

▶ Mr. Lee tried three *differents* approaches.

Adverbs modify verbs, adjectives, and other adverbs, as well as whole clauses.

▶ The financial analyst settled down *comfortably* in her new job.

▶ The patient is demanding a *theoretically* impossible treatment.

▶ *Apparently,* the experiment was a success.

45a Forms of adjectives and adverbs

No single rule indicates the correct form of all adjectives and adverbs.

Adverb: adjective + -*ly* Many adverbs are formed by adding -*ly* to an adjective: *soft/softly; intelligent/intelligently.* Sometimes when -*ly* is added, a spelling change occurs: *easy/easily; terrible/terribly.*

Adjectives ending in -*ic* To form an adverb from an adjective ending in -*ic*, add -*ally* (*basic/basically; artistic/artistically*), except for *public*, whose adverb form is *publicly*.

Adjectives ending in -*ly* Some adjectives, such as *friendly, lovely, timely,* and *masterly,* already end in -*ly* and have no distinctive adverb form.

adjective
▶ She is a friendly person.

┌─ adverbial phrase ─┐
▶ She spoke to me in a friendly way.

Irregular adverb forms Certain adjectives do not add -*ly* to form an adverb:

Adjective	Adverb
good	well
fast	fast
hard	hard

adjective
▶ He is a hard worker.

adverb
▶ He works hard.

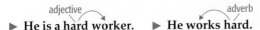

adjective   adverb

▶ **He is a hard worker.**   ▶ **He works hard.**

[*Hardly* is not the adverb form of *hard*. Rather, it means "barely," "scarcely," or "almost not at all": *I could* hardly *breathe in that stuffy room.*]

Note: Well can also function as an adjective, meaning "healthy" or "satisfactory": *A* well *baby smiles often. She feels* well.

45b When to use adjectives and adverbs

In speech, adjectives (particularly *good, bad*, and *real*) are often used to modify verbs, adjectives, or adverbs. This is nonstandard usage. Use an adverb to modify a verb or an adverb.

                                      really well.

▶ **The webmaster fixed the**   ▶ **The chorus sings** ~~real good.~~

     well.

link ~~good.~~

                clearly.   badly.

▶ **The guide speaks very** ~~clear.~~   ▶ **They dance** ~~bad.~~

45c Adjectives after linking verbs

After linking verbs (*be, seem, appear, become*), use an adjective to modify the subject.

▶ **Sharon Olds's poems are** *lyrical.*

▶ **The book seems** *repetitive.*

Some verbs (*appear, look, feel, smell, taste*) are sometimes used as linking verbs, sometimes as action verbs. If the modifier tells about the subject, use an adjective. If the modifier tells about the action of the verb, use an adverb.

ADJECTIVE   **The analyst looks** *confident* **in her new job.**

ADVERB   **The lawyer looks** *confidently* **at all the assembled partners.**

ADJECTIVE   **The waiter feels** *bad.*

              The steak smells *bad.*

ADVERB   **The chef smelled the lobster** *appreciatively.*

Note: Use a hyphen to connect two words used as an adjective when they appear before a noun. Do not use a hyphen when the words follow a linking verb with no noun complement.

▶ **Sonny Rollins is a** *well-known* **saxophonist.**

▶ **Sonny Rollins is** *well known.*

45d Compound adjectives

A compound adjective consists of two or more words used as a unit to describe a noun. Many compound adjectives contain the past participle *-ed* verb form: *flat-footed, barrel-chested, broad-shouldered, old-fashioned, well-dressed, left-handed.* Note the form when a compound adjective is used before a noun: hyphen, past participle (*-ed*) form where necessary, and no noun plural (*-s*) ending.

▶ **They have a** *five-year-old* **daughter.** [Their daughter is five years old.]

▶ **She gave me a** *five-dollar* **bill.** [She gave me five dollars.]

▶ **He is a** *left-handed* **pitcher.** [He pitches with his left hand.]

For more on hyphenation with compound adjectives, see 56b.

45e Position of adverbs

An adverb can be placed in various positions in a sentence.

▶ *Enthusiastically,* **she ate the sushi.**

▶ **She** *enthusiastically* **ate the sushi.**

▶ **She ate the sushi** *enthusiastically.*

ESL NOTE

Adverb Placement

Do not place an adverb between a verb and a short direct object (62b).

▶ She ate *enthusiastically* the sushi.

Put adverbs that show frequency (*always, usually, frequently, often, sometimes, seldom, rarely, never*) in one of four positions:

1. At the beginning of a sentence

   ▶ *Sometimes* I just sit and daydream instead of writing.

   When *never, seldom,* or *rarely* occurs at the beginning of the sentence, word order is inverted (see also 34d and 43d).

   ▶ *Never* will I let that happen.

2. Between the subject and the main verb

   ▶ They *always* arrive half an hour late.

3. After a form of *be* or any auxiliary verb (such as *do, have, can, will, must*)

   ▶ The writing center is *always* open in the evening.

   ▶ The tutors are *seldom* late for training.

   ▶ There has *never* been an available computer during exam week.

4. In the final position

   ▶ Amira checks her e-mail *frequently.*

Note: Never place the adverb *never* in the final position.

45f Conjunctive adverbs (*however, therefore,* etc.)

There are two important points to remember about conjunctive adverbs such as *however, therefore,* and *moreover.*

1. When a conjunctive adverb occurs in the middle of a clause, set it off with commas.

   ▶ The president's course of action has, **therefore**, been severely criticized.

2. When it occurs between independent clauses, use a semicolon to end the first clause and put a comma after the adverb.

▶ **The hearings were contentious; however, the Supreme Court Justice was approved.**

See also 2d, 31c, 39c, and 47e.

45g No double negatives

Adverbs like *hardly*, *scarcely*, and *barely* are considered negatives, and the contraction *-n't* stands for the adverb *not*. Some languages and dialects allow the use of more than one negative to emphasize an idea, but Standard English allows only one negative in a clause. Avoid double negatives.

DOUBLE NEGATIVE	**We do*n't* have *no* excuses.**
REVISED	**We do*n't* have *any* excuses. [or] We have *no* excuses.**
DOUBLE NEGATIVE	**She did*n't* say *nothing*.**
REVISED	**She did*n't* say *anything*. [or] She said *nothing*.**
DOUBLE NEGATIVE	**City residents ca*n't hardly* afford the sales tax.**
REVISED	**City residents can *hardly* afford the sales tax.**

45h Comparative and superlative forms of adjectives and adverbs

Adjectives and adverbs have three forms: positive, comparative, and superlative. Use the comparative form to compare two people, places, things, or ideas; use the superlative to compare more than two.

Regular forms Add the ending *-er* to form the comparative and *-est* to form the superlative of both short adjectives (those that have one syllable or those that have two syllables and end in *-y* or *-le*) and one-syllable adverbs. (Change *-y* to *-i* if *-y* is preceded by a consonant: *icy, icier, iciest.*) Generally, a superlative form is preceded by *the* (*the shortest distance*).

Positive	Comparative (Comparing two)	Superlative (Comparing more than two)
short	shorter	shortest
pretty	prettier	prettiest
simple	simpler	simplest
fast	faster	fastest

With longer adjectives and with adverbs ending in *-ly*, use *more* (for the comparative) and *most* (for the superlative). Note that *less* (comparative) and *least* (superlative) are used with adjectives of any length (*less bright, least bright; less effective, least effective*).

Positive	Comparative	Superlative
intelligent	more intelligent	most intelligent
carefully	more carefully	most carefully
dangerous	less dangerous	least dangerous

If you cannot decide whether to use *-er/-est* or *more/most*, consult a dictionary. If there is an *-er/-est* form, the dictionary will say so.

Note: Do not use the *-er* form along with *more* or the *-est* form along with *most.*

▶ The first poem was ~~more~~ better than the second.

▶ Boris is the ~~most~~ fittest person I know.

Irregular forms   The following common adjectives and adverbs have irregular comparative and superlative forms:

Positive	Comparative	Superlative
good	better	best
bad	worse	worst
much/many	more	most
little	less	least
well	better	best
badly	worse	worst

***Than* with comparative forms** To compare two people, places, things, or ideas, use the comparative form and the word *than*. If you use a comparative form in your sentence, you need the word *than* to let readers know what you are comparing with what.

▶ This course of action is more efficient‸ than the previous one.

Comparative forms are also used without *than* in an idiomatic way.

▶ The *harder* he tries, the *more satisfied* he feels.

▶ The *more,* the *merrier.*

Absolute adjectives Do not use comparative and superlative forms of adjectives that imply absolutes: *complete, empty, full, equal, perfect, priceless,* or *unique.* In addition, do not add intensifying adverbs such as *very, totally, completely,* or *absolutely* to these adjectives. To say that something is "perfect" implies an absolute rather than something measured in degrees.

▶ He has ~~the most~~ *a* perfect view of the ocean.

▶ They bought a ~~totally~~ unique quilt at an auction.

45i Faulty or incomplete comparisons

Make sure that you state clearly what items you are comparing. Some faulty comparisons can give readers the wrong idea. See 40h, 44a, 44b.

INCOMPLETE **He likes the parrot better than his wife.**

To avoid suggesting that he prefers the parrot to his wife, clarify the comparison by completing the second clause.

REVISED **He likes the parrot better *than his wife does.***

Edit sentences like the following:

▶ My essay got a higher grade than Maria‸'s. [Compare the two essays, not your essay and Maria.]

▶ **Williams's poem gives a more objective depiction of the**

painting than Auden 's. [To compare Williams's poem with
Auden's poem, you need to include an apostrophe; otherwise,
you compare a poem to the poet W. H. Auden.]

Comparisons must also be complete. If you say that something
is "more efficient," your reader wonders, "More efficient than
what?"

▶ **Didion shows us a home that makes her feel more tied to her**

roots than her home in Los Angeles does. [Include the other part of the comparison.]

Chapter **46**

Relative Clauses and Relative Pronouns

A relative clause relates to an antecedent in a nearby clause.

relative clause

▶ **The girl** *who* **can't dance says the band can't play.**
—Yiddish proverb

46a Relative pronouns

When deciding whether to use *who, whom, which,* or *that,* use the following table as a guide. Your choice of pronoun will depend on these
three factors:

1. The function of the relative pronoun in its clause
2. Whether the relative pronoun refers to a human or nonhuman
   antecedent
3. Whether the clause is restrictive or nonrestrictive (see 46b for this
   distinction)

Relative Pronouns and Antecedents

Antecedent	Function of Relative Pronoun		
	Subject	Object	Possessive
Human antecedent	*who*	*whom* (can be omitted)	*whose*
Nonhuman antecedent	*that* or *which* (see 46b)	*that* (can be omitted) or *which* (see 46b)	*of which* (formal) *whose* (informal)

HUMAN

SUBJECT: The teachers *who* challenge us are the ones we remember.

OBJECT: The players [*whom*] the spectators boo often end up in the minor leagues.

POSSESSIVE: Spectators *whose* cell phones ring will be asked to leave.

NONHUMAN

SUBJECT: The dog *that* kept barking all night drove the neighbors crazy.

OBJECT: They stayed at a hotel [*that*] their friends had recommended.

POSSESSIVE: We stayed in a picturesque town the name *of which* I can't remember.

We stayed in a picturesque town *whose* name I can't remember.

Watch out! Do not rename the subject in the independent clause.

► The teachers who challenge us ~~they~~ are the ones we remember.

Remember that an inserted phrase does not affect the function of a pronoun.

► Let's reward contestants who we realize have not been coached.

Do not use *what* as a relative pronoun.

▶ The deal ~~what~~ the CEO was trying to make turned out to be
     that
crooked.

46b Restrictive and nonrestrictive relative clauses

The two types of relative clauses, restrictive and nonrestrictive, fulfill
different functions and need different punctuation (47d).

RESTRICTIVE   **The people *who live in the apartment above mine* make
a lot of noise at night.**

NONRESTRICTIVE **The Sullivans, *who live in the apartment above mine,*
make a lot of noise at night.**

Restrictive relative clause   A restrictive relative clause provides
information essential for identifying the antecedent and restricting
its scope.

FEATURES

1. The clause is not set off with commas.
2. An object relative pronoun can be omitted.
3. *That* (rather than *which*) is used for reference to nonhuman
   antecedents.

▶ **The teachers *who challenge us* are the ones we remember.**
[The independent clause—"The teachers are the ones"—leads
us to ask, "Which teachers?" The relative clause provides
information that is essential to completing the meaning of the
subject; it restricts the meaning from "all teachers" to "the
teachers who challenge us."]

▶ **The book [*that*] *you gave me* was fascinating.** [The relative
pronoun *that* is the direct object in its clause ("You gave me
the book") and can be omitted.]

Nonrestrictive relative clause   A nonrestrictive relative clause
provides information that is not essential for understanding the antecedent. It refers to and describes a proper noun (which names a
specific person, place, or thing and begins with a capital letter) or a
noun that is identified and unique.

FEATURES

1. The antecedent is a unique, designated person or thing.
2. The clause is set off by commas.
3. *Which* (not *that*) is used to refer to a nonhuman antecedent.
4. An object relative pronoun cannot be omitted.

> ▶ The book *War and Peace,* **which you gave me, was fascinating.** [The independent clause—"The book *War and Peace* was fascinating"—does not promote further questions, such as "Which book?" The information in the relative clause ("which you gave me") is almost an aside and not essential for understanding the independent clause.]

A nonrestrictive relative clause with a quantity word   Relative clauses beginning with a quantity word such as *some, none, many, much, most,* or *one* followed by *of which* or *of whom* are always nonrestrictive.

> ▶ **They selected five candidates,** *one of whom* **would get the job.**

> ▶ **The report mentioned five names,** *none of which* **I recognized.**

ESL NOTE

Relative vs. Personal Pronouns

You need only the relative pronoun, not a personal pronoun in addition.

>   *most of whom*
> ▶ **I tutored some students,** ~~which most of them~~ **were my classmates.**

46c   Agreement of verb with relative pronoun

Determine subject-verb agreement within a relative clause by asking whether the antecedent of a subject relative pronoun is singular or plural.

>   —— relative clause ——
> ▶ **The book that** *is* **at the top of the bestseller list gives advice about health.** [The singular noun *book* is the antecedent of *that,* the subject of the singular verb *is* in the relative clause.]

▶ The books that *are* at the top of the bestseller list give advice about health, success, and making money. [The plural noun *books* is the antecedent of *that*, the subject of the plural verb *are* in the relative clause.]

Note: The phrase *one of* is followed by a plural noun phrase. However, the verb can be singular or plural, depending on the meaning.

▶ Juan is one of the employees who *work* long hours. [Several employees work long hours. Juan is one of them. The plural noun *employees* is the antecedent of *who*, the subject of the plural verb *work* in the relative clause.]

▶ Juan is the only one of the employees who *works* long hours. [Only Juan works long hours.]

46d Relative clauses with prepositions

When a relative clause contains a relative pronoun within a prepositional phrase, do not omit the preposition. Keep in mind these three points:

1. Directly after the preposition, use *whom* or *which,* never *that.*

▶ The man *for whom* we worked last year has just retired.

2. If you place the preposition after the verb, use *that* (or you can omit *that*), but do not use *whom* or *which.*

[that]
▶ The security measures ~~which~~ the mayor had insisted on made him unpopular.

3. Do not add an extra personal pronoun object after the preposition at the end of the relative clause.

▶ The theater company [that] they are devoted to ~~it~~ has produced six new plays this season.

46e Position of relative clause

To avoid ambiguity, place a relative clause as close as possible to its antecedent. (See also 40b on misplaced modifiers.)

AMBIGUOUS   **He searched for the notebook all over the house that his friend had forgotten.** [Had his friend forgotten the house?]

REVISED   **He searched all over the house for the notebook that his friend had forgotten.**

46f *Where* and *when* as relative pronouns

When you refer to actual or metaphoric places and times, you can use *where* to replace *in which*, *at which*, or *to which*, and you can use *when* to replace *at which*, *in which*, or *on which*. Do not use a preposition with *where* or *when*.

▶ **The morning on which she graduated was warm and sunny.**

▶ **The morning *when* she graduated was warm and sunny.**

▶ **The village in which he was born honored him last year.**

▶ **The village *where* he was born honored him last year.**

Use *where* or *when* only if actual time or physical location is involved.

                                                    according to which
▶ **The influence of the Sapir-Whorf hypothesis, ~~where~~ behavior is regarded as influenced by language, has declined.**

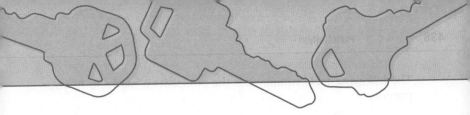

Punctuation serves to regulate the flow of information through a sentence, showing readers how to read your ideas. The following headline from the *New York Times,* "Stock Fraud Is Easier, and Easier to Spot," says that stock fraud is not only easy to engage in but also easy to detect. Without the comma, however, the sentence would send a different message: it would say that detecting stock fraud is becoming increasingly easy.

Try reading the following without the benefit of the signals a reader usually expects.

> When active viruses especially those transmitted by contact can spread easily within the world health organization hard working doctors are continually collaborating to find treatments for several infectious diseases sars avian flu and hepatitis.

Conventional punctuation and mechanics clarify the meaning:

> When active, viruses—especially those transmitted by contact—can spread easily; within the World Health Organization, hard-working doctors are continually collaborating to find treatments for several infectious diseases: SARS, avian flu, and hepatitis.

The following table summarizes the punctuation marks to fit your purpose.

How Punctuation Shows Meaning

What Do You Want to Do?	Options
Overall purpose: To end a sentence	
• To mark where a sentence ends	Period, question mark, or exclamation point (.?!), 51a, 51b
• To indicate the end of a sentence with a close connection to the next sentence	Semicolon (;), 50a
Overall purpose: To separate	
• To separate independent clauses only when a connecting word (*and, but, or, nor, so, for,* or *yet*) is used	Comma (,), 47b
• To separate introductory words, a phrase, or a clause from a following independent clause	Comma (,), 47c
• To separate items (words, phrases, clauses) in a list (*x, y,* and *z*)	Comma (,), 47f
• To separate items in a list that contains internal commas (*x, x; y, y;* and *z*)	Semicolon (;), 50a
• To separate certain adjectives	Comma (,), 47g
• To separate a verb from a quoted statement that follows or precedes it	Comma (,), 47h
• To separate lines of poetry written as running text	Slash (/), 51f
Overall purpose: To insert	
• To insert a word, words, or an "extra information" (nonrestrictive) phrase or clause into a sentence	Commas (, ,), 47d
• To give more emphasis to the insert	Dashes (—), 51c

How Punctuation Shows Meaning

What Do You Want to Do?	Options
• To insert a change within a quotation	Square brackets [ ], 51e
• To insert explanatory information	Parentheses ( ), 51d
Overall purpose: To anticipate an explanation or a list	Colon (:), 50b
Overall purpose: To quote	
• To quote exact words or give the title of a story, a poem, or an article	Double quotation marks (" "), 49b
• To enclose a quotation within another quotation	Single quotation marks (' '), 49d
Overall purpose: To delete from a quotation	Ellipsis dots (. . .), 51g
Overall purpose: To indicate possession	
• For most words	Apostrophe + s ('s), 48b
• For nouns forming the plural with s	Apostrophe after the s (s'), 48c, 48e

Chapter **47**

Commas

A comma separates parts of a sentence; a comma alone does not separate one sentence from another. When readers see a comma, they know that the parts of the sentence are being separated for a reason. When you really can't decide whether to use commas, follow this general principle: "When in doubt, leave them out." Readers find excessive use of commas more distracting than a few missing ones.

47a Two checklists—comma: yes, comma: no

The two checklists provide general rules of thumb. Details and more examples of each rule follow in the rest of chapter 47. Note that in the sample sentences in this chapter, yellow shading means, "No comma here."

KEY POINTS

Comma: Yes

1. Before a coordinating conjunction (*and, but, or, nor, so, for, yet*) to connect independent clauses, including commands, but optional in British English and if the clauses are short (*Wharton entertained and James visited*). See 47b.

   ▶ He frowned, but she did not understand why he was worried.

2. After most introductory words, phrases, or clauses (47c)

   ▶ After the noisy party, the neighbors complained.

3. To set off extra (nonrestrictive) information included in a sentence ("extra commas with extra information") (47d)

   ▶ Her father, a computer programmer, works late at night.

4. To set off a transitional expression or an explanatory insert (47e)

   ▶ The ending, however, is disappointing.

5. To separate three or more items in a series (47f)

   ▶ The fans applauded, cheered, and whistled.

6. Between adjectives that can be reversed and connected with *and* (coordinate adjectives) (47g)

   ▶ We ate a delicious, well-prepared meal.

7. After a verb that introduces a quotation (47h)

   ▶ She gasped, "We haven't a moment to lose!"

KEY POINTS

Comma: No (see also 47i)

1. Not between subject and verb

   ▶ The actor in *Get Shorty* plays Tony in *The Sopranos*.

   However, use two commas to set off any extra information inserted between subject and verb (see 47d).

2. Not before part of a compound structure that is not an independent clause

   ▶ **She won the trophy and accepted it graciously.**

3. Not *after* a coordinating conjunction connecting two independent clauses, but *before* it

   ▶ **The movie tried to be engaging, but it failed miserably.**

4. Not between two independent clauses without a coordinating conjunction (use either a period and a capital letter or a semicolon instead)

   ▶ **He won; she was delighted.**

5. Not between an independent clause and a following dependent clause introduced by *after, before, because, if, since, unless, until,* or *when* (neither before nor after the subordinating conjunction)

   ▶ **She will continue working for the city until she has saved enough for graduate school.**

6. Not before a clause beginning with *that*

   ▶ **They warned us that the meeting would be difficult.**

7. Not before and after essential, restrictive information

   ▶ **The player who scored the goal became a hero.**

8. Not between a verb and its object or complement

   ▶ **The best gifts are food and clothes.**

9. Not after *such as*

   ▶ **Popular fast food items, such as hamburgers and hot dogs, tend to be high in fat.**

47b Use a comma before a coordinating conjunction (*and, but,* etc.) that connects independent clauses.

When you connect independent clauses with a coordinating conjunction (*and, but, or, nor, so, for, yet*), place a comma before the conjunction.

▶ The managers are efficient, but personnel turnover is high.

▶ The juggler juggled seven plates, and we all cheered.

However, when the clauses are short, many writers omit the comma.

▶ He offered to help and he meant it.

47c Use a comma after most introductory phrases and clauses.

The comma signals to readers that the introductory part of the sentence has ended. It says, in effect, "Now wait for the independent clause."

▶ If you blow out all the candles, your wishes will come true.

▶ More than seventeen years ago, Burma was renamed Myanmar.

The comma after the introductory material tells readers to expect the subject and verb of the independent clause. After one word or a short phrase, the comma can be omitted: *Immediately the fun began.* However, in some sentences, omitting the comma can lead to a serious or humorous misreading:

▶ While the guests were eating a mouse ran across the floor.

47d Use commas to set off an extra (nonrestrictive) phrase or clause.

When a phrase or clause provides extra information that could be omitted without changing the meaning of the independent clause, the phrase or clause is said to be *nonrestrictive*. Use commas to set off a nonrestrictive element. Doing so signals that the extra information it presents does not limit the meaning of the independent clause. A phrase or clause that limits or restricts the meaning of the independent clause is said to be *restrictive*. Do not use commas with restrictive information.

NONRESTRICTIVE **We'll attend, even though we'd rather not.** [We will definitely attend. The *even though* clause does not restrict the meaning.]

RESTRICTIVE **We'll attend if we have time.** [We will attend only if circumstances permit. The *if* clause restricts the meaning.]

Commas around appositive phrases Use commas to set off a descriptive or explanatory phrase, called an *appositive phrase*. If the phrase were omitted, readers might lose some interesting details but would still be able to understand the message.

appositive
┌─ phrase ─┐
▶ **She loves her car, a red Toyota.**

┌──── appositive phrase ────┐
▶ **His dog, a big Labrador retriever, is afraid of mice.**

▶ **Salinger's first novel, *The Catcher in the Rye,* captures the language and thoughts of teenagers.** [The commas are used because the title provides supplementary information about the first novel, not information that identifies which novel the writer means. See also 47i, item 8.]

Commas around nonrestrictive participle phrases Nonrestrictive participle phrases add extra descriptive, but not essential, information.

▶ **My boss, wearing a red tie and a green shirt, radiated the holiday spirit.** [The participle phrase does not restrict the meaning of *boss* by distinguishing one boss from another.]

Commas around extra information in nonrestrictive relative clauses When you give nonessential information in a relative clause introduced by *who, whom,* or *which* (never *that*), set the clause off with commas.

▶ **My boss, who wears bright colors, is a cheerful person.** [The independent clause "My boss is a cheerful person" does not lead readers to ask "Which boss?" The relative clause does not restrict the meaning of *boss*.]

▶ His recent paintings, which are hanging in our local restaurant, show dogs in various disguises. [The relative clause, introduced by *which*, merely provides the additional fact that his recent paintings are on display in the restaurant.]

Note: Do not use commas to set off essential, restrictive information (46d and 47i).

┌ restricts *people* to a subgroup ┐
▶ People who wear bright colors send an optimistic message. [The relative clause, beginning with *who*, restricts "people" to a subgroup: not all people send an optimistic message; those who wear bright colors do.]

47e Use commas to set off transitional expressions and explanatory insertions.

Transitional expressions and conjunctive adverbs connect or weave together the ideas in your writing and act as signposts for readers. See 2d for a list of these expressions. Use commas to set off a transitional expression from the rest of the sentence.

▶ Most Labrador retrievers, however, are courageous.

Note: When you use a transitional expression such as *however, therefore, nevertheless, above all, of course,* or *in fact* at the beginning of an independent clause, end the previous clause with a period or a semicolon. Then place a comma after the transitional expression.

▶ The party was a success. In fact, it was still going on at 2 a.m.

You may sometimes choose to insert a phrase or a clause to make a comment, offer an explanation, drive a point home, or point out a contrast. Insertions used for these purposes are set off by commas.

▶ The consequences will be dire, I think.

▶ The best, if not the only, solution is to apologize and start over.

▶ Seasonal allergies, such as those caused by ragweed, are
common.

▶ Unlike SUVs, compact cars do not guzzle gas.

47f Use commas to separate three or more items in a series.

Readers see the commas between items in a series (words, phrases, or clauses) and realize, "This is a list." If you said the sentence aloud, you would pause between items; in writing, you use commas to separate them. Journalists and British writers often omit a comma before the final *and*.

▶ Searching through the drawer, the detective found a key, a
stamp, three coins, and a photograph.

See also 50a for when to use semicolons in place of commas in a list.

47g Use commas to separate coordinate adjectives.

Adjectives are *coordinate* when their order can be reversed and the word *and* can be inserted between them without any change in meaning. Coordinate adjectives (such as *beautiful, delicious, exciting, noisy*) make subjective and evaluative judgments rather than providing objectively verifiable information about, for instance, size, shape, color, or nationality. Separate coordinate adjectives with commas.

▶ He hires people who are energetic, efficient, and polite.

Do not, however, put a comma between the final adjective of a series and the noun it modifies.

▶ Energetic, efficient, and polite salespeople are in demand.

Note that no comma is necessary to separate adjectives that are cumulative, modifying the whole noun phrase that follows (see 62g for the order of these adjectives).

▶ Entering the little old stone house brought back memories
of her childhood.

47h Use a comma between a direct quotation and the preceding or following clause.

The independent clause may come either before or after the quotation.

- ▶ When asked what she wanted to be later in life, she replied, "An Olympic swimmer."

- ▶ "I want to be an Olympic swimmer," she announced confidently. [The comma is inside the quotation marks.]

However, omit the comma if the quotation is a question or exclamation.

- ▶ "Do you want to be a swimmer?" she asked.

In addition, do not insert a comma before a quotation that is integrated into your sentence:

- ▶ The advertisers are promoting "a healthier lifestyle."

47i When not to use commas: Ten rules of thumb

1. Do not use a comma to separate a verb from its subject.

- ▶ The gifts she received from her colleagues made her realize her value to the company.

- ▶ Interviewing so many women in the United States helped the researcher understand the "American dream."

Between a subject and verb, you may need to put two commas around inserted material, but never use just one comma.

- ▶ The engraved plaque, given to her by her colleagues on her last day of work, made her feel proud.

(subject: The engraved plaque; verb: made)

2. Do not use a comma when the second part of a compound structure is not an independent clause.

- ▶ Amy Tan has written novels and adapted them for the screen.

- ▶ Tan has written about her mother and the rest of her family.

3. Do not use a comma *after* a coordinating conjunction that connects two sentences. The comma goes *before* the conjunction, not after it.

▶ *Mad Hot Ballroom* is supposed to be good, but I missed it when it came to my local movie theater.

4. Do not use a comma to connect two independent clauses when no coordinating conjunction is present. Instead, end the first clause with a period and make the second clause a new sentence, or insert a semicolon between the clauses. Use a comma only if you connect the clauses with a coordinating conjunction. See chapter 39 for ways to correct a comma splice, the error that results when two independent clauses are incorrectly connected with a comma.

▶ Amy Tan has written novels; they have been adapted for the screen.

Some writers, however, use a comma between two independent clauses when the clauses use parallel structures to point out a contrast (40j).

▶ She never insults, she just criticizes.

If you do not know readers' expectations on this point, it may be best to play it safe and separate the clauses with a period or a semicolon.

5. Do not use a comma to separate an independent clause from a following dependent clause introduced by *after, before, because, if, since, unless, until,* or *when*.

▶ The test results were good because all the students had studied in groups.

6. Do not use a comma after *although*.

▶ Although the oboist had a cold, she performed well.

7. Do not use a comma to separate a clause beginning with *that* from the rest of the sentence.

▶ The girl in Tan's story tried to convey to her mother that she did not have to be a child prodigy.

Note: A comma can appear before a *that* clause when it is the second comma of a pair before and after extra information inserted as a non-restrictive phrase.

▶ He skates so fast, despite his size, that he will probably break the world record.

8. Do not use commas around a phrase or clause that provides essential, restrictive information.

▶ Alice Walker's essay "Beauty: When the Other Dancer Is the Self" discusses coping with a physical disfigurement.
[Walker has written more than one essay. The title restricts the noun *essay* to one specific essay.]

Similarly, a restrictive relative clause introduced by *who, whom, whose, which,* or *that* is never set off by commas. The clause provides essential, identifying information (see 46d and 47d).

▶ The teachers praised the children who finished on time. [The teachers didn't praise all the children; they praised only the ones who finished on time.]

9. Do not use a comma to separate a verb from its object or complement.

▶ The qualities required for the job are punctuality, efficiency, and the ability to work long hours.

10. Do not use a comma after *such as*.

▶ They bought kitchen supplies such as detergent, paper towels, and garbage bags.

47j Special uses of commas

To prevent misreading Use a comma to separate elements in a sentence that may otherwise be confusing.

▶ He who can, does. He who cannot, teaches.
  —George Bernard Shaw, *Man and Superman*
[Usually a comma is not used to separate a subject from the verb. Here the comma is necessary to prevent confusion.]

With an absolute phrase Use a comma to set off a phrase that modifies the whole sentence (an absolute phrase).

> ┌─────── absolute phrase ───────┐
> ▶ The audience looking on in amusement, the valedictorian blew kisses to all her favorite instructors.

With a date Use a comma to separate the day from the year in a date.

> ▶ On May 14, 1998, the legendary singer Frank Sinatra died.
> [Do not use a comma before the year when the day precedes the month: 14 May 1998.]

With numbers Use a comma (never a period) to divide numbers into thousands.

> ▶ 1,200   ▶ 515,000   ▶ 34,000,000

No commas are necessary in years (2002), numbers in addresses (3501 East 10th Street), or page numbers (page 1008).

With titles Use commas around a person's title or degree when it follows the name.

> ▶ Stephen L. Carter, Ph.D., gave the commencement speech.

With the parts of an address

> ▶ Alice Walker was born in Eatonton, Georgia, in 1944.

However, do not use a comma before a ZIP code: Newton, MA 02159.

With a conversational tag or tag question

> ▶ Yes, Salinger's daughter, like others before her, has produced a memoir.

> ▶ She has not won a Pulitzer Prize, has she?

With a direct address or salutation

> ▶ Whatever you build next, Mr. Trump, will cause controversy.

Chapter **48**

Apostrophes

An apostrophe indicates ownership or possession: *Fred's books, the government's plans, a year's pay* (the books belonging to Fred, the plans of the government, the pay for a year). It can also signal omitted letters (*who's, can't*).

48a Two checklists—apostrophe: yes, apostrophe: no

> ### KEY POINTS
> **Apostrophe: Yes**
>
> 1. Use *-'s* for the possessive form of all nouns except plural nouns that end with *-s*: *the hero's misfortune, the journalist's sources, the people's advocate.*
> 2. Use an apostrophe alone for the possessive form of plural nouns that end with *-s*: *many politicians' lives, the heroes' misfortunes.*
> 3. Use an apostrophe to indicate the omission of letters in contracted forms such as *didn't, they're,* and *let's.*
> 4. Use *it's* only for "it is" or "it has": *It's a good idea; it's been a long time.* (The possessive form of the pronoun *it* is spelled with no apostrophe: *The house lost its roof.*)

> ### KEY POINTS
> **Apostrophe: No**
>
> 1. Generally, do not use an apostrophe to form the plurals of nouns. (See 48e for rare exceptions.)
> 2. Never use an apostrophe before an *-s* ending on a verb. Note that *let's* is a contracted form for *let us*; the *-s* is not a verb ending.
> 3. Do not write possessive pronouns (*hers, its, ours, yours, theirs*) with an apostrophe.
> 4. Do not use an apostrophe to form the plural of names: *the Browns.*
> 5. With inanimate objects and concepts, writers sometimes prefer to use *of* in place of an apostrophe: *the back of the desk, the end of the garden, the cost of the service.*

48b Use -'s to signal possession.

As a general rule, to signal possession, use -'s with singular nouns, with indefinite pronouns (43h), and with plural nouns that do not form the plural with -*s*.

the child's books	anybody's opinion
the children's toys	today's world
this month's budget	Mr. Jackson's voice
someone else's idea	their money's worth

Individual and joint ownership   To indicate individual ownership, make each owner possessive.

▶ **Updike's and Roth's recent works received glowing reviews.**

To show joint ownership, make only the last owner possessive: *Sam, Sue, and Pat's house.*

Compound nouns   Add -'s to the last word in a compound noun.

▶ **my brother-in-law's car**

Singular nouns ending in -*s*   When a singular noun ends in -*s*, add -'s as usual for the possessive.

▶ **Thomas's toys**   ▶ **my boss's instructions**

However, when a singular noun ending in -*s* is a long word or ends with a *z* or *eez* sound, an apostrophe alone is sometimes used: *Erasmus' rhetoric, Euripides' dramas, Jesus' disciples.*

48c Use only an apostrophe to signal possession in plural nouns already ending in -*s*.

Add only an apostrophe when a plural noun already ends in -*s*.

▶ **the students' suggestions**   ▶ **my friends' ambitions**
   [more than one student]   [more than one friend]

Remember to include an apostrophe in comparisons with a noun understood (40h and 45h):

▶ **His views are different from other professors'.**
[... from other professors' views]

48d Use an apostrophe in contractions.

In a contraction (*shouldn't, don't, haven't*), the apostrophe appears where letters have been omitted. To test whether an apostrophe is in the correct place, mentally replace the missing letters. The replacement test, however, will not help with the following:

won't   will not

Note: Some readers may object to contractions in formal academic writing, especially scientific writing, because they view them as colloquial and informal. It is safer not to use contractions unless you know the conventions of the genre and your readers' preferences.

can't	cannot	they'd	they had *or* they would
didn't	did not		
he's	he is *or* he has	they're	they are
's	is, has, *or* does (How's it taste?)	it's	it is *or* it has
		let's	let us (Let's go.)

Never place an apostrophe before the *-s* ending of a verb:

▶ **The author let~~'~~s his characters take over.**

An apostrophe can also take the place of the first part of a year or decade.

▶ **the greed of the '80s** [the 1980s]

▶ **the Spirit of '76** [the year 1776]

Note: Fixed forms spelled with an apostrophe, such as *o'clock* and the poetic *o'er*, are contractions ("of the clock," "over").

48e Use -'s for plurals only in two instances.

A general rule is never to use an apostrophe to form a plural. However, in the following instances an apostrophe is sometimes used.

1. Use -'s for the plural form of letters of the alphabet. Italicize only the letter, not the plural ending (52c).

▶ Maria picked all the *M*'s out of her alphabet soup.

▶ Georges Perec's novel called *A Void* has no *e*'s in it at all.

2. Use -'s for the plural form of a word referred to as the word itself. Italicize the word named as a word, but do not italicize the -'s ending (52c).

▶ You have too many *but*'s in that sentence.

MLA and APA prefer no apostrophe in the plural form of numbers, acronyms, and abbreviations (54f).

the 1900s   the 1990s   CDs   FAQs   BAs

However, you may see such plurals spelled with -'s. In all cases, be consistent in your usage.

Never use an apostrophe to signal the plural of common nouns or personal names: *big bargains, the Jacksons.*

48f Distinguish between *it's* and *its.*

When deciding whether to use *its* or *it's*, think about meaning. *It's* is a contraction meaning "it is" or "it has." *Its* is the possessive form of the pronoun *it* and means "belonging to it." See also 44b.

▶ It's a good idea.   ▶ The committee took its time.

Chapter **49**

Quotation Marks

In American English, double quotation marks indicate where someone's exact words begin and end. For long quotations, see 49f.

49a Guidelines for using quotation marks

KEY POINTS

Quotation Marks: Basic Guidelines

1. Quote exactly the words used by the original speaker or writer.
2. Pair opening quotation marks with closing quotation marks to indicate where the quotation ends and your ideas begin.
3. Use correct punctuation to introduce and end a quotation, and place other marks of punctuation carefully in relation to the quotation marks.
4. Enclose the titles of articles, short stories, songs, and poems in quotation marks.
5. Enclose any added or changed material in square brackets (51e); indicate omitted material with ellipsis dots (51g).

49b Punctuation introducing and ending a quotation

After an introductory verb, such as *say, state,* or *write,* use a comma followed by a capital letter to introduce a direct quotation.

▶ It was Erma Bombeck who said, "Families aren't dying. They're merging into conglomerates."

— "Empty Fridge, Empty Nest"

Use a colon after a complete sentence introducing a quotation, and begin the quotation with a capital letter.

▶ Woody Allen always tries to make us laugh even about serious issues like wealth and poverty: "Money is better than poverty, if only for financial reasons."

— *Without Feathers*

When a quotation is integrated into the structure of your own sentence, use no special introductory punctuation other than the quotation marks.

▶ Phyllis Grosskurth comments that "anxiety over money was driving him [Byron] over the brink."

—*Byron*

Put periods and commas inside quotation marks, even if these punctuation marks do not appear in the original quotation.

▶ When Henry Rosovsky characterizes Bloom's ideas as "mind-boggling," he is not offering praise.

—*The University*

In a documented paper, when you use parenthetical citations after a short quotation at the end of a sentence, put the period at the end of the citation, not within the quotation. See 49f for long quotations.

▶ Geoffrey Wolff observes that when his father died, there was nothing to indicate "that he had ever known another human being" (11).

—*The Duke of Deception*

Put question marks and exclamation points inside the quotation marks if they are part of the original source, with no additional period.   When your sentence is a statement, do not use a comma or period in addition to a question mark or exclamation point.

▶ She asked, "Where's my mama?"

Put a question mark, exclamation point, semicolon, or colon outside the closing quotation marks.   If your sentence contains punctuation that is your own, not part of the original quotation, do not include it within the quotation marks.

▶ The chapter focuses on this question: Who are "the new American dreamers"?

49c Quotation marks in dialogue

Do not add closing quotation marks until the speaker changes or you interrupt the quotation. Begin each new speaker's words with a new paragraph.

interruption
┌── of quotation ──┐
▶   "I'm not going to work today," he announced. "Why should I? I worked all weekend. My boss is away on vacation. And I have a headache."

┌──────── change of speaker ────────┐
"Honey, your boss is on the phone," his wife called from the bedroom.

If a quotation from one speaker continues for more than one paragraph, place *closing* quotation marks at the end of only the *final* paragraph of the quotation. However, place *opening* quotation marks at the beginning of every paragraph so that readers realize that the quotation is continuing.

49d A quotation within a quotation

Enclose quotations in double quotation marks. Use single quotation marks to enclose a quotation or a title of a short work within a quotation. (The reverse is the case in British English!)

▶ Margaret announced, "I have read 'The Lottery' already."

▶ The comedian Steven Wright once said, "I have an existential map. It has 'You are here' written all over it."

49e Quotation marks with titles, definitions, and translations

For a translation or definition, use quotation marks:

▶ The abbreviation *p.m.* means "after midday."

KEY POINTS
Titles: Quotation Marks or Italics/Underlining?

1. Quotation marks with the title of an article, short story, poem, song, or chapter: "Kubla Khan"; "Lucy in the Sky with Diamonds"; "The Yellow Wallpaper"; "America: The Multinational Society."

2. Italics or underlining with the title of a book, journal, magazine, newspaper, film, play, or long poem published alone: The Tipping Point, *Newsweek, The Hours,* Beowulf (52a). (MLA style prefers underlining.)

3. No quotation marks and no italics or underlining with the title of your own essay (49f): Safety First.

For more on capital letters with titles, see 53d.

49f When not to use quotation marks

Note that in the sample sentences, yellow shading means "no quotation marks here."

Do not put quotation marks around indirect quotations.

> ▶ One woman I interviewed said that her husband argued like a lawyer.

Do not put quotation marks around clichés, slang, or trite expressions.   Instead, revise to eliminate the cliché, slang, or trite expression. See also 33d and 33g.

> involvement.
> ▶ All they want is ~~"a piece of the action."~~
>   ^

Do not put quotation marks at the beginning and end of long indented quotations.   When you use MLA style to quote more than three lines of poetry or four typed lines of prose, indent the whole passage one inch (or ten spaces) from the left margin. Indent five spaces in APA or *Chicago* style. Do not enclose the quoted passage in quotation marks, but retain any internal quotation marks. See 10f and chapters 13, 16, and 19 for examples.

On the title page of your own paper, do not put quotation marks around your essay title. Use quotation marks in your title only when your title contains a quotation or the title of a short work.

▶ **Charles Baxter's "Gryphon" as an Educational Warning**

Chapter **50**

Semicolons and Colons

A colon (:) may look like a semicolon (;). A colon is two dots; the semicolon, a dot above a comma. However, they are used in different ways, and they are not interchangeable. Note the use of the semicolon and colon in the following passage discussing the musical number "Cheek to Cheek" in the Fred Astaire and Ginger Rogers film *Top Hat*:

[Ginger] Rogers is perhaps never more beautiful than when she's just listening; she never takes her eyes off him and throughout this scene I don't think she changes her expression once. The modesty of the effect makes her look like an angel: such a compliant, unasking attitude, handsome beyond expectation in such a fierce woman.

—Arlene Croce,
*The Fred Astaire and Ginger
Rogers Book*

Ginger Rogers and Fred Astaire

50a Two checklists—semicolon: yes, semicolon: no

A period separates independent clauses with finality; a semicolon, such as the one you have just seen in the previous example, provides a less distinct separation and indicates that an additional related thought or item will follow immediately. As essayist Lewis Thomas comments in his "Notes on Punctuation":

> The period tells you that that is that; if you didn't get all the meaning you wanted or expected, anyway you got all the writer intended to parcel out and now you have to move along. But with a semicolon there you get a pleasant little feeling of expectancy; there is more to come.

KEY POINTS
Semicolon: Yes

1. Between closely connected independent clauses when no coordinating conjunction (*and, but, or, nor, so, for, yet*) is used

   ▶ **Biography tells us about the subject; biographers also tell us about themselves.**

   (Do not overuse semicolons in this way.) A comma between the two independent clauses would produce a comma splice, and no punctuation at all would produce a run-on sentence (see chapter 39). Do not use a capital letter to begin a clause after a semicolon.

2. Between independent clauses connected with a transitional expression like *however, moreover, in fact, nevertheless, above all,* or *therefore* (see the list in 2d)

   ▶ **The results of the study support the hypothesis; however, further research with a variety of tasks is necessary.**

   (If the transitional expression is in the middle or at the end of its clause, the semicolon still appears between the clauses: *The results support the hypothesis; further research, however, is necessary.*)

(Continued)

(Continued)

3. To separate items in a list containing internal commas

▶ **When I cleaned out the refrigerator, I found a chocolate cake, half-eaten; some canned tomato paste, which had a blue fungus growing on the top; and some possibly edible meat loaf.**

KEY POINTS

Semicolon: No

1. Not in place of a colon to introduce a list or an explanation

▶ **Ellsworth Kelly has produced a variety of works of art⁄ drawings, paintings, prints, and sculptures.**

2. Not after an introductory phrase or dependent clause, even if the phrase or clause is long. Using a semicolon would produce a fragment. Use a comma instead.

▶ **Because the training period was so long and arduous for all the players⁄the manager allowed one visit by family and friends.**

3. Not before an appositive phrase

▶ **The audience cheered the Oscar winner⁄Philip Seymour Hoffman.**

4. Not in place of a comma before *and, but, or, nor, so, for,* or *yet* joining independent clauses

▶ **The thrift shop in the church basement needed a name⁄ and the volunteers chose Attic Treasures.**

50b Two checklists—colon: yes, colon: no

A colon signals anticipation. It follows an independent clause and introduces information that readers will need. A colon tells readers, "What comes next will define, illustrate, or explain what you have just read." Use one space after a colon. Note that in the sample sentences, yellow shading means "no colon here."

KEY POINTS

Colon: Yes

1. After an independent clause to introduce a list

   ▶ The students included three pieces of writing in their portfolios: a narrative, an argument, and a documented paper.

2. After an independent clause to introduce an explanation, expansion, or elaboration

   ▶ After an alarming cancer diagnosis and years of treatment, Lance Armstrong was victorious: he won the Tour de France seven times.

   Some writers prefer to use a capital letter after a colon introducing an independent clause. Whatever you choose to do, be consistent in your usage.

3. To introduce a rule or principle, which may begin with a capital letter

   ▶ The main principle of public speaking is simple: Look at the audience.

4. To introduce a quotation not integrated into your sentence and not introduced by a verb such as *say*

   ▶ Emily Post has provided an alternative to attempting to outdo others: "To do *exactly as your neighbors do* is the only sensible rule."

   A colon also introduces a long quotation set off from your text (9g).

5. In salutations, precise time notations, titles, and biblical citations

   ▶ Dear Chancellor Witkin:

   ▶ To: The Chancellor

   ▶ 7:20 p.m.

   ▶ *Backlash: The Undeclared War against American Women*

   ▶ Genesis 37:31–35 [Here, a period could be used in place of the colon.]

KEY POINTS
Colon: No

1. Not directly after a verb (such as a form of *be* or *include*)

   ▶ The two main effects were the improvement of registration and an increase in the numbers of advisers.

   ▶ The book includes a preface, an introduction, an appendix, and an index.

2. Not after a preposition (such as *of, except,* and *regarding*) or the phrase *such as*

   ▶ The essay consisted of a clear beginning, middle, and end.

   ▶ The novel will please many readers except linguists and lawyers.

   ▶ They packed many different items for the picnic, such as taco chips, salsa, bean salad, pita bread, and egg rolls.

3. Not after *for example, especially,* or *including*

   ▶ His varied taste is shown by his living room furnishings, including antiques, modern art, and art deco lighting fixtures.

Chapter **51**

Other Punctuation Marks

51a Periods

In British English, a period is descriptively called a "full stop." The stop at the end of a sentence is indeed full—more of a stop than a comma provides. Periods are also used with abbreviations, decimals, and amounts of money, as in items 3 and 4 on page 463.

1. Use a period to end a sentence that makes a statement or gives a command.

▶ The interviewer asked the manager about the company's finances.

▶ Note the use of metaphor in the last paragraph.

The Web site of the Modern Language Association (MLA), in its list of Frequently Asked Questions, recommends leaving one space after a punctuation mark at the end of a sentence but sees "nothing wrong with using two spaces after concluding punctuation marks." Ask your instructor for her or his preference.

For periods used with sentences within parentheses, see 53a.

2. Use a period, not a question mark, to end a sentence concluding with an indirect question.

▶ The interviewer asked the manager how much the company made last year. [See also 40d, 4li, and 62d.]

3. Use a period to signal an abbreviation.

Mr.   Mrs.   Dr.   Rev.   Tues.   etc.

Use only one space after the period: Mr. Lomax. Some abbreviations contain internal periods. Do not include a space after the first internal period.

e.g.   i.e.   a.m.   p.m.   (or **A.M.**   **P.M.**)

Note: For some abbreviations with capital letters, you can use periods or not. Just be consistent.

A.M. or AM   P.M. or PM   U.S.A. or USA

When ending a sentence with an abbreviation, do not add an extra period: *The plane left at 7 a.m.*

However, MLA style recommends that no periods be used with initials of names of government agencies (HUD) or other organizations (ACLU), acronyms (abbreviations pronounced as words: NASA, AIDS), Internet abbreviations (URL), abbreviations for states (CA, NJ), or common time indicators (BC, AD) (54b).

4. Use a period with decimals and with amounts of money over a dollar: 3.7, $7.50.

51b Question marks and exclamation points

Question marks (?)   A question mark at the end of a sentence signals a direct question. Do not use a period in addition to a question mark.

▶ **What is he writing?**

If questions in a series are not complete sentences, you still need question marks. A question fragment may begin with a capital letter or not. Just make your usage consistent.

▶ **Are the characters in the play involved in the disaster? Indifferent to it? Unaware of it?**

▶ **Are the characters in the play involved in the disaster? indifferent to it? unaware of it?**

However, after an indirect question, use a period, not a question mark (51a).

▶ **I wonder what he is writing.**

Questions are useful devices to engage readers' attention. You ask a question and then provide an answer.

▶ **Many cooks nowadays are making healthier dishes. How do they do this? For the most part, they use unsaturated oil.**

A question mark is sometimes used to express uncertainty about a date or to indicate a query.

▶ **"She jumped in?" he wondered.** [Note that no comma is needed after a question mark that is part of a quotation.]

▶ **Plato (427?–347 BC) founded the Academy at Athens.**

Exclamation points (!)   An exclamation point at the end of a sentence indicates that the writer considers the statement amazing, surprising, or extraordinary. As novelist F. Scott Fitzgerald said, "An exclamation point is like laughing at your own joke." Let your words and ideas carry the force of any emphasis you want to communicate.

NO   The last act of her play is really impressive!

YES   The last act resolves the crisis in an unexpected and dramatic way.

If you feel you absolutely have to include an exclamation point to get your point across in dialogue or with an emphatic command or statement, do not use it along with an additional comma or period.

► "Just watch the ball!" the coach yelled.

Note: An exclamation point (or a question mark) can be used with a period that signals an abbreviation:

► The match didn't end until 1 a.m.!

Avoid using a question mark or an exclamation point enclosed in parentheses to convey irony or sarcasm.

NO   The principal, that great historian (?), has proposed a new plan for the history curriculum.

YES   The principal, who admits he is no historian, has proposed a new plan for the history curriculum.

51c Dashes

A dash (—) alerts readers to an explanation, to something unexpected, or to an interruption. Form a dash by typing two hyphens, putting no extra space before, between, or after them. Recent software will transform the two hyphens into one continuous dash. A dash should be followed by a phrase, not a clause.

► Armed with one weapon—his wit—he faced the crowd.

► The accused gasped, "But I never—" and fainted.

► In America there are two classes of travel—first class and with children.
                    —Robert Benchley, in Robert E. Drennan, *The Algonquin Wits*

Commas can be used to set off an appositive phrase, but a pair of dashes is preferable when appositive phrases form a list containing commas.

► The contents of his closet—torn jeans, frayed jackets, and suits shiny on the seat and elbows—made him reassess his priorities.

Overusing the dash may produce a staccato effect. Use it sparingly.

51d Parentheses

Use parentheses to mark an aside or provide additional information.

▶ **Everyone admired Lance Armstrong's feat (winning the Tour de France seven times).**

Also use parentheses to enclose citations in a documented paper and to enclose numbers or letters preceding items in a list.

▶ **(3) A journalist reports that in the course of many interviews, he met very few people who were cynical about the future of the country (Lamb 5).**

At the end of a sentence, place the period inside the last parenthesis only when a separate new sentence is enclosed (see also 53a).

▶ **Lance Armstrong's feat led to greater visibility for competitive cycling in the United States. (He won the Tour de France seven times.)**

51e Brackets

Square brackets ([ ]) When you insert words or comments or make changes to words within a quotation, enclose the inserted or changed material in square brackets. Be careful to insert only words that help the quotation fit into your sentence grammatically or that offer necessary explanation. Do not insert words that substantially change the meaning.

▶ **According to Ridley, "the key to both of these features of life [the ability to reproduce and to create order] is information."**

On occasion, you may need to use brackets to insert the Latin word *sic* (meaning "thus") into a quoted passage in which an error occurs. Using *sic* tells readers that the word or words that it follows were present in the original source and are not your own.

▶ **Richard Lederer tells of a man who did "exercises to strengthen his abominable [sic] muscles."**

Square brackets can also be used in MLA style around ellipsis dots that you add to signal an omission from a source that itself contains ellipsis dots (51g).

Angle brackets (< >)   Use angle brackets to enclose e-mail addresses and URLs, particularly in an MLA-style works-cited list. See 12e and 57a.

51f   Slashes

Use a slash (/) to separate two or three lines of poetry quoted within your own text. For quoting more than three lines of poetry, see 10f.

> ▶ **Philip Larkin asks a question that many of us relate to: "Why should I let the toad *work* / Squat on my life?"**

Slashes are also used in expressions such as *and/or* and *he/she* to indicate options. Be careful not to overuse these expressions.

51g   Ellipsis dots

When you omit material from a quotation, indicate the omission—the ellipsis—by using spaced dots (. . .). (MLA style recommends using square brackets around ellipsis dots if the passage you quote from itself contains an ellipsis.) The following passage by Ruth Sidel, on page 27 of *On Her Own,* is used in the examples that follow.

> These women have a commitment to career, to material well-being, to success, and to independence. To many of them, an affluent lifestyle is central to their dreams; they often describe their goals in terms of cars, homes, travel to Europe. In short, they want their piece of the American Dream.

Words omitted from the middle of a quotation   Use three ellipsis dots when you omit material from the middle of a quotation.

> ▶ **Ruth Sidel reports that the women in her interviews "have a a commitment to career . . . and to independence" (27).**

Words omitted at the end of your sentence   When you omit part of a quotation and the omission occurs at the end of your own sentence, insert ellipsis dots after the sentence period, followed by the closing quotation marks, making four dots in all.

▶ **Ruth Sidel presents interesting findings about jobs and money: "These women have a commitment to career, to material well-being. . . ."**

When a parenthetical reference follows the quoted passage, put the final sentence period after the parenthetical reference:

▶ **Ruth Sidel presents interesting findings about jobs and money: "These women have a commitment to career, to material well-being . . ." (27).**

Complete sentence omitted   When you omit a complete sentence or more, insert three ellipsis dots.

▶ **Sidel tells us how "an affluent life-style is central to their dreams; . . . they want their piece of the American dream" (27).**

Line of poetry omitted   When you omit one or more lines of poetry from a long, indented quotation, indicate the omission with a line of dots.

▶ **This poem is for the hunger of my mother**
. . . . .
who read the Blackwell's catalogue
like a menu of delights
and when we moved from Puerto Rico to the States
we packed 100 boxes of books and 40 of everything else.
                                    —Aurora Levins Morales, *Class Poem*

When not to use ellipsis dots   Do not use ellipsis dots when you quote only a word or a phrase because it will be obvious that material has been omitted:

▶ **The women Sidel interviewed see an "affluent life-style" in their future.**

Note: Use three dots to indicate a pause in speech or an interruption.

▶ **The doctor said, "The good news is . . ." and then turned to take a phone call.**

Chapter **52**

Italics and Underlining

Use italic type or underlining to highlight a word, phrase, or title in your own writing. In manuscript form, underlining is more distinctive and therefore preferred, particularly in MLA bibliographical lists and in material to be graded or typeset. Ask your instructor which to use. For underlining when writing online, see 57b.

52a   Italicize or underline titles of long, whole works.

In the body of an essay, italicize or underline the titles of books, journals, magazines, newspapers, plays, films, TV series, long poems, musical compositions, Web sites, online databases, and works of art.

- ▶ <u>**The Sun Also Rises**</u>   ▶ *The Daily Show*   ▶ <u>Newsweek</u>

- ▶ *Nickel and Dimed*   ▶ <u>Mona Lisa</u>   ▶ *Wikipedia*

In the body of your text, do not italicize or underline the names of sacred works such as the Bible and the Koran (Qur'an), though these will be underlined in an MLA citation (11c, item R) and in a works-cited list (12c, item 18). Also do not italicize or underline the books of the Bible (Genesis, Psalms) or the titles of documents and laws, such as the Declaration of Independence, the Constitution, and the Americans with Disabilities Act.

Do not italicize or underline the titles of short works, such as poems, short stories, essays, and articles; use quotation marks (49e). Do not italicize or underline the title of your own essay (49e).

See MLA, APA, CSE, and *Chicago* styles for the conventions of italics or underlining in a list of references (chapters 12–19).

52b   Italicize or underline names of ships, trains, airplanes, and spacecraft.

- ▶ <u>**Mayflower**</u>   ▶ *Silver Meteor*   ▶ *Mir*   ▶ <u>Columbia</u>

Do not underline or italicize the abbreviations sometimes preceding them: USS *Constitution*.

52c   Italicize or underline letters, numerals, and words referring to the words themselves, not to what they represent.

▶ The sign had a large <u>P</u> in black marker and a <u>3</u> in red.

▶ *Zarf* is a useful word for some board games.

52d   Italicize or underline words from other languages.

Expressions not commonly used in English should be italicized or underlined. Do not overuse such expressions because they tend to sound pretentious.

▶ The author's *Weltanschauung* promotes gloom.

Do not italicize common expressions: et al., croissant, film noir, etc.

52e   Do not use italics or underlining for emphasis.

Select a word that better conveys the idea you want to express.

▶ The climb was ~~so scary~~.
                ^

Chapter 53

Capitalization

53a   Capitalize *I* and the first word of a sentence.

Always use a capital letter for the pronoun *I* and for the first word of a sentence. E-mail correspondence without any capitals may annoy some readers (see also 57c). However, do not use a capital letter for the first word after a semicolon except for *I* or a proper noun. In addition, use no capital letter if you insert a complete sentence into another sentence, using parentheses:

▶ **The Web site provides further historical information (just click on the icon).**

But use a capital letter if the sentence within parentheses stands alone:

▶ **The Web site provides further historical information. (Just click on the icon.)**

Note also the placing of the periods in the examples above (51d).

53b Capitalize proper nouns and proper adjectives.

Begin the names of specific people, places, and things with a capital letter. For the use of *the* with proper nouns, see 60f.

Types of Proper Nouns and Adjectives	Examples
People	Albert Einstein, Madonna, T. S. Eliot, Bill Gates (but bell hooks)
Nations, continents, planets, stars, and galaxies	Hungary, Asia, Mercury, the North Star, the Milky Way
Mountains, rivers, and oceans	Mount Everest, the Thames, the Pacific Ocean
Public places and regions	Golden Gate Park, the Great Plains, the Midwest, the South (but no capital for direction, as in "Drive south on the turnpike")
Streets, buildings, and monuments	Rodeo Drive, the Empire State Building, the Roosevelt Memorial
Cities, states, and provinces	Toledo, Kansas, Nova Scotia
Days of the week and months	Wednesday, March
Holidays	Labor Day, the Fourth of July
Organizations, companies, and search engines	the Red Cross, Microsoft Corporation, AltaVista, eBay (internal capital)

Types of Proper Nouns and Adjectives	Examples
Institutions (including colleges, departments, schools, government offices, and courts of law)	University of Texas, Department of English, School of Business, Defense Department, Florida Supreme Court
Historical events, named periods, and documents	the Civil War, the Renaissance, the Roaring Twenties, the Declaration of Independence
Religions, deities, revered persons, and sacred texts	Buddhism, Islam, Muslim, Baptist, Jehovah, Mohammed, the Torah, the Koran (Qur'an)
Races, tribes, nations, nationalities, and languages	the Navajo, Greece, Greek, Spain, Spanish, Syrian, Farsi
Registered trademarks	Kleenex, Apple, Bic, Nike, Xerox
Names of ships, planes, and spacecraft	the USS *Kearsarge,* the *Spirit of St. Louis,* the *Challenger*
Titles of courses	English Composition, Introduction to Sociology

Note: Do not capitalize nouns naming general classes or types of people, places, things, or ideas: *government, jury, mall, prairie, utopia, traffic court, the twentieth century, goodness, reason.* Also, do not capitalize the names of seasons (*next spring*) or subjects of study, except for languages (*She is interested in geology and Spanish.*). For the use of capital letters in online writing, see 57c.

53c   Capitalize a title before a person's name.

▶ The reporter interviewed Senator Thompson.

▶ The residents cheered Grandma Jones.

Do not use a capital letter when a title is not attached to a person's name.

▶ Each state elects two senators.

▶ My grandmother is ninety years old.

When a title substitutes for the name of a known person, a capital letter is often used.

▶ Have you spoken with the Senator [senator] yet?

53d Capitalize major words in a title.

In titles of published books, journals, magazines, essays, articles, films, poems, and songs, use a capital letter at the beginning of all words. However, do not use a capital letter for articles (*the, a, an*), coordinating conjunctions (*and, but, or, nor, so, for, yet*), *to* in an infinitive (*to stay*), and prepositions unless they begin or end the title or subtitle.

▶ "With a Little Help from My Friends"

▶ *Reflections from the Keyboard: The World of the Concert Pianist*

For more on titles, see the Key Points box in 49e.

53e Capitals with colons and quotations

Should a capital letter be used at the beginning of a clause after a colon? Usage varies. Usually a capital letter is used if the clause states a rule or principle (50b). Make your usage consistent.

Should a capital letter be used at the beginning of a quotation? Capitalize the first word of a quoted sentence if it is capitalized in the original passage.

▶ Quindlen says, "This is a story about a name," and thus tells us the topic of her article.

Do not capitalize when you quote part of a sentence.

▶ When Quindlen says that she is writing "a story about a name," she is telling us the topic of her article.

Chapter **54**

Abbreviations

For abbreviations commonly used in online writing, see 57e.

54a   Abbreviate titles used with people's names.

Use an abbreviation, followed by a period, for titles before or after names. The following abbreviated titles precede names: *Mr., Mrs., Ms., Prof., Dr., Gen.,* and *Sen.* The following abbreviated titles follow names: *Sr., Jr., PhD, MD, BA,* and *DDS.* Do not use a title both before and after a name: *Dr. Benjamin Spock* or *Benjamin Spock, MD.* Do not abbreviate a title if it is not attached to a specific name.

> ► Pat Murphy Sr. went to the ~~dr.~~ twice last week.
>   *doctor*

54b   Abbreviate the names of familiar institutions, countries, tests, diseases, diplomas, individuals, and objects.

Use capitalized abbreviations of the names of well-known institutions (*UCLA, YWCA, FBI, UN*), countries (*USA* or *U.S.A.*), tests and diplomas (*SAT, GED*), diseases (*MS, HIV*), individuals (*FDR*), TV and radio networks and stations (*PBS, WQXR*), and objects (*DVD*). If you use a specialized abbreviation, first use the term in full followed by the abbreviation in parentheses; then use the abbreviation.

> ► The Graduate Record Examination (GRE) is required by many graduate schools. GRE preparation is therefore big business.

54c   Abbreviate terms used with numbers.

Use the abbreviations such as *BC, AD, a.m., p.m., $, mph, wpm, mg, kg,* and other units of measure only when they occur with specific numbers.

▶ **35 BC** [meaning "before Christ," now often replaced with *BCE*, "before the Common Era"]

▶ **AD 1776** [*anno domini*, "in the year of the Lord," now often replaced with *CE*, "Common Era," used after the date: 1776 CE]

▶ **2:00 a.m./p.m.** [*ante* or *post meridiem*, Latin for "before or after midday"] Alternatives are A.M./P.M. or AM/PM. Be consistent.

Do not use these abbreviations and other units of measure when no number is attached to them.

▶ His family gave him a wallet full of <del>$</del> money to spend on vacation.

▶ They arrived late in the <del>p.m.</del> afternoon.

54d Abbreviate common Latin terms.

In notes, parentheses, and source citations, use abbreviations for common Latin terms. In the body of your text, use the English meaning.

Abbreviation	Latin	English Meaning
etc.	et cetera	and so on
i.e.	id est	that is
e.g.	exempli gratia	for example
cf.	confer	compare
NB	nota bene	note well
et al.	et alii	and others

54e Do not abbreviate familiar words to save time and space.

In formal writing, write in full expressions such as the following:

&	and
bros.	brothers [Use "Bros." only if it is part of the official name of a business.]

chap.	chapter
Mon.	Monday
nite	night
NJ	New Jersey [Abbreviate the name of a state only in an address, a note, or a reference.]
no.	number [Use the abbreviation only with a specific number: "No. 17 on the list was deleted."]
Oct.	October [Write names of days and months in full, except in some works-cited lists.]
soc.	sociology [Write names of academic subjects in full.]
thru	through
w/	with

54f Use *-s* (not *-'s*) for the plural form of an abbreviation.

Do not use an apostrophe to make an abbreviation plural (48e).

▶ **She has over a thousand CDs.**

▶ **Both his SUVs are at the repair shop.**

Chapter **55**

Numbers

Conventions for using numerals (actual figures) or words vary across the disciplines.

55a Use the conventions of the discipline in which you are writing.

In the humanities and in business letters

Use words for numbers expressible in one or two words and for fractions (*nineteen, fifty-six, two hundred, one-half*).

Use numerals for longer numbers (*326; 5,625; 7,642,000*).

Use a combination of words and numerals for whole millions, billions, and so on (*45 million, 1 billion*).

In scientific and technical writing

Use numerals for all numbers above nine.

Use numerals for numbers below ten only when they show precise measurement, as when they are grouped and compared with other larger numbers (*5 of the 39 participants*), or when they precede a unit of measurement (*6 cm*), indicate a mathematical function (*8%; 0.4*), or represent a specific time, date, age, score, or number in a series.

Use words for fractions: *two-thirds.*

55b Spell out numbers that begin a sentence.

▶ **One hundred twenty-five members voted for the new bylaws.**

▶ **Six thousand fans have already bought tickets.**

 ESL NOTE

Number before *Hundred, Thousand,* and *Million*

Even after plural numbers, use the singular form of *hundred, thousand,* and *million*. Add *-s* only when there is no preceding number.

▶ **Five *hundred* books were damaged in the flood.**

▶ ***Hundreds* of books were damaged in the flood.**

55c Use numerals for giving the time and dates and in other special instances.

In nonscientific writing, use numerals for the following:

Time and dates	6 p.m. on 31 May 1995
Decimals	20.89
Statistics	median score 35

Addresses	16 East 93rd Street
Chapter, page, scene, and line numbers	chapter 5, page 97
Quantities appearing with abbreviations or symbols	6°C (for temperature Celsius), $21, 6'7"
Scores	The Knicks won 89–85.

For percentages and money, numerals and the symbol (*75%, $24.67*) are usually acceptable, or you can spell out the expression if it is fewer than four words (*seventy-five percent, twenty-four dollars*).

55d Use *-s* (not *-'s*) for the plural form of numerals.

▶ **in the 1980s**   ▶ **They scored in the 700s in the SATs.**

Chapter **56**

Hyphens

Use hyphens to divide a word or to form a compound. For the use of hyphens online, see 57d.

56a Hyphens with prefixes

Many words with prefixes are spelled without hyphens: *cooperate, nonrestrictive, unnatural*. Others are hyphenated: *all-inclusive, anti-intellectual, self-effacing*. Always use a hyphen when the main word is a number or a proper noun: *all-American, post-1990*. If you are unsure about whether to insert a hyphen after a prefix, check a big dictionary to see if it lists the word as hyphenated.

56b Hyphens in compound words

Some compound nouns are written as one word (*toothbrush*), others as two words (*coffee shop*), and still others with one or more hyphens (*role-playing, father-in-law*). Always check an up-to-date dictionary.

Similarly, check a dictionary for compound verbs (*cross-examine, overemphasize*).

Hyphenate compound adjectives preceding a noun: *a well-organized party, a law-abiding citizen, a ten-page essay.* When the modifier follows the noun, no hyphen is necessary: *The party was well organized. Most citizens try to be law abiding. The essay was ten pages long.*

Do not insert a hyphen between an *-ly* adverb and an adjective or after an adjective in its comparative (*-er*) or superlative (*-est*) form: *a tightly fitting suit, a sweeter sounding melody.*

Treat a series of hyphenated prefixes like this:

▶ **Many second- and third-generation Americans celebrate their origins.**

56c Hyphens in spelled-out numbers

Use hyphens when spelling out two-word numbers from twenty-one to ninety-nine. (See chapter 55 for more on spelling out numbers.)

▶ **Twenty-two applicants arrived early in the morning.**

Also use a hyphen in spelled-out fractions: *two-thirds of a cup.*

56d End-of-line hyphens

Most word processors either automatically hyphenate words or automatically wrap words around to the next line. Choose the latter option to avoid the strange and unacceptable word division that sometimes appears with automatic hyphenation. Do not insert a hyphen into a URL to split it across lines (see 57d).

Chapter 57

Online Guidelines

57a Punctuation in URLs

Punctuation marks communicate essential information in Web site addresses—uniform resource locators (URLs)—and in e-mail addresses. Be sure to include all marks when you write an address, and if you need to spread a URL over more than one line, split it after a slash (MLA style) or before a punctuation mark. Do not split the protocol (<http://>). In a print source, use angle brackets to enclose e-mail and Web addresses.

▶ **The Modern Language Association, whose Web site is at <http://www.mla.org>, provides examples of documenting Web sources.**

Do not include any additional punctuation within the angle brackets (57d).

57b Underlining and italics online

In an online source, URLs are hyperlinked and therefore appear as underlined on the screen. When you write for publication on the Web, always use italics to indicate titles and other usually underlined expressions.

57c Capital letters online

Don't let the speed and informal nature of e-mail delude you into thinking that no rules or conventions matter anymore. Especially in academic and business settings, e-mail messages written with no capitals for the first word of a sentence, for proper nouns, or for *I* will send readers the somewhat insulting signal that you have not bothered to check what you send them.

Overdoing capitals is as bad as (maybe worse than) including none at all. Writing a whole message in capital letters can be perceived by readers as the online equivalent of shouting. In order not to offend readers in e-mail communications and online discussion groups, avoid the prolonged use of capital letters. See also 22a.

57d Hyphens online

Some e-mail addresses and URLs include hyphens, so never add a hyphen to indicate that you have split an address between lines. When an online address includes a hyphen, do not break the line at a hyphen because readers will not know whether the hyphen is part of the address. Break the line after @ or after a slash.

Technological vocabulary changes quickly. You will find both *e-mail* and *email*. The MLA prefers the hyphenated spelling, *e-mail*, but the tendency is for common words like this to move toward closing up. Whichever form you use, use it consistently.

57e Abbreviations online

Many abbreviations in the electronic world have become standard fare: CD-ROM, RAM, PIN, and more. In addition, the informal world of online communication leads to informal abbreviations, at least in personal e-mail messages. Abbreviations such as *BTW* ("by the way"), *IMHO* ("in my humble opinion"), and *TTYTT* ("to tell you the truth") are used in informal e-mail, but you should avoid them in formal contexts.

Chapter **58**

Spelling

Get into the habit of using a dictionary and a word processor with a spelling-check program. Even if you check your spelling with computer software, you still need to proofread. A program will not alert you to a correctly spelled word used in the wrong place (such as *cite* used in place of *sight* or *site*). However, you may be called upon to write spontaneously without access to a spelling program or a dictionary, so learn the basic rules in 58a–58e.

58a Plurals of nouns

Regular plural forms   The regular plural of nouns is formed by adding *-s* or *-es* to the singular word.

essay, essays   match, matches

To form the plural of a compound noun, attach the *-s* to the main noun in the phrase.

mothers-in-law   passersby

Proofread carefully for plural forms that form the plural with -s but make other changes, too, such as the following:

-f or -fe ⟶ -ves	(*Exceptions:* beliefs, roofs, chiefs)
thief, thieves	
wife, wives	

-o ⟶ -oes	**-o ⟶ -os**
potato, potatoes	hero (sandwich), heros
tomato, tomatoes	photo, photos
hero (human), heroes	piano, pianos

Consonant + -y ⟶ -ies	**Vowel + -y ⟶ -ys**
family, families	toy, toys
party, parties	monkey, monkeys

Irregular plural forms (no -s ending)

man, men	foot, feet
woman, women	tooth, teeth
child, children	mouse, mice

Plural forms borrowed from other languages   Words borrowed from other languages, particularly Greek and Latin words, frequently borrow the plural form of the language, too.

basis, bases	nucleus, nuclei
thesis, theses	vertebra, vertebrae
hypothesis, hypotheses	alumnus (m.), alumni
criterion, criteria	alumna (f.), alumnae

Plural forms with no change   Some words have the same form in singular and plural: *moose, deer, sheep, species.*

58b Doubling consonants

Doubled consonants form a link between spelling and pronunciation because the doubling of a consonant signals a short vowel sound.

Double the consonant when the verb stem contains one vowel plus one consonant in one syllable.

slip, slipping, slipped   hop, hopping, hopped

The doubled consonant preserves the short vowel sound. Compare the pronunciation of *hop, hopping, hopped* with *hope, hoping, hoped.* Compare the vowel sounds in *write, writing,* and *written.*

Double the consonant when the verb stem contains two or more syllables with one vowel plus one consonant in the final stressed syllable.

refer, referring, referred   control, controlling, controlled

Compare *traveling* and *traveled* with the stress on the first syllable. (British English usage, however, is *travelling* and *travelled.*)

Double the consonant when the suffix *-er* or *-est* is added to one-syllable adjectives ending in one vowel plus one consonant.

big, bigger, biggest   hot, hotter, hottest

Double the *l* when adding *-ly* to an adjective that ends in one *-l.*

careful, carefully   successful, successfully

58c Spelling with *-y* or *-i*

Verb Ends in Consonant + *-y*	*-ies*	*-ying*	*-ied*
cry	cries	crying	cried
study	studies	studying	studied

Verb Ends in Vowel + *-y*	*-ys*	*-ying*	*-yed*
play	plays	playing	played

Exceptions: pay/paid, say/said, lay/laid

Verb Ends in Vowel + *-e*	*-ies*	*-ying*	*-ied*
die	dies	dying	died

Two-Syllable Adjective Ends in -y	-i with a Suffix
happy	happier, happily, happiness

Two-Syllable Adjective Ends in -ly	-lier	-liest
friendly	friendlier	friendliest

58d Internal *ie* or *ei*

This traditional rhyme helps with the decision about whether to use *ie* or *ei*: "I before *e*/Except after *c*/Or when sounded like *ay*/As in *neighbor* and *weigh*." The following examples illustrate those guidelines:

i before *e*	*e* before *i* after *c*	*e* before *i* when sounded like *ay*
believe	receive	vein
relief	ceiling	reign
niece	deceive	sleigh

But note the exceptions:

i before *e* even after *c*	*e* before *i*, not after *c*	
conscience	height	seize
science	either/neither	foreign
species	leisure	weird

58e Adding a suffix

Keep a silent *-e* before an *-ly* suffix.

immediate, immediately   sure, surely

Exceptions: true, truly; whole, wholly; due, duly

Keep a silent *-e* before a suffix beginning with a consonant.

state, statement   force, forceful   rude, rudeness

Exceptions: acknowledge, acknowledgment; judge, judgment; argue, argument

Drop a silent *-e* before a suffix beginning with a vowel.

hope, hoping   observe, observant

write, writing   remove, removable

Exceptions: enforce, enforceable; change, changeable. Retaining the *-e* preserves the soft sound of the preceding consonant.

With adjectives ending in *-le*, drop the *-le* when adding *-ly*.

sensible, sensibly

With adjectives ending in *-ic*, add *-ally* to form the adverb.

basic, basically   characteristic, characteristically

Exception: public, publicly

Pay attention to the suffixes *-able*, *-ible*, *-ant*, *-ent*, *-ify*, and *-efy*. More words end in *-able* than in *-ible*. Here are some of the most common *-ible* words:

eligible	incredible	irresistible	legible
permissible	responsible	terrible	visible

Unfortunately, there are no rules of thumb to help you decide whether to use the suffix *-ant* or *-ent*. Learn common words with these suffixes, and have your dictionary handy for others.

-ant	*-ent*
defiant	confident
observant	convenient
relevant	existent
reluctant	imminent
resistant	independent

The suffix *-ify* is more common than *-efy*. Learn the four *-efy* words:

liquefy   putrefy   rarefy   stupefy

58f Multinational characters: Accents, umlauts, tildes, and cedillas

Words and names in languages other than English may be spelled with special marks over or under a letter, such as an accent (é or è), an umlaut or dieresis (ö), a tilde (ñ), or a cedilla (ç). Your word processing program probably provides these characters (in Microsoft Word, go to Insert/Symbol/Subset). If it does not, insert them by hand.

TECH NOTE

A Useful Web Site for Writing in Other Languages

International Accents and Diacriticals: Theory, Charts, and Tips, prepared by Irene Starr of the Foreign Language Resource Center at the University of Massachusetts, is a useful site that provides charts of how to use Word, Wordperfect, or a Macintosh computer to produce multinational characters; instructions on accessing and using the International English keyboard; and links to sites useful for those writing non-Roman alphabets.

Online Study Center   **Mechanics** Writing in other languages

earning to write well often means learning to write for readers of many different linguistic and cultural backgrounds; it may also mean writing in more than one language and even in more than one local version of a language.

Chapter **59**

Writing across Cultures

59a English and Englishes

At the same time as we are becoming more aware of diversity and other countries' languages and cultures, we are also experiencing a spread in the use of English. More than 380 million people speak English as their first language, and more than a billion use English as a common language for special communicative, educational, and business purposes within their own communities. However, languages are not fixed and static, and the users of English in their various locations adapt the language for their own use, as the Circle of World English (37c) shows. For example, a *cell phone* in the United States is a *mobile phone* in England and a *handphone* in Singapore.

The concept of one English or a "standard" language is thus becoming more fluid, focused more on the context and the language users than on one set of rules. Consequently, the English regarded as standard in North America is not necessarily standard in Australia, the United Kingdom, Hong Kong, Singapore, Indonesia, India, or Pakistan. Scholars see Englishes—varieties of English—in place of a monolithic English with an immutable set of rules.

Varieties of English spoken in different geographical locations even have their own names: Spanglish (Spanish English), Singlish (Singaporean English), and Taglish (Tagalog English, spoken in the Philippines) are just a few examples of language varieties that have developed. English is thus being reinvented around the world, sometimes to the dismay of academics and government officials, sometimes with the approval of citizens who see the adaptation as an act of freedom, even rebellion. The Filipino poet Gemino Abad has claimed: "The English language is now ours. We have colonized it."

Nevertheless, to reach the expectations of the largest number of academic readers, a sense of a standard vocabulary, syntax, and grammar still prevails across boundaries.

59b Difference, not deficit

Students in colleges in North America who grew up speaking another language are often called students of English as a Second Language (ESL), and the abbreviation is commonly used in college curricula, professional literature, and the press. However, this term is not broad enough. Many so-called second-language students speak three or four languages, depending on their life and educational circumstances and the languages spoken at home. Along with being bilingual or multilingual, such students frequently are multicultural, equipped with all the knowledge and experience that those terms imply.

Whether your first language is a variety of English or a totally different language, it is a good idea to see your knowledge of language and culture as an advantage rather than a problem. Unlike many monolingual writers (individuals who know only one version of one language), you are able to know different cultures in depth and to switch at will among varied linguistic and rhetorical codes. Rather than having only one language, one culture, and one culturally bound type of writing, you have a broader perspective—more to think about, more to write about, more resources to draw on as you write, and far more comparisons to make among languages, writers, writing, and culture. You bring your culture with you into your writing, and as you do so, you help shape and reshape the culture of North America.

Remember, too, that in many situations, the readers you write for will be culturally and linguistically diverse, not all emerging from one educational background. In formal settings, always aim to make your ideas clear to *all* readers by using Standard English, avoiding slang and jargon, and choosing a style appropriate to your subject matter.

59c Learning from errors

Even for students who have been learning a new language or the conventions of a standard dialect for a while, errors are inevitable. Welcome and embrace your errors; study them; learn from them. Errors show learning in progress. If you make no errors while you are learning to speak or write a new language or a standard version of English, perhaps you are being too careful and using only what you know is correct. Be willing to take risks and try new words, new expressions, new combinations. That is the way to expand your repertoire.

TECH NOTE

Web Sites on Language and Writing

The Web sites listed here provide useful information.

- ESL Resources, Handouts, and Exercises from Purdue University's Online Writing Lab at <http://owl.english.purdue.edu/handouts/esl/index.html>.

- Guide to Grammar and Writing at <http://grammar.ccc.commnet.edu/grammar/>. On this Capital Community College site, you will find information and quizzes on words, paragraphs, and essays. The Grammar Logs in "Ask Grammar" contain people's questions and answers and cover interesting points.

When you make an error, write a note about it. Consider why you made the error—was it, for example, transfer from your home language, a guess, a careless mistake? Or was it the employment of a logical but erroneous hypothesis about Standard English (such as "Many verbs form the past tense with -ed; therefore, the past tense form of *swear* is probably *sweared*")? Analyzing the causes of errors will help you understand how to edit them and avoid them in the future. (By the way, the past tense form of *swear* is *swore*.)

59d Editing guide to multilingual transfer errors

Errors in writing in a new language can occur when you are grappling with new subject matter and difficult subjects. You concentrate on ideas and clarity, but because no writer can do everything at once, you fail to concentrate on editing.

The editing guide that follows identifies several problem areas for multilingual/ESL writers. It shows grammatical features (column 1) of specific languages (column 2), features that lead to an error when transferred to English (column 3). An edited Standard English version appears in column 4. Of course, the guide covers neither all linguistic problem areas nor all languages. Rather, it lists a selection, with the goal of being useful and practical. Use the guide to raise your awareness about your own and other languages.

 **Online Study Center**   **ESL** ESL center

Editing Guide

Language Features	Languages	Sample Transfer Errors in English	Edited Version
ARTICLES (60c–60f)			
No articles	Chinese, Japanese, Russian, Swahili, Thai, Urdu	*Sun is hot.* *I bought book.* *Computer has changed our lives.*	*The sun is hot.* *I bought a book.* *The computer has changed our lives.*
No indefinite article with profession	Arabic, French, Japanese, Korean, Vietnamese	*He is student.* *She lawyer.*	*He is a student.* *She is a lawyer.*
Definite article with days, months, places, idioms	Arabic	*She is in the bed.* *He lives in the Peru.*	*She is in bed.* *He lives in Peru.*
Definite article used for generalization	Farsi, French, German, Greek, Portuguese, Spanish	*The photography is an art.* *The books are more expensive than the disks.*	*Photography is an art.* *Books are more expensive than disks.*
Definite article used with proper noun	French, German, Portuguese, Spanish	*The Professor Brackert teaches in Frankfurt.*	*Professor Brackert teaches in Frankfurt.*

Language Features	Languages	Sample Transfer Errors in English	Edited Version
No definite article	Hindi, Turkish	*Store on corner is closed.*	*The store on the corner is closed.*
No indefinite article	Korean (uses *one* for *a;* depends on context)	*He ran into one tree.*	*He ran into a tree.*

VERBS AND VERB FORMS (chapter 61)

Language Features	Languages	Sample Transfer Errors in English	Edited Version
Be can be omitted.	Arabic, Chinese, Greek, Russian	*India hotter than Britain.* *She working now.* *He cheerful.*	*India is hotter than Britain.* *She is working now.* *He is cheerful.*
No progressive forms	French, German, Greek, Russian	*They still discuss the problem.* *When I walked in, she slept.*	*They are still discussing the problem.* *When I walked in, she was sleeping.*
No tense inflections	Chinese, Thai, Vietnamese	*He arrive yesterday.* *When I was little, I always walk to school.*	*He arrived yesterday.* *When I was little, I always walked to school.*
No inflection for third person singular	Chinese, Japanese, Korean, Russian, Thai	*The singer have a big band.* *She work hard.*	*The singer has a big band.* *She works hard.*
Past perfect formed with *be*	Arabic	*They were arrived when I called.*	*They had arrived when I called.*
Different tense boundaries from English	Arabic, Chinese, Farsi, French	*I study here for a year.* *He has left yesterday.*	*I have been studying here for a year.* *He left yesterday.*

(Continued)

Language Features	Languages	Sample Transfer Errors in English	Edited Version
Different limits for passive voice	Japanese, Korean, Russian, Thai, Vietnamese	*They were stolen their luggage.*	*Their luggage was stolen.*
		My name base on Chinese characters.	*My name is based on Chinese characters.*
		The mess clean up quick.	*The mess was cleaned up quickly.*
		A miracle was happened.	*A miracle (has) happened.*
No -ing (gerund)/ infinitive distinction	Arabic, Chinese, Farsi, French, Greek, Portuguese, Spanish, Vietnamese	*She avoids to go.*	*She avoids going.*
		I enjoy to play tennis.	*I enjoy playing tennis.*
Infinitive not used to express purpose	Korean	*People exercise for losing weight.*	*People exercise to lose weight.*
Overuse of progressive forms	Hindi, Urdu	*I am wanting to leave now.*	*I want to leave now.*

WORD ORDER AND SENTENCE STRUCTURE (chapter 62)

Verb precedes subject.	Arabic, Hebrew, Russian, Spanish (optional), Tagalog	*Good grades received every student in the class.*	*Every student in the class received good grades.*
Verb-subject order in dependent clause	French	*I knew what would propose the committee.*	*I knew what the committee would propose.*

Language Features	Languages	Sample Transfer Errors in English	Edited Version
Verb after subject and object	Bengali, German (in dependent clause), Hindi, Japanese, Korean, Turkish	. . . *(when) the teacher the money collected.*	. . . *(when) the teacher collected the money.*
Coordination favored over subordination	Arabic	Frequent use of *and* and *so*	
Relative clause or restrictive phrase precedes noun it modifies.	Chinese, Japanese, Korean, Russian	*The enrolled in college student . . .*	*The student (who was) enrolled in college . . .*
		A nine-meter-high impressive monument . . .	*An impressive monument that is nine meters high . . .*
		He gave me a too difficult for me book.	*He gave me a book that was too difficult for me.*
Adverb can occur between verb and object or before verb.	French, Spanish, Urdu (before verb)	*I like very much clam chowder.*	*I like clam chowder very much.*
		They efficiently organized the work.	*They organized the work efficiently.*
That clause rather than an infinitive	Arabic, French, Hindi, Russian, Spanish	*I want that you stay.*	*I want you to stay.*
		I want that they try harder.	*I want them to try harder.*
Inversion of subject and verb (rare)	Chinese	*She is leaving and so I am.*	*She is leaving, and so am I.*

(Continued)

Language Features	Languages	Sample Transfer Errors in English	Edited Version
Conjunctions occur in pairs.	Chinese, Farsi, Vietnamese	*Although she is rich, but she wears simple clothes.* *Even if I had money, I would also not buy that car.*	*Although she is rich, she wears simple clothes.* *Even if I had money, I would not buy that car.*
Subject (especially *it* pronoun) can be omitted.	Chinese, Italian, Japanese, Portuguese, Spanish, Thai	*Is raining.*	*It is raining.*
Commas set off a dependent clause.	German, Russian	*He knows, that we are right.*	*He knows that we are right.*
No exact equivalent of *there is/there are*	Japanese, Korean, Portuguese, Russian, Thai (adverb of place and *have*)	*This article says four reasons to eat beans.* *In the garden has many trees.*	*This article says [that] there are four reasons to eat beans.* *There are many trees in the garden.*

NOUNS, PRONOUNS, ADJECTIVES, ADVERBS (chapters 44, 45, 60)

Language Features	Languages	Sample Transfer Errors in English	Edited Version
Personal pronouns restate subject.	Arabic, Gujarati, Spanish (optional)	*My father he lives in California.*	*My father lives in California.*
No human/ nonhuman distinction for relative pronoun (*who/which*)	Arabic, Farsi, French, Russian, Spanish, Thai	*Here is the student which you met her last week.* *The people which arrived . . .*	*Here is the student [whom] you met last week.* *The people who arrived . . .*
Pronoun object included in relative clause	Arabic, Chinese, Farsi, Hebrew	*The house [that] I used to live in it is big.*	*The house that I used to live in is big.*

Language Features	Languages	Sample Transfer Errors in English	Edited Version
No distinction between subject and object forms of some pronouns	Chinese, Gujarati, Korean, Thai	*I gave the forms to she.*	*I gave the forms to* her. *Or* I *gave her the forms.*
Nouns and adjectives have same form.	Chinese, Japanese	*She is beauty woman.* *They felt very safety on the train.*	*She is a* beautiful *woman.* *They felt very* safe *on the train.*
No distinction between *he* and *she*, *his* and *her*	Bengali, Farsi, Gujarati, Spanish (*his* and *her* only), Thai	*My sister dropped his purse.*	*My sister dropped* her *purse.*
No plural form after a number	Creole, Farsi	*He has two dog.*	*He has two* dogs.
No plural (or optional) forms of nouns	Chinese, Japanese, Korean, Thai	*Several good book . . .*	*Several good* books *. . .*
No relative pronouns	Korean	*The book is on the table is mine.*	*The book that is on the table is mine.*
Different perception of countable/ uncountable	Japanese, Russian, Spanish	*I bought three furnitures.*	*I bought three* pieces of *furniture. Or* I *bought three chairs.*
		She has red hairs.	*She has* red hair.
Adjectives show number.	Russian, Spanish	*I have helpfuls friends.*	*I have* helpful *friends.*
Negative before verb	Spanish	*Jack no like meat.*	*Jack* does not *like meat.*
Double negatives used routinely	Spanish	*They don't know nothing*	*They don't know* anything. *Or* They *know* nothing.

59e Editing guide to vernacular Englishes

Many of the varieties of English shown in the Circle of English in 37c differ from Standard American English in their use of words and grammatical conventions. Speakers of these Englishes have to do a kind of translating, called *code switching*, when they speak or write in Standard English, just as we all switch codes between levels of formality when we interact with different audiences. Consider, for example, situations when you might say, "'Sup?" ("What's up?") rather than "Good morning." As David Crystal, author of *The Stories of English*, points out, "We need to be very sure of our ground (or very drunk) before we say, 'Yo, Officer.'"

The following table shows some of the common features that confront speakers of African American Vernacular (AAV), Creole, and other varieties of English in North America when they move back and forth between their home culture and the academic world.

Vernaculars and Standard English

Linguistic Feature of Vernacular	Example (Nonstandard)	Edited for Standard English
Omitted form of *be*	*Maxine studying.*	*Maxine is studying.*
Use of *be* for habitual action	*Ray be working at home.*	*Ray usually works at home.*
Use of *been* without *have*	*I been sleeping all day.*	*I have (I've) been sleeping all day.*
Omitted *-ed*	*The books arrive this morning.*	*The books arrived this morning.*
No *-s* ending for third person singular present tense verb	*That model have a big smile.*	*That model has a big smile.*
No plural form after a plural number	*Jake own two dog.*	*Jake owns two dogs.*
Verb inversion before indefinite pronoun subject	*Can't nobody do that.*	*Nobody can do that.*

Linguistic Feature of Vernacular	Example (Nonstandard)	Edited for Standard English
They instead of possessive *their*	*The players grabbed they gear.*	*The players grabbed their gear.*
Hisself instead of *himself*	*That musician promote hisself too much.*	*That musician promotes himself too much.*
Personal pronoun restates subject.	*His instructor, she strict.*	*His instructor is strict.*
No apostrophe + -s for possessive	*She my brother wife.*	*She is my brother's wife.*
It used in place of *there*	*It's a gate at the entrance.*	*There is (There's) a gate at the entrance.*
Double negative	*You don't know nothing.*	*You don't know anything./You know nothing.*

Chapter **60**

Nouns and Articles

60a Categories of nouns

Nouns in English fall into various categories. A *proper noun* names a unique person, place, or thing and begins with a capital letter: *Walt Whitman, Lake Superior, Grand Canyon, Vietnam Veterans Memorial, Tuesday* (53b, 60f). A *common noun* names a general class of persons, places, or things and begins with a lowercase letter: *bicycle, furniture, plan, daughter, home, happiness.* Common nouns can be further categorized as countable and uncountable.

A *countable noun* can have a number before it (*one, two,* and so on) and has a plural form. Countable nouns frequently add -s to indicate the plural: *picture, pictures; plan, plans.*

An *uncountable noun* cannot be directly counted. It has no plural form: *furniture, advice, information.*

Common Nouns

Countable	Uncountable
tool, hammer (tools, hammers)	equipment
chair, desk (chairs, desks)	furniture
necklace, earring (necklaces, earrings)	jewelry
view, scene (views, scenes)	scenery
tip, suggestion (tips, suggestions)	advice

The concept of countability varies across languages. Japanese, for example, makes no distinction between countable and uncountable nouns. In French, Spanish, and Chinese, the word for *furniture* is a countable noun; in English, it is not. In Russian, the word for *hair* is countable and used in the plural.

60b Uncountable nouns

Some nouns are usually uncountable in English and are commonly listed as such in a language learners' dictionary such as *The American Heritage English as a Second Language Dictionary.* Learn the most common uncountable nouns, and note the ones that end in -*s* but are nevertheless singular:

> *A mass made up of parts:* clothing, equipment, furniture, garbage, homework, information, jewelry, luggage, machinery, money, scenery, traffic, transportation
>
> *Abstract concepts:* advice, courage, education, fun, happiness, health, honesty, information, knowledge
>
> *Natural substances:* air, blood, cotton, heat, ice, sunshine, water, wood, wool
>
> *Diseases:* diabetes, influenza, measles
>
> *Games:* checkers, chess, soccer, tennis
>
> *Subjects of study:* biology, economics, history, physics

Note the following features of uncountable nouns.

1. An uncountable noun has no plural form:

> *some*
> ► She gave me several informations.

> ► The couple bought a lot of new furnitures.

2. An uncountable noun subject is always followed by a singular verb:

▶ Their advice ~~are~~ useful.
    ^{is}

3. You can give an uncountable noun a countable sense—that is, indicate a quantity of it—by adding a word or phrase that indicates quantity. The noun itself will always remain singular: three pieces of *furniture,* two items of *information,* many pieces of *advice.*

4. Some nouns can be countable in one context and uncountable in another. Always examine the context.

GENERAL CLASS (UNCOUNTABLE)

▶ He loves *chocolate.* [all chocolate, in whatever form]

▶ *Time* flies.

▶ He has red *hair.*

A COUNTABLE ITEM OR ITEMS

▶ She gave him a *chocolate.* [one piece of candy from a box of many chocolates]

▶ They are having *a good time.*

▶ There is a *long grey hair* on her pillow.

KEY POINTS

What to Use before an Uncountable Noun

Use

The zero article (generalization)	Furniture is expensive.
The (specific reference)	*The* furniture she bought is hideous.
This, that	*This* furniture is tacky.
A possessive pronoun: *my, his, their,* etc.	*Their* furniture is modern.
A quantity word: *some, any, much, less, more, most, a little, a great deal (of), all, other* (43i)	She has bought *some* new furniture.

(Continued)

(Continued)

Do not use	
A/an (except in phrases *a little* or *a great deal of*)	The room needs ~~a~~ new furniture.
Each, every, another	All furniture ~~Every furniture~~ should be practical.
These, those	That furniture is ~~Those furnitures are~~ elegant.
Numerals: *one, two, three,* etc.	two pieces of furniture. They bought ~~two furnitures.~~
A plural quantity word: *several, many, a few*	a little furniture. She took only ~~a few furniture~~ with her to her new apartment.

60c Basic rules for articles (*a, an,* and *the*)

1. Use *the* whenever a reference to a common noun is specific and unique for writer and reader (see 60d).

   　the
   ▶ He loves⌃museum that Rem Koolhaas designed.

2. Do not use *a* or *an* with a plural countable noun.

   ▶ They cited ~~a~~ reliable surveys.

3. Do not use *a* or *an* with an uncountable noun.

   ▶ He gave ~~a~~ helpful advice.

4. Use *a* before a consonant sound: *a bird, a house, a sonnet.* Use *an* before a vowel sound: *an egg, an ostrich, an hour, an ugly vase.* Take special care with the sounds associated with the letters *h* and *u,* which can have either a consonant or a vowel sound: *a housing project, an honest man; a unicorn, an uprising.*

5. To make a generalization about a countable noun, do one of the following:

   ■ Use the plural form: *Lions are majestic.*

   ■ Use the singular with *a* or *an*: *A lion is a majestic animal.*

   ■ Use the singular with *the* to denote a classification: *The lion is a majestic animal.*

6. A countable singular noun can never stand alone, so make sure that a countable singular noun is preceded by an article or by a demonstrative pronoun (*this, that*), a number, a singular word expressing quantity, or a possessive.

> A (Every, That, One, Her) nurse
> ▶ ~~Nurse~~ has a difficult job.
>   ^

7. In general, though there are many exceptions, use no article with a singular proper noun (*Mount Everest*), and use *the* with a plural proper noun (*the Himalayas*). See 60f.

60d *The* for a specific reference

When you write a common noun that both you and your readers know refers to one or more specific persons, places, things, or concepts, use the article *the*. The reference can be specific in two ways: outside the text or inside it.

Specific reference outside the text

▶ **I study *the* earth, *the* sun, and *the* moon.** [the ones in our solar system]

▶ **She closed *the* door.** [of the room she was in]

▶ **Her husband took *the* dog out for a walk.** [the dog belonging to the couple]

Specific reference inside the text

▶ ***The* kitten that her daughter brought home had a distinctive black patch above one eye.** [a specific kitten—one that was brought home]

▶ **Her daughter found *a* kitten. When they were writing a lost-and-found ad that night, they realized that *the* kitten had a distinctive black patch above one eye.** [The second mention is of a specific kitten identified earlier—the one her daughter had found.]

▶ **He bought *the most expensive* bicycle in the store.** [A superlative makes a reference to one specific item.]

60e   Which article? Four basic questions

Multilingual writers often have difficulty choosing among the articles *a, an,* and *the* and the *zero article* (no article at all). Languages vary greatly in their representation of the concepts conveyed by English articles (see the Editing Guide to Multilingual Transfer Errors in 59d).

The Key Points box lists four questions to ask about a noun to decide whether to use an article and, if so, which article to use.

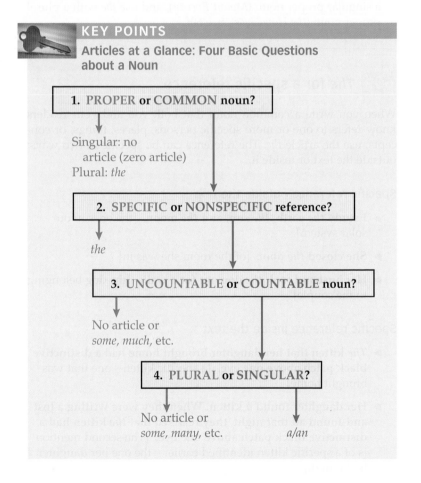

KEY POINTS

Articles at a Glance: Four Basic Questions about a Noun

1. **PROPER or COMMON noun?**

Singular: no article (zero article)
Plural: *the*

2. **SPECIFIC or NONSPECIFIC reference?**

the

3. **UNCOUNTABLE or COUNTABLE noun?**

No article or *some, much,* etc.

4. **PLURAL or SINGULAR?**

No article or *some, many,* etc.   *a/an*

You can use the questions to decide which article, if any, to use with the noun *poem* as you consider the following sentence:

▶ Milton wrote __?__ moving poem about the blindness that afflicted him before he wrote some of his greatest works.

1. Is the noun (*poem*) a proper noun or a common noun?

   COMMON   **Go to question 2.**

2. Does the common noun refer to a specific person, place, thing, or idea known to both writer and reader as unique, or is the reference nonspecific?

   NON-SPECIFIC   [*Poem* is not identified to the reader in the same way that *blindness* is. We know the reference is to the blindness that afflicted Milton before he wrote some of his greatest works. However, there is more than one "moving poem" in literature. The reference would be specific for readers only if the poem had been previously discussed.] **Go to question 3.**

3. Is the noun uncountable or countable?

   COUNTABLE   [We can say *one poem, two poems*.] **Go to question 4.**

4. Is the noun plural or singular?

   SINGULAR   [The first letter in the noun phrase *moving poem* is *m*, a consonant sound.] **Use *a* as the article.**

   ▶ Milton wrote *a* moving poem about the blindness that afflicted him before he wrote some of his greatest works.

60f Proper nouns and articles

Singular proper nouns: Use no article   As a general rule, capitalize singular proper nouns and use no article. Examples are *Stephen King, Central America, Africa, Islam, Golden Gate Park, Hollywood Boulevard, Cornell University, Lake Temagami, Mount St. Helens, Thursday, July*. There are, however, many exceptions.

EXCEPTIONS: SINGULAR PROPER NOUNS WITH *THE*

Proper nouns with a common noun and *of* as part of the name: *the University of Texas, the Fourth of July, the Museum of Modern Art, the Statue of Liberty*

Highways: *the New Jersey Turnpike, the Long Island Expressway*

Buildings: *the Eiffel Tower, the Prudential Building*

Bridges: *the Golden Gate Bridge*

Hotels and museums: *the Hilton Hotel, the Guggenheim Museum*

Countries named with a phrase: *the United Kingdom, the Dominican Republic, the People's Republic of China*

Parts of the globe: *the North Pole, the West, the East, the Riviera*

Seas, oceans, gulfs, rivers, and deserts: *the Dead Sea, the Atlantic Ocean, the Persian Gulf, the Yangtze River, the Mojave Desert*

Historical periods and events: *the Enlightenment, the October Revolution, the Cold War*

Groups: *the Taliban, the Chicago Seven*

Plural proper nouns: Use *the* Examples are *the United States, the Great Lakes, the Himalayas, the Philippines, the Chinese* (people) (53b).

Chapter **61**

Verbs and Verb Forms

A clause needs a complete verb consisting of one of the five verb forms (41a) and any necessary auxiliaries. Some forms derived from a verb (*verbals*) cannot serve as the main verb of a clause: an *-ing* form, a past participle (ending in *-ed* for a regular verb), or an infinitive (*to* + base form). Because readers get so much information from verbs, they have a relatively low level of tolerance for error, so make sure you edit with care and use auxiliary verbs whenever necesssary.

61a The *be* auxiliary

Inclusion (See also 41c.) The *be* auxiliary must be included in a verb phrase in English, though in languages such as Chinese, Russian, and Arabic it can be omitted.

> are
> ▶ They͜studying this evening.

> been
> ▶ They have͜studying since dinner.

Sequence (See also 41c.) What comes after a *be* auxiliary?

■ The *-ing* form follows a verb in the active voice: He *is sweeping* the floor.

■ The past participle follows a verb in the passive voice: The floor *was swept* yesterday.

61b Modal auxiliary verbs: Form and meaning

The nine modal auxiliary verbs are *will, would, can, could, shall, should, may, might,* and *must.* Note the following three important points.

1. The modals do not change form.

2. The modals never add an *-s* ending.

3. Modals are always followed by a base form without *to: could go, should ask, must arrive, might have* seen, *would be* sleeping.

▶ The committee must ~~to~~ vote tomorrow.

▶ The proposal might improve~~s~~ the city.

▶ The residents could disapprove~~d~~.

Meanings of Modal Verbs

Meaning	Present and Future	Past
1. Intention	*will, shall*	*would*
	She *will* explain. [*Shall* is used mostly in questions: *Shall I buy that big green ceramic horse?*]	She said that she *would* explain.
2. Ability	*can* (am/is/are able to)	*could* (was/were able to)
	He *can* cook well. [Do not use *can* and *able to* together: *He is able to cook well.*]	He *could* not read until he was eight. [He was not able to read until he was eight.]

(Continued)

Meaning	Present and Future	Past
3. Permission	*may, might, can, could*	*might, could*
	May I refer to Auden again? [*Might* or *could* is more tentative.]	Her instructor said she *could* use a dictionary.
4. Polite question	*would, could*	
	Would readers please indulge me for a moment?	
	Could you try not to read ahead?	
5. Speculation	*would, could, might*	*would* or *could* or *might* + *have* + past participle
	If he had more talent, he *could* become a professional pianist. [See also 16f.]	If I had studied, I *might have* passed the test.
6. Advisability	*should*	*should* + *have* + past participle
	You *should* go home and rest.	You *should have* taken your medication. [Implied here is "but you did not."]
7. Necessity (stronger than *should*)	*must* (or *have to*)	*had to* + base form
	Applicants *must* apply for a mortgage.	Theo van Gogh *had to* support his brother.
8. Prohibition	*must* + *not*	
	Participants *must not* leave until all the questions have been answered.	

Meaning	Present and Future	Past
9. Expectation	*should*	*should* + *have* + past participle
	The author *should* receive a check soon.	You *should have* received your check a week ago.
10. Possibility	*may, might*	*might* + *have* + past participle
	The technician *may* be working on the problem now.	She *might* already *have* revised the ending.
11. Logical assumption	*must*	*must* + *have* + past participle
	She's late; she *must* be stuck in traffic.	She *must have* taken the wrong route.
12. Repeated past action		*would* (or *used to*) + base form
		When I was a child, I *would* spend hours drawing.

61c Infinitive after verbs and adjectives

Some verbs are followed by an infinitive (*to* + base form or base form alone). Some adjectives also occur with an infinitive. Such combinations are highly idiomatic. You need to learn each one individually as you find it in your reading.

Verb + infinitive These verbs are commonly followed by an infinitive (*to* + base form):

agree	choose	fail	offer	refuse
ask	claim	hope	plan	venture
beg	decide	manage	pretend	want
bother	expect	need	promise	wish

Note any differences between English and your native language. For example, the Spanish word for *refuse* is followed by the equivalent of an *-ing* form.

▶ He refused ~~criticizing~~ the system.
to criticize

Position of a negative   In a verb + infinitive pattern, the position of the negative affects meaning. Note the difference in meaning that the position of a negative (*not, never*) can create.

▶ He did *not* decide to buy a new car. His wife did.

▶ He decided *not* to buy a new car. His wife was disappointed.

Verb + noun or pronoun + infinitive   Some verbs are followed by a noun or pronoun and then an infinitive. See also 18a for a pronoun used before an infinitive.

▶ The librarian *advised them to use* a better database.

Verbs that follow this pattern are *advise, allow, ask, cause, command, convince, encourage, expect, force, help, need, order, persuade, remind, require, tell, urge, want, warn.*

   Spanish and Russian use a *that* clause after verbs like *want*. In English, however, *want* is followed by an infinitive.

▶ Rose wanted ~~that~~ her son ~~would~~ become a doctor.
to

Make, let, and have   After these verbs, use a noun or pronoun and a base form of the verb (without *to*).

▶ He *made his son practice* for an hour.

▶ They *let us leave* early.

▶ She *had her daughter wash* the car.

Note the corresponding passive voice structure with *have*:

▶ She usually *has the car washed* once a month.

Adjective + infinitive   Some adjectives are followed by an infinitive. The filler subject *it* often occurs with this structure.

▶ It is dangerous *to hike* alone in the woods.

Adjectives Followed by Infinitive

anxious	(in)advisable	sorry
dangerous	likely	(un)fair
eager	lucky	(un)just
essential	powerless	(un)kind
foolish	proud	(un)necessary
happy	right	wrong
(im)possible	silly	

61d Verbs followed by an *-ing* verb form used as a noun

▶ I can't help *laughing* at Jon Stewart.

The *-ing* form of a verb used as a noun is known as a *gerund*. The verbs that are systematically followed by an *-ing* form make up a relatively short and learnable list.

admit	consider	enjoy	miss	resist
appreciate	delay	finish	postpone	risk
avoid	deny	imagine	practice	suggest
be worth	discuss	keep	recall	tolerate
can't help	dislike			

inviting
▶ We considered ~~to invite~~ his parents.

hearing
▶ Most people dislike ~~to hear~~ cell phones at concerts.

Note that a negation comes between the verb and the *-ing* form:

▶ During their vacation, they enjoy *not* getting up early every day.

61e Verbs followed by an infinitive or an *-ing* verb form

Some verbs can be followed by either an infinitive or an *-ing* verb form (a gerund) with almost no discernible difference in meaning: *begin, continue, hate, like, love, start.*

▶ **She loves** *cooking.*   ▶ **She loves** *to cook.*

The infinitive and the *-ing* form of a few verbs (*forget, remember, try, stop*), however, signal different meanings:

▶ **He remembered** *to mail* **the letter.** [an intention]

▶ **He remembered** *mailing* **the letter.** [a past act]

61f *-ing* and *-ed* forms used as adjectives

Both the present participle (*-ing* verb form) and the past participle (ending in *-ed* in regular verbs) can function as adjectives (see 41a and 41g). Each form has a different meaning: the *-ing* adjective indicates that the word modified produces an effect; the past participle adjective indicates that the word modified has an effect produced on it.

▶ **The** *boring* **cook served baked beans yet again.** [The cook produces boredom. Everyone is tired of baked beans.]

▶ **The** *bored* **cook yawned as she scrambled eggs.** [The cook felt the emotion of boredom as she did the cooking, but the eggs could still be appreciated.]

Produces an Effect	Has an Effect Produced on It
amazing	amazed
amusing	amused
annoying	annoyed
confusing	confused
depressing	depressed
disappointing	disappointed
embarrassing	embarrassed
exciting	excited
interesting	interested
satisfying	satisfied
shocking	shocked
surprising	surprised
worrying	worried

Note: Do not drop the *-ed* ending from a past participle. Sometimes in speech it blends with a following *t* or *d* sound, but in writing the *-ed* ending must be included.

▶ I was surprise to see her wild outfit.
　　　　　　　d

▶ The researchers were ~~worry~~ that the results were contaminated.
　　　　　　worried

 Chapter **62**

Word Order and Sentence Structure

62a Inclusion of a subject

In some languages, a subject can be omitted. In English, you must include a subject in every clause, even just a filler subject such as *there* or *it*.

▶ When the director's business partners lost money, were immediate effects on the share prices.
　　　　　　　　　　　　　　　　　　　　　there

▶ He went bankrupt because was too easy to borrow money.
　　　　　　　　　　　　　it

Do not use *it* to point to a long subject that follows.

▶ We can say that ~~it~~ does not matter the historical period of the society.

62b Order of sentence elements

Order of subject, verb, object　Languages vary in their basic word order for the sentence elements of subject (S), verb (V), and direct object (DO). In English, the most commonly occurring sentence pattern is S + V + DO ("Children like candy"). See also 37d.

▶ ~~Good grades received every~~ student in the class.
　　　　　Every　　　　　　　　　*received good grades.*

Expressions of time and place Put adverbs and adverb phrases of time and place at the beginning or end of a clause, not between the verb and its direct object.

▶ The quiz show host congratulated ⎡many times⎤ the winner.

Descriptive adjective phrases Put a descriptive adjective phrase after, not before, the noun it modifies.

▶ I would go to ⎡known only to me⎤ places.

62c Direct and indirect objects

Some verbs—such as *give, send, show, tell, teach, find, sell, ask, offer, pay, pass,* and *hand*—can be followed by both a direct object and an indirect object. The indirect object is the person or thing to whom or to which, or for whom or for which, something is done. It follows the verb and precedes the direct object (37d).

```
          ┌── IO ──┐ ┌── DO ──┐
```
▶ He gave his mother some flowers.

```
    IO   ┌── DO ──┐
```
▶ He gave her some flowers.

An indirect object can be replaced with a prepositional phrase that *follows* the direct object:

```
    ┌──── DO ────┐  prepositional phrase
```
▶ He gave some flowers to his mother.

Some verbs—such as *explain, describe, say, mention,* and *open*—are never followed by an indirect object. However, they can be followed by a direct object and a prepositional phrase with *to* or *for*:

```
                              to me.
```
▶ She explained ~~me~~ the election process⸝

```
                    to us.
```
▶ He described ~~us~~ the menu⸝

Note that *tell,* but not *say,* can take an indirect object.

```
        told
```
▶ She ~~said~~ him the secret.

62d Direct and indirect quotations and questions

In a direct quotation or direct question, the exact words used by the speaker are enclosed in quotation marks. In an indirect quotation or indirect question, the writer reports what the speaker said, and quotation marks are not used. Changes also occur in pronouns, time expressions, and verb tenses (41i).

┌─────── direct quotation ───────┐
▶ **He said, "I have lost my notebook."**

┌─────── indirect quotation ───────┐
▶ **He said that he had lost his notebook.**

┌─────── direct question ───────┐
▶ **He asked, "Have you seen it?"**

┌── indirect question ──┐
▶ **He asked if we had seen it.**

Direct and indirect quotations   Usually you must make several changes when you use an introductory verb in the past tense to report a direct quotation as an indirect quotation. You will do this often when you write college papers and report the views of others. Avoid shifts from direct to indirect quotations (40d).

Direct and Indirect Quotations

Change	Direct/ Indirect Quotation	Example	Explanation
Punctuation and tense	Direct	The young couple said, "The price *is* too high."	Exact words within quotation marks
	Indirect	The young couple said that the price *was* too high.	No quotation marks; tense change (16e)
Pronoun and tense	Direct	He insisted, "*I understand* the figures."	First person pronoun and present tense
	Indirect	He insisted that *he understood* the figures.	Change to third person pronoun; tense change

(Continued)

Change	Direct/ Indirect Quotation	Example	Explanation
Command to statement	Direct	"Cancel the payment," her husband said.	
	Indirect	Her husband *told* her *to* cancel the payment.	Verb (*tell, instruct*) + *to*
Expressions of time, place, and tense	Direct	The bankers said, "We *will* work on *this* deal *tomorrow*."	
	Indirect	The bankers said *they would* work on *that* deal *the next day*.	Expressions of time and place not related to speaker's perspective; tense change (16e); change to third person pronoun
Colloquial to formal	Direct	The clients said, "Well, no thanks; *we won't* wait."	
	Indirect	The clients thanked the bankers but said *they would not* wait.	Spoken words and phrases omitted or rephrased; also a tense change

Direct and indirect questions　When a direct question is reported indirectly, it loses the word order of a question (V + S) and the question mark. Sometimes changes in tense are necessary (see also 41i).

DIRECT QUESTION

　　　　　　　　V　　　　　S
The buyer asked, "*Are* the goods ready to be shipped?"

INDIRECT QUESTION

　　　　　　　　　　　　S　　　　V
The buyer asked if the goods *were* ready to be shipped.

	V S	
DIRECT QUESTION	The boss asked, "What *are* they doing?"	

		S V	
INDIRECT QUESTION	The boss asked what they *were* doing.	

	V *did* S V	
DIRECT QUESTION	"Why *did* they *send* a letter instead of a fax?" her secretary asked.	

	S V V	
INDIRECT QUESTION	Her secretary asked why they [*had*] *sent* a letter instead of a fax.	

Use only a question word such as *why* or the word *if* or *whether* to
introduce an indirect question. Do not use *that* as well.

▶ Her secretary asked ~~that~~ why they sent a letter instead of
a fax.

Direct and Indirect Questions

	Introductory Words	Auxiliary Verb	Subject	Auxiliary Verb(s)	Main Verb and Rest of Clause
DIRECT	What	are	they		thinking?
INDIRECT	Nobody knows what		they	are	thinking.
DIRECT	Where	does	he		work?
INDIRECT	I can't remember where		he		works.
DIRECT	Why	did	she		write that poem?
INDIRECT	The poet does not reveal why		she		wrote that poem. *(Continued)*

	Introductory Words	Auxiliary Verb	Subject	Auxiliary Verb(s)	Main Verb and Rest of Clause
DIRECT		Have	the diaries	been	published yet?
INDIRECT	The Web site does not say if (whether)		the diaries	have been	published yet.
DIRECT		Did	the space program		succeed?
INDIRECT	It is not clear if		the space program		succeeded.

62e Dependent clauses with *although* and *because*

In some languages, a subordinating conjunction (such as *although* or *because*) can be used along with a coordinating conjunction (*but, so*) or a transitional expression (*however, therefore*) in the same sentence. In English, only one is used.

NO
> *Although* he loved his father, *but* he did not have much opportunity to spend time with him.

POSSIBLE REVISIONS
> *Although* he loved his father, he did not have much opportunity to spend time with him.

> He loved his father, *but* he did not have much opportunity to spend time with him.

NO
> *Because* she had been trained in the church, *therefore* she was sensitive to the idea of audience.

POSSIBLE REVISIONS
> *Because* she had been trained in the church, she was sensitive to the idea of audience.

> She had been trained in the church, *so* she was sensitive to the idea of audience.

> She had been trained in the church; *therefore,* she was sensitive to the idea of audience.

See 47e for the punctuation of transitional expressions.

62f Unnecessary pronouns

Do not restate the simple subject of a sentence as a pronoun. See also 40i.

> ▶ Visitors to the Statue of Liberty ~~they~~ have worn the steps down.

> ▶ The counselor who told me about dyslexia ~~he~~ is a man I will never forget.

In a relative clause introduced by *whom, which,* or *that,* do not include a pronoun that the relative pronoun has replaced. See also 46f.

> ▶ The house that I lived in ~~it~~ for ten years has been sold.

62g Order of adjectives

When you use cumulative adjectives (the word *and* cannot be inserted between them as each modifies the whole noun phrase that follows it), follow the conventional sequence before the head noun: (1) size, (2) shape, (3) age, (4) color, (5) region or geographical origin, (6) architectural style or religion, (7) material, (8) noun used as adjective to modify the head noun.

>   1   3   5   7   head noun
> ▶ the big old Italian stone house

>   2   4   6   8   head noun
> ▶ our rectangular green Art Deco storage chest

Do not use commas between cumulative adjectives. For punctuation with other (coordinate) adjectives, see 47g.

Chapter **63**

Prepositions and Idioms

Prepositions appear in phrases with nouns and pronouns, and they also combine with adjectives and verbs in various ways. Learn the idioms one by one as you come across them.

63a Expressions with three common prepositions

Learn the uses of prepositions by writing them down in lists when you come across them in your reading. Here is a start:

In

in July, in 2007, in the morning, in the drawer, in the closet, in Ohio, in Milwaukee, in the cookie jar, in the library stacks, singing in the rain, in the United States, in his pocket, in bed, in school, in class, in Spanish, in time (to participate in an activity), in love, the letter in the envelope

On

on the menu, on the library shelf, on Saturday, on 9 September 2006, on Union Street, on the weekend, on the roof, a ring on her finger, an article on education, on the moon, on earth, on occasion, on time (punctual), on foot, on the couch, knock on the door, the address on the envelope

At

at 8 o'clock, at home, at a party, at night, at work

63b Adjective + preposition

When you are writing, use a dictionary to check the specific prepositions used with an adjective.

▶ The botanist is *afraid of* spiders.

▶ E. O. Wilson was *interested in* ants.

Some idiomatic adjective + preposition combinations are *afraid of, ashamed of, aware of, fond of, full of, jealous of, proud of, suspicious of, tired of, interested in, grateful to* (someone), *grateful for* (something), *responsible to* (someone), *responsible for* (something), *anxious about, content with,* and *satisfied with.*

63c Verb + preposition

Some idiomatic verb + preposition combinations are *concentrate on, congratulate* (someone) *on* (success or good fortune), *depend on, insist on, rely on, consist of, take care of, apologize to* (someone) *for* (an offense or error), *blame* (someone) *for* (an offense or error), *thank* (someone) *for* (a gift or favor), *complain about, worry about, laugh at, smile at,* *explain* (facts) *to* (someone), *throw* (an object) *to* (someone waiting to catch it), *throw* (an object) *at* (someone not expecting it), *arrive in* (a country or city), and *arrive at* (a building or an event). Keep a list of others you notice.

63d Phrasal verbs

Prepositions and a few adverbs (such as *away* and *forward*) can combine with verbs in such a way that they no longer function as prepositions or ordinary adverbs. They are then known as *particles*. Only a few languages other than English—Dutch, German, and Swedish, for example—have this verb-plus-particle (preposition or adverb) combination, which is called a *phrasal verb*. Examples of English phrasal verbs are *put off* and *put up with*.

The meaning of a phrasal verb is entirely different from the meaning of the verb alone. Note the idiomatic meanings of some common phrasal verbs.

break down [stop functioning]	run across [meet unexpectedly]
get over [recover from]	run out [become used up]
look into [examine]	take after [resemble]

Always check the meanings of such verbs in a specialized dictionary such as *The American Heritage English as a Second Language Dictionary*.

A particle can be followed by a preposition to make a three-word combination:

▶ She *gets along with* everybody. [She is friendly toward everybody.]

Other three-word verb combinations are

catch up with [draw level with]	look up to [admire]
look down on [despise]	put up with [endure]
look forward to [anticipate]	stand up for [defend]

Position of direct objects with two-word phrasal verbs Some two-word transitive phrasal verbs are separable. The direct object of these verbs can come between the verb and the accompanying particle.

▶ She *put off* her dinner party. [She postponed her dinner party.]

▶ She *put* her dinner party *off*.

When the direct object is a pronoun, however, always place the pronoun between the verb and the particle.

▶ She *put* it *off*.

Some commonly used phrasal verbs that follow that principle are listed here. They can be separated by a noun as a direct object; they must be separated when the direct object is a pronoun.

call off [cancel]	give up [surrender]	make up [invent]
fill out [complete]	leave out [omit]	turn down [reject]
find out [discover]	look up [locate]	turn off [stop]

Most dictionaries list phrasal verbs that are associated with a particular verb, along with their meanings and examples. Develop your own list of such verbs from your reading.

63e Preposition + -*ing* verb form used as a noun

The -*ing* verb form that functions as a noun (the *gerund*) frequently occurs after a preposition.

▶ They congratulated him *on winning* the prize.

▶ Sue expressed interest *in participating* in the fundraiser.

▶ He ran three miles *without stopping*.

▶ The cheese is the right consistency *for spreading*.

Note: Take care not to confuse *to* as a preposition with *to* used in an infinitive. When *to* is a preposition, it is followed by an object—a noun, a pronoun, a noun phrase, or an -*ing* verb form, not by the base form of a verb.

⌐ infinitive ¬
▶ They want *to adopt* a child.

preposition + -*ing* form (gerund)
▶ They are looking forward *to adopting* a child.

Check which to use by testing whether a noun replacement fits the sentence:

▶ They are looking forward to *parenthood*.

Note also *be devoted to, be/get used to* (see 64h).

Chapter **64**

Frequently Asked ESL Editing Questions

64a When do I use *no* and *not*?

Not is an adverb that negates a verb, an adjective, or another adverb. *No* is an adjective and therefore modifies a noun.

▶ She is *not* wealthy.   ▶ She is *not* really poor.

▶ The author does *not* intend to deceive the reader.

▶ The author has *no* intention of deceiving the reader.

64b What is the difference between *too* and *very*?

Both *too* and *very* intensify an adjective or adverb, but they are not interchangeable. *Too* indicates excess. *Very* indicates degree, meaning "extremely."

▶ It was *very* hot.

▶ It was *too* hot to sit outside. [*Too* occurs frequently in the pattern *too* + adjective or adverb + *to* + base form of verb.]

▶ The Volvo was *very* expensive, but he bought it anyway.

▶ The Volvo was *too* expensive, so he bought a Ford instead.

64c Does *few* mean the same as *a few*?

A few is the equivalent of *some*. *Few* is the equivalent of *hardly any*; it has more negative connotations than *a few*. Both expressions are used with countable plural nouns. Although *a* is not generally used with plural nouns, the expression *a few* is an exception.

some

▶ She feels fortunate because she has *a few* helpful colleagues.

hardly any

▶ She feels depressed because she has *few* helpful colleagues.

You might prefer to use only the more common *a few* and use *hardly any* in sentences where the context demands *few.* Similar expressions used with uncountable nouns are *little* and *a little.*

> ⌐some⌐
> ► She has *a little* time to spend on work-related projects.

> hardly any
> ► She has *little* time to spend on recreation.

64d How do I distinguish *most, most of,* and *the most*?

Most expresses a generalization, meaning "nearly all."

> ► *Most* Americans like ice cream.

When a word like *the, this, these, that,* or *those* or a possessive pronoun (such as *my, their*) precedes the noun to make it specific, *most of* is used. The meaning is "nearly all of."

> ► I did *most of* this needlework.

> ► *Most of* his colleagues work long hours.

The most is used to compare more than two people or items.

> ► Bill is *the most* efficient of all the technicians.

64e What structures are used with *easy, hard,* and *difficult*?

The adjectives *easy, hard,* and *difficult* cause problems for speakers of Japanese and Chinese. All of the following patterns are acceptable in English.

> ► It is *easy* for me to change a fuse.

> ► It is *easy* to change a fuse.

> ► To change a fuse is *easy* for me.

> ► To change a fuse is *easy.*

> ► Changing a fuse is *easy* for me.

> ► Changing a fuse is *easy.*

> ► I find it *easy* to change a fuse.

However, a sentence like the following needs to be edited in English into one of the patterns listed above or as follows:

> think it is
> ► I ~~am~~ *easy* to change a fuse.
>   ^

64f How do I use *it* and *there* to begin a sentence?

Use *there* to indicate that something exists (or existed) or happens (or happened). See also 30b.

> There
> ► ~~It~~ was a royal wedding in my country two years ago.
>   ^
> There
> ► ~~It~~ is a tree on the corner of my block.
>   ^

Use *it* for weather, distance, time, and surroundings.

> ► It is a long way to Tipperary.   ► It is hot.

Use *it* also in expressions such as *it is important, it is necessary,* and *it is obvious,* emphasizing the details that come next. See also 30b.

> ► It is essential for all of you to sign your application forms.

It or *there* cannot be omitted as a filler subject.

> it
> ► As you can see, is dark out already.
>   ^

64g Which possessive pronoun do I use: *His* or *her*?

In some languages, the form of the pronoun used to indicate possession changes according to the gender of the noun that follows it, not according to the pronoun's antecedent. In French, for instance, *son* or *sa* means "his" or "her," and in Spanish *su* means *his* or *her,* the form being determined by the noun the pronoun modifies.

> ► Marie et sa mère [Marie and her mother]

> ► Pierre et sa mère [Pierre and his mother]

> ► Pierre et son père [Pierre and his father]

In English, however, the gender of a possessive (*his, her,* or *its*) is always determined by the antecedent.

▶ I met Marie and her mother.

▶ I met Pierre and his mother.

64h What is the difference between *get used to* and *used to*?

For multilingual writers of English, the distinction between *used to* + base form and *be/get used to* + *-ing* (gerund) is difficult.

▶ He *used to work* long hours. [He did in the past but doesn't anymore. The infinitive form follows *used* in this sense.]

▶ Air traffic controllers *are used to dealing* with emergencies. [They are accustomed to it. The *-ing* form follows *be/get used to.*]

Chapter 65

Glossary of Usage

Listed in this glossary are words that are often confused (*affect/effect, elicit/illicit*) or misspelled (*it's/its*). Also listed are nonstandard words (*irregardless, theirself*) and colloquial expressions (*OK*) that should be avoided in formal writing.

a, an Use *an* before words that begin with a vowel sound (the vowels are *a, e, i, o,* and *u*): *an apple, an hour* (silent *h*). Use *a* before words that begin with a consonant sound: *a planet, a yam, a ukelele, a house* (pronounced *h*).

accept, except, expect *Accept* is a verb: *She accepted the salary offer. Except* is usually a preposition: *Everyone has gone home except my boss. Expect* is a verb: *They expect to visit New Mexico on vacation.*

adapt, adopt *Adapt* means "to adjust" and is used with the preposition *to: It takes people some time to adapt to the work routine after college. Adopt* means "to take into a family" or "to take up and follow": *The couple adopted a three-year-old child. The company adopted a more aggressive policy.*

adverse, averse *Adverse* is an adjective describing something as hostile, unfavorable, or difficult. *Averse* indicates opposition to something and usually takes the preposition *to. The bus driver was averse to driving in the adverse driving conditions.*

advice, advise *Advice* is a noun: *Take my advice and don't start smoking. Advise* is a verb: *He advised his brother to stop smoking.*

affect, effect In their most common uses, *affect* is a verb, and *effect* is a noun. To *affect* is to have an *effect* on something: *Pesticides can affect health. Pesticides have a bad effect on health. Effect,* however, can be used as a verb meaning "to bring about": *The administration hopes to effect new health care legislation. Affect* can also be used as a noun in psychology, meaning "a feeling or emotion."

aisle, isle You'll find an *aisle* in a supermarket or a church. An *isle* is an island.

all ready, already   *All ready* means "totally prepared": *The students were all ready for their final examination.* *Already* is an adverb meaning "by this time": *He has already written the report.*

all right, alright   *All right* (meaning "satisfactory") is standard. *Alright* is nonstandard. However, *alright* is used in popular culture to mean "wonderful."

all together, altogether   *All together* is used to describe acting simultaneously: *As soon as the boss had presented the plan, the managers spoke up all together.* *Altogether* is an adverb meaning "totally," often used before an adjective: *His presentation was altogether impressive.*

allude, elude   *Allude* means "to refer to": *She alluded to his height.* *Elude* means "to avoid": *He eluded her criticism by leaving the room.*

allusion, illusion   The noun *allusion* means "reference to": *Her allusion to his height made him uncomfortable.* The noun *illusion* means "false idea": *He had no illusions about being Mr. Universe.*

almost, most   Do not use *most* to mean *almost*: *Almost* [not *Most*] *all my friends are computer literate.*

alot, a lot of, lots of   *Alot* is nonstandard. *A lot of* and *lots of* are regarded by some as informal for *many* or *a great deal of*: *They have performed many research studies.*

aloud, allowed   *Aloud* is an adverb meaning "out loud": *She read her critique aloud.* *Allowed* is a form of the verb *allow*: *Employees are not allowed to participate in the competition.*

ambiguous, ambivalent   *Ambiguous* is used to describe a phrase or act with more than one meaning: *The ending of the movie is ambiguous; we don't know if the butler really committed the murder.* *Ambivalent* describes uncertainty and the coexistence of opposing attitudes and feelings: *The committee is ambivalent about the proposal for restructuring the company.*

among, between   Use *between* for two items, *among* for three or more: *I couldn't decide between red or blue. I couldn't decide among red, blue, or green.*

amoral, immoral   *Amoral* can mean "neither moral nor immoral" or "not caring about right or wrong," whereas *immoral* means "morally wrong": *Some consider vegetarianism an amoral issue, but others believe eating meat is immoral.*

amount, number   *Amount* is used with uncountable expressions: *a large amount of money, work, or effort.* *Number* is used with countable plural expressions: *a large number of people, a number of attempts.* See 60b.

an See *a*.

ante-, anti- *Ante-* is a prefix meaning "before," as in *anteroom*. *Anti-* means "against" or "opposite," as in *antiseptic* or *antifreeze*.

anyone, any one *Anyone* is a singular indefinite pronoun meaning "anybody": *Can anyone help me?* *Any one* refers to one from a group and is usually followed by *of* + plural noun: *Any one* [as opposed to any two] *of the suggestions will be considered acceptable.*

anyplace The standard *anywhere* is preferable.

anyway, anywhere, nowhere; anyways, anywheres, nowheres *Anyway, anywhere,* and *nowhere* are standard forms. The others, ending in *-s,* are not.

apart, a part *Apart* is an adverb: *The old book fell apart.* *A part* is a noun phrase: *I'd like to be a part of that project.*

as, as if, like See *like*.

as regards See *in regard to*.

assure, ensure, insure All three words mean "to make secure or certain," but only *assure* is used in the sense of making a promise: *He assured us everything would be fine.* *Ensure* and *insure* are interchangeable, but only *insure* is commonly used in the commercial or financial sense: *We wanted to ensure that the rate we paid to insure our car against theft would not change.*

awful Avoid using *awful* to mean "bad" or "extremely": not *He's awful late* but *He's extremely late.*

a while, awhile *A while* is a noun phrase: *a while ago; for a while. Awhile* is an adverb meaning "for some time": *They lived awhile in the wilderness.*

bad, badly *Bad* is an adjective, *badly* an adverb. Use *bad* after linking verbs (such as *am, is, become, seem*): *They felt bad after losing the match.* Use *badly* to modify a verb: *They played badly.*

bare, bear *Bare* is an adjective meaning "naked": the *bare* facts, a *bare*-faced lie. *Bear* is a noun (the animal) or a verb meaning "to carry" or "to endure": *He could not bear the pressure of losing.*

barely Avoid creating a double negative (such as *can't barely type*). *Barely* should always take a positive verb: *She can barely type. They could barely keep their eyes open.* See *hardly*.

because, because of *Because* is a subordinating conjunction used to introduce a dependent clause: *Because it was raining, we left early. Because of* is a two-word preposition: *We left early because of the rain.*

being as, being that   Avoid. Use *because* instead: *Because* [not *Being as*] *I was tired, I didn't go to class.*

belief, believe   *Belief* is a noun: *She has radical beliefs. Believe* is a verb: *He believes in an afterlife.*

beside, besides   *Beside* is a preposition meaning "next to": *Sit beside me. Besides* is a preposition meaning "except for": *He has no assistants besides us. Besides* is also an adverb meaning "in addition": *I hate horror movies. Besides, there's a long line.*

better   See *had better.*

between   See *among.*

brake, break   When we apply the *brake* in a car, we can *break* a window or even get a bad *break.*

breath, breathe   The first word is a noun, the second a verb: *Take three deep breaths. Breathe in deeply.*

bring, take   Use *bring* to suggest carrying something from a farther place to a nearer one, and *take* for any other transportation: *First bring me a cake from the store, and then we can take it to the party.*

can't hardly   This expression is nonstandard. See *hardly.*

censor, censure   The verb *censor* refers to editing or removing from public view. *Censure* means to criticize harshly. *The new film was censored for graphic content, and the director was censured by critics for his irresponsibility.*

cite, site, sight   *Cite* means "to quote or mention"; *site* is a noun meaning "location"; *sight* is a noun meaning "view": *She cited the page number in her paper. They visited the original site of the abbey. The sight of the skyline from the plane produced applause from the passengers.*

compare to, compare with   Use *compare to* when implying similarity: *They compared the director to Alfred Hitchcock.* Use *compare with* when examining similarities or differences: *She wrote an essay comparing Hitchcock with Orson Welles.*

complement, compliment   As verbs, *complement* means "to complete or add to something," and *compliment* means "to make a flattering comment about someone or something": *The wine complemented the meal. The guests complimented the hostess on the fine dinner.* As nouns, the words have meanings associated with the verbs: *The wine was a fine complement to the meal. The guests paid the hostess a compliment.*

compose, comprise *Compose* means "to make up"; *comprise* means "to include." *The conference center is composed of twenty-five rooms. The conference center comprises twenty-five rooms.*

conscience, conscious *Conscience* is a noun meaning "awareness of right and wrong." *Conscious* is an adjective meaning "awake" or "aware." *Her conscience troubled her after the accident. The victim was still not conscious.*

continual, continuous *Continual* implies repetition; *continuous* implies lack of a pause. *The continual interruptions made the lecturer angry. Continuous rain for two hours stopped play.*

could care less This expression is often used but is regarded by some as nonstandard. In formal English, use it only with a negative: *They could not care less about their work.*

council, counsel A *council* is a group formed to consult, deliberate, or make decisions. *Counsel* is advice or guidance. *The council was called together to help give counsel to the people. Counsel* can also be a verb: *We counseled the students to withdraw from the course.*

credible, creditable, credulous *Credible* means "believable": *The jury found the accused's alibi to be credible and so acquitted her. Creditable* means "deserving of credit": *A B+ grade attests to a creditable performance. Credulous* means "easily taken in or deceived": *Only a child would be so credulous as to believe that the streets are paved with gold.* See also *incredible, incredulous.*

criteria, criterion *Criteria* is the plural form of the singular noun *criterion*: *There are many criteria for a successful essay. One criterion is sentence clarity.*

curricula, curriculum *Curricula* is the plural form of *curriculum. All the departments have well-thought-out curricula, but the English Department has the best curriculum.*

custom, customs, costume All three words are nouns. *Custom* means "habitual practice or tradition": *a family custom. Customs* refers to taxes on imports or to the procedures for inspecting items entering a country: *go through customs at the airport.* A *costume* is "a style of dress": *a Halloween costume.*

dairy, diary The first word is associated with cows and milk, the second with daily journal writing.

decease, disease *Decease* is a verb or noun meaning "die" or "death." *Disease* is an illness: *The disease caused an early decease.*

decent, descent, dissent *Decent* is an adjective meaning "good" or "respectable": *decent clothes, a decent salary. Descent* is a noun meaning "way down" or "lineage": *She is of Scottish descent. Dissent,* used both as a noun and a verb, refers to disagreement: *The dissent about freedom led to civil war.*

desert, dessert *Desert* can be pronounced two ways and can be a noun with the stress on the first syllable (*the Mojave Desert*) or a verb with the stress on the second syllable: *When did he desert his family?* The noun *desert* means "a dry, often sandy, environment." The verb *desert* means "to abandon." *Dessert* (with stress on the second syllable) is the sweet course at the end of a meal.

device, devise *Device* is a noun: *He said they needed a device that could lift a car. Devise* is a verb: *She began to devise a solution to the problem.*

different from, different than Standard usage is *different from*: *She looks different from her sister.* However, *different than* appears frequently in speech and informal writing, particularly when *different from* would require more words: *My writing is different than* [in place of *different from what*] *it was last semester.*

differ from, differ with To *differ from* means "to be unlike": *Lions differ from tigers in several ways, despite being closely related.* To *differ with* means to "disagree with": *They differ with each other on many topics but are still good friends.*

discreet, discrete *Discreet* means "tactful": *Be discreet when you talk about your boss. Discrete* means "separate": *He writes on five discrete topics.*

disease See *decease.*

disinterested, uninterested *Disinterested* means "impartial or unbiased": *The mediator was hired to make a disinterested settlement. Uninterested* means "lacking in interest": *He seemed uninterested in his job.*

dissent See *decent.*

do, due *Do* is a verb. Do not write "*Do* to his absences, he lost his job"; instead use the two-word preposition *due to* or *because of.*

drag, dragged Use *dragged* for the past tense of the verb *drag. Drug* is nonstandard.

drown, drowned The past tense of the verb *drown* is *drowned; drownded* is not a word: *He almost drowned yesterday.*

due to the fact that, owing to the fact that Wordy. Use *because* instead: *They stopped the game because* [not *due to the fact that*] *it was raining.*

each, every   These are singular pronouns; use them with a singular verb. See also 43h and 44d.

each other, one another   Use *each other* with two; use *one another* with more than two: *The twins love each other. The triplets all love one another.*

effect   See *affect.*

e.g.   Use *for example* or *for instance* in place of this Latin abbreviation.

elicit, illicit   *Elicit* means "to get or draw out": *The police tried in vain to elicit information from the suspect's accomplice. Illicit* is an adjective meaning "illegal": *Their illicit deals landed them in prison.*

elude   See *allude.*

emigrate, immigrate   *Emigrate from* means "to leave a country"; *immigrate to* means "to move to another country": *They emigrated from Ukraine and immigrated to the United States.* The noun forms *emigrant* and *immigrant* are derived from the verbs.

eminent, imminent   *Eminent* means "well known and noteworthy": *an eminent lawyer. Imminent* means "about to happen": *an imminent disaster.*

ensure   See *assure.*

etc.   This abbreviation for the Latin *et cetera* means "and so on." Do not let a list trail off with *etc.* Rather than *They took a tent, a sleeping bag, etc.,* write *They took a tent, a sleeping bag, cooking utensils, and a stove.*

every, each   See *each.*

everyday, every day   *Everyday* (one word) is an adjective meaning "usual": *Their everyday routine is to break for lunch at 12:30. Every day* (two words) is an adverbial expression of frequency: *I get up early every day.*

except, expect   See *accept.*

explicit, implicit   *Explicit* means "direct": *She gave explicit instructions. Implicit* means "implied": *A tax increase is implicit in the proposal.*

farther, further   Both words can refer to distance: *She lives farther (further) from the campus than I do. Further* also means "additional" or "additionally": *The management offered further incentives. Further, the union proposed new work rules.*

female, male   Use these words as adjectives, not as nouns in place of *man* and *woman: There are only three women* [not *females*] *in my class. We are discussing female conversational traits.*

few, a few   *Few* means "hardly any": *She feels depressed because she has few helpful colleagues. A few* means "some"; it has more positive connotations than *few*: *She feels fortunate because she has a few helpful colleagues* (64c).

fewer, less   Formal usage demands *fewer* with plural countable nouns (*fewer holidays*), *less* with uncountable nouns (*less sunshine*). However, in informal usage, *less* with plural nouns commonly occurs, especially with *than*: *less than six items, less than ten miles, fifty words or less*. In formal usage, *fewer* is preferred.

first, firstly   Avoid *firstly, secondly,* and so on, when listing reasons or examples. Instead, use *first, second.*

flammable, inflammable, nonflammable   Both *flammable* and *inflammable* mean the same thing: able to be ignited easily. *Nonflammable* means "unable to be ignited easily." *Dry wood is flammable* or *Dry wood is inflammable. Asbestos is nonflammable.*

flaunt, flout   *Flaunt* means "to show [something] off," or "to display in a proud or boastful manner." *Flout* means "to defy or to show scorn for." *When she flaunted her jewels, she flouted good taste.*

former, latter   These terms should be used only in reference to a list of two people or things: *We bought lasagna and rhubarb, the former for dinner and the latter for dessert.* For more than two items, use *first* and *last*: *I had some pasta, a salad, and rhubarb; though the first was very filling, I still had room for the last.*

get married to, marry   These expressions can be used interchangeably: *He will get married to his fiancée next week. She will marry her childhood friend next month.* The noun form is *marriage: Their marriage has lasted thirty years.*

go, say   Avoid replacing the verb *say* with *go*, as this is nonstandard usage: *Jane says* [not *goes*], *"I'm tired of this game."*

good, well   *Good* is an adjective; *well* is an adverb: *If you want to write well, you must use good grammar.* See 45a.

had better   Include *had* in Standard English, although it is often omitted in advertising and in speech: *You had better* [not *You better*] *try harder.*

hardly   This is a negative word. Do not use it with another negative: <u>not</u> *He couldn't hardly walk* <u>but</u> *He could hardly walk.*

have, of   Use *have*, not *of*, after *should, could, might,* and *must: They should have* [not *should of*] *appealed.*

height   Note the spelling and pronunciation: not *heighth.*

heroin, heroine   Do not confuse these words. *Heroin* is a drug; *heroine* is a brave woman. *Hero* may be used for an admirable person of either sex.

hisself   Nonstandard; instead, use *himself.*

hopefully   This word is an adverb meaning "in a hopeful manner" or "with a hopeful attitude": *Hopefully, she e-mailed her résumé.* Avoid using *hopefully* in place of *I hope that:* not *Hopefully, she will get the job* but *I hope that she will get the job.* The former usage is, however, quite common.

I, me   Do not confuse *I* and *me.* Use *I* only in the subject position, and use *me* only in the object position. To check subjects and objects using *and,* simply drop any additional subject or object so that only the pronoun remains: not *The CFO and me were sent to the conference* but *The CFO and I were sent* (I was sent); not *Please send copies to my secretary and I* but *Please send copies to my secretary and me* (send copies to me). See 44a.

illicit   See *elicit.*

illusion   See *allusion.*

immigrate   See *emigrate.*

imminent   See *eminent.*

implicit   See *explicit.*

imply, infer   *Imply* means "to suggest in an indirect way": *He implied that further layoffs were unlikely.* *Infer* means "to guess" or "to draw a conclusion": *I inferred that the company was doing well.*

incredible, incredulous   *Incredible* means "difficult to believe": *The violence of the storm was incredible.* *Incredulous* means "skeptical, unable to believe": *They were incredulous when he told them about his daring exploits in the whitewater rapids.*

infamous   *Infamous* is an adjective meaning "notorious": *Blackbeard's many exploits as a pirate made him infamous along the American coast.* Avoid using it as a synonym for "not famous."

inflammable   See *flammable.*

in regard to, as regards   Use one or the other. Do not use the nonstandard *in regards to.*

insure   See *assure.*

irregardless   Nonstandard; instead use *regardless: He selected a major regardless of the preparation it would give him for a career.*

it's, its   The apostrophe in *it's* signals not a possessive but a contraction of *it is* or *it has*. *Its* is the possessive form of the pronoun *it*: *The city government agency has produced its final report. It's available upon request.* See also 48f.

kind, sort, type   In the singular, use each of these nouns with *this* and a singular noun: *this type of book*. Use in the plural with *these* and a plural noun: *these kinds of books*.

kind of, sort of   Do not use these to mean "somewhat" or "a little." *The pace of the baseball game was somewhat* [not *kind of*] *slow.*

knew, new   *Knew* is the past tense of the verb *know*. *New* is an adjective meaning "not old."

lend, loan   *Lend* is a verb, and *loan* is ordinarily used as a noun: *Our cousins offered to lend us some money, but we refused the loan.*

less   See *fewer*.

lie, lay   Be sure not to confuse these verbs. *Lie* does not take a direct object; *lay* does. See 41b.

like, as, as if   In formal usage, *as* and *as if* are subordinating conjunctions and introduce dependent clauses: *She walks as her father does. She looks as if she could eat a big meal. Like* is a preposition and is followed by a noun or pronoun, not by a clause: *She looks like her father.* In speech, however, and increasingly in writing, *like* is often used where formal usage dictates *as* or *as if*: *She walks like her father does. He looks like he needs a new suit.* Know your audience's expectations.

likely, liable   *Likely* means "probably going to," while *liable* means "at risk of" and is generally used to describe something negative: *Eddie plays the guitar so well he's likely to start a band. If he keeps playing that way, he's liable to break a string. Liable* also means "responsible": *The guitar manufacturer cannot be held liable.*

literally   Avoid overuse: *literally* is an adverb meaning "actually" or "word for word" and should not be used in conjunction with figurative expressions such as *my jaw literally hit the floor* or *he was literally bouncing off the walls. Literally* should be used only when the words describe exactly what is happening: *He was so scared his face literally went white.*

loan   See *lend*.

loose, lose   *Loose* is an adjective meaning "not tight": *This jacket is comfortable because it is so loose. Lose* is a verb (the past tense form and past participle are *lost*): *Many people lose their jobs in a recession.*

lots of   See *alot*.

man, mankind Avoid using these terms, as they are gender-specific. Instead, use *people, human beings, humankind, humanity,* or *men and women.*

marital, martial *Marital* is associated with marriage, *martial* with war.

may be, maybe *May be* consists of a modal verb followed by the base form of the verb *be; maybe* is an adverb meaning "perhaps." If you can replace the expression with *perhaps,* make it one word: *They may be there already,* or *maybe they got caught in traffic.*

me, I See *I.*

media, medium *Media* is the plural form of *medium: Television and radio are both useful communication media, but his favorite medium is the written word.*

most See *almost.*

myself Use only as a reflexive pronoun (*I told them myself*) or as an intensive pronoun (*I myself told them*). Do not use *myself* as a subject pronoun: not *My sister and myself won* but *My sister and I won.*

no, not *No* modifies a noun: *The author has no intention of deceiving the reader. Not* modifies a verb, adjective, or adverb: *She is not wealthy. He does not intend to deceive.*

nonflammable See *flammable.*

nowadays All one word. Be sure to include the final -*s.*

nowhere, nowheres See *anyway.*

number See *amount.*

off, off of Use only *off,* not *off of: She drove the car off* [not *off of*] *the road.*

oftentimes Do not use. Prefer *often.*

OK, O.K., okay Reserve these forms for informal speech and writing. Choose another word in a formal context: not *Her performance was OK* but *Her performance was satisfactory.*

one another See *each other.*

owing to the fact that See *due to the fact that.*

passed, past *Passed* is a past tense verb form: *They passed the deli on the way to work. He passed his exam. Past* can be a noun (*in the past*), an adjective (*in past times*), or a preposition (*She walked past the bakery*).

peak, peek, pique *Peak* is the top of a summit: *She has reached the peak of her performance. Peek* (noun or verb) means "glance": *A peek through the* *window is enough.* Pique (also a noun or a verb) has to do with feeling indignation: *Feeling insulted, he stormed out in a fit of pique.*

personal, personnel   *Personal* is an adjective meaning "individual," while *personnel* is a noun referring to employees or staff: *It is my personal belief that a company's personnel should be treated like family.*

phenomena, phenomenon   *Phenomena* is the plural form of the noun *phenomenon*: *Outer space is full of celestial phenomena, one spectacular phenomenon being the Milky Way.*

plus   Do not use *plus* as a coordinating conjunction or a transitional expression. Use *and* or *moreover* instead: *He was promoted, and* [not *plus*] *he received a bonus.* Use *plus* as a preposition meaning "in addition to": *His salary plus his dividends placed him in a high tax bracket.*

pore, pour   To *pore* is to read carefully or to ponder: *I saw him poring over the want ads before he poured himself a drink.*

precede, proceed   *Precede* means "to go or occur before": *The Roaring Twenties preceded the Great Depression. Proceed* means "to go ahead": *After you pay the fee, proceed to the examination room.*

prejudice, prejudiced   *Prejudice* is a noun. *Prejudice is harmful to society. Prejudiced* is a past participle verb form: *He is prejudiced against ethnic minorities.*

pretty   Avoid using *pretty* as an intensifying adverb. Use *really, very, rather,* or *quite: The stew tastes very* [not *pretty*] *good.* Often, however, the best solution is to avoid using any adverb: *The stew tastes good.*

principal, principle   *Principal* is a noun (*the principal of a school*) or an adjective meaning "main" or "most important": *His principal motive was monetary gain. Principle* is a noun meaning "standard or rule": *He always acts on his principles.*

quite, quiet   Do not confuse the adverb *quite,* meaning "very," with the adjective *quiet* ("still" or "silent"): *We were all quite relieved when the audience became quiet.*

quote, quotation   *Quote* is a verb. Do not use it as a noun; use *quotation: The quotation* [not *quote*] *from Walker tells the reader a great deal.*

real, really   *Real* is an adjective; *really* is an adverb. Do not use *real* as an intensifying adverb: *She acted really* [not *real*] *well.*

reason is because   Avoid *the reason is because.* Instead, use *the reason is that* or rewrite the sentence. See 40f.

regardless   See *irregardless.*

respectable, respectful, respective   *Respectable* means "presentable, worthy of respect": *Wear some respectable shoes to your interview.* *Respectful* means "polite or deferential": *Parents want their children to be respectful to adults.* *Respective* means "particular" or "individual": *The friends of the bride and the groom sat in their respective seats in the church.*

respectfully, respectively   *Respectfully* means "showing respect": *He bowed respectfully when the queen entered.* *Respectively* refers to items in a list and means "in the order mentioned": *Horses and birds gallop and fly, respectively.*

rise, raise   *Rise* is an intransitive verb: *She rises early every day.* *Raise* is a transitive verb: *We raised alfalfa last summer.* See 41b.

sale, sell   *Sale* is a noun: *The sale of the house has been postponed.* *Sell* is a verb: *They are still trying to sell their house.*

should (could, might) of   Nonstandard; instead use *should have: You should have paid.* See 41c, pages 385–86.

since   Use this subordinating conjunction only when time or reason is clear: *Since you insist on helping, I'll let you paint this bookcase.* Unclear: *Since he got a new job, he has been happy.*

site, sight   See *cite.*

sometimes, sometime, some time   The adverb *sometimes* means "occasionally": *He sometimes prefers to eat lunch at his desk.* The adverb *sometime* means "at an indefinite time": *I read that book sometime last year.* The noun phrase *some time* consists of the noun *time* modified by the quantity word *some: After working for Honda, I spent some time in Brazil.*

sort, type   See *kind.*

sort of   See *kind of.*

stationary, stationery   *Stationary* is an adjective meaning "not moving" (*a stationary vehicle*); *stationery* is a noun referring to writing paper.

supposedly   Use this, not *supposably: She is supposedly a great athlete.*

taught, thought   Do not confuse these verb forms. *Taught* is the past tense and past participle form of *teach; thought* is the past tense and past participle form of *think: The students thought that their professor had not taught essay organization.*

than, then   *Then* is a time word; *than* must be preceded by a comparative form: *bigger than, more interesting than.*

their, there, they're   *Their* is a pronoun indicating possession; *there* indicates place or is used as a filler in the subject position in a sentence;

they're is the contracted form of *they are*: *They're over there, guarding their luggage.*

theirself, theirselves, themself   Nonstandard; instead, use *themselves.*

threat, treat   These words have different meanings: *She gave the children some cookies as a treat. The threat of an earthquake was alarming.*

thusly   Incorrect form of *thus.*

to, too, two   Do not confuse these words. *To* is a sign of the infinitive and a common preposition; *too* is an adverb meaning *also*; *two* is the number: *She is too smart to agree to report to two bosses.*

undoubtedly   This is the correct word, not *undoubtably.*

uninterested   See *disinterested.*

unique   The adjective *unique* means "the only one of its kind" and therefore should not be used with qualifying adjectives like *very* or *most*: *His recipe for chowder is unique* [not *most unique* or *quite unique*]. See 45h, "Absolute adjectives."

used to, get (become) used to   These expressions share the common form *used to.* But the first, expressing a past habit that no longer exists, is followed by the base form of a verb: *He used to wear his hair long.* (Note that after *not*, the form is *use to*: *He did not use to have a beard.*) In the expression *get (become) used to, used to* means "accustomed to" and is followed by a noun or an *-ing* verb form: *She couldn't get used to driving on the left when she was in England.* See also 64h.

way, ways   Use *way* to mean "distance": *He has a way to go. Ways* in this context is nonstandard.

wear, were, we're   *Wear* is a verb meaning "to have on as covering adornment or protection" (*wearing a helmet*); *were* is a past tense form of *be*; *we're* is a contraction for *we are.*

weather, whether   *Weather* is a noun; *whether* is a conjunction: *The weather will determine whether we go on the picnic.*

whose, who's   *Whose* is a possessive pronoun: *Whose goal was that? Who's* is a contraction of *who is* or *who has*: *Who's the player whose pass was caught? Who's got the ball?*

your, you're   *Your* is a pronoun used to show possession. *You're* is a contraction for *you are*: *You're wearing your new shoes today, aren't you?*

Chapter **66**

Glossary of Grammatical Terms

absolute phrase   A phrase consisting of a noun phrase followed by a verbal or a prepositional phrase and modifying an entire sentence: *Flags flapping in the wind,* the stadium looked bleak.

acronym   A pronounceable word formed from the initials of an abbreviation: *NATO, MADD, NOW.* 51a.

active voice   Attribute of a verb when its grammatical subject performs the action: The dog *ate* the cake. 42.

adjective   The part of speech that modifies a noun or pronoun: She wears *flamboyant* clothes. His cap is *orange.* 37d, 45, 62g. See also *comparative; coordinate adjective; cumulative adjective; superlative; parts of speech.*

adjective clause   A dependent clause beginning with a relative pronoun (*who, whom, whose, which,* or *that*) and modifying a noun or pronoun: The writer *who won the prize* was elated. Also called a *relative clause.* 37d, 46.

adverb   The part of speech that modifies a verb, an adjective, another adverb, or a clause: She ran *quickly.* He is *really* successful. The children were *well* liked. Many adverbs end in *-ly.* 37d, 45. See also *comparative; conjunctive adverb; frequency adverb; parts of speech; superlative.*

adverb clause   A dependent clause that modifies a verb, an adjective, or an adverb and begins with a subordinating conjunction: He left early *because he was tired.* 37d.

agent   The person or thing doing the action described by a verb: *His sister* won the marathon. The marathon was won by *his sister.* 42a.

agreement   The grammatical match in person, number, and gender between a verb and its subject or between a pronoun and its antecedent (the word the pronoun refers to): The *benefits continue; they are* pleasing. The *benefit continues; it is* pleasing. 43, 44d.

antecedent   The noun that a pronoun refers to: My son who lives nearby found a *kitten. It* was black and white. 44c, 44d, 46a.

appositive phrase   A phrase occurring next to a noun and used to describe it: His father, *a factory worker,* is running for office. 38a, 44a, 47d.

article *A, an* (indefinite articles), or *the* (definite article). Also called a *determiner*. 60c, 60d, 60e.

auxiliary verb A verb that joins with another verb to form a complete verb. Auxiliary verbs are forms of *do, be,* and *have,* as well as the modal auxiliary verbs. 37d, 41c. See also *modal auxiliary verb.*

base form The dictionary form of a verb, used in an infinitive after *to: see, eat, go, be.* 41a.

clause A group of words that includes a subject and a verb. 37d. See also *dependent clause; independent clause.*

cliché An overused, predictable expression: *as cool as a cucumber.* 33g.

collective noun A noun naming a collection of people or things that are regarded as a unit: *team, jury, family.* For agreement with collective nouns, see 43f, 44d.

comma splice The error that results when two independent clauses are incorrectly joined with only a comma. Chapter 39.

common noun A noun that does not name a unique person, place, or thing. Chapter 60. See also *proper noun.*

comparative The form of an adjective or adverb used to compare two people or things: *bigger, more interesting.* 45h. See also *superlative.*

complement A *subject complement* is a word or group of words used after a linking verb to refer to and describe the subject: Harry looks *happy.* An *object complement* is a word or group of words used after a direct object to complete its meaning: They call him a *liar.* 37d, 43c.

complete verb A verb that shows tense. Some verb forms, such as *-ing* (present) participles and past participles, require auxiliary verbs to make them complete verbs. *Going* and *seen* are not complete verbs; *are going* and *has been seen* are complete. 38c, 41c.

complex sentence A sentence that has one independent clause and one or more dependent clauses: *He wept when he won the marathon.* 34c.

compound adjective An adjective formed of two or more words often connected with hyphens: a *well-constructed* house. 45d, 56b.

compound-complex sentence A sentence that has at least two independent clauses and one or more dependent clauses: *She works in Los Angeles, but her husband works in San Diego, where they both live.* 34c.

compound noun A noun formed of two or more words: *toothbrush, merry-go-round.* 56b.

compound predicate   A predicate consisting of two or more verbs and their objects, complements, and modifiers: He *whistles and sings in the morning.* 38d, 40h.

compound sentence   A sentence that has two or more independent clauses: *She works in Los Angeles, but her husband works in San Diego.* 34c.

compound subject   A subject consisting of two or more nouns or pronouns and their modifiers: *My uncle and my aunt* are leaving soon. 43g, 44a.

conditional clause   A clause introduced by *if* or *unless,* expressing conditions of fact, prediction, or speculation: *If we earned more,* we would spend more. 41j.

conjunction   The part of speech used to link words, phrases, or clauses. 37d, 38b. See also *coordinating conjunction; correlative conjunctions; parts of speech; subordinating conjunction.*

conjunctive adverb   A transitional expression used to link two independent clauses. Some common conjunctive adverbs are *moreover, however,* and *furthermore.* 2d, 37d.

connotation   The meanings and associations suggested by a word, as distinct from the word's denotation, or dictionary meaning. 33c.

contraction   The shortened form that results when an apostrophe replaces one or more letters: *can't* (for *cannot*), *he's* (for *he is* or *he has*), *they're* (for *they are*). 48d.

coordinate adjective   Evaluative adjective modifying a noun. When coordinate adjectives appear in a series, their order can be reversed, and they can be separated by *and.* Commas are used between coordinate adjectives: the *comfortable, expensive car.* 47g.

coordinating conjunction   The seven coordinating conjunctions are *and, but, or, nor, so, for,* and *yet.* They connect sentence elements that are parallel in structure: He couldn't call, *but* he wrote a letter. 31c, 37d, 47b.

coordination   The connection of two or more ideas to give each one equal emphasis: *Sue worked after school, so she didn't have time to jog.* 31c.

correlative conjunctions   A pair of conjunctions joining equivalent elements. The most common correlative conjunctions are *either . . . or, neither . . . nor, both . . . and,* and *not only . . . but also: Neither* my sister *nor* I could find the concert hall. 40j.

countable noun   A common noun that has a plural form and can be used after a plural quantity word (such as *many* or *three*): one *book,* three *stores,* many *children.* 60a, 60e.

cumulative adjective   An adjective that modifies a noun and occurs in a conventional order with no comma between adjectives: a *new red plastic* bench. 62g.

cumulative sentence   A sentence that adds elements after the independent clause. 34c.

dangling modifier   A modifier that fails to modify the noun or pronoun it is intended to modify: <u>not</u> *Turning the corner,* the lights went out. <u>but</u> *Turning the corner, we* saw the lights go out. 40c.

demonstrative pronoun   The four demonstrative pronouns are *this, that, these,* and *those: That* is my glass. 43j.

denotation   A word's dictionary meaning. See also *connotation.* 33b, 33c.

dependent clause   A clause that cannot stand alone as a complete sentence and needs to be attached to an independent clause. A dependent clause begins with a subordinating word such as *because, if, when, although, who, which,* or *that: When it rains,* we can't take the children outside. 37d, 38b.

diction   Choice of appropriate words and tone. Chapter 33.

direct object   The person or thing that receives the action of a verb: They ate *cake* and *ice cream.* 37d, 62c.

direct quotation   A person's words reproduced exactly and placed in quotation marks: *"I won't be home until noon,"* she said. 10f, 40d, 62d.

double negative   The use of two negative words in the same sentence: He does *not* know *nothing.* This usage is nonstandard and needs to be avoided: *He does not know anything. He knows nothing.* 45g.

ellipsis   Omission of words from a quotation, indicated by three dots: "I pledge allegiance to the flag . . . and to the republic for which it stands . . ." 51g.

etymology   The origin of a word. 33b.

euphemism   A word or phrase used to disguise literal meaning: She *is in the family way* [meaning "pregnant"]. 33g.

faulty predication   The error that results when subject and verb do not match logically: <u>not</u> The *decrease* in stolen cars *has diminished* in the past year. <u>but</u> The *number* of stolen cars *has decreased* in the past year. 40e.

figurative language   The use of unusual comparisons or other devices to draw attention to a specific meaning. See *metaphor; simile.* 5b, 33e.

filler subject *It* or *there* used in the subject position of a clause, followed by a form of *be: There are* two elm trees on the corner. 30b, 43d, 64f.

first person The person speaking or writing: *I* or *we.* 44a.

fragment A group of words that is punctuated as if it were a sentence but is grammatically incomplete because it lacks a subject or a predicate or begins with a subordinating word: *Because it was a sunny day.* Chapter 38.

frequency adverb An adverb that expresses time (such as *often, always,* or *sometimes*). It can be the first word in a sentence or be used between the subject and the main verb, after an auxiliary verb, or as the last word in a sentence. 45e.

fused sentence See *run-on sentence.*

gender Classification of a noun or pronoun as masculine (*Uncle John, he*), feminine (*Ms. Torez, she*), or neuter (*book, it*). 44e, 64g.

generic noun A noun referring to a general class or type of person or object: A *student* has to write many papers. 44d.

gerund The *-ing* verb form used as a noun: *Walking* is good for your health. 43e, chapter 61, 63e. See also *verbal.*

helping verb See *auxiliary verb.*

imperative mood Verb mood used to give a command: *Follow* me. 34b.

indefinite pronoun A pronoun that refers to a nonspecific person or thing: *anybody, something.* 43h, 44d.

independent clause A clause that has a subject and predicate and is not introduced by a subordinating word. An independent clause can function as a complete sentence. *Birds sing. The old man was singing a song.* Hailing a cab, *the woman used a silver whistle.* 31c, 37d.

indicative mood Verb mood used to ask questions or make statements. It is the most common mood. 34b.

indirect object The person or thing to whom or to which, or for whom or for which, an action is performed. It comes between the verb and the direct object: He gave his *sister* some flowers. 37d, 62c.

indirect question A question reported by a speaker or writer, not enclosed in quotation marks: They asked *if we would help them.* 62d.

indirect quotation A description or paraphrase of the words of another speaker or writer, integrated into a writer's own sentence and not enclosed in quotation marks: He said *that they were making money.* 40d, 62d.

infinitive The base form, or dictionary form, of a verb, preceded by *to*: *to see, to smile.* 41a, 61c, 61e.

infinitive phrase An infinitive with its objects, complements, or modifiers: *To wait for hours* is unpleasant. He tries hard *to be punctual.* 38a, 43e.

intensive pronoun A pronoun ending in *-self* or *-selves* and used to emphasize its antecedent: They *themselves* will not attend. 44h.

interjection The part of speech that expresses emotion and is able to stand alone: *Aha! Wow!* Interjections are seldom appropriate in academic writing. 37d.

interrogative pronoun A pronoun that introduces a direct or indirect question: *Who* is that? I don't know *what* you want. 44i.

intransitive verb A verb that does not take a direct object: Exciting events *have occurred.* He *fell.* 37d, 42a. See also *transitive verb.*

inverted word order The presence of the verb before the subject in a sentence; used in questions or for emphasis: *Do you expect* an award? Not only *does she do* gymnastics, she also wins awards. 30b, 43d.

irregular verb A verb that does not form its past tense and past participle with *-ed*: *sing, sang, sung; grow, grew, grown.* 41a.

linking verb A verb connecting a subject to its complement. Typical linking verbs are *be, become, seem,* and *appear*: He *seems* angry. A linking verb is intransitive; it does not take a direct object. 37d, 41c, 44a, 45c.

mental activity verb A verb not used in a tense showing progressive aspect: *prefer, want, understand:* <u>not</u> He *is wanting to leave.* <u>but</u> He *wants* to leave. 41d.

metaphor A figure of speech implying a comparison but not stating it directly: a *gale* of laughter. 5b, 33e.

misplaced modifier An adverb (particularly *only* and *even*) or a descriptive phrase or clause positioned in such a way that it modifies the wrong word or words: She showed the ring to her sister *that her aunt gave her.* 40b.

mixed structure A sentence with two or more types of structures that clash grammatically: *By doing* her homework at the last minute *caused* Meg to make many mistakes. 40a, 40e, 40f.

modal auxiliary verb The nine modal auxiliaries are *will, would, can, could, shall, should, may, might,* and *must.* They are followed by the base form of a verb: *will go, would believe*. Modal auxiliaries do not change form. 41c, 61b.

modifier   A word or words that describe another noun, adverb, verb, phrase, or clause: He is a *happy* man. He is smiling *happily*. Chapter 45.

mood   The mood of a verb tells whether the verb states a fact (*indicative*: She *goes* to school); gives a command (*imperative: Come* back soon); or expresses a condition, wish, or request (*subjunctive:* I wish you *were* not leaving). 41j. See also *imperative mood; indicative mood; subjunctive mood.*

nonrestrictive phrase or clause   A phrase or clause that adds extra or nonessential information to a sentence and is set off with commas: His report, *which he gave to his boss yesterday,* received enthusiastic praise. 46b, 47d.

noun   The part of speech that names a person, place, thing, or idea. Nouns are proper or common and, if common, countable or uncountable. 37d, chapter 60. See also *collective noun; common noun; compound noun; countable noun; generic noun; noun clause; parts of speech; proper noun; uncountable noun.*

noun clause   A dependent clause that functions as a noun: I like *what you do. Whoever scores a goal* will be a hero. 37d.

noun phrase   A noun with its accompanying modifiers and articles: *a brilliant, hard-working student.* 37d.

number   The indication of a noun or pronoun as singular (one person, place, thing, or idea) or plural (more than one). 43a, 44d.

object of preposition   The noun or pronoun (along with its modifiers) that follows a preposition: on *the beach.* 37d.

paragraph   A group of sentences set off in a text, usually on one topic. 2b, 2c.

parallelism   The use of coordinate structures that have the same grammatical form: She likes *swimming* and *playing* tennis. 40j.

participle phrase   A phrase beginning with an *-ing* verb form or a past participle: The woman *wearing a green skirt* is my sister. *Baffled by the puzzle,* he gave up. 34e. See also *verbal.*

particle   A word (frequently a preposition or adverb) that combines with a verb to form a phrasal verb, a verb with an idiomatic meaning: get *over,* take *after.* 63d.

parts of speech Eight traditional categories of words used to form sentences: noun, pronoun, verb, adjective, adverb, conjunction, preposition, and interjection. See 37d and the listing for each in this glossary.

passive voice Attribute of a verb when its grammatical subject is the receiver of the action that the verb describes: The book *was written* by my professor. 30c, chapter 42. See also *active voice*.

past participle A verb form that in regular verbs ends with *-ed*. The past participle needs an auxiliary verb to function as the complete verb of a clause: *has chosen, was cleaned, might have been told*. The past participle can function alone as an adjective. 41a, 41c, 41d, 41g, 61f.

perfect progressive tense forms Verb tenses that show actions in progress up to a specific point in present, past, or future time. For active voice verbs, use forms of the auxiliary *have been* followed by the *-ing* form of the verb: *has/have been living, had been living, will have been living*. 41d.

perfect tense forms Verb tenses that show actions completed by present, past, or future time. For active voice verbs, use forms of the auxiliary *have* followed by the past participle of the verb: *has/have arrived, had arrived, will have arrived*. 41d.

periodic sentence A sentence that uses words and phrases to build up to the independent clause. 34c.

person The form of a pronoun or verb that indicates whether the subject is doing the speaking (first person, *I* or *we*), is spoken to (second person, *you*), or is spoken about (third person, *he, she, it,* or *they*). 43a, 44a.

phrasal verb An idiomatic verb phrase consisting of a verb and a preposition or adverb called a *particle*: *put off, put on.* 63d.

phrase A group of words that lacks a subject or predicate and functions as a noun, verb, adjective, or adverb: *under the tree, has been singing, amazingly simple.* 37d. See also *absolute phrase; appositive phrase; infinitive phrase; participle phrase; prepositional phrase*.

possessive The form of a noun or pronoun that indicates ownership. Possessive pronouns include *my, his, her, their, theirs,* and *whose: my* boat, *your* socks. The possessive form of a noun is indicated by an apostrophe or an apostrophe and *-s: Mario's* car, the *children's* nanny, the *birds'* nests. 43j, 44b, 48a, 48b.

predicate The part of a sentence that contains the verb and its modifiers and that comments on or makes an assertion about the subject. To be complete, a sentence needs a subject and a predicate. 37d.

prefix Letters attached to the beginning of a word that change the word's meaning: *un*necessary, *re*organize, *non*stop. 56a.

preposition The part of speech used with a noun or pronoun in a phrase to indicate time, space, or some other relationship. 37d, 46d, chapter 63. The noun or pronoun is the object of the preposition: *on the table, after dinner, to her.*

prepositional phrase A phrase beginning with a preposition and including the object of the preposition and its modifiers: The head *of the electronics company* was waiting *for an hour.* 37d, 38a, 46d.

present participle The *-ing* form of a verb, showing an action as being in progress or continuous: They are *sleeping.* Without an auxiliary, the *-ing* form cannot function as a complete verb but can be used as an adjective: *searing* heat. When the *-ing* form is used as a noun, it is called a *gerund: Skiing* can be dangerous. 41a, 43e, 61d, 61f. See also *verbal.*

progressive tense forms Verb tenses that show actions in progress at a point or over a period of time in past, present, or future time. They use a form of *be* + the *-ing* form of the verb: They *are working;* he *will be writing.* 41d, 41e, 41f.

pronoun The part of speech that takes the place of a noun, a noun phrase, or another pronoun. 37d, 43h, chapter 44. See *parts of speech.*

pronoun reference The connection between a pronoun and its antecedent. Reference should be clear and unambiguous: Mr. Estern picked up *his* hat and left. 44c.

proper noun The capitalized name of a specific person, place, or thing: *Golden Gate Park, University of Kansas.* 37d, 53b, 60f. See also *common noun.*

quantity word A word expressing the idea of quantity, such as *each, every, several, many,* and *much.* Subject-verb agreement is tricky with quantity words: *Each* of the students *has* a different assignment. 43i. See also *agreement.*

reflexive pronoun A pronoun ending in *-self* or *-selves* and referring to the subject of a clause: They incriminated *themselves.* 44h.

regular verb Verb that ends with *-ed* in its past tense and past participle forms. 41a.

relative clause   See *adjective clause.*

relative pronoun   Pronoun that introduces a relative clause: *who, whom, whose, which, that.* 46a.

restrictive phrase or clause   A phrase or clause that provides information essential for identifying the word or phrase it modifies. A restrictive phrase or clause is not set off with commas: The book *that is first on the bestseller list* is a memoir. 46b, 47i.

run-on sentence   The error that results when two independent clauses are not separated by a conjunction or by any punctuation: <u>not</u> *The dog ate the meat the cat ate the fish.* <u>but</u> *The dog ate the meat; the cat ate the fish.* Also called a *fused sentence.* Chapter 39.

second person   The person addressed: *you.* 44a, 44g.

shifts   Inappropriate switches in grammatical structure, such as from one tense to another or from statement to command or from indirect to direct quotation: <u>not</u> Joan asked *whether I was warm enough* and *did I sleep well* <u>but</u> *Joan asked whether I was warm enough and had slept well.* 40d, 41h.

simile   A figure of speech that makes a direct comparison: She has a laugh *like a fire siren.* 5b, 33e.

simple tense forms   Verb tenses that show present, past, or future time with no perfect or progressive aspects: they *work,* we *worked,* she *will work.* 41d, 41e, 41f.

split infinitive   An infinitive with a word or words separating *to* from the base verb form: *to successfully complete.* This structure has become acceptable. 40b.

Standard English   "The variety of English that is generally acknowledged as the model for the speech and writing of educated speakers." This *American Heritage Dictionary,* 4th edition, definition warns that the use of the term is "highly elastic and variable" and confers no "absolute positive evaluation." 33d, 37c.

subject   The noun or pronoun that performs the action of the verb in an active voice sentence or receives the action of the verb in a passive voice sentence. To be complete, a sentence needs a subject and a verb. 37d, 38d, 40i, 62a.

subjunctive mood   Verb mood used in conditions and in wishes, requests, and demands: I wish he *were* here. She demanded that he *be* present. 41j.

subordinate clause   See *dependent clause.*

subordinating conjunction   A conjunction used to introduce a dependent adverb clause: *because, if, when, although, since, while.* 31c, 37d, 38b.

suffix   Letters attached to the end of a word that change the word's function or meaning: gentle*ness,* humor*ist,* slow*er,* sing*ing.* 58e.

superlative   The form of an adjective or adverb used to compare three or more people or things: *biggest; most unusual; least effectively.* 45g, 60d. See also *comparative.*

synonym   A word that has the same or nearly the same meaning as another word.

tense   The form of a verb that indicates time. Verbs change form to distinguish present and past time: he *goes;* he *went.* Various structures are used to express future time, mainly *will* + the base form, or *going to* + the base form. 41d. See also *perfect progressive tense forms; perfect tense forms; progressive tense forms; simple tense forms.*

third person   The person or thing spoken about: *he, she, it, they,* or nouns. 43a, 44a.

topic chain   Repetition of key words or related words throughout a passage to aid cohesion. 31a, 42d.

transitional expression   A word or phrase used to connect two independent clauses, such as *for example, however,* and *similarly.* 2d, 47e, 50a.

transitive verb   A verb that takes an object—the person or thing that receives the action (in the active voice): Dogs *chase* cats. When transitive verbs are used in the passive voice, the subject receives the action of the verb: Cats *are chased* by dogs. 37d, 41b, 42a, 42b. See also *intransitive verb.*

uncountable noun   A common noun that cannot follow a plural quantity word (such as *several* or *many*) is never used with *a* or *an,* is used with a singular third person verb, and has no plural form: *furniture, happiness, information.* 43e, 60b.

verb   The part of speech that expresses action or being and tells (in the active voice) what the subject of the clause is or does. The complete verb in a clause might require auxiliary or modal auxiliary verbs to complete its meaning. 37d, chapter 41, chapter 61.

verbal   A form, derived from a verb, that cannot function as the main verb of a clause. The three types of verbals are the infinitive, the *-ing* participle, and the past participle (for example, *to try, singing, stolen*). A verbal can function in a phrase as a noun, adjective, or adverb. Chapter 61, 63e.

verb chain   Combination of an auxiliary verb, a main verb, and verbals: She *might have promised to leave;* they *should deny having helped* him. Chapter 61.

verb phrase   A complete verb formed by auxiliaries and the main verb: *should have waited.* 37d.

voice   Transitive verbs (verbs that take an object) can be used in the active voice (*He is painting the door*) or the passive voice (*The door is being painted*). Chapter 42.

zero article   The lack of an article (*a, an,* or *the*) before a noun. Uncountable nouns are used with the zero article when they make no specific reference. 60b, 60d, 60e.

Index

Note: An asterisk (*) refers to a page number in the Glossary of Grammatical Terms.

TEXT CREDITS

Part 1:   Pages 6–7, from "The Economics of Fair Play" by Karl Sigmund, Ernst Fehr, and Martin A. Nowak. Copyright © 2002 by Scientific American. All rights reserved; page 32, from *The Columbia Encyclopedia*, ed. Paul Lagasse, © 2006 Columbia University Press. Reprinted with the permission of the publisher; page 33, Matthew Gilbert, "All Talk, All the Time," *Boston Globe Magazine*, June 4, 2000, p. 9. Reprinted courtesy of The Boston Globe; page 39, excerpt from Malcolm Gladwell, "The Moral-Hazard Myth," *New Yorker*, August 29, 2005, p. 49. Reprinted by permission of the author; page 82, from "Stopping by Woods on a Snowy Evening" by Robert Frost, in *The Poetry of Robert Frost*, ed. Edward Connery Lathem (New York: Henry Holt and Company, Inc., 1979). Copyright © 1951 by Robert Frost, copyright © 1969 by Henry Holt and Company, Inc. Reprinted by permission of Henry Holt and Company.

Part 2:   Page 107, reprinted courtesy of Google; page 113, image reproduced with permission of EBSCO Publishing; page 115, courtesy of The City University of New York; page 126, courtesy of ReclaimDemocracy.org; pages 134–137, reprinted by permission of the author. Ellen Laird teaches in the English Department at Hudson Valley Community College; pages 138–139, "Marketers Tap Chatty Young Teens, and Hit a Hot Button" by Clayton Collins. Excerpted with permission from the March 30, 2005 issue of the *Christian Science Monitor* (www.csmonitor.com). © 2005 The Christian Science Monitor. All rights reserved.

Part 3:   Page 181, image reproduced with permission of EBSCO Publishing; page 185, Reprinted by permission of CNN ImageSource.

Part 4:   Page 227, reprinted by permission of the H. W. Wilson Company. Copyright © 2006. Material reproduced with permission of the publisher, page 230, screen shot reprinted by permission from Blizzard Entertainment Inc., <http://www.blizzard.com>.

Part 5:   Pages 270–273, screen shots reprinted by permission from Microsoft; page 281, Linda J. Sax et al., *The American Freshman: National Norms for Fall 2002*, Los Angeles, Higher Education Research Institute, UCLA, 2003 http://www.gseis.ucla.edu/heri/norms_charts.pdf. Data are weighted responses of 282,549 students at 437 higher education institutions. Reprinted by permission; page 294, reprinted courtesy of the InterReligious Council of Central New York and Daniel Sauve; pages 297–298, permission to reprint granted by Charles Mak and the LaGuardia Center for Teaching and Learning, coordinators of the e-portfolio initiative at LaGuardia Community College, CUNY, available at <http://www.lagcc.cuny.edu/ctl>; pages 305, 307, 308, adapted from Scot Ober, *Business Communication*, Fifth Edition. Used with permission from Houghton Mifflin Company; page 310, courtesy of Ben & Jerry's.

Part 7:   Page 356, definition of "Standard English," from *American Heritage Dictionary of the English Language*, 4th ed. Copyright © 2000 by Houghton Mifflin. Reproduced by permission; page 356, from Tom McArthur, "The English Languages?," in *English Today* (July 1987), p. 11. Reprinted with the permission of Cambridge University Press.

Part 8:   Page 467, The quotation from "Toads" by Philip Larkin is reprinted from *The Less Deceived* by permission of Marvell Press, England and

Australia; page 468, "Class Poem" by Aurora Levins Morales, from *Getting Home Alive* by Aurora Morales and Rosario Morales (Firebrand Books, 1986). Reprinted by permission of Firebrand Books.

Part 10:   Page 552, definition of "Standard English," from *American Heritage Dictionary of the English Language*, 4th ed. Copyright © 2000 by Houghton Mifflin. Reproduced by permission.

PHOTO CREDITS

Part 1:   Page 29, © Reuters NewMedia, Inc./Corbis; page 34, (top) Corbis; page 34, (bottom) The Library of the London School of Economics and Political Science; page 58, image courtesy of Scenic Hudson; design by Pentagram; page 58, courtesy Columbia Action Now; writer and designer Douglas Welch; page 69, courtesy www.Adbusters.org.

Part 3:   Page 171, from *Uniforms: Why We Are What We Wear* by Paul Fussell. Copyright © 2002 by Paul Fussell. Excerpted and reprinted by permission of Houghton Mifflin Company. All rights reserved; page 177, copyright 2004 by the National Council of Teachers of English. Reprinted with permission; page 198, photo by Don Pierce/Uvic Photo Service, University of Victoria.

Part 4:   Page 219, from *Naturalist* by E. O. Wilson. Copyright © 1994 by Island Press. Reproduced by permission of Island Press, Washington, DC; page 223, table of contents courtesy Scientific American, Inc./Illustration: Tom Draper Design.

Part 5:   Page 273, James Estrin/The New York Times; pages 302 and 303, courtesy of Horizons for Homeless Children (formerly the Horizons Initiative), 1705 Columbus Avenue, Roxbury, MA 02119, www.horizonsforhomelesschildren.org.

Part 6:   Page 336, © The New Yorker Collection 1981, Charles Barsotti from cartoonbank.com. All rights reserved.

Part 7:   Page 393, © The New Yorker Collection 2001, Mick Stevens from cartoonbank.com. All rights reserved.

Part 8:   Page 458, Hulton Archives/Getty Images.

Language and Culture Boxes

Tech Notes

ESL
Notes

Source Shots

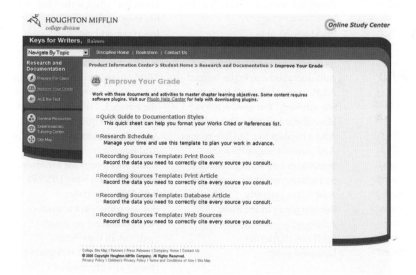

COMMON EDITING AND PROOFREADING MARKS

Symbol	Example (change marked)	Example (change made)
⌒o	Correct a typo.	Correct a typo.
⌒r⌒/m⌒/⌒o	Correct more than one typo.	Correct more than one typo.
t	Insert a letter.	Insert a letter.
or words	Insert a word.	Insert a word or words.
℘	Make a deletion.	Make a deletion.
℘	Delete and close up space.	Delete and close up space.
⌒	Close up extra space.	Close up extra space.
#	Insert proper spacing.	Insert proper spacing.
# / ⌒	Insert space and close up.	Insert space and close up.
tr	Transpose letters indicated.	Transpose letters indicated.
tr	Transpose as words indicated.	Transpose words as indicated.
tr	Reorder shown as words several.	Reorder several words as shown.
⊏	⊏ Move text to left.	Move text to left.
⊐	⊐ Move text to right.	Move text to right.
⌑	⌐Indent for paragraph.	Indent for paragraph.
no ⌑	⊏ No paragraph indent.	No paragraph indent.
run in	Run back turnover lines.	Run back turnover lines.
⌐	Break line when it runs far too long.	Break line when it runs far too long.
⊙	Insert period here.	Insert period here.
∧	Commas commas everywhere.	Commas, commas everywhere.
∨	Its in need of an apostrophe.	It's in need of an apostrophe.
∜ / ∜	Add quotation marks he begged.	"Add quotation marks," he begged.
;	Add a semicolon don't hesitate.	Add a semicolon; don't hesitate.
:	She advised "You need a colon."	She advised: "You need a colon."
?	How about a question mark	How about a question mark?
⁻=⁻	Add a hyphen to a bill like receipt.	Add a hyphen to a bill-like receipt.
⟨/⟩	Add parentheses as they say.	Add parentheses (as they say).
lc	Sometimes you want Lowercase.	Sometimes you want lowercase.
caps	Sometimes you want upperCASE.	Sometimes you want UPPERCASE.
ital	Add italics instantly.	Add italics *instantly.*
rom	But use roman in the main.	But use roman in the main.
bf	Add boldface if necessary.	Add **boldface** if necessary.
sp	Spell out all 3 terms.	Spell out all three terms.
stet	Let stand as is.	Let stand as is. (This retracts a change already marked.)

Note: Numbers refer to sections in the book.

Abbreviation	Meaning/Error
ab or abbr	abbreviation, **54**, **57e**
adj	adjective, **37d**, **45**
adv	adverb, **37d**, **45**
agr	agreement, **43**, **44d**
apos	apostrophe, **40h**, **48**
arg	argument error, **4e–4j**
art	articles, **60**
awk	awkward, **30**, **31**, **40**
bias	biased or sexist language, **33f**, **44e**
ca or case	case, **44a**
cap (ṯom)	use capital letter, **53**, **57c**, **60f**
coh	coherence, **2d**
comp	comparative, **45h**, **45i**
coord	coordination, **31c**, **47b**
cs	comma splice, **39**
d	diction, **33**
db neg	double negative, **45g**
dev	development, **2c**
dm	dangling modifier, **40c**
doc	documentation, **11–19**
-ed	error with *-ed* ending, **41g**
exact	exactness, **33c**
frag	sentence fragment, **38**
fs	fused sentence, **39**
gen	gender bias, **33f**, **44e**
hyph	hyphenation, **56**, **57d**
id	idiom, **63**
inc	incomplete sentence or construction, **40h**, **62a**
ind quot	indirect quotation, **41i**, **62d**
-ing	error with *-ing* ending, **61**
ital	italics/underlining, **12a**, **15a**, **18c**, **19a**, **52**, **57b**
jar	jargon, **33d**
lc (Ṁe)	use a lowercase letter, **53**
log	logic, **4h**, **4i**, **4j**

Abbreviation	Meaning/Error
mix or mixed	mixed construction, **40a**
mm	misplaced modifier, **40b**
ms	manuscript form, **3f**, **26**, **27**
nonst	nonstandard usage, **37c**, **38–46**
num	faulty use of numbers, **55**
//	parallelism, **40j**
p	punctuation, **47–51**, **57a**
pass	passive voice, **30c**, **42**
prep	preposition, **37d**, **63**
pron	pronoun, **37d**, **44**
quot	quotation, **10f**, **49**
ref	pronoun reference, **44c**
rel cl	relative clause, **46**
rep or red	repetitive or redundant, **29a**, **29d**
-s	error with *-s* ending, **43**
shift	needless shift, **40d**, **41h**
sp	spelling, **58**
s/pl	singular/plural, **43a**, **43h**, **58a**
sub	subordination, **31c**, **62e**
sup	superlative, **45h**
s-v agr	subject-verb agreement, **43**
t	verb tense, **41d**
trans	transition, **2d**, **47e**
und	underlining/italics, **12a**, **52**, **57b**
us	usage, **65**
v or vb	error with verb, **41**
var	[sentence] variety, **34**
w	wordy, **29**
wc	word choice, **33**
wo	word order, **34d**, **62b**, **62g**
ww	wrong word, **33**

CONTENTS